Navigating the Intersection of AI Policy, Technology, and Governance

Alaa Youssef
School of Medicine, Stanford University, USA

Ayse Arslan
Independent Researcher, USA

IGI Global
Scientific Publishing
Publishing Tomorrow's Research Today

Vice President of Editorial Melissa Wagner
Director of Acquisitions Mikaela Felty
Director of Book Development Jocelynn Hessler
Production Manager Mike Brehm
Cover Design Jose Rosado

Published in the United States of America by
IGI Global Scientific Publishing
701 East Chocolate Avenue
Hershey, PA, 17033, USA
Tel: 717-533-8845
Fax: 717-533-7115
Website: https://www.igi-global.com E-mail: cust@igi-global.com

Library of Congress Cataloging-in-Publication Data

Names: Youssef, Alaa, 1992- editor | Arslan, Ayse, 1979- editor
Title: Navigating the intersection of AI policy, technology, and governance / edited by Alaa Youssef, Ayse Arslan, Engineering Science Reference.
Other titles: Navigating the intersection of artificial intelligence policy, technology, and governance
Description: Hershey, PA : IGI Global Scientific Publishing, 2025. | Includes bibliographical references and index. | Summary: "The primary objective of this book is to provide a comprehensive, interdisciplinary exploration of the critical issues at the intersection of Artificial Intelligence (AI) and policy"-- Provided by publisher.
Identifiers: LCCN 2025005795 (print) | LCCN 2025005796 (ebook) | ISBN 9798337312101 hardcover | ISBN 9798337312118 paperback | ISBN 9798337312125 ebook
Subjects: LCSH: Artificial intelligence--Law and legislation | Artificial intelligence--Government policy | Machine learning | Database management | LCGFT: Law materials
Classification: LCC K564.C6 N39 2026 (print) | LCC K564.C6 (ebook) | DDC 343.09/998--dc23/eng/20250808
LC record available at https://lccn.loc.gov/2025005795
LC ebook record available at https://lccn.loc.gov/2025005796

British Cataloguing in Publication Data
A Cataloguing in Publication record for this book is available from the British Library.

Table of Contents

Detailed Table of Contents

Quantum computing represents a transformative paradigm in modern computation, leveraging the principles of quantum mechanics to solve complex problems beyond the reach of classical computers. With applications across diverse fields, quantum computing plays a pivotal role in advancing cryptography, artificial intelligence, drug discovery and etc..Additionally, quantum computing enhances artificial intelligence by optimizing machine learning models, improves financial modeling, and supports climate simulation by processing vast datasets and intricate algorithms at unprecedented speeds. Its potential also extends to revolutionizing secure communications, personalized medicine, and sustainable energy solutions. As researchers and industries increasingly explore this field, quantum computing is poised to address previously intractable problems and redefine technological innovation. This chapter highlights its diverse and impactful applications, underscoring its promise to reshape industries and create groundbreaking advancements.

A number of industries including IoT, blockchain, and AI are merging to redesign various industry standards in intelligence, security, and productivity. AI advances Blockchain's key distinctives, and open ledgers by changing data processing and pattern recognition alongside decision-making. Blockchain technology reduces such vulnerabilities as tampering and illegitimate accessing by providing a decentralized immutable platform for data sharing. This has the effect of improving the reliability of the data used by AI models and in turn the reliability of the predictions made by those models. The one that Decentralized applications for which smart contracts or decentralized AI markets are another example, have is also based on blockchain in combination with artificial intelligence. But scalability, energy efficiency and ethical issues are still issues that need to be resolved. IoT has enabled the security provided by the blockchain, and have greatly contributed to enhancing the advancement of Industry 4.0.blockchain integration with AI governance, and in quantum computing.

The integration of artificial intelligence (AI) and machine learning (ML) in database management systems (DBMS) is revolutionizing how data is managed and analyzed. This review highlights the role of AI/ML in enhancing DBMS functions such as intelligent transaction scheduling (e.g., conflict prediction in OLTP), adaptive query optimization (e.g., reinforcement learning for plan selection), and automated configuration tuning (e.g., workload-aware systems like RocksDB). Key components include data preprocessing (feature extraction, normalization), architectural integration (embedding ML into optimizers, use of federated learning), and evaluation using metrics such as query latency, throughput, and model accuracy. While these innovations offer greater efficiency and scalability, ethical considerations such as data privacy, bias, and system transparency are crucial. This paper emphasizes the need for responsible AI adoption in DBMS to support real-time analytics, operational efficiency, and intelligent data-driven applications.

AI technologies have impacted the academic performance and skill development of marketing students. This study investigates how AI technologies affected the academic performance and the skills in marketing students. The research paper provides insight about AI technologies' role in changing marketing education for students. The research aims to identify the usage patterns of AI in marketing students, evaluating the impact of AI education on marketing students' performance and the impact on the non-academic skill developments. To investigate the changes in the skills and academics primary and secondary data has been used. The primary data includes the survey which was done using convenient and snow-ball sampling. The secondary data was collected using the research papers and studies done earlier by researchers. There were three main aims, while collecting the secondary data, which are understanding consumer sentiments, improving market performance with AI and AI's influence on non-academic skill development.

This chapter explores the future potential of generative AI (GenAI) and the key challenges it presents. It highlights opportunities in creativity, education, healthcare, and industry, while also addressing major risks such as fake content, privacy issues, and algorithmic bias. The chapter emphasizes the need for clear communication with non-expert audiences and examines evolving AI policy-making processes. It offers insights into managing risks and maximizing benefits, helping stakeholders better navigate GenAI's complexities. With practical recommendations for transparency and responsible use, this chapter serves as a valuable guide for academics, policymakers, industry leaders, and educators working to understand and manage the societal impact of generative AI.

This chapter examines the environmental impact of artificial intelligence (AI) and explores strategies to align AI development with sustainability goals. As AI-driven technologies expand, their energy consumption and carbon footprint present significant challenges, particularly in the operation of data centers and high-performance computing infrastructure. This chapter analyzes AI's dual role as both a contributor to environmental challenges and a tool for sustainability. It discusses AI's carbon footprint and AI's potential to drive climate action. Policy interventions, such as financial incentives, regulations for data centers, and carbon offset initiatives, are also examined. By integrating sustainability into AI development, this chapter

Preface

The rapid evolution of artificial intelligence (AI) is fundamentally reshaping the technological, economic, and social landscapes of our era. As AI systems become increasingly intertwined with critical infrastructures-spanning telecommunications, healthcare, finance, and security-the imperative to understand and govern these technologies with foresight and responsibility grows ever more urgent. The convergence of AI policy, technology, and governance now stands at the forefront of global discourse, demanding a multidisciplinary approach that bridges technical innovation with robust ethical, legal, and societal frameworks.

This volume, *Navigating the Intersection of AI Policy, Technology, and Governance*, seeks to illuminate the complex interplay between cutting-edge technological advancements and the policies and governance structures that shape their development and deployment. The chapters collected herein traverse a diverse array of topics: from the transformative potential of 5G and 6G networks and the integration of AI in next-generation antenna and sensor technologies, to the profound implications of quantum computing, cryptography, and the ethical challenges posed by AI-driven systems in domains such as healthcare, finance, and public infrastructure.

At its core, this book recognizes that AI is not merely a technical phenomenon but a sociotechnical force-one shaped by the values, interests, and power structures of its creators, regulators, and users. The governance of AI thus extends beyond algorithmic design to encompass transparency, accountability, fairness, and democratic oversight, as well as the anticipation and mitigation of emerging risks. The global nature of AI innovation further necessitates a nuanced understanding of international regulatory frameworks, techno-politics, and the distribution of benefits and risks across societies.

The chapters that follow are organized to provide both foundational insights and specialized explorations of key issues at the intersection of AI and policy. Readers will encounter analyses of network technologies and their role in enabling AI-driven applications, investigations into the security and privacy challenges of interconnected systems, and critical examinations of the ethical and legal dimensions of AI governance. By bringing together perspectives from engineering, policy, law, and ethics, this book aims to equip scholars, practitioners, and policymakers with the knowledge and tools necessary to navigate the evolving landscape of AI with rigor and responsibility.

As we stand at a pivotal moment in the trajectory of AI, the need for informed, collaborative, and adaptive governance has never been greater. It is our hope that this volume will serve as a catalyst for thoughtful engagement and constructive action at the intersection of AI policy, technology, and governance.

ORGANIZATION OF THE BOOK

In the opening chapter, *Applications of Quantum Computing in AI*, we introduce the transformative synergy between quantum computing and artificial intelligence. This chapter illustrates how quantum principles are revolutionizing AI, enabling the resolution of complex challenges in cryptography, climate modeling, drug discovery, and sustainable energy. By highlighting how quantum computing enhances machine learning models and data processing capabilities, the chapter sets the tone for the profound technological shifts explored throughout the book.

Chapter 2, *AI, Blockchain, and IoT Driving Innovation in Connected Ecosystems*, examines the convergence of three disruptive technologies. It explores how AI enhances blockchain integrity and intelligence, while IoT infrastructure accelerates data exchange and operational efficiency. The authors critically analyze how these technologies coalesce to form the backbone of Industry 4.0, acknowledging the unresolved challenges of scalability, energy use, and ethics that demand attention.

In Chapter 3, *Impact of Artificial Intelligence and Machine Learning Techniques in Database Management System Components*, the focus shifts to AI's role in optimizing core data systems. The chapter provides a comprehensive review of how machine learning methods are transforming traditional DBMS functions—such as query optimization, automated tuning, and intelligent transaction scheduling—while emphasizing the importance of addressing bias, privacy, and system transparency.

Chapter 4, *Artificial Intelligence and the Performance of Students*, brings an applied lens to AI's educational impact. Through empirical research on marketing students, the chapter investigates how AI tools influence academic achievement and non-academic skill development. By analyzing primary and secondary data, it highlights AI's role in reshaping modern pedagogy, consumer understanding, and student competencies.

In Chapter 5, *Designing the Future with Generative AI by Overcoming Challenges and Maximizing Opportunities*, we delve into the dual promise and peril of generative AI. The chapter outlines the current capabilities and risks—ranging from content authenticity to privacy—and emphasizes the importance of clear communication and evolving policy. It offers actionable strategies to guide stakeholders toward a responsible and beneficial integration of GenAI into various sectors.

Chapter 6, *Green AI: Balancing Innovation with Environmental Sustainability*, shifts the conversation to the ecological impact of AI. It underscores AI's growing carbon footprint while also positioning the technology as a potential ally in sustainability efforts. Through an exploration of data center policies, carbon offset strategies, and green design principles, the chapter presents a framework for aligning AI innovation with global environmental goals.

Ethics and governance take center stage in Chapter 7, *Balancing Innovation and Regulation: Ethical Frameworks for AI Policy and Governance*. This chapter articulates the tension between fostering technological advancement and ensuring responsible oversight. It introduces dynamic governance models and ethical frameworks that can guide policy development, offering a roadmap for inclusive, value-aligned AI ecosystems.

Chapter 8, *Navigating AI Governance: National and International Legal and Regulatory Frameworks*, deepens the discussion by comparing the regulatory approaches of different jurisdictions. With a focus on the EU's proactive legislative models and the US's sector-specific strategies, the chapter offers insight into global efforts to regulate AI. It emphasizes the urgency of creating adaptable and harmonized legal frameworks that support innovation without compromising ethical standards.

The international perspective continues in Chapter 9, *Global AI Governance and Collaboration: The Role of International Bodies in AI Regulation*. This chapter stresses the necessity of transnational cooperation in establishing ethical norms for AI. It acknowledges institutional and geopolitical hurdles while advocating for collaborative strategies that ensure AI serves the global public good and upholds human rights.

Finally, Chapter 10, *Navigating the Intersection of AI Models, State Surveillance, National Security, and AI Regulation in the Indian Technological Landscape*, offers a critical case study from India. The chapter explores how generative AI intersects with national security, surveillance, and citizen privacy. By analyzing domestic and international regulatory responses, it presents recommendations for robust governance mechanisms that protect individual rights while managing technological risks.

Together, these ten chapters present a rich, multidisciplinary exploration of the opportunities, risks, and responsibilities that define our AI-driven future. Through a blend of technical insight, ethical reflection, and policy analysis, this volume aims to inform and guide scholars, practitioners, and policymakers as they navigate the evolving landscape of artificial intelligence and its interconnected technologies.

Alaa Youssef

School of Medicine, Stanford University, USA

Ayse Arslan
Independent Researcher, USA

Chapter 1
Applications of Quantum Computing in AI

Swathi Mummadi
https://orcid.org/0000-0001-7078-5729
BV Raju Institute of Technology, Narsapur, India &Universiti Malaysia Perlis, Malaysia

Asral Bahari Jambek
Universiti Malaysia Perlis, Malaysia

Akshaya Siripuram
BV Raju Institute of Technology, Narsapur, India

Srivardhan Vadla
BV Raju Institute of Technology, Narsapur, India

Nawaz Mohammed
BV Raju Institute of Technology, Narsapur, India

ABSTRACT

Quantum computing represents a transformative paradigm in modern computation, leveraging the principles of quantum mechanics to solve complex problems beyond the reach of classical computers. With applications across diverse fields, quantum computing plays a pivotal role in advancing cryptography, artificial intelligence, drug discovery and etc..Additionally, quantum computing enhances artificial intelligence by optimizing machine learning models, improves financial modeling, and supports climate simulation by processing vast datasets and intricate algorithms at unprecedented speeds. Its potential also extends to revolutionizing secure communications, personalized medicine, and sustainable energy solutions. As researchers and industries increasingly explore this field, quantum computing is poised to ad-

DOI: 10.4018/979-8-3373-1210-1.ch001

dress previously intractable problems and redefine technological innovation. This chapter highlights its diverse and impactful applications, underscoring its promise to reshape industries and create groundbreaking advancements.

INTRODUCTION

Within the quickly changing field of innovation, quantum computing speaks to a progressive move that challenges the confinements of classical computing. Quantum computers utilize qubits, which can exist in superposition, meaning they can be both and 1 simultaneously, in differentiation to classical computers, which utilize bits that can exist in one of two states: 0 or 1, (Nielsen, Michael, & Isaac, 2010). Because of this characteristic, quantum computers can simultaneously analyze enormous volumes of data, making them exponentially more powerful than classical systems for certain computational tasks. Additionally, entanglement, another fundamental quantum property, enables qubits to be intrinsically linked regardless of distance, allowing for highly efficient and coordinated data processing, (Shor, 1994).

Quantum computing holds considerable potential and could greatly impact multiple fields, especially in cryptography, optimization, and logical investigation. Shor's calculation (1997), for instance, illustrates the ability of quantum computers to factor large numbers exponentially faster than classical computers, posing a challenge to current encryption methods. Similarly, Grover's calculation gives a quadratic speedup for database looks, making quantum computers prevalent for certain problem-solving errands, (Grover, 1996). In addition, quantum reenactments have the potential to revolutionize chemistry and fabric science by precisely modeling atomic intuition, something that classical computers battle with due to computational complexity, (Aspuru-Guzik et al., 2005). In drug discovery, for example, quantum computers could model complex protein structures to predict new pharmaceutical compounds, potentially decreasing the time required for unused medication advancement from decades to a fair number of a long time.

Despite these headways, quantum computing is still in its formative stages, confronting challenges such as quantum decoherence, clamor, and the requirements for blunder adjustment. Maintaining quantum states for extended periods requires highly controlled environments, and scalable quantum hardware remains a significant hurdle, (Preskill, 1998). Additionally, the cost of developing and maintaining quantum systems is prohibitively high, with advanced quantum processors requiring ultra-low temperatures near supreme zero (-273°C) to preserve steadiness. Nevertheless, ongoing research and major investments from technology giants like IBM, Google, and startups worldwide are rapidly progressing quantum computing. As this innovation proceeds to advance, it is anticipated that the longer term of computation, opening conceivable outcomes that were once regarded inconceivable. This chapter will give a clear understanding of the nuts and bolts of quantum computing and its applications.

KEY CONCEPTS IN QUANTUM COMPUTING

Quantum computing is built upon crucial standards of quantum mechanics that empower it to perform computations in ways that classical computers cannot. Not at all like classical computers, which depend on the deterministic double rationale, quantum computers use the probabilistic nature of quantum mechanics to prepare and examine data on a very basic level in diverse ways. By utilizing quantum bits or qubits, which can exist in multiple states simultaneously due to superposition, quantum computers are capable of handling a vast number of computations in parallel. This parallelism allows them to outperform classical computers in solving certain types of problems that would otherwise take an impractical amount of time using traditional methods.

These foundational standards allow quantum computers interesting preferences in an assortment of spaces. In cryptography, quantum computing has the potential to break broadly utilized encryption plans, such as RSA, by proficiently figuring expansive numbers utilizing calculations like Shor's calculation. Then again, quantum cryptography itself, especially through quantum key dispersion (QKD), offers unused strategies for making profoundly secure communication systems that are safe to listen stealthily. In optimization, quantum computers can illuminate complex combinatorial issues that emerge in coordination, budgetary modeling, and machine learning, where classical approaches battle due to exponential complexity. So also, fabric science and chemistry stand to advantage gigantically from quantum recreations, which can demonstrate atomic intelligence at an exceptional level of exactness, driving headways in medicate disclosure, nanotechnology, and renewable vitality arrangements. In counterfeit insights and machine learning, quantum computing can quicken information investigation, design acknowledgment, and decision-making forms, opening unused capabilities in areas such as healthcare, cybersecurity, and computerization.

Underneath are a few of the foremost vital concepts in quantum computing.

Quantum Superposition: The Power of Parallelism

One of the foremost principal standards of quantum computing is quantum superposition, which permits a qubit to exist in a combination of both 0 and 1 states at the same time. This wonder may be a result of the wave-like nature of quantum particles, as described by Schrödinger's equation. Mathematically, a qubit's state is represented as: $|\psi\rangle = \alpha|0\rangle+\beta|1\rangle$

Where α and β are complex likelihood amplitudes. These amplitudes decide the likelihood of the qubit collapsing into a specific state when measured. Superposition empowers quantum computers to handle numerous conceivable outcomes at the same time, driving exponential speedups in certain computational errands. For this case, Shor's calculation utilizes superposition to effectively figure expansive numbers, which poses a noteworthy challenge to classical encryption systems, (Shor, 1996). Moreover, Grover's calculation abuses superposition to look through an unsorted database in $O(\sqrt{N})$ time, giving a quadratic speedup compared to classical look algorithms, (Grover, 1996). Figure 1 gives you a comparison between classical bits and quantum bits, where the quantum bits are in superposition.

Figure 1. Classical bits vs quantum bits (in superposition)

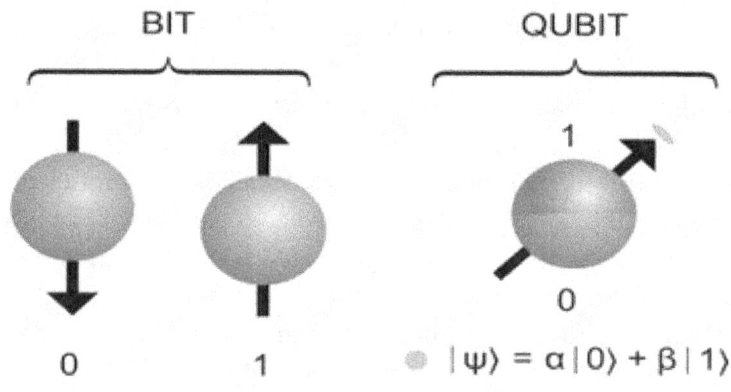

Real-world applications of superposition incorporate quantum chemistry recreations, where quantum computers demonstrate atomic intelligence remotely more productively than classical computers. This capacity has significant suggestions for sedate revelation, fabric science, and climate displaying, where complex frameworks must be analyzed at the quantum level. Furthermore, businesses such as funds and coordinations are starting to investigate quantum-based optimization strategies to fathom complex issues such as supply chain productivity and hazard administration.

Quantum Entanglement: The Mysterious Connection

The quantum trap is one of the foremost charming and crucial marvels in quantum mechanics. It depicts a one-of-a-kind relationship between two or more quantum particles, such as qubits, wherein their states are inherently connected in any case of the physical separation isolating them. This implies that measuring the state of one molecule momentarily decides the state of its entrapped partner, indeed in case they are light-years separated. Albert Einstein broadly alluded to this wonder as "spooky action at a separate," because it apparently resists classical standards of territory and causality, (Einstein *et al.,* 1935).

The noteworthiness of quantum ensnarement amplifies past hypothetical material science into viable applications, especially within the areas of quantum computing and quantum communication. In quantum cryptography, ensnarement serves as a pivotal asset for secure communication conventions. Quantum Key Dissemination (QKD) plans, such as BB84 and E91, use ensnarement to empower the secure trade of cryptographic keys, guaranteeing that any endeavor at listening in disturbs the framework and is promptly perceptible. These conventions offer hypothetically unbreakable encryption, making them profoundly profitable for secure communications in areas like defense, back, and information security, (Bennett & Brassard, 1984).

Within the quantum domain, this picture captures the substance of ensnared states—two particles whose wavefunctions are not distinct, shaping a single nonlocal substance. The brilliant structures speak to qubits, each existing in a superposition of premise states $|0\rangle$ and $|1\rangle$, yet intrinsically correlated through an entanglement operator.

The connecting energy threads symbolize the shared quantum state, mathematically described by the entangled Bell states:

Or similar maximally entangled configurations. Measurement on one qubit instantaneously collapses the wavefunction, forcing the correlated outcome in the remote qubit, irrespective of spatial separation—a direct consequence of nonlocality in quantum mechanics.

The infinity-like topology suggests the preservation of entanglement across time and space, constrained only by decoherence mechanisms. The surrounding Hamiltonian expressions hint at the unitary evolution governing the system, while the wave-like structures reflect the probability amplitudes of state evolution in Hilbert space. The general visual representation captures the puzzling nature of the quantum trap and its hypothetical noteworthiness.

Another groundbreaking application of quantum trap is quantum teleportation. Not at all like the teleportation depicted in science fiction, quantum teleportation does not include the exchange of physical matter but maybe the momentary transmission of quantum states from one area to another. By utilizing entrapped particles and classical communication, the state of a qubit can be duplicated at a far-off area without physically moving the first qubit. This phenomenon plays a significant part in the improvement of quantum systems and the imagined worldwide quantum web. Strikingly, later tests have effectively illustrated quantum teleportation over separations surpassing 1,200 kilometers, exhibiting the potential for long-distance quantum communication, (Briegel et al., 1998).

Ensnarement moreover plays a crucial part in quantum computing, where it empowers quantum calculations to perform complex calculations exponentially quicker than classical computers. Specifically, ensnared qubits permit superdense coding and improved parallelism, clearing the way for headways in areas such as fabric science, cryptography, and manufactured insights.

Quantum Interference: The Engine of Quantum Speedup

Quantum impedances may be an essential guideline that underpins the capacity of quantum computers to realize critical computational speedups. This phenomenon arises due to the inherent wave-like nature of quantum states, which allows their probability amplitudes to interact constructively or destructively. By carefully controlling this interference, quantum algorithms can enhance the likelihood of obtaining the correct computational outcomes while simultaneously canceling out incorrect paths. Without interference, Quantum obstructions may be a principal rule that underpins the capacity of quantum computers to realize noteworthy computational speedups, (Aaronson, 2013).

One of the foremost outstanding applications of quantum impedances is in Grover's look calculation, where impedance instruments open up the probability of coming to the proper arrangement, viably lessening the number of emphases required to find a target component inside an unsorted database. So also, in the Quantum Fourier Transform (QFT), which serves as a key building block of Shor's factoring algorithm, interference enables efficient manipulation of quantum states, leading to exponential speedup in integer factorization problems, (Deutsch, 1985). The ability to exploit interference in such algorithms highlights its critical role in distinguishing quantum computation from classical approaches, making it a cornerstone of quantum advantage in solving complex computational tasks.

Quantum Tunnelling: Breaking Classical Barriers

One of the foremost captivating and irrational marvels in quantum mechanics is quantum tunneling, which permits subatomic particles to pass through vitality obstructions that would be inconceivably beneath classical material science. This impact emerges from the standards of wave-particle duality and is numerically portrayed by Schrödinger's wave condition. In classical mechanics, a molecule must have adequate vitality to cross a potential boundary. Be that as it may, within the quantum realm, particles show wave-like behavior, which implies there's a limited likelihood that they can burrow through a boundary and rise on the other side, indeed when their classical vitality is inadequate to overcome it. This marvel has been tentatively watched in different areas, such as atomic combination in stars, semiconductor gadgets, and checking tunneling microscopy, where electrons burrow through a potential obstruction, empowering high-resolution imaging of surfaces at the nuclear level.

Within the space of quantum computing, quantum tunneling plays an essential part in quantum strengthening, a computational worldview outlined for fathoming complex optimization issues. Not at all like conventional gate-based quantum computers, which control qubits through an arrangement of unitary operations, quantum annealers—such as those created by D-Wave Systems—harness the impacts of quantum tunneling to investigate different potential arrangements simultaneously, (Farhi et al., 2014). This approach permits quantum annealers to traverse energy landscapes more efficiently by tunneling through local minima, rather than being trapped like classical optimization methods. As a result, quantum annealing has demonstrated promise in solving logistics, financial modeling, artificial intelligence, and other combinatorial optimization challenges, where classical algorithms often struggle due to computational bottlenecks, (Kadowaki & Nishimori, 1998).

By leveraging quantum tunneling, researchers are continuously expanding the frontiers of computation, unlocking new possibilities for solving real-world problems that demand extreme computational efficiency. As quantum advances advance, the commonsense applications of tunneling-based strategies are anticipated to develop, advertising inventive arrangements to a few of the foremost complex optimization challenges confronted by numerous businesses.

Quantum Teleportation: Instantaneous State Transfer

Quantum teleportation may be a groundbreaking wonder in quantum mechanics that empowers the exact exchange of quantum states between far-off areas by leveraging the standards of quantum traps and classical communication. Not at all like routine information transmission, which includes the physical exchange of information-carrying particles, quantum teleportation permits the precise replication of a quantum state at another area without the requirement to coordinate the physical development of the initial particle. This interesting capability is pivotal for the improvement of quantum communication and computing innovations because it jams the fragile quantum properties that are regularly misplaced in classical transmission strategies.

The teleportation process consists of three fundamental steps. First, an entangled pair of qubits is generated, forming a quantum link between the sender and receiver, (Zeilinger et al., 2007). Next, the sender performs a joint measurement on the original qubit and one of the entangled qubits, effectively collapsing their states in a way that correlates with the target qubit at the receiving end, (Bouwmeester et al., 1997). Since the measurement alters the state of the original qubit irreversibly, the quantum information is effectively "transferred" rather than duplicated, preserving the no-cloning theorem. Finally, the sender transmits classical information about the measurement results to the receiver, who then applies the necessary corrective operations to the remaining entangled qubits, subsequently recreating the precise quantum state of the first molecule at the inaccessible location, (Pan et al., 2010).

Quantum teleportation may be a key enabler of quantum organizing because it permits the secure exchange of quantum data without requiring coordinated physical transport. This has significant suggestions for the advancement of the quantum web, where quantum states can be handed off over tremendous separations with tall devotion. Later tests have effectively illustrated satellite-based quantum teleportation over separations surpassing 1,200 kilometers, checking a critical turning point in long-distance quantum communication and demonstrating the possibility of a future worldwide quantum network, (Ren et al., 2017). As investigations advance, quantum teleportation is anticipated to play a central part in empowering secure quantum cryptographic conventions, disseminated quantum computing, and large-scale quantum systems.

QUANTUM ERROR CORRECTION: OVERCOMING DECOHERENCE

One of the foremost impressive challenges within the improvement of quantum computing is the issue of quantum blunder redress (QEC), which is planned to neutralize the negative impacts of decoherence—the progressive misfortune of quantum data due to undesirable intelligence with the encompassing environment. Not at all like classical computing frameworks, where mistakes can be moderated by presenting repetition (such as putting away numerous duplicates of a bit), quantum frameworks work beneath the limitations of quantum mechanics, where the no-cloning hypothesis forbids the precise duplication of a self-assertive quantum state. This makes conventional blunder adjustment strategies incapable, requiring the improvement of specialized quantum mistake adjustment codes that can protect data without damaging crucial quantum principles, (Knill et al., 1996) (Gottesman, 1996).

One of the foremost broadly investigated and promising quantum blunder redress methods is the surface code, which encodes a consistent qubit by conveying its quantum data over numerous physical qubits. This strategy depends on equality checks to distinguish and rectify blunders while guaranteeing that the encoded quantum data remains steady despite the nearness of clamor and decoherence, (Kitaev, 2003) (Dennis et al., 2002). By ceaselessly observing the framework for blunders without straightforwardly measuring or exasperating the consistent qubit, the surface code empowers quantum computers to maintain quantum coherence for longer durations.

Figure 2. Visualisation of quantum error correction

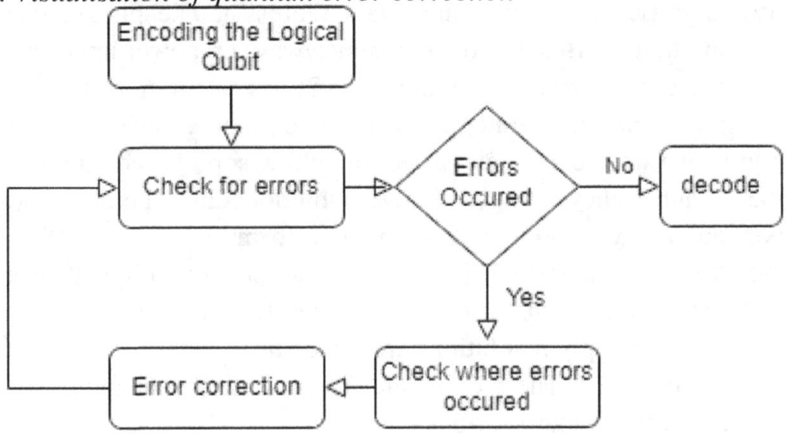

Effective quantum error correction is a fundamental requirement for the practical realization of large-scale quantum computing. Without robust error correction mechanisms, quantum systems would be too fragile to perform computations reliably, limiting their scalability and usefulness for real-world applications. Recent advancements in QEC protocols and hardware implementation have brought researchers closer to achieving fault-tolerant quantum systems, clearing the way for breakthroughs in cryptography, fabric science, optimization, and counterfeit insights, (Terhal, 2015) (Aliferis et al., 2008). Additionally, experimental progress in topological quantum error correction and surface code architectures has demonstrated improved error thresholds, further advancing the feasibility of large-scale quantum computing, (Bombin & Martin-Delgado, 2006) (Brown et al., 2019). As quantum innovations proceed to advance, moving forward blunder rectification procedures will stay a basic center to open the total potential of quantum computing.

QUANTUM GATES: THE BUILDING PIECES OF QUANTUM COMPUTING

Quantum doors serve as the basic operations in quantum computing, practically equivalent to classical rationale doors but with noteworthy contrasts due to the standards of quantum mechanics. Not at all like classical entryways that prepare double bits deterministically, quantum doors work on qubits, leveraging properties such as superposition, trap, and quantum obstructions to perform computations past classical capabilities, (Mermin, 2007). These doors are numerically spoken to by unitary frameworks, guaranteeing that all quantum operations are reversible, a property that recognizes quantum computing from its classical partner. This reversibility is significant for quantum mistake redress and keeping up coherence in quantum computations. Besides, quantum entryways empower interesting computational pathways that permit calculations like Shor's calculation and Grover's look calculation to beat classical strategies in certain domains, (Steane, 1996).

Quantum entryways can be classified into a few sorts based on their work and the number of qubits they act upon. Single-qubit doors incorporate principal operations like Pauli entryways (X, Y, Z), which perform bit and stage flips (Barenco et al., 1995), the Hadamard door (H), which makes superposition (Watrous, 2018), the Stage doors (S, T), which present stage shifts (DiVincenzo, 2000), and the Rx, Ry, Rz doors, which apply revolutions around distinctive tomahawks of the Bloch sphere (Feynman, 1986). These doors are fundamental for quantum state control and planning quantum superpositions.

Multi-qubit entryways work on two or more qubits and incorporate vital doors just like the CNOT (Controlled-NOT) entryway, which flips the target qubit in the event that the control qubit is in Childs et al. (2002), and the CZ (Controlled-Z) door, which presents a stage move based on the control qubit's state, (Montanaro, 2016). More complex controlled entryways just like the Toffoli (CCNOT) entryway and the Fredkin (CSWAP) entryway expand control to numerous qubits, playing key parts in quantum rationale and blunder correction, (Harrow et al., 2009). Swap entryways permit qubits to trade states, which is valuable for reordering quantum registers in computations, (Zurek, 2003).

A detailed explanation of these gates is given below.

The Pauli Gates

Pauli doors are crucial single-qubit quantum entryways that are broadly utilized in quantum computing. They compare to the three Pauli matrices—Pauli-X, Pauli-Y, and Pauli-Z—which portray turns around the x, y, and z tomahawks of the Bloch circle, individually. These doors are unitary and Hermitian, meaning they can be utilized to develop reversible quantum operations. Pauli doors play a key part in quantum data handling, counting quantum mistake adjustment, cryptographic conventions, and quantum algorithms, (Schuld & Petruccione, 2018). The Bloch circle representation of Pauli doors is given in Figure 3.

Figure 3. Bloch sphere representation of Pauli gates (X, Y, Z)

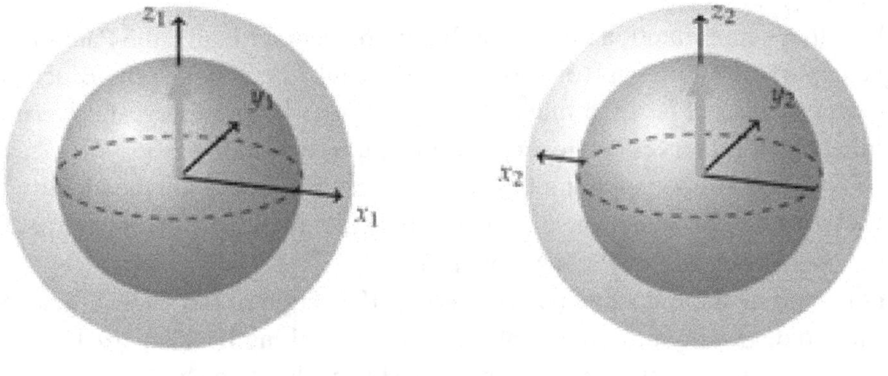

Pauli-X Gate

The Pauli-X door could be a principal quantum door that serves as the quantum analog of the classical NOT door. It flips the computational premise states of a qubit, meaning it changes $|0\rangle$ into $|1\rangle$ and bad habit versa. This change can be numerically communicated as $X|0\rangle=|1\rangle$, $X|1\rangle=|0\rangle$.

The lattice representation of the Pauli-X door is given in Figure 5. Geometrically, the Pauli-X door compares to a turn of π (or 180°) around the x-axis of the Bloch sphere, (Frank et al., 2019). The unitary nature of the Pauli-X entryway guarantees that quantum data is protected, meaning that applying the door twice comes about within the character operation. Matrix representations of Pauli-X gate is $X = \begin{bmatrix} 1 & 0 \\ 0 & 1 \end{bmatrix}$

When applied to a normal qubit state like: $|\psi\rangle=\alpha|0\rangle+\beta|1\rangle$, the Pauli-X gate swaps the likelihood amplitudes of the two premise states: $X|\psi\rangle=\alpha|1\rangle+\beta|0\rangle$. It flips the qubit state, comparable to a classical NOT entryway.

Another pivotal property of the Pauli-X entryway is that it is Hermitian, meaning its conjugate transpose is equal to itself: $X\dagger=X$, and also it is unitary, satisfying the condition: $XX\dagger=I$. These properties make the Pauli-X entryway an essential component of quantum circuits and algorithms, playing a key part in quantum computation and quantum error correction, (Blais et al., 2021) (Zhang et al., 2020).

Pauli-Y Gate

The Pauli-Y door may be a crucial single-qubit quantum entryway that performs both a bit-flip and a phase-flip operation. It alters the state of a qubit by exchanging the computational basis states while introducing a complex phase factor. When applied to the standard basis states, the transformations are expressed as $Y|0\rangle = i|1\rangle$, $Y|1\rangle = -i|0\rangle$.

Its lattice representation is given in Figure 6. Geometrically, the Pauli-Y entryway compares to a turn of π (or 180°) approximately the y-axis of the Bloch circle, (Kandala et al., 2017). Like other Pauli gates, it is both unitary and Hermitian, meaning that it preserves the norm of the quantum state and satisfies $Y^\dagger = Y$ as well as $YY^\dagger = I$. In addition, applying the Pauli-Y gate twice results in the identity operation confirming its self-inverse property, (Chen et al., 2020) (Montanaro, 2021). Matrix representations of Pauli-Y gate is $Y = \begin{bmatrix} 0 & -i \\ i & 0 \end{bmatrix}$

For a common qubit state $|\psi\rangle = \alpha|0\rangle + \beta|1\rangle$, the action of the Pauli-Y gate swaps the amplitudes while introducing phase factors, resulting in: $Y|\psi\rangle = \alpha i|1\rangle - \beta i|0\rangle$. It presents a complex phase stage move at the side of the state flip.

Pauli-Z Gate

The Pauli-Z door could be an essential single-qubit quantum entryway that performs a phase-flip operation. Not at all like the Pauli-X and Pauli-Y entryways, the Pauli-Z door does not change the likelihood of measuring a qubit within the computational premise. Instep, it presents a stage move of π to the $|1\rangle$ state whereas clearing out $|0\rangle$ unaltered. This change is spoken to numerically as $Z|0\rangle = |0\rangle$, $Z|1\rangle = -|1\rangle$

Its framework representation is given in Figure 7. Geometrically, the Pauli-Z door compares to a revolution of π (or 180°) around the z-axis of the Bloch sphere, (Krantz et al., 2019). Just like the other Pauli entryways, the Pauli-Z entryway is unitary, satisfying $ZZ^\dagger = I$, and Hermitian, meaning $Z^\dagger = Z$. Additionally, applying the Pauli-Z gate twice results in the identity operation. Matrix representations of Pauli-Z gate is $Z = \begin{bmatrix} 1 & 0 \\ 0 & -1 \end{bmatrix}$

It applies a stage flip without changing the qubit's plentifulness. Since the Pauli-Z door as it were influences the stage of the quantum state without modifying estimation probabilities within the computational premise, it plays a significant part in quantum calculations and quantum blunder adjustment, (Gambetta et al., 2017).

The Hadamard Gate

The Hadamard door could be a significant single-qubit quantum door that makes superposition states, a foundation of quantum computation. Its unitary network representation is given as in Figure 7. The change produces an equal superposition of the $|0\rangle$ and $|1\rangle$ states, an operation that's vital for quantum parallelism and obstructions, (Kjaergaard et al., 2020). It transforms the computational basis states as

$H = \frac{|0\rangle \pm |1\rangle}{\sqrt{2}}$ for both positive and negative phases. Hadamard gate matrix representation is is $H = \frac{1}{\sqrt{2}}\begin{bmatrix} 1 & 1 \\ 1 & -1 \end{bmatrix}$

The Hadamard entryway isn't as it were unitary but moreover, self-inverse, meaning that applying it twice returns the framework to its unique state. This property ensures that it preserves the overall probability amplitudes, making it a fundamental tool for preparing qubits in a balanced superposition before further quantum operations. The ability of the Hadamard gate to interconvert between the computational basis and the superposition basis is essential in many quantum algorithms, such as those used for quantum Fourier transforms and search algorithms, (McEwen et al., 2019).

Besides, the geometric elucidation of the Hadamard entryway on the Bloch circle is especially shrewd, as it appears in Figure 4. The door maps the premise state $|0\rangle$ to a point on the equator of the circle, where the state has broken even with likelihood amplitudes for measuring $|0\rangle$ and $|1\rangle$. This visualization emphasizes the gate's role in generating quantum interference, a critical feature that underpins the speed-up in various quantum algorithms, (Kjaergaard et al., 2020).

Figure 4. Hadamard gate bloch sphere

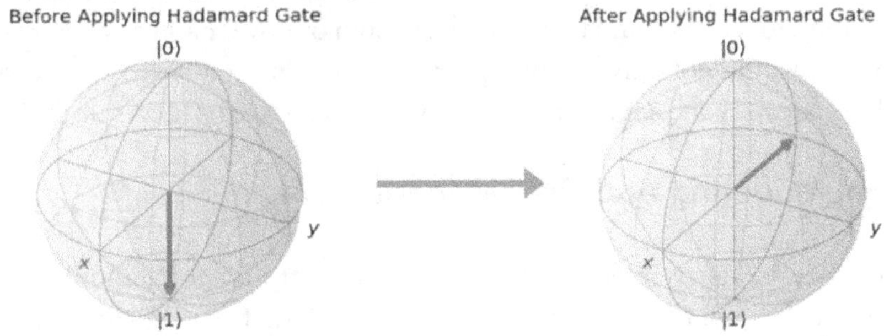

Phase Gates

The stage entryway could be a principal single-qubit operation that applies a controlled stage move to the quantum state without modifying its estimation probabilities. This door takes off the $|0\rangle$ state unaltered whereas duplicating the $|1\rangle$ state by a complex stage calculates eiΦ. Its framework representation is given by:

$P(\Phi) = \begin{bmatrix} 1 & 0 \\ 0 & e^{i\Phi} \end{bmatrix}$. When applied to a general qubit state $|\ \psi\rangle = \alpha\ |\ 0\rangle + \beta\ |\ 1\rangle$, the phase gate transforms it into $P(\varphi)\ |\ \psi\rangle = \alpha\ |\ 0\rangle + \beta e\text{^}i\Phi\ |\ 1\rangle$.

This operation effectively rotates the state about the z-axis of the Bloch sphere by an angle φ, altering the relative phase between the basis states while leaving their amplitudes—and thus the probabilities of measuring $|0\rangle$ or $|1\rangle$—unchanged. In practice, special cases of the phase gate are commonly used: for example, when $\varphi=\pi/2$ the door is known as the S entryway, and when $\varphi=\pi/4$ it is alluded to as the T entryway or $\pi/8$ entryway. These variations play a basic part in quantum impedances and blunder redress schemes, (Wang et al., 2020).

APPLICATIONS OF QUANTUM COMPUTING

Quantum Chemistry and Sedate Revelation

Quantum computing is set to revolutionize quantum chemistry by mimicking atomic frameworks that are right now unmanageable for classical computers. Classical approaches struggle with the exponential scaling of electron–nucleus interactions in large molecules, making high-precision calculations both time- and resource-intensive. Quantum computers, however, operate on qubits that naturally encode the quantum states of molecules, thereby enabling a more accurate simulation of chemical reactions, binding energies, and electron correlations. These enhanced simulations could dramatically accelerate the drug discovery process, reduce reliance on costly laboratory trials, and facilitate the design of novel catalysts and materials. Such progress would not only advance pharmaceuticals but also drive innovation in sustainable materials and energy solutions, (Orús et al., 2020) (McArdle et al., 2020).

Financial Modeling and Risk Management

The finance industry is poised to gain significantly from quantum computing through more efficient and accurate models. Modern financial markets require the solving of high-dimensional optimization problems and stochastic differential equations, where classical techniques often resort to approximations that may oversimplify market dynamics. Quantum algorithms leverage quantum parallelism to evaluate a vast number of scenarios simultaneously, thereby enabling more precise risk assessments, portfolio optimizations, and derivative pricing. This quantum advantage can yield a competitive edge by enhancing decision-making processes and reducing systemic risk in complex financial systems, (Pirandola, 2020).

Machine Learning and Data Analytics

Quantum computing guarantees to convert machine learning and huge information analytics by significantly quickening the preparation and execution of complex models. Conventional machine learning calculations are constrained by the computational fetch of preparing high-dimensional information, frequently driving to long preparation periods and compelled to show complexity. By misusing the high-dimensional Hilbert space accessible in quantum frameworks, quantum machine learning calculations can perform perplexing direct variable-based math operations—such as framework reversal and eigenvalue decomposition—more productively. This potential speedup may lead to strides in design acknowledgment, speedier merging of neural systems, and the disclosure of more unobtrusive information relationships. The integration of quantum circuits into classical ML systems is anticipated to open unused wildernesses in counterfeit intelligence, (Pirandola, 2020) (Biamonte et al., 2017).

Cybersecurity and Cryptography

Quantum computing has a dual role in cybersecurity: it both poses significant threats to classical cryptography and offers new avenues for secure communication. On the one hand, powerful quantum algorithms, such as Shor's algorithm, can potentially break widely deployed encryption methods like RSA, rendering current public-key systems vulnerable. On the other hand, quantum key dissemination (QKD) tackles the interesting properties of quantum mechanics to empower secure communication channels that can distinguish any listening endeavors. QKD conventions ensure that any capture attempts change the quantum state, subsequently alarming clients to potential breaches. This inborn security is driving the advancement of post-quantum cryptographic strategies to protect data within the quantum era, (Zhang et al., 2021) (Scarani et al., 2009).

Logistics and Supply Chain Optimization

Proficient coordination and supply chain administration include understanding profoundly complex optimization issues where the number of potential courses or plans develops exponentially with arranged estimates. Classical calculations can end up overpowered by the endless arrangement space, coming about in imperfect asset assignment. Quantum optimization techniques—such as quantum strengthening and variational quantum algorithms—employ quantum obstructions to assess numerous arrangements concurrently. By doing so, they guarantee to distinguish ideal techniques more rapidly and precisely, which may lead to noteworthy taking a toll on reserve funds and productivity changes in businesses like transportation, fabricating, and retail. Additionally, quantum recreation strategies are being investigated to handle NP-hard issues that are something else unfavorably utilizing classical computation, (Bauer et al., 2016) (Lloyd, 1996).

Materials Science and Advanced Simulation

In materials science, understanding the properties of modern compounds requires recreating nuclear and electronic intuitions with extraordinary accuracy. Classical strategies regularly drop brief when tending to the complexities of electron relationships and quantum elements, especially in frameworks with numerous association particles. Quantum computers, be that as it may, can natively reenact these quantum marvels, giving bits of knowledge into superconductivity, attraction, and chemical reactivity that are troublesome or inconceivable to realize with classical reenactments. Such propels are anticipated to quicken the revelation of high-performance materials for applications in vitality capacity, hardware, and aviation, in this manner driving advancement and supporting maintainable technologies, (Babbush et al., 2021).

Fundamental Physics and High-Energy Simulations

Quantum computing is interestingly situated to progress our understanding of principal material science by mimicking complex quantum frameworks that oversee the universe. High-energy material science, quantum field hypothesis, and many-body quantum frameworks include intelligence with a tremendous number of degrees of flexibility, rendering classical recreations illogical. Quantum computers can speak to these intelligent straightforwardly, permitting analysts to reenact marvels such as quantum chromodynamics, extraordinary stages of matter, and indeed angles of quantum gravity. These reenactments give not as it were a window into the inward workings of nature but moreover offer assistance refine hypothetical models and drive the advancement of modern advances that abuse quantum mechanical principles, (Georgescu, Ashhab, & Nori, 2014).

Weather Forecasting and Climate Modeling

Quantum computing has the potential to revolutionize climate determining and climate modeling by preparing endless sums of air information with higher exactness and speed than classical supercomputers. Traditional weather models rely on numerical methods to solve complex partial differential equations governing fluid dynamics and thermodynamics. However, the chaotic nature of the atmosphere and the enormous number of interacting variables make long-term predictions extremely challenging for classical methods, (Tennie & Palmer, 2023).

Quantum computers can enhance these models by leveraging quantum parallelism to simulate atmospheric interactions on a finer scale, reducing uncertainties in predictions. Quantum machine learning techniques can also help analyze historical climate data to identify patterns and improve the accuracy of extreme weather event predictions, such as hurricanes, heatwaves, and droughts. These advancements could significantly benefit disaster preparedness, agricultural planning, and climate change mitigation strategies, ultimately leading to more resilient and sustainable societies, (Schwabe et al., 2025).

CONCLUSION

Quantum computing is rising as a transformative innovation capable of understanding challenges that are, as of now, past the reach of classical strategies. Its applications span a wide extend of domains—from revolutionizing medicate revelation and money-related modelling to upgrading machine learning, reinforcing cybersecurity, optimizing coordination, progressing materials science, and extending our understanding of crucial material science. As quantum equipment and calculations proceed to advance, these breakthroughs will reshape businesses and drive uncommon logical advances. To bridge the hole between near-term quantum gadgets and real-world applications, half-breed quantum-classical approaches are, as of now, being investigated. With progressing progressions in quantum calculations and equipment models, businesses around the world are on the brink of a worldview move fueled by quantum computing.

REFERENCES

Aaronson, S. (2013). *Quantum Computing Since Democritus*. Cambridge University Press. DOI: 10.1017/CBO9780511979309

Aliferis, P., & Preskill, J. (2008). Fault-Tolerant Quantum Computation Against Biased Noise. *Physical Review A, 78*(5), 052331. DOI: 10.1103/PhysRevA.78.052331

Arute, F., Arya, K., Babbush, R., Bacon, D., Bardin, J. C., Barends, R., Biswas, R., Boixo, S., Brandao, F. G. S. L., Buell, D. A., Burkett, B., Chen, Y., Chen, Z., Chiaro, B., Collins, R., Courtney, W., Dunsworth, A., Farhi, E., Foxen, B., & Martinis, J. M. (2019). Quantum supremacy using a programmable superconducting processor. *Nature, 574*(7779), 505–510. DOI: 10.1038/s41586-019-1666-5 PMID: 31645734

Aspuru-Guzik, A., Dutoi, A. D., Love, P. J., & Head-Gordon, M. (2005). Simulated quantum computation of molecular energies. *Science, 309*(5741), 1704–1707. DOI: 10.1126/science.1113479 PMID: 16151006

Babbush, R.. (2021). Quantum Algorithms for Scientific Applications. *Science Advances, 7*(25), eabg5656.

Barenco, A., Bennett, C. H., Cleve, R., DiVincenzo, D. P., Margolus, N., Shor, P., Sleator, T., Smolin, J. A., & Weinfurter, H. (1995). Elementary gates for quantum computation. *Physical Review A, 52*(5), 3457–3467. DOI: 10.1103/PhysRevA.52.3457 PMID: 9912645

Bauer, B., Wecker, D., Hastings, M. B., & Troyer, M. (2016). Hybrid Quantum-Classical Approach to Quantum Dynamics. *Physical Review X, 6*(3), 031015. DOI: 10.1103/PhysRevX.6.031045

Bennett, C. H., & Brassard, G. "Quantum Cryptography: Public Key Distribution and Coin Tossing." *Proceedings of IEEE International Conference on Computers, Systems and Signal Processing*, Bangalore, India, 1984, pp. 175–179.

Bharti, K., Cervera-Lierta, A., Kyaw, T., Haug, T., Alperin-Lea, S., Anand, A., Degroote, M., Heimonen, H., Kottmann, J. S., Menke, T., Mok, W.-K., Sim, S., Kwek, L.-C., & Aspuru-Guzik, A. (2022). Noisy Intermediate-Scale Quantum Algorithms. *Reviews of Modern Physics, 94*(1), 015004. DOI: 10.1103/RevModPhys.94.015004

Biamonte, J., Wittek, P., Pancotti, N., Rebentrost, P., Wiebe, N., & Lloyd, S. (2017). Quantum Machine Learning. *Nature, 549*(7671), 195–202. DOI: 10.1038/nature23474 PMID: 28905917

Blais, A., Grimsmo, A. L., Girvin, S. M., & Wallraff, A. (2021). Circuit quantum electrodynamics. *Reviews of Modern Physics, 93*(2), 025005. DOI: 10.1103/RevModPhys.93.025005

Bombin, H., & Martin-Delgado, M. A. (2006). Topological Quantum Distillation. *Physical Review Letters, 97*(18), 180501. DOI: 10.1103/PhysRevLett.97.180501 PMID: 17155532

Bouwmeester, D., Pan, J.-W., Mattle, K., Eibl, M., Weinfurter, H., & Zeilinger, A. (1997). Experimental Quantum Teleportation. *Nature, 390*(6660), 575–579. DOI: 10.1038/37539

Briegel, H. J., Dür, W., Cirac, J. I., & Zoller, P. (1998). Quantum Repeaters: The Role of Imperfect Local Operations in Quantum Communication. *Physical Review Letters, 81*(26), 5932–5935. DOI: 10.1103/PhysRevLett.81.5932

Brown, B. J.. (2019). Fault-Tolerant Handling of Qubit Loss in Surface Codes. *Physical Review X, 9*(3), 031041.

Chen, Y.. (2020). Variational quantum simulation of the Heisenberg model on a superconducting quantum processor. *Physical Review. A, 101*(3), 032329.

Childs, A. M.. (2002). Quantum algorithms for algebraic problems. *Quantum Information & Computation, 2*(3), 181–191. DOI: 10.26421/QIC2.3-1

Dennis, E., Kitaev, A., Landahl, A., & Preskill, J. (2002). Topological Quantum Memory. *Journal of Mathematical Physics, 43*(9), 4452–4505. DOI: 10.1063/1.1499754

Deutsch, D. (1985). Quantum theory, the Church–Turing principle and the universal quantum computer. Proceedings of the Royal Society of London. A. Mathematical and Physical Sciences, 400(1818), 97-117.

DiVincenzo, D. P. (2000). The physical implementation of quantum computation. *Fortschritte der Physik, 48*(9-11), 771–783. DOI: 10.1002/1521-3978(200009)48:9/11<771::AID-PROP771>3.0.CO;2-E

Einstein, A., Podolsky, B., & Rosen, N. (1935). Can Quantum-Mechanical Description of Physical Reality Be Considered Complete? *Physical Review, 47*(10), 777–780. DOI: 10.1103/PhysRev.47.777

Farhi, E., Goldstone, J., & Gutmann, S. (2014). A quantum approximate optimization algorithm. arXiv preprint arXiv:1411.4028.

Feynman, R. P. (1986). Quantum mechanical computers. *Foundations of Physics, 16*(6), 507–531. DOI: 10.1007/BF01886518

Gambetta, J. M., Chow, J. M., & Steffen, M. (2017). Building logical qubits in a superconducting quantum computing system. npj quantum information, 3(1), 2.

Georgescu, I. M., Ashhab, S., & Nori, F. (2014). Quantum Simulation. *Reviews of Modern Physics*, *86*(1), 153–185. DOI: 10.1103/RevModPhys.86.153

Gottesman, D. (1996). Class of Quantum Error-Correcting Codes Saturating the Quantum Hamming Bound. *Physical Review A*, *54*(3), 1862–1868. DOI: 10.1103/PhysRevA.54.1862 PMID: 9913672

Grover, L. K. (1996, July). A fast quantum mechanical algorithm for database search. In *Proceedings of the twenty-eighth annual ACM symposium on Theory of computing* (pp. 212-219).

Harrow, A. W., Hassidim, A., & Lloyd, S. (2009). Quantum algorithm for linear systems of equations. *Physical Review Letters*, *103*(15), 150502. DOI: 10.1103/PhysRevLett.103.150502 PMID: 19905613

Kadowaki, T., & Nishimori, H. (1998). Quantum Annealing in the Transverse Ising Model. *Physical Review E: Statistical Physics, Plasmas, Fluids, and Related Interdisciplinary Topics*, *58*(5), 5355–5363. DOI: 10.1103/PhysRevE.58.5355

Kandala, A., Mezzacapo, A., Temme, K., Takita, M., Brink, M., Chow, J. M., & Gambetta, J. M. (2017). Hardware-efficient variational quantum eigensolver for small molecules and quantum magnets. *Nature*, *549*(7671), 242–246. DOI: 10.1038/nature23879 PMID: 28905916

Kitaev, A. Y. (2003). Fault-Tolerant Quantum Computation by Anyons. *Annals of Physics*, *303*(1), 2–30. DOI: 10.1016/S0003-4916(02)00018-0

Kjaergaard, M., Schwartz, M. E., Braumüller, J., Krantz, P., Wang, J. I., Gustavsson, S., & Oliver, W. D. (2020). Superconducting Qubits: Current State of Play. *Annual Review of Condensed Matter Physics*, *11*(1), 369–395. DOI: 10.1146/annurev-conmatphys-031119-050605

Knill, E.. (1996). Resilient Quantum Computation: Error Correction or Purification? *Physical Review Letters*, *77*(13), 2575–2578.

Krantz, P., Kjaergaard, M., Yan, F., Orlando, T. P., Gustavsson, S., & Oliver, W. D. (2019). A quantum engineer's guide to superconducting qubits. *Applied Physics Reviews*, *6*(2), 021318. DOI: 10.1063/1.5089550

Lloyd, S. (1996). Universal Quantum Simulators. *Science*, *273*(5278), 1073–1078. DOI: 10.1126/science.273.5278.1073 PMID: 8688088

McArdle, S.. (2020). Quantum Chemistry on Quantum Computers. *Reviews of Modern Physics*, *92*(1), 015003. DOI: 10.1103/RevModPhys.92.015003

McEwen, M.. (2019). Gate performance characterization of the Hadamard operation on superconducting qubits. *Physical Review Applied*, *12*(2), 024043.

Mermin, N. (2007). *David. Quantum Computer Science: An Introduction*. Cambridge University Press. DOI: 10.1017/CBO9780511813870

Montanaro, A. (2016). Quantum algorithms: an overview. npj Quantum Information, 2(1), 1-8.

Nielsen, M. A., & Chuang, I. L. (2010). *Quantum Computation and Quantum Information*. Cambridge University Press.

Orús, R.. (2020). Quantum Computing for Finance: Overview and Prospects. *Reviews in Physics*, *5*, 100–115.

Pan, J.-W.. (2010). Experimental Free-Space Quantum Teleportation. *Nature Photonics*, *4*(6), 376–381. DOI: 10.1038/nphoton.2010.87

Pirandola, S., Andersen, U. L., Banchi, L., Berta, M., Bunandar, D., Colbeck, R., Englund, D., Gehring, T., Lupo, C., Ottaviani, C., Pereira, J. L., Razavi, M., Shamsul Shaari, J., Tomamichel, M., Usenko, V. C., Vallone, G., Villoresi, P., & Wallden, P. (2020). Advances in Quantum Cryptography. *Advances in Optics and Photonics*, *12*(4), 1012–1236. DOI: 10.1364/AOP.361502

Preskill, J. (1998). *Fault-tolerant quantum computation*. Introduction to Quantum Computation and Information. DOI: 10.1142/9789812385253_0008

Ren, J.-G., Xu, P., Yong, H.-L., Zhang, L., Liao, S.-K., Yin, J., Liu, W.-Y., Cai, W.-Q., Yang, M., Li, L., Yang, K.-X., Han, X., Yao, Y.-Q., Li, J., Wu, H.-Y., Wan, S., Liu, L., Liu, D.-Q., Kuang, Y.-W., & Pan, J.-W. (2017). Ground-to-Satellite Quantum Teleportation. *Nature*, *549*(7670), 70–73. DOI: 10.1038/nature23675 PMID: 28825708

Scarani, V., Bechmann-Pasquinucci, H., Cerf, N. J., Dušek, M., Lütkenhaus, N., & Peev, M. (2009). The Security of Practical Quantum Key Distribution. *Reviews of Modern Physics*, *81*(3), 1301–1350. DOI: 10.1103/RevModPhys.81.1301

Schuld, M., & Petruccione, F. (2018). *Supervised Learning with Quantum Computers*. Springer. DOI: 10.1007/978-3-319-96424-9

Schwabe, M., Pastori, L., de Vega, I., Gentine, P., Iapichino, L., Lahtinen, V., . . . Eyring, V. (2025). Opportunities and challenges of quantum computing for climate modelling. arXiv preprint arXiv:2502.10488.

Shor, P. W. (1994, November). Algorithms for quantum computation: discrete logarithms and factoring. In *Proceedings 35th annual symposium on foundations of computer science* (pp. 124-134). Ieee.

Shor, P. W. (1996, October). Fault-tolerant quantum computation. In *Proceedings of 37th conference on foundations of computer science* (pp. 56-65). IEEE.

Shor, P. W. (1997). Polynomial-time algorithms for prime factorization and discrete logarithms on a quantum computer. *SIAM Journal on Computing*, *26*(5), 1484–1509. DOI: 10.1137/S0097539795293172

Steane, A. (1996). Error Correcting Codes in Quantum Theory. *Physical Review Letters*, *77*(5), 793–797. DOI: 10.1103/PhysRevLett.77.793 PMID: 10062908

Tennie, F., & Palmer, T. N. (2023). Quantum Computers for Weather and Climate Prediction: The Good, the Bad, and the Noisy. *Bulletin of the American Meteorological Society*, *104*(2), E488–E500. DOI: 10.1175/BAMS-D-22-0031.1

Terhal, B. M. (2015). Quantum Error Correction for Quantum Memories. *Reviews of Modern Physics*, *87*(2), 307–346. DOI: 10.1103/RevModPhys.87.307

Wang, Y.. (2020). High-Fidelity Phase Gates for Superconducting Qubits. *Physical Review Applied*, *12*(3), 034034.

Watrous, J. (2018). *The Theory of Quantum Information*. Cambridge University Press. DOI: 10.1017/9781316848142

Zeilinger, A.. (2007). Quantum Entanglement and Teleportation. *Reviews of Modern Physics*, *79*(3), 777–787.

Zhang, J.. (2020). Experimental quantum simulation of fermion-antifermion scattering via boson exchange in a superconducting quantum circuit. *Nature Communications*, *11*(1), 1–8. PMID: 31911652

Zhang, Y., Zhang, S., & Wang, X. (2021). Quantum Optimization for Complex Systems. *Journal of Quantum Information*, *7*(2), 45–67.

Zurek, W. H. (2003). Decoherence, einselection, and the quantum origins of the classical. *Reviews of Modern Physics*, *75*(3), 715–775. DOI: 10.1103/RevModPhys.75.715

Chapter 2
AI, Blockchain, and IoT Driving Innovation in Connected Ecosystems

Sreelekha Paul
https://orcid.org/0009-0007-5524-1919
Brainware University, India

Anindita Chakraborty
Brainware University, India

ABSTRACT

A number of industries including IoT, blockchain, and AI are merging to redesign various industry standards in intelligence, security, and productivity. AI advances Blockchain's key distinctives, and open ledgers by changing data processing and pattern recognition alongside decision-making. Blockchain technology reduces such vulnerabilities as tampering and illegitimate accessing by providing a decentralized immutable platform for data sharing. This has the effect of improving the reliability of the data used by AI models and in turn the reliability of the predictions made by those models. The one that Decentralized applications for which smart contracts or decentralized AI markets are another example, have is also based on blockchain in combination with artificial intelligence. But scalability, energy efficiency and ethical issues are still issues that need to be resolved. IoT has enabled the security provided by the blockchain, and have greatly contributed to enhancing the advancement of Industry 4.0.blockchain integration with AI governance, and in quantum computing.

DOI: 10.4018/979-8-3373-1210-1.ch002

INTRODUCTION

The three technologies that are pushing technological advancement across industries include; Artificial intelligence, Blockchain, and the Internet of things (IoT). Due to AI, systems can process data, analyse it, and assert wise judgment, which includes machine learning, natural language processing, and computer visions (Russell et al., 2020 & Norvig, 2020). Its uses are as vast as self-contained microsystems in manufacturing right down to prognosis models in healthcare. Blockchain is a distributed ledger database that records secure, transparent, and safe P2P transactions and protects the information with cryptographic algorithms. Some obvious uses include supply chain audit trails and cryptocurrency control (Nakamoto et al., 2008). IoT, in contrast, connects billions of devices globally for making intelligent automation decisions and for real-time data exchange. IoT has transformed operation performance and human interface in smart homes, industrial IoT and many others (Atzori et al., 2010). These technologies coalesce to construct compelling ecosystems proactively addressing barriers to scale, security, and real-time decision making and opening up new horizons of possibility.

Strategic Importance of Convergence

All three technologies rely on each other to provide the best results that IoT offers, the decentralized approach of blockchain, and the complex analysing ability of AI. Through the conversion of big data, AI enables IoT alongside enhancing automation and deploying predictive analysis (Gubbi et al., 2013). In this way, Blockchain fosters the evolution of IoT by providing data guarantee, managing trustless environments, and providing security digitization (Christidis et al., 2016 & Devetsikiotis, 2016). Connectivity can be described as the central idea and an enabling platform through which IoT supports merging of systems and devices for real-time interactions. This alliance ensures that there is creation of new ideas in areas such as supply chain, smart city and personalized healthcare since questions of scale, security and performance are addressed. The potential of the three together redefines digital ecosystems.

Global Trends and Vision

Due to technology advancements and enabling legal systems, there is an increasing uptake of AI, Blockchain, and IoT globally. The various technologies that the countries are priorities are as follows; – blockchain technology that enables the safe transaction, – IoT technology leads to connectivity in smart cities, – project AI in healthcare and finance industries lead. The EU's proposed AI Act also heavily relies on the significance of interoperability and ethical usage across the globe in IoT standardisation activities (European Commission, 2021). Since practical solutions for creating a consistent and stable technological system to suggest solutions for their integration are a major part of this chapter, this chapter will consider their intersection, strengths, and issues.

BACKGROUND

Three critical technologies are merging to transform modern technology ecosystems; blockchain, artificial intelligence (AI) and the Internet of Things (IoT). While individually these inventions help a lot in achieving improvements, their joint implementation reveals their full value. Machine learning, natural language processing, and computer vision are transforming many industries, from predictive healthcare to accurate manufacturing, through AI's a variety of capabilities (Russell & Norvig, 2020). As Nakamoto et al. (2008) put it, 'A blockchain is a decentralised cryptographically-secure ledger showing the immutable, visible record of transactions necessary for digital identity management, supply chain management, and banking'. Meanwhile, IoT makes possible smooth instantaneous communication between billions of devices that support applications from industrial automation to smart cities (Atzori et al., 2010). Never before seen is the value that is released when these technologies are strategically integrated. The ability of machine learning and data analytics of AI allows the IoT systems to make more accurate as well as predictive judgments over and above the resource management and operational efficiency (Gubbi et al., 2013). In even situations where trust is absent, blockchain's decentralized nature and cryptographic strength make possible IoT networks with assured safe data transfers (Christidis et al., 2016; Devetsikiotis, 2016). Through solving vital questions, such as scalability, security, and latency, our partnership creates the possibilities for revolutionary use cases in areas of decentralized banking, smart manufacturing industries, as well as customized healthcare. The fusion of these emerging technologies will reconfigure the digital ecosystems as they evolve, which will serve as a template for intelligent digital infrastructures, scalable, and robust.

SYNERGIES AND INNOVATIONS IN CONVERGENCE

It shows that IoT, blockchain, and AI are combined to create opportunities for further development of various spheres. By supplementing large information for the purpose of predictive analytics, AI enhances IoT by enabling a more infrastructural and complex system. More so, (Christidis et al., 2016 and Devetsikiotis, 2016) it is argued that in the Internet of Things, blockchain improves the security of the system and trust since it is able to protect data and restrict unauthorized access. When used in synergy, the mentioned technologies enable smart contracting, which provides decentralized intelligence in complex procedures. For example, blockchain ensures shifting clean energy transparently, and AI enabled IoT objects in smart cities might unilaterally control energy systems (Li et al., 2018). There are new forms such as federated learning which makes it possible to train collaborative AI models on distributed IoT devices. Through making provision for scalability, latency and data security among other challenges this integrated platform encourages more advanced healthcare applications.

AI-Driven IoT Data Analytics

The integration of AI into IoT networks offers crucial features of enhanced predictive features coupled with real-time responses to data analytics and decision-making procedures. Connecting devices generates huge volumes of data used to identify patterns, estimate further development, and enhance performance by AI systems. In the case of industrial IoT systems, the use of AI to analyze data from sensors is employed in the assessment of possible equipment failures, reduction of losses due to the same and cost savings (Lee et al., 2019). Moreover, real-time anomaly detection using AI techniques assures dynamic reaction mechanisms, which are obligatory for certain applications such as healthcare and smart grid application. In healthcare IoT, AI detects mismatched patterns in a patient's condition and in return gives out alerts to healthcare givers (Ramesh et al., 2020).

Table 1. Small example

Example Use Case	AI Role	IoT Contribution
Predictive Maintenance.	Analyzing sensor data trends.	Providing real-time equipment data.
Smart Healthcare Monitoring.	Detecting anomalies in vitals.	Delivering continuous health metrics.

Blockchain-Enhanced IoT Security and Trust

Blockchain technology addresses individual security challenges such as data integrity, authentication, and privacy enhancing IoT systems, quoting from (Christidis et al., 2016 and Devetsikiotis, 2016), the decentralized and unalterable character of the ledger minimizes the risk of data leaks and cyber terrorism since it provides a secure method to record IoT information. Device authentication by blockchain minimizes the danger posed by SPOFs by eliminating dependency on central hosts.

To prevent the vulnerability to unauthorized intrusion, gadgets in a smart home context can employ the Blockchain technique to confirm their device identity in a cryptographic manner (Zhang et al., 2021). Other features found in Blockchain include secure data encryption that shields private IoT data as it is being transmitted and stored.

Table 2. Blockchain's integration fosters trust, enhancing IoT adoption in domains like healthcare, logistics, and energy management

Example Use Case	Blockchain Role	IoT Contribution
Smart Home Authentication.	Decentralized identity management.	Device-to-device communication security.
Supply Chain Transparency	Immutable transaction records.	Real-time asset tracking.

Blockchain and AI Fusion for Decentralized Intelligence

Blockchain integrated AI enhances decentralized intelligence and helps to solve complex problems such as automation, data accuracy, and model interpretability. The problem of oversight of changes in training the model, as well as decision making are solved in the blockchain as the system provides a transparent and immutable ledger of changes to the AI model. This is especially crucial for sensitive sectors such as the medical and the financial sectors (Zhang et al., 2021). That is why, by being transparent, there is a significantly lower likelihood of manipulative or biased AI outcomes. For example, AI is capable of predicting the likelihood of stock-outs in the supply chains where smart contracts based on the blockchain are used and as a result, new orders for supplies will be made (Christidis et al., 2016 & Devetsikiotis, 2016).

Table 3. This fusion paves the way for robust, transparent, and self-operating systems across industries

Example Use Case	Blockchain Role	AI Contribution
Predictive Maintenance.	Secure logging of AI insights.	Failure predictions.
Automated Supply Chains.	Smart contract execution.	Demand forecasting.

The Role of Edge Computing and Federated Learning

Blending AI and Blockchain, edge computing reduces both latency and the load on central servers because data is partially analyzed close to IoT devices (Shi et al., 2016). This is important for applications where quick decisions are vital including manufacturing process automation and self-driving cars. In other words, the blockchain optimizes edge computing by providing safe decentralized data exchange between edge nodes, protection against manipulation / unwanted access. Devices in the IoT ecosystem, due to federated learning, may jointly train models without sharing their raw data at all while optimizing the communication cost and privacy preservation (Li et al., 2020).

Table 4. This integration enables scalable, secure, and efficient decentralized systems for IoT applications

Use Case	Edge Computing Role	Federated Learning Role	Blockchain Contribution
Autonomous Vehicles	Real-time decision-making.	Collaborative model training.	Secure data sharing between nodes.
Healthcare Diagnostics	Localized data processing.	Privacy-preserving AI model updates.	Immutable training records.

INDUSTRY APPLICATIONS AND TRANSFORMATIONS

Due to its constructive impact on productivity and reduction of barriers to openness and creativity, the hybrid of AI, Blockchain and IoT is surging progressive advancements in many fields. Patients' health is monitored through real-time readings generated by IoT devices, and an assessment of the readings is done through AI. Blockchain ensures data integrability and safeguards patient data that includes the medical records (Zhang et al., 2021). Internet of things keeps an eye on the consignment, leverages artificial intelligence for anticipating shifts in demand, and uses blockchain to ensure that products' track records are preserved for excellence in supply chain, and this reduces frauds and inefficiencies as outlined (Casino et al., 2019). Through safe data transfers via block chain, IoT and energy efficiency in Smart Cities, and also through AI self-organised traffic flow for Smart Cities, the three parties' benefit.

For instance, in agriculture, the fields record the supply chain information to prove the genuine origin of food products, and IoT records the soil state; deep learning algorithms recommend how best to cultivate plants. Due to this junction, industries ensure change in needs, improvement of processes, and gain trust, hence transforming conventional systems into smart interconnected industries.

Smart Cities and Sustainable Urbanization

With energy efficiency, optimum utilization of resources along with smart governing, the trio of AI, Blockchain, and IoT is revolutionizing smart cities. To reduce energy inefficiencies, decrease loss, and enhance water supplies, Internet of Things systems that harness AI analyze real-time data collected by urban sensors (Batty et al., 2012). For instance, smart grids use AI techniques in predicting the energy needs in the society and ensure adequate supply, minimization of wastage. The ability to shield data from IoT sensors and provide an immutable, public ledger of public service functioning enhances urban management greatly through the use of blockchain. Examples include; efficient and accountable land registry systems and citizen interface Institutions (Reyna et al., 2018).

Healthcare 4.0

Technologies are integrated into the concept of healthcare 4.0, for intelligent, efficient, and safe medical options for patients. The use of artificial intelligence in IoT devices enables the diagnosis or early identification of illness risks since client vital signs are permanently checked in real-time (Ramesh et al., 2020). For instance, smart clothing employing AI algorithms integrated through its design and capability can detect uncharacteristic heart rates and alert physicians to immediate action. Blockchain solves key issues such as security and data sharing of patient records by implementing the EHR by decentralized and distributed structure, patient record privacy is ensured and many administrative problems are eliminated (Zhang et al., 2021). Trust is further cultivated by the assurance that user-specific information as well as other sensitive information exchanged between patient and provider is safe with blockchain.

Global Supply Chain Resilience

This paper discusses how the integration of the blockchain system with AI enhances the reliability of worldwide supply chains through enhancing the predictability, security, and transparency of the supply chain. Downtime is minimized and demand is expected by integrating the analysis of real time IoT data for better inventory and logistics (Choi et al., 2018). In fraud detection and compliance, blockchain ensures that product provenance is met since records on origin, transport, and handling are well protected (Casino et al., 2019). For instance, AI can predict when there will be supply chain disruptions, which will lead to smart contracts secured by blockchain to restock products. Smart IoT sensors check the conditions required for storage in the supply chain of foods and blockchain ensures quality to ascertain safety and originality.

For example: The pharmaceutical supply chain's resilience is increased through the use of AI, Blockchain, and IoT, which make it possible for predictive logistics, product traceability, and environmental condition monitoring. Blockchain stores unchangeable information to stop fake medications, IoT monitors environmental conditions to maintain product quality, and AI evaluates IoT sensor data to predict delays.

Next-Generation Financial Systems

Blockchain, AI, and IoT are being used in synergy to develop intelligent decentralization and unheard-of fluidity that is revolutionizing financial institutions. DeFi is an application of blockchain solutions that eliminates intermediaries and replaces them with smart contracts to ensure that financial services are automatic, transparent and safe. AI enhances operations on decentralized platforms, protects against fraud, offers personalized information regarding users' financial operations, and addresses the problem of risk management. The IoT payment solutions enable device to device immediate peer to peer transactions, which are required in auto-governed systems like smart appliances or connected autos. An example includes a smart wallet which is secured with blockchain and IoT based which will enable a connected automobile to pay tolls or refuel on its own.

CHALLENGES AND LIMITATIONS IN INTEGRATION

Although combining AI, blockchain, and IoT technologies could lead to a complete transformation of the world, we should remember that the presence of particular little-known impediments could be a barrier to the whole process. The operations model that takes place during the manufacturing process creates the demand for evermore complex and capable asset management solutions to regulate and optimize the practice.

Scalability and Interoperability

Keeping up with the demand of maintaining the decentralized nature of blockchain is also a way to deal with scaling issues. Sharing the details of a blockchain network presents scalability issues with other devices and IoT platforms (Nguyen et al., 2020). Energy wastage is caused by all the challenges in the scalability of the clouds. Also, most AI (machine and deep learning) algorithms require it. often unevenly distributed and random data schemes. Lower power nano-gates that will control the current through the magnets and look for other ways how electricity is used is another way to take advantage of the scalability of an edge system. A multidimensional interaction of data should be taken into account so that flexibility can be achieved. Blockchain is too rigid to support the fleeting IoT as Blockchain has no operational logic capability. IoT networks run on private blockchains, which have been designed to support local devices in a particular application area. However, Blockchain is considered as an unscalable technology. Scaling problems arise mainly from widespread IoT attacks such as Botnets, botnet detection, and countermeasures in the cloud to defend against them. Perimeter networks can enhance the security of IoT platforms through the Epigrammatic (2017) security approach, which is a decentralized and authenticated topology. The majority of AI models could be applied to the edge.

Energy Efficiency and Sustainability

Diverse range of IoT devices, but some Blockchain protocols might not react to dynamic IoT networks. Another problem is that with Bitcoin and other cryptocurrencies, the secure IoT payments have increased the amount of electricity used. Additionally, multiple standards and protocols create difficulties in integrating IoT, blockchain, and AI models. Automation and AI integration are the future possibilities that can be offered through IoT. In healthcare wearables gain traction because patients are becoming active participants in their own HealthMap can play an important role in the deployment of IoT devices across various platforms. By building a common interconnection the interoperability of all the platforms will be improved. The big challenge for the developers and Stanley also suggests a way for AI models to self-optimize by improving their parallelism and learning tools. "For Re-training, both software code and the model must be changed. The one with a more specific job has a larger area of operation, and the learning rate is too low.

For example, when people talk to chatbots, they expect more real-time responses than browsing the internet, hence processing latency affects usability. This is due to the reason that a short time window demands higher processing power and longer time CAD a lower one.

Data Privacy and Security

The acquisition and processing of data from IoT sensors need to be less energy-intensive by using new Digital Signal Processing technology. Other methods that will lessen the power. Demanding Mining is done both on blockchains and in the training of AI models. Together, they have been reported to cause a high amount of carbon emissions, thus becoming one of the main contributors of environmental pollution. The algorithms like GPT-3 demand a significant amount of power for both training and inference. Computer Scientists have proposed several approaches to address blockchain technology's energy efficiency concerns. Such techniques include

(a) the introduction of cap-and-trade taxing schemes,
(b) the use of renewable energy sources,
(c) the use of Proof-of-Stake (PoS)/PoW-based consensus algorithms, and
(d) the deployment of more efficient processors. Because the PoW algorithm on blockchains uses as high as little states.

This is why energy consumption is much higher than expected. The other AI method, such as the GPT-3 models, also requires large amounts. Only about 25% is used in training, and 75% is used in inference. Updating these and introducing the AI engines in the hospital may be much more cost-effective and result in significantly better patient care. The importance of Devices keeps collecting user data, but the badly performed treatment of this data can result in abuse or surveillance that creates privacy issues (Roman et al., 2018). Also, blockchain is immutable, which is one of the reasons' leading to noncompliance with such regulations as GDPR, the user's right to be forgotten, for instance. Limitations of Blockchain Immutability can be seen as an advantage of blockchain technology, but it also hides from us some of the challenges we have to deal with. While updates necessary for dynamic IoT data can be done, they are, however, not easy to carry out on immutable Blockchain ledgers. Furthermore, it is still tricky to incorporate Blockchain with privacy-preserving alternative frameworks, such as differential privacy.

Implications for Ethics and Society Bias

In AI and Blockchain Documents Biases can unconsciously be included in the decision-making process of AI models. Immutable blockchain records cannot be updated and remove biases. For example, a database based on the Blockchain technology that contains biased recruiting algorithms might continue to discriminate. Blockchain has a built-in solution so that such problems arise only for the human. A transparent but immutable system (Mehrabi et al., 2021). Fairness in Adoption

Equity is a worldwide prevalent issue in the integration of tech devices. The poor of the world may lack proper information technology which can lead to separating them from the rest of their world, (leaving an exploitation gap). The ethical aspects of the societal impact of technology are among other things such as the automated society aspect, which includes the loss of human voice and job dislocation.

EMERGING TRENDS

Based on new technologies such as autonomy, collaboration systems, quantum computing the examined interconnections between AI, Blockchain, and IoT proceed. Improving the scalability, integrating interoperability and underlining the principles of moral, human approach are the purposes of these developments.

Blockchain and AI with Quantum Computing

Blockchain; and divergent optimization of the Internet of Things devices is among the fields where the application of quantum computing is evolutionary. By increasing the cryptographic computations along with the consensus procedure, such quantum procedures like Shor's algorithm highly improves the scalability of blockchains as discussed (Yuan et al., 2020). For instance, regarding the increasing Blockchain complexity, using quantum-based key distribution may enhance its security and at the same time reduce the process load.

The use of quantum computing in AI allows in providing solutions to multi-variable optimization problems inherent in Internet of Things systems. A quantum-artificial intelligence combined system, for instance, is expected to reduce latency and energy consumption when used to optimize routing of IoT devices in a smart city.

Self-Contained and Integrated Systems

Aviation is an example of the autonomous system, which incorporates drones, robots, and smart cars to be operated with the help of Artificial Intelligence of things coupled with IoT networks through Blockchain technology. While blockchain ensures the protection of decentralised, public regulation of autonomous activities, artificial intelligence (AI) enables real-time decision-making (Christidis et al., 2016 & Devetsikiotis, 2016).

For example, a fleet of drones can organize an array of battened operations on disaster management, share the information in real-time with the help of Internet of Things sensors, and use blockchain for the transparent registration and distribution of sources. This was established to ensure efficiency and self-assurance in performing core duties.

Partnerships and Ecosystem Creation

Through the development of multi-industry platforms with established shared systems, such as blockchain, IoT, and AI, innovation is promoted. For instance, co-operation between logistics and healthcare industries enables the use of Blockchain to safely track medical equipment and supplies; IoT provides real time tracking; and AI optimizes the routes.

This is why standardization organizations such as the IEEE are so important because they come up with the architecture that supports interaction between the systems (IEEE Standards Association, 2021). These initiatives bring innovation and global acceptance.

Human-Centric AI and Privacy-First Design

There are emerging trends that suggest a shift towards moral models of AI's which are open, designed for responsible use, and pay great attention to user privacy. Thus, by making the judgments understandable, the XAI models reduce the probability of obtaining bias outcomes (Gunning et al., 2019). Blockchain improves this by providing structures for IoT devices where user's data privacy is preserved at the same time being ensured safe decentralized management of data.

Blockchain, for instance, may obscure patent de-identification in the health sector while enabling artificial intelligence to analyse the health of the population in the society. This does so in a perfect way that equally balances between innovation and privacy.

STRATEGIC IMPLICATIONS

More information about the strategic implications of integration of the AI, Blockchain, and IoT across the industries presented in this chapter. This coincides on how these two concepts complement each other to extend safe and scalable systems, improve on operations and result in innovation. These technologies solve challenges like integration, power use, and information protection to offer fresh ideas from making smart cities to redesigning supply chains. In addition, all these new developments, such as the autonomy systems and quantum computers, the chapter provides organizations with knowledge on preparedness of prepared strategies.

Lastly, it stresses that for all of these great technologies to reach their full potential, ethics, laws and sectors collaboration must be observed.

Synergies and Innovations

Blockchain-AI- IoT integration is one of the most significant present technical enablers with applications across industries and there is a clear synergistic result when all three are integrated. Connecting Things of the Internet of Things means that it can make connectivity and data gathering commonplace; intelligent decision making and data analysis through Artificial Intelligence systems balances this out. These are complemented by blockchain, which ensures decentralized, secure and immutable systems. The merging of these technologies is helping shape the foundation for dealing with present day concerns such as; size, cost, and data protection concerns (Christidis et al., 2016 & Devetsikiotis, 2016). Significant outcomes that were highlighted are the minimization of latency through edge computing, data security through the use of block chain, and use of artificial intelligence in prediction on IoT networks. Hyped technologies such as quantum computing enhance IoT performance and Blockchain solutions improve Blockchain capacity for IoT, and autonomous systems apply Artificial Intelligence to make real-time responses for innovative IoT devices while building trust frameworks based on blockchain (Yuan et al., 2020). Besides, all the human-centered designs put more emphasis on ethical and even privacy issues solutions. In order to ensure that there is accountability and transparency, then AI models should be implemented (Gunning et al., 2019).

Use cases which redefine an industry like supply chain, smart city or even the improvement of healthcare, all stem from these synergies. All these solutions prove effectiveness of cooperation and innovation initiatives within a company because they address many of the key obstacles such as interoperability and power consumption and provide a winsomely ethical and sustainable approach to digital transformation.

Multidisciplinary Collaboration

AI, Blockchain, IoT cannot be adopted without significant collaboration between technologists, legislators, and researchers. These revolutionary technologies have brought up technological, legal and even sociological issues and these interdisciplinary collaborations are therefore necessary in order to address them. Thus, technologists contribute to innovation by designing solutions that can grow alongside society, solid algorithms for privacy entailment, and overall, safe frameworks. Meanwhile, the legislators develop policies good for the creators while also addressing moral concerns such as data protection and privacy, as well as equal access to the technologies (Floridi et al., 2018). About new developments, the researchers offer recommendations for solutions, proving them with evidence, to ensure that knowledge is attainable and sustainable. For example, the development of standards to ensure reliability and compatibility in cross-OS environments, to be pursued by scholars studying Blockchain and AI in the context of IoT networks the development of standards to ensure reliability and compatibility in cross-OS ecosystems, to be advanced by scholars researching the use of Blockchain and AI in IoT networks (IEEE Standards Association, 2021). Program trials can be carried out through collaborative efforts with a number of involved parties such as decentralised health care systems or smart city infrastructure, to better understand practical applicability and expansion capability.

Several fields have to join forces in order to develop this vision that would unify the technical aspects with the social requirements. There are, however, challenges if the stakeholder is to make the advantages of integration attainable to the larger population, these challenges include; bias, energy use, and digital divides may be addressed through open dialogue and value creation.

Vision for a Secure and Intelligent Digital Future

The three technologies of AI, Blockchain, and IoT bring in a new age of revolution, paving a way for Industry 5.0 and beyond. This new paradigm focuses much on the intelligent, secure, and human-centred technologies which enhance the interaction between humans and machines. They are personalised, sustainable and ethical inventions of Industry 5.0, in contrast to Industry 4.0, which focuses on automation. AI is used for better analysis, blockchain for security and trust and IoT for integration (Breque et al., 2021). With real-time optimization and intelligent decision-making and predictive maintenance, AI-based IoT sensors are expected to enhance industrial practices. These systems will be considerably enhanced through blockchain technology, with data integrity to underlie the systems and block-chain based frameworks for safe and open transactions. Thus, AI integrated robots, for example, might complement humans in smart manufacturing, while blockchain guards IoT and operating data Sensors help resource allocations.

Collectively in the future the above technologies have the potential to address sophisticated problems such as digital public services access and energy management. Ethical consideration and sustainable measures shall be incorporated in the future digital ecosystem in order to shape prosperity and social well-being by innovation. The former type of vision requires great cooperation among academicians, engineering technologists and politicians in order to construct sound and versatile systems for promoting the advance of the standard of living in every part of the globe.

ADVANCE FEATURES

- On the basis of modern elements, this chapter aims at improving the understanding of the integration of AI, Blockchain, and IoT successfully and provides valuable advice on such integration.
- The substantive sized case descriptions offer samples of the full application, like Singapore smart city initiatives with blockchain ensuring safe data handling, IoT devices and AI program in energy efficiency of data and city planning.
- Currently, IBM's Food Trust Blockchain that enhances food safety and discourages fraud in the market has revealed enhanced supply chain traceability and better global supply chain transparency.
- Blockchain safeguards the updated software and operational information and AI controlled IoT in the Tesla cars is a good example of the innovation of self-driving cars. Such systems rely on employment of real-time data for this purpose. These examples show how these technologies might transform a few industries and there are numerous applications of these technologies.

CONCLUSION

The chapter employs frameworks and graphics to enhance understanding of the interacted relationship between the blockchain, IoT and AI. These illustrations pinpoint their roles in scalability, efficiency and security while their coordinated interaction is methodologically comprehensible. In an attempt to be forward-looking, I have included speculative yet evidence-based scenarios of Industry 5.0 and beyond in the chapter. To increase the reliability of global trade, it, for instance, envisions an intelligent supply chain that employs Blockchain for secure transactions; IoT for monitoring the conditions; and AI for risk prognosis. The chapter gives a good roadmap for how to use AI, Blockchain and IoT in building safe and smart future digital domain by integrating today's popular features with futuristic use cases. This is even more effective as besides the training it also promotes innovation within the entire organization.

FUTURE DIRECTION

While the field AI+Blockchain+IoT is rich in opportunities, its future depends on how the current challenges are addressed, and the opportunities for creating new applications are understood. Subsequent research and development of these technologies should emphasize on issues of scalability, sustainability and ethically acceptable uses of the technologies as they are enhanced.

- **Development of quantum enhanced systems:** One of these includes the design of enhancing systems for various applications, one of which is the development of quantum enhanced systems. Increased consensus processes across the trek as well as enhanced cryptographic safety stand to revolutionize the blockchain mechanism through quantum computing. It also indicates opportunities in optimizing IoT – Smart City energy distribution or Self-driving cars – by addressing multi-variable problems. The mystery of how to apply quantum algorithms in today's frameworks may present levels of efficiency unprecedented in the past.
- **Edge and federated computing models:** Such elements as edge and federated computing models are also a positive trend. They also work on the data at source so that the latency is reduced and data privacy is optimized. reference. Future systems could utilize Federated learning and blockchain technology to build safe flexible decentralised AI networks for use in disaster relief, healthcare and financial sectors.
- **Cross Industry Integration Standards:** It will also help to have Industry interfacing and development of standards. The Cross Industry Integration Standards vendors and industry reference models will accelerate the integration of multiple industries, including transportation and agriculture. When it comes to addressing ethical and regulatory questions as well as enhancing fairness and sustainability of adoption across the globe, collaborative projects by professionals, engineers, lawmakers, as well as scholars might be implemented.
- **Human oriented AI systems:** For AI to be accepted by individuals and organizations in the society there is need for human oriented AI systems with privacy as a priority. AI's next gen must utilize Blockchain for storing their data securely and privately; and must incorporate transparency, accountability, and justice into the algorithms it employs. These guidelines are essential in the applications such as healthcare where dealing with sensitive information is inevitable to accompany the best moral standards.
- **Uses across Industry 5.0:** Last of all, the further development of uses across Industry 5.0 and more will alter the way technology extends and bears on people and the world. The focus on sustainable utilization of resources will remain the driving force and innovation enablers proposed for these systems are blockchain for transparent management and AI/ IoT for efficient use and allocation of the available resources. For instance, blockchain may offer trust,

AI may enhance distribution, renewable resources can be incorporated into self-supply systems.

REFERENCES

Atzori, L., Iera, A., & Morabito, G. (2010). The Internet of Things: A survey. *Computer Networks*, *54*(15), 2787–2805. DOI: 10.1016/j.comnet.2010.05.010

Batty, M., Axhausen, K. W., Giannotti, F., Pozdnoukhov, A., Bazzani, A., Wachowicz, M., Ouzounis, G., & Portugali, Y. (2012). Smart cities of the future. *The European Physical Journal. Special Topics*, *214*(1), 481–518. DOI: 10.1140/epjst/e2012-01703-3

Breque, M., De Nul, L., & Petridis, A. (2021). Industry 5.0: Towards a sustainable, human-centric, and resilient European industry. European Commission Report.

Casino, F., Dasaklis, T. K., & Patsakis, C. (2019). A systematic literature review of blockchain-based applications: Current status, classification, and open issues. *Telematics and Informatics*, *36*, 55–81. DOI: 10.1016/j.tele.2018.11.006

Choi, T. M., Wallace, S. W., & Wang, Y. (2018). Big data analytics in operations management. *Production and Operations Management*, *27*(10), 1868–1881. DOI: 10.1111/poms.12838

Christidis, K., & Devetsikiotis, M. (2016). Blockchains and smart contracts for the Internet of Things. *IEEE Access : Practical Innovations, Open Solutions*, *4*, 2292–2303. DOI: 10.1109/ACCESS.2016.2566339

European Commission. (2021). *Proposal for a Regulation Laying Down Harmonized Rules on Artificial Intelligence*. EUR-Lex.

Floridi, L., Cowls, J., Beltrametti, M., Chatila, R., Chazerand, P., Dignum, V., Luetge, C., Madelin, R., Pagallo, U., Rossi, F., Schafer, B., Valcke, P., & Vayena, E. (2018). AI4People—An ethical framework for a good AI society: Opportunities, risks, principles, and recommendations. *Minds and Machines*, *28*(4), 689–707. DOI: 10.1007/s11023-018-9482-5 PMID: 30930541

Gubbi, J., Buyya, R., Marusic, S., & Palaniswami, M. (2013). Internet of Things (IoT): A vision, architectural elements, and future directions. *Future Generation Computer Systems*, *29*(7), 1645–1660. DOI: 10.1016/j.future.2013.01.010

Gunning, D., & Aha, D. W. (2019). DARPA's explainable artificial intelligence (XAI) program. *AI Magazine*, *40*(2), 44–58. DOI: 10.1609/aimag.v40i2.2850

IEEE Standards Association. (2021). *Advancing interoperability in AI systems*. IEEE Reports.

Lee, J., Bagheri, B., & Kao, H. A. (2019). A cyber-physical systems architecture for Industry 4.0-based manufacturing systems. *Manufacturing Letters*, *3*(1), 18–23.

Li, S., Da Xu, L., & Zhao, S. (2018). The Internet of Things: A survey. *Information Systems Frontiers*, *17*(2), 243–259. DOI: 10.1007/s10796-014-9492-7

Li, T., Sahu, A. K., Talwalkar, A., & Smith, V. (2020). Federated learning: Challenges, methods, and future directions. *IEEE Signal Processing Magazine*, *37*(3), 50–60. DOI: 10.1109/MSP.2020.2975749

Mehrabi, N., Morstatter, F., Saxena, N., Lerman, K., & Galstyan, A. (2021). A survey on bias and fairness in machine learning. *ACM Computing Surveys*, *54*(6), 1–35. DOI: 10.1145/3457607

Nakamoto, S. (2008). Bitcoin: A Peer-to-Peer Electronic Cash System. *Bitcoin.org*.

Nguyen, Q. K.. (2020). A survey on blockchain applications in IoT. *IEEE Access : Practical Innovations, Open Solutions*, *7*, 164–173.

Ramesh, A., Kambhampati, C., Monson, J. R. T., & Drew, P. J. (2020). Artificial intelligence in medicine. *Annals of the Royal College of Surgeons of England*, *86*(5), 334–338. DOI: 10.1308/147870804290 PMID: 15333167

Reyna, A., Martín, C., Chen, J., Soler, E., & Díaz, M. (2018). On blockchain and its integration with IoT. Challenges and opportunities. *Future Generation Computer Systems*, *88*, 173–190. DOI: 10.1016/j.future.2018.05.046

Roman, R.. (2018). Privacy and security in the Internet of Things: A review. *Future Generation Computer Systems*, *78*, 826–837.

Russell, S., & Norvig, P. (2020). *Artificial Intelligence: A Modern Approach* (4th ed.). Pearson.

Shi, W., Cao, J., Zhang, Q., Li, Y., & Xu, L. (2016). Edge computing: Vision and challenges. *IEEE Internet of Things Journal*, *3*(5), 637–646. DOI: 10.1109/JIOT.2016.2579198

World Economic Forum. (2020). The Global Technology Governance Report 2020. World Economic Forum.

Yuan, X., Lu, Y., & Wang, X. (2020). Quantum-enhanced Blockchain and its applications. *Quantum Engineering*, *2*(1), e49.

Zhang, P., White, J., Schmidt, D. C., Lenz, G., & Rosenbloom, S. T. (2021). FHIRChain: Applying Blockchain to securely and scalably share clinical data. *Computers in Biology and Medicine*, *104*, 132–141.

Chapter 3
Impact of Artificial Intelligence and Machine Learning Techniques in Database Management System Components

J. Vijaya
https://orcid.org/0000-0002-9948-8573
International Institute of Information Technology, Naya Raipur, India

Suvankar Paul
International Institute of Information Technology, Naya Raipur, India

Rohan Sharma
International Institute of Information Technology, Naya Raipur, India

ABSTRACT

The integration of artificial intelligence (AI) and machine learning (ML) in database management systems (DBMS) is revolutionizing how data is managed and analyzed. This review highlights the role of AI/ML in enhancing DBMS functions such as intelligent transaction scheduling (e.g., conflict prediction in OLTP), adaptive query optimization (e.g., reinforcement learning for plan selection), and automated configuration tuning (e.g., workload-aware systems like RocksDB). Key components include data preprocessing (feature extraction, normalization), architectural integration (embedding ML into optimizers, use of federated learning), and evaluation using metrics such as query latency, throughput, and model accuracy. While these innovations offer greater efficiency and scalability, ethical considerations such as

DOI: 10.4018/979-8-3373-1210-1.ch003

data privacy, bias, and system transparency are crucial. This paper emphasizes the need for responsible AI adoption in DBMS to support real-time analytics, operational efficiency, and intelligent data-driven applications.

INTRODUCTION

The convergence of AI and DBMS has become a focal point for research and innovation, reshaping how organizations manage, analyze, and leverage data. As the demand for data-driven decision-making intensifies, the traditional limitations of relational databases especially in handling vast and unstructured datasets have become increasingly apparent. Concurrently, the rapid advancement of machine learning (ML) technologies presents both opportunities and challenges for optimizing data processing and retrieval. AI is revolutionizing the database landscape by automating routine tasks such as configuration tuning, backups, and performance monitoring, (Wannalai & Mekruksavanich, 2019). This automation not only minimizes human error but also significantly reduces operational overhead. Moreover, AI's predictive analytics capabilities empower organizations to anticipate trends and enhance decision-making processes. As database systems incorporate these intelligent solutions, they improve data quality by identifying inconsistencies and bolstering security through anomaly detection and threat analysis, (Openko et al., 2019) (Sanca & Ailamaki, 2024). On the other hand, the complexities of modern DBMSs characterized by numerous adjustable parameters necessitate efficient tuning methods that can often overwhelm human administrators. Recent advancements in ML offer promising solutions, allowing databases to learn from historical data and autonomously recommend optimal configurations, thus streamlining performance management. The reciprocal relationship between AI and DBMSs is noteworthy: AI enhances database intelligence, optimizing query processing and automating index selection, while DBMS technologies simplify the deployment of AI models, reducing complexity and fostering innovation. This dual paradigm, often referred to as AI for DB (AI for databases) and DB for AI (databases for AI), underscores the potential for collaborative advancements that can reshape industries, (Wang et al., 2024) (Unuriode et al., 2023). Additionally, the integration of AI within DBMSs addresses pressing challenges, such as ensuring data security and privacy in an era of stringent regulatory demands. Advanced encryption methods can allow for complex queries on encrypted data, safeguarding sensitive information while maintaining functionality.

This paper aims to explore the evolution, challenges, and innovations at the intersection of AI and DBMSs. We will examine empirical evaluations of ML pipelines executed directly within database environments, utilizing frameworks like MASQ (Machine Learning AS Query) to translate trained models into standard SQL. Through this exploration, we will highlight the collective potential of AI and DBMSs to enhance operational efficiency and address the complexities of modern data environments, ultimately paving the way for the next generation of intelligent database systems. Additionally, integrating AI into DBMSs aids in addressing crucial concerns such protecting data security and privacy, particularly in light of expanding regulatory requirements. Sensitive information is safeguarded while remaining accessible for analysis thanks to modern AI-driven encryption approaches that allow databases to do sophisticated queries on encrypted data.

BACKGROUND

The research methodology employed in this review focuses on systematically exploring and analyzing the integration of AI and ML within DBMS. The methodology consists of several stages, including Fundamental of AI and DBMS, Traditional DBMS approaches, Literature review, (Chaudhuri, 1998) (Abbasi et al., 2024) (Van Aken et al., 2017) (Nookala, 2021) (Tsesmelis & Simitsis, 2022) (Gadde, 2024) (Kumar, Boehm, & Yang, 2017) (Ma, 2022) (Ramakrishnan & Gehreke, 2002) (Wang et al., 2016) (Munappy et al., 2019) (Shen et al., 2022) (Miao et al., 2017) (Cebi et al., 2020) (Paganelli et al., 2023) (Nanda, Bajaj, & Gupta, 2020) (Nihalani, Silakari, & Motwani, 2009) (Huang, Gao, & Chen, 2024) (Xuan et al., 2022) (Bai, 2023) (Hao, 2021) (Zhou et al., 2020) (Li, Zhou, & Cao, 2021) (Wu et al., 2022) (Khan et al., 2024) (Al-Khassawneh & Alaya, 2023) (Rosa et al., 2024) (Ding et al., 2019) (Pulivarthy, 2024) (Kandolo, 2024), data collection, analysis, and evaluation of findings from both theoretical and practical perspectives.

1. **Fundamental of AI and DBMS:** An analytical framework is developed to systematically evaluate the role of AI and ML in DBMS across various dimensions such as query optimization, data security, data quality management, and maintenance automation. Comparative analysis is conducted to identify common themes, technologies, and challenges in integrating AI and ML into traditional DBMS. Factors such as performance improvement, scalability, and security are assessed in relation to AI and ML technologies used is shown in Figure 1.

Figure 1. Knowledge modeling of the proposed methodology

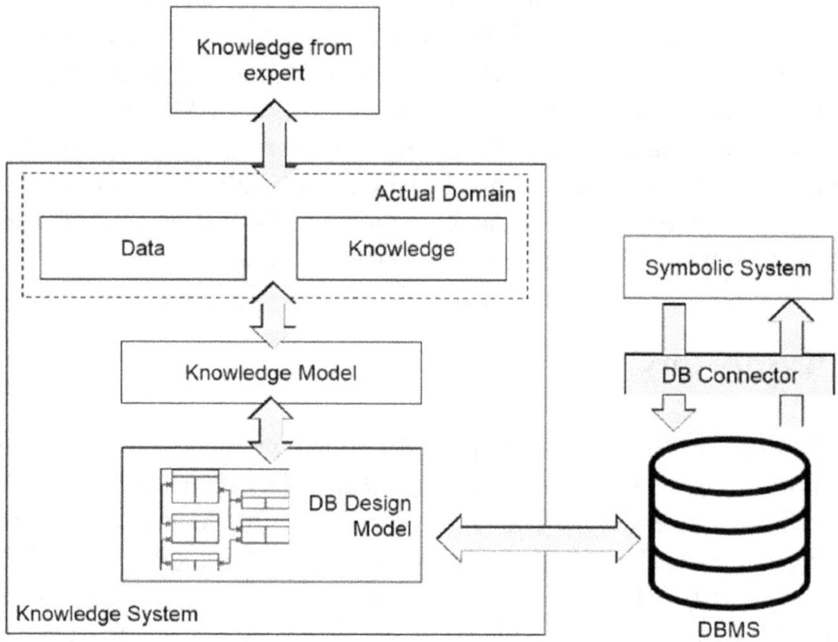

2. Traditional DBMS approaches
   a) **Hierarchical DBMS:** The hierarchical database model organizes data in a tree-like structure, where each record has a single parent and potentially many children. This model is suitable for applications with clear parent-child relationships, such as organizational charts or file systems. While it allows for fast data retrieval through predefined paths, it lacks flexibility — especially in handling complex many-to-many relationships — and requires knowledge of the structure during querying.
   b) **Network DBMS:** The network model extends the hierarchical model by allowing many-to-many relationships using a graph structure. Records are connected through sets (pointers), enabling more flexible data navigation. Although it offers better representation of real-world relationships compared to the hierarchical model, it introduces complexity in schema design and query execution, as developers must manually manage the data paths.
   c) **Relational DMBS:** The relational model, introduced by E.F. Codd, revolutionized database design by storing data in tables (relations) consisting of rows and columns. It uses SQL (Structured Query Language) for data

manipulation and retrieval. RDBMS provides simplicity, data independence, and strong support for ACID (Atomicity, Consistency, Isolation, and Durability) properties. This model has become the most widely adopted due to its balance of flexibility, robustness, and ease of use, though it can struggle with massive unstructured or semi-structured data.

d) **Object Oriented DBMS:** Object-Oriented DBMS integrates database capabilities with object-oriented programming principles. Data is stored in the form of objects, supporting inheritance, polymorphism, and encapsulation. This model is useful for complex applications like CAD, multimedia, and scientific research. However, OODBMSs are less common in practice due to lack of standardization and challenges in integrating with traditional relational systems.

e) **File based System (Pre-DBMS):** Before formal DBMS models, data were stored in flat files, often managed manually by custom application code. These systems suffered from data redundancy, inconsistency, poor scalability, and minimal data security. There was no standard way to query or relate data, making maintenance difficult and error-prone. The limitations of file-based systems led to the evolution of structured DBMS models

3. **Literature survey:** The distribution of articles according to the suggested classification model for the function of machine learning (ML) and artificial intelligence (AI) in diverse industries in DBMS is shown in Table 1.

Table 1. Distribution of articles used in this study

Topic	Number of Papers	Techniques	References
Intelligent Data base management system	5	Intelligent DB & Future Direction	(Wannalai & Mekruksavanich, 2019) (Openko et al., 2019) (Sanca & Ailamaki, 2024) (Wang et al., 2024) (Unuriode et al., 2023)
Fundamental of DBMS and Evaluation	2	Data collection & Evaluation parameters	(Chaudhuri, 1998) (Abbasi et al., 2024)
Data Base Automation	3	Automated DB using AI	(Van Aken et al., 2017) (Nookala, 2021) (Tsesmelis & Simitsis, 2022)
Data Base Real Time Processing	1	Real Time Processing	(Gadde, 2024)
Data Base Analytics	2	AI models, DL and ML models	(Kumar, Boehm, & Yang, 2017) (Ma, 2022)
Data Base Management System	1	Data Management Techniques and Models	(Ramakrishnan & Gehreke, 2002)

continued on following page

Table 1. Continued

Topic	Number of Papers	Techniques	References
Integration of DL in DB	5	DL techniques for Real-time Data Processing	(Wang et al., 2016) (Munappy et al., 2019) (Shen et al., 2022) (Miao et al., 2017) (Cebi et al., 2020)
Integration of ML in DB	10	ML techniques for Real-time Data Processing	(Paganelli et al., 2023) (Nanda, Bajaj, & Gupta, 2020) (Nihalani, Silakari, & Motwani, 2009) (Huang, Gao, & Chen, 2024) (Xuan et al., 2022) (Bai, 2023) (Hao, 2021) (Zhou et al., 2020) (Li, Zhou, & Cao, 2021) (Wu et al., 2022)
Integration of AI in DB	1	AI-DB Integration Approaches	(Khan et al., 2024)
Application of DB and Limitation of Integration	5	Challenges in Integration	(Al-Khassawneh & Alaya, 2023) (Rosa et al., 2024) (Ding et al., 2019) (Pulivarthy, 2024) (Kandolo, 2024)

Recent research highlights the growing interest and challenges in integrating intelligent techniques within modern Database Management Systems (DBMS). Wannalai and Mekruksavanich (2019) explore the application of intelligent databases for enhancing information management, emphasizing the potential of AI to improve data retrieval and decision-making processes. Openko et al. (2019) discuss the critical considerations in selecting appropriate DBMS solutions in contemporary information systems, underscoring the need for adaptability and efficiency. Sanca and Ailamaki (2024) examine the evolving challenges and opportunities in model-relational data management, particularly focusing on optimizing performance and scalability in complex data environments. Wang et al. (2024) provide a qualitative study on automating DBMS functions, identifying key obstacles and potential solutions in the automation process, including query optimization and system tuning. Lastly, Unuriode et al. (2023) review the integration of artificial intelligence into database systems, offering a comprehensive overview of AI-driven advancements and their implications for future database architectures. Together, these works collectively highlight both the progress and ongoing challenges in blending AI and ML techniques with DBMS to meet the demands of increasingly complex and data-intensive applications.

Recent research in the field of database management systems (DBMS) demonstrates substantial progress in the integration of artificial intelligence (AI) and machine learning (ML) techniques to enhance the efficiency, scalability, and adaptability of traditional database architectures. The pioneering work of Chaudhuri (1998) laid the groundwork by investigating the crucial intersection between data mining and database systems, which has since evolved into a broader exploration of intelligent data management. More contemporary studies, such as those by Abbasi et al. (2024) and

Van Aken et al. (2017), delve deeply into the design and implementation of adaptive and scalable DBMS frameworks, which leverage machine learning algorithms to automate tasks like query optimization, resource allocation, and performance tuning. The study by Nookala (2021) highlights how machine learning can automate and optimize data warehouse operations, improving efficiency. Tsesmelis and Simitsis (2022) explore the evolution of database optimizers, emphasizing a shift from static rules to adaptive learning-based strategies. Both works underscore AI/ML's growing role in enhancing DBMS performance and adaptability. Additionally, applied research by Gadde (2024) and Ma (2022) has showcased the tangible benefits of AI-augmented database management systems in real-time data analytics and intelligent system control, illustrating how AI can drive more responsive and context-aware data operations in increasingly complex and dynamic environments. Kumar, Boehm, and Yang (2017) highlight key data management challenges in machine learning, such as data cleaning, integration, and labeling. They also review emerging systems and techniques that address these issues to streamline the ML pipeline, (Gadde, 2024) (Kumar, Boehm, & Yang, 2017) (Ma, 2022). The incorporation of deep learning methods into DBMS introduces further dimensions of complexity and opportunity, addressing challenges in multidimensional data processing, lifecycle management, and system security as highlighted by Wang et al. (2016), Munappy et al. (2019), and Cebi et al. (2020). Wang et al. (2016) discuss the intersection of databases and deep learning, identifying challenges like data heterogeneity, model management, and system optimization.

Shen et al. (2022) propose a framework integrating deep learning with multidimensional databases to enhance mass data processing efficiency. Miao et al. (2017) advocate for a unified approach to data and lifecycle management in deep learning, emphasizing the need for system-level integration to support iterative model development. These works collectively underline the importance of bridging data systems and ML workflows for scalability and performance.

Alongside these technical innovations, comprehensive reviews and surveys, including those by Zhou et al. (2020) and Li et al. (2021), offer valuable syntheses of current machine learning methodologies tailored specifically for database applications. These works emphasize the growing reliance on ML to support a variety of data management functions, from transaction scheduling to anomaly detection and predictive analytics. More recent advancements by Paganelli et al. (2023) and Huang et al. (2024) illustrate cutting-edge efforts to seamlessly embed machine learning predictions and reinforcement learning-based strategies within core DBMS operations, such as automated index selection and dynamic query planning, thereby facilitating more intelligent and autonomous database management. Simultaneously, the emergence of AI in databases has surfaced critical concerns around data privacy and security, with researchers like Al-Khassawneh (2023) and Kandolo (2024) addressing the imperative need for robust AI-driven data access controls and secure handling of sensitive information. Collectively, this extensive body of research not only underscores the rapid advancements achieved in intelligent database systems but also brings to light the complex challenges and open research questions that continue to drive innovation in the field, especially as data volumes grow and applications demand more sophisticated and real-time analytical capabilities.

The integration of Artificial Intelligence (AI) and Machine Learning (ML) into database systems has led to transformative advancements across various dimensions of data management. Nanda et al. (2020) survey the use of ML in transaction scheduling, demonstrating its potential to enhance concurrency and adaptability. Nihalani et al. (2009) explore intelligent database systems by combining AI with traditional DBMS to support decision-making. Cao et al. (2022) introduce ML-based techniques to safeguard databases from electromagnetic radiation threats, highlighting a novel security application. Bai (2023) emphasizes the role of NoSQL databases and Ajax technology in AI-driven information systems, facilitating more scalable and interactive architectures. Hao (2021) develops a database mining system powered by AI algorithms to improve data discovery and pattern recognition. Wu et al. (2022) review ML tools and databases for drug combination prediction, showcasing how AI can drive biomedical research. Khan et al. (2024) discuss AI's role in managing big databases, focusing on storage efficiency and automated analytics. Rosa et al. (2024) present a hybrid approach integrating IoT and big data analytics with ML to build intelligent DBMS architectures. Ding et al. (2019) propose leveraging AI for optimizing index recommendations using query execution data, reflecting automation in performance tuning. Lastly, Pulivarthy (2024) examines how generative AI is reshaping the database industry through innovative tools and services. Collectively, these studies underscore the profound impact of AI/ML in enhancing database performance, security, scalability, and intelligence across diverse application domains.

MAIN FOCUS OF THE CHAPTER

According to AI for DBMS consist of four dimensions: 1) Database Automation 2) Database Real-time Processing 3) Database Analysis 4) Database Management is shown in Figure 2.

Figure 2. Classification framework for AI and ML technique in database

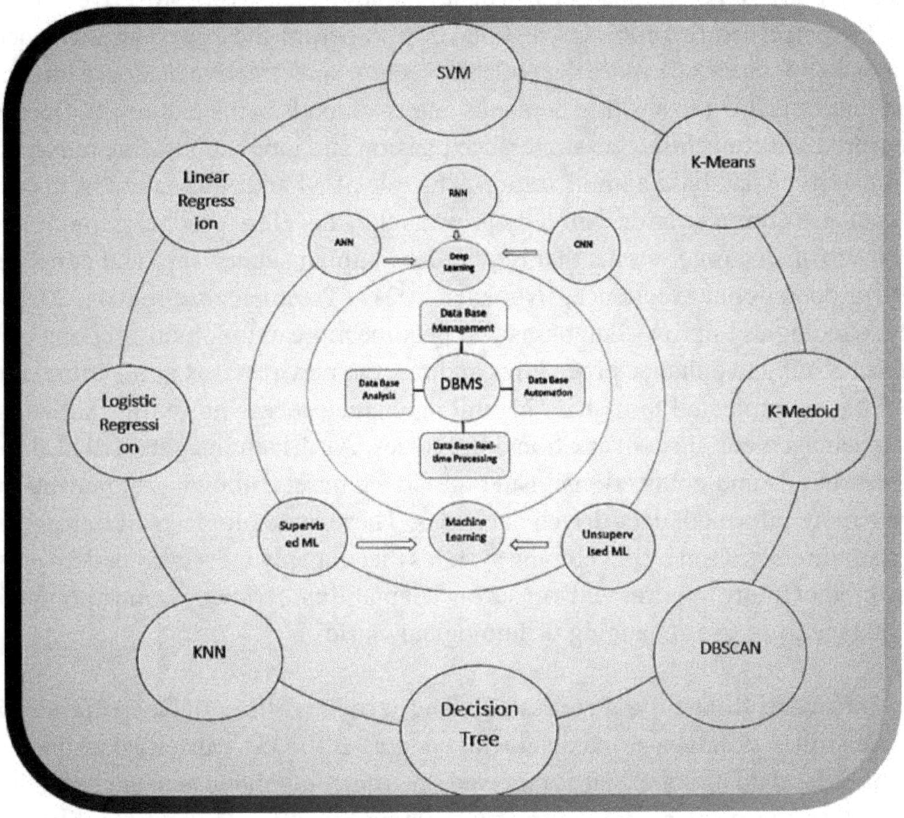

1. **Database Automation:** Database automation reduces the need for manual intervention and boosts operational efficiency by streamlining and optimizing database management operations using cutting-edge software tools, artificial intelligence, and machine learning technologies. Automating regular tasks like provisioning, backups, patching, performance tweaking, scaling, and security management are essential elements of database automation. Through the reduction of human error and the facilitation of uniform performance across environments, these automated technologies improve database operations' speed and accuracy. Businesses may improve scalability, speed up recovery times, and save a lot of money by automating processes like resource allocation, query optimization, and data movement. By regularly checking for vulnerabilities and deploying fixes, automation also increases security by guaranteeing compliance and lowering the possibility of breaches, (Van Aken *et al.*, 2017).

An extra layer of intelligence is added by AI-driven features like self-healing systems and predictive analytics, which enable databases to proactively identify and fix performance problems or breakdowns before they have an influence on company operations. A more dependable, secure, and effective database infrastructure that can adjust to shifting demands and workloads is the end result, freeing up enterprises to concentrate on strategic expansion and innovation while reducing the complexity of database administration. The role of AI and automation technologies in database administration will only grow as they develop, producing more intelligent, self-managing systems that require less human supervision and consistently deliver operational excellence, (Nookala, 2021) (Tsesmelis & Simitsis, 2022). As AI technologies improve, databases will become more autonomous, relying on machine learning to enhance procedures and react to new patterns in real time. Future systems are projected to include natural language processing (NLP), allowing for easy management via conversational interfaces. AI-driven insights will also reveal hidden trends and connections inside massive datasets, allowing organizations to make more informed, data-driven decisions. These technologies will transform database administration by developing systems that not only meet current demands but also predict future requirements, ensuring adaptability, efficiency, and a competitive advantage in an ever-changing technological world.

2. **Database Real-time Processing:** The term"real-time database processing" describes a database management systems (DBMS) capacity to handle and process data as soon as it is received, guaranteeing that users can immediately access the most recent information. Time-sensitive applications like online transactions, live analytics, and real-time monitoring systems are supported by real-time processing, which enters, processes, and makes available data virtually instantly. For sectors where judgments or actions must be made on the most recent data, such as e-commerce, banking, and the Internet of Things, this kind of processing is crucial. Because real-time databases are designed for high throughput, low latency, and constant data updates, they allow businesses to provide smooth user experiences, analyze data instantly, and respond to changing circumstances as they arise, (Gadde, 2024). Real-time database processing is getting even more potent as AI technologies advance, using machine learning algorithms to forecast patterns and automate decision-making. By spotting trends and abnormalities more quickly than with conventional techniques, AI-driven analytics can increase the value of real-time data and empower companies to take preventative action.
3. **Database Analysis:** In Database Management Systems (DBMS), database analysis for AI entails processing and organizing vast amounts of data using sophisticated analytical techniques, which are then used to improve the function-

ality and performance of AI models. To increase the effectiveness of machine learning algorithms, data analysis for AI in DBMS usually includes obtaining pertinent features, spotting trends, and refining data structures. By automating processes like anomaly detection, data cleaning, and predictive modelling, AI-driven analysis enables DBMS to scale and adapt as necessary. In order to ensure quicker and more accurate decision-making, AI can also automate indexing strategies, optimize query performance, and fine-tune database setups based on real-time data analysis. Businesses can extract more value from their data for intelligent applications thanks to the synergy between AI and DBMS, which improves data-driven insights, (Kumar, Boehm, & Yang, 2017) (Ma, 2022).

4. **Database Management:** Optimizing and organizing data processing, retrieval, and storage systems to meet the needs of AI applications is known as database management for AI. Databases in this situation need to manage enormous data quantities, guarantee effective querying, and sustain optimal performance for real-time processing and analytics. Utilizing strategies like data indexing, partitioning, and normalization, effective database management for AI entails arranging data to enable simple access and rapid analysis. Additionally, data pretreatment and administration are crucial since AI models frequently need clean, structured, and well-organized data for training. Organizations may improve resource allocation, automate data cleansing, optimize queries, and allow predictive analytics by integrating AI with database management systems (DBMS). This will ultimately guarantee the seamless operation of AI-driven applications and speed up insights, (Ramakirshnan & Gehrke, 2002). In order to manage the scalability and flexibility needed by AI applications, database administration for AI also entails utilizing cutting-edge technologies like distributed database systems, NoSQL databases, and in-memory databases. These systems are made to effectively analyze both structured and unstructured data, allowing AI algorithms to glean insightful information from a variety of data sources.

Additionally, automating schema evolution, improving anomaly detection in data streams, and optimizing indexing are all possible with the integration of machine learning techniques within database management systems. Sensitive data is protected and regulatory compliance is ensured by using AI-driven data governance and security solutions. Organizations may increase decision-making speed and fully utilize their data assets by utilizing AI-powered data orchestration and real-time processing capabilities.

AI Framework in DBMS

Figure 3 provides an in-depth exploration of how ML and AI are transforming 1) Database Automation 2) Database Real-time Processing 3) Database Analysis 4) Database Management. It covers:

Figure 3. Framework for AI and ML technique in database application

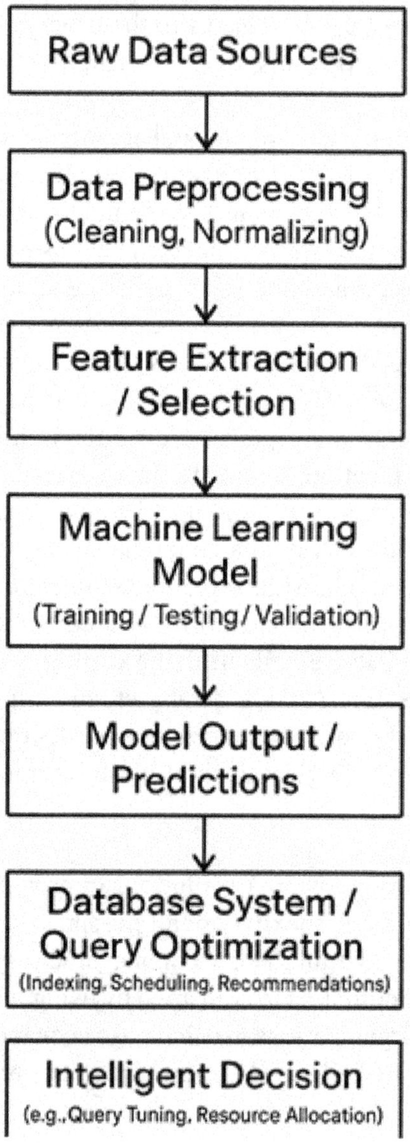

1. **Data Sources:** Data collection in DBMS is the first step where data is gathered from different sources like user inputs, sensors, applications, or files and stored into a database table for further processing.
2. **Data Pre-processing:** In Database Management Systems (DBMS), raw data sources often contain **missing or incomplete information**, which can lead to inaccurate queries or analytics. AI and ML techniques help solve this problem by predicting missing values using models trained on historical data, improving data reliability. Another common issue is **duplicate records**, which can arise due to multiple entries of the same data in different formats. Traditional rule-based methods struggle with slight variations, but ML algorithms can intelligently detect and merge such duplicates by learning patterns from existing data. DBMS also deals with **unstructured data** such as emails, social media content, or scanned documents. AI technologies like Natural Language Processing (NLP) and computer vision help convert these raw inputs into structured formats that databases can store and process efficiently. **Data anomalies or outliers**, which may indicate fraud or data entry errors, are difficult to detect manually in large datasets. ML models trained on normal behavior can automatically identify unusual patterns, making anomaly detection faster and more accurate.
3. **Feature Extraction: Feature extraction** in the context of **DBMS** refers to the process of **identifying and transforming important data attributes (features)** from large, raw datasets stored in a database. These features are then used for **data mining, machine learning, or analytics** tasks. Feature extraction means selecting key pieces of information (columns or patterns) from a database table that best represent the data for further analysis or prediction.
4. **Model Building:** In this explain Machine Learning models such as supervised and unsupervised model and some of the deep learning model used in DBMS.
   a) **Machine Learning:** In Database Management Systems (DBMS), ML entails incorporating sophisticated algorithms that enable databases to learn from past data and gradually enhance performance, query optimization, and decision-making. A DBMS may automatically find trends, forecast query execution times, improve indexing strategies and spot abnormalities in big datasets by utilizing ML techniques. This makes it possible for the system to react in real time for improved resource usage and quicker data retrieval in response to shifting workloads and data patterns. Machine learning may also improve forecasting, classification, and data cleansing, which can result in more precise insights and more effective data management. Continuous learning makes machine learning algorithms in DBMS more intelligent and responsive to changing business requirements by automating repetitive processes, lowering the need for human interaction, and increasing overall database efficiency, (Paganelli *et al.,* 2023).

i) **Supervised Learning:** Supervised learning relies on a dataset containing input/output pairs, where the objective is to train a model that predicts outputs for new inputs while minimizing errors. This approach works best in scenarios with sample training data and well-defined input-output mappings, (Nanda, Bajaj, & Gupta, 2020).

- **Decision Tree:** One popular machine learning approach that is important to database management systems (DBMS) is the decision tree. It facilitates decision-making by displaying data in a tree-like, hierarchical structure, with each internal node signifying an attribute test, each branch reflecting a test result, and each leaf node signifying a categorization or judgment. Decision trees are especially helpful in DBMS for tasks including data classification, indexing, and query optimization. Decision trees improve database operations by enabling effective prediction and clustering through the analysis of patterns and correlations in the data. Additionally, they can help with decision-making process automation, lowering manual labour, and increasing accuracy in jobs like recommendation systems, fraud detection, and customer segmentation. Decision trees further improve the intelligence and adaptability of DBMS when combined with AI, leading to improved insights and increased operational efficiency, (Nihalani, Silakari, & Motwani, 2009).
- **Linear Regression:** A basic statistical technique with many uses in database management systems (DBMS), linear regression is particularly useful when paired with artificial intelligence. By fitting a linear equation to the data, it simulates the relationship between one or more independent factors and a dependent variable. By using linear regression in DBMS for forecasting, trend analysis, and predictive analytics, databases are able to extract useful information from their stored data. Based on past data, it can assist in forecasting future sales, user behaviour, or system performance, for example. DBMS can automate the examination of complicated datasets, optimize queries, and improve decision-making processes by combining AI and linear regression. Databases are no longer merely repositories but also instruments for strategic insights because to this synergy, which enables more

intelligent, data-driven operations, (Huang, Gao, & Chen, 2024).

- **Logistic Regression:** Database management systems (DBMS) frequently employ logistic regression, a potent statistical method, for categorization tasks. By simulating the likelihood of a particular event occurring, logistic regression forecasts categorical outcomes as opposed to linear regression, which predicts continuous outcomes. It is extensively used in DBMS for jobs like customer segmentation, fraud detection, and binary classification issues like determining the legitimacy of a transaction. Logistic regression improves DBMS's capacity to process and analyze big datasets effectively when paired with AI, allowing for precise forecasts and automated decision-making. It is a useful tool for incorporating predictive analytics into database systems and enabling more intelligent data-driven solutions because of its ease of use, interpretability, and scalability, (Cao et al., 2022).
- **Support Vector Machines**: SVM are sophisticated machine learning algorithms that are essential for managing intricate classification and regression tasks in database management systems (DBMS). SVM is very useful in situations with high dimensional data since it finds the best hyperplane to divide data points into discrete classes. SVM is utilized in DBMS for tasks like text categorization, anomaly detection, and predictive modelling, which allow systems to find patterns and trends in big datasets. By producing reliable and accurate predictions even when dealing with noisy or unbalanced data, SVM improves the analytical powers of DBMS when used with AI. This combination turns traditional databases into intelligent data-driven systems by enabling better decision-making, automatic insights, and smarter query processing, (Bai, 2023). Additionally, Support Vector Machines (SVMs) are excellent at jobs like feature selection, which helps find the most pertinent characteristics in big datasets, increasing database query efficiency and lowering computational cost. They are adaptable for a range of database applications, such as fraud detection and consumer segmentation, due to their capacity to manage non-linear relationships through kernel functions. SVMs can also be incorporated into database systems for real-time analytics, giving complex queries quick

and precise answers. SVMs can be combined with other machine learning methods to create hybrid models that improve database systems' scalability and flexibility. Additionally, SVMs ensure the robustness of the database environment by spotting possible breaches or unusual activity, which helps to protect data. This integration demonstrates how SVMs are revolutionizing AI-driven database management systems and empowering them to satisfy the needs of contemporary data-centric applications.

- **K-Nearest Neighbours:** A straightforward yet powerful machine learning technique, the k-Nearest Neighbours (KNN) algorithm is used in database management systems (DBMS) for tasks including regression and classification. Based on a selected distance measure, KNN finds the data points that are closest to a query point (neighbours) and uses their values to forecast results. It is extensively utilized in DBMS for tasks including anomaly detection, recommendation systems, clustering, and data retrieval. Because it is non-parametric, it can handle multi-dimensional, complicated data that is kept in databases. While paired with AI, KNN improves DBMS's capacity to provide individualized insights, better data indexing, and facilitate real-time decision-making. This makes databases more intelligent and flexible while handling and analyzing massive amounts of data. By effectively locating related records, the k-Nearest Neighbours (KNN) technique can also be used to increase query efficiency in databases. This is especially helpful in applications like product suggestions and consumer profiling. It is ideal for managing both structured and unstructured data, including text, video, and images, that are kept in contemporary databases because of its versatility and ease of use. KNN can also be used for dynamic clustering, which allows adaptive database partitioning for better query execution by instantly identifying groups of related data points. Additionally, KNN is perfect for real-time analytics, where new data points are constantly being added to the database, because it can work with incremental data difficulties. KNN is a useful tool for today's data management problems since it can be used in AI-driven DBMS to provide improved predictive capabilities, individualized user experiences, and more effective data retrieval procedures, (Hao, 2021).

ii) **Unsupervised Learning:** In unsupervised learning, models are trained on input data without explicit output labels. The goal is to uncover hidden structures or patterns within the data. Common applications include clustering and density estimation.

- **K-Means:** A common clustering method for organizing and analyzing big datasets in database management systems (DBMS) is the K-means algorithm. By reducing the distance between data points and the centroids of each cluster, it divides the data into a predetermined number of clusters. K-means is used in database management systems (DBMS) for tasks including anomaly detection, pattern identification, and customer segmentation. This allows databases to find hidden structures in the data. It is perfect for managing high-dimensional data kept in databases because of its ease of use and effectiveness. When combined with AI, K-means improves DBMS's analytical capabilities by facilitating automated clustering, better query optimization, and actionable insights. This process turns unstructured data into structured, relevant information that can be used to make decisions. The K-means technique can also be used for real-time dynamic clustering, which allows databases to adjust to changing trends and patterns in data without a lot of manual work. This is especially helpful in applications like market basket analysis, which groups and analyzes consumer purchase patterns to improve inventory control and product suggestions. By finding and classifying related data points, K-means can also help with data preprocessing, making later analytical tasks like regression or classification easier. Because of its scalability, it may be used with large-scale distributed databases, where clustering is done across several nodes to effectively manage enormous datasets. K-means can be integrated into AI-driven DBMS to improve resource allocation, indexing methods, and data visualization, which will ultimately turn raw data into useful, actionable insights for companies and organizations, (Zhou et al., 2020).

- **K-Medoid:** Database management systems (DBMS) frequently employ the K-Means clustering technique, which helps organize data into discrete clusters according to their commonalities. Data points are allocated to a predetermined number of clusters, and cluster centroids are iteratively updated to minimize variance within each cluster. K-means is used in DBMS for tasks like trend analysis, data compression, and customer segmentation, which facilitate effective information organization and retrieval. It is a popular option for exploratory data analysis in databases because of its capacity to manage huge datasets. By automating data grouping, revealing hidden patterns, and increasing the effectiveness of data-driven decision-making processes, K-means, when paired with AI, improves the DBMS, (Wang et al., 2024). Database management systems (DBMS) commonly use K-Medoids, a reliable substitute for K-Means, for clustering jobs, especially when working with datasets that contain outliers or non-Euclidean distance metrics. K-Medoids is more robust to noise and anomalies than K-Means since it chooses real data points as cluster representatives rather than relying on centroids. Because of this feature, K-Medoids are perfect for applications where outliers are important, such fraud detection. By combining related data points, K-Medoids can also be used to optimize database indexing, which will shorten search times and enhance query performance. K-Medoids improves DBMS when used with AI by facilitating more precise clustering in high-dimensional spaces and offering more profound understanding of intricate datasets. K-Medoids is a potent tool for contemporary, AI-driven database systems because of this integration, which facilitates sophisticated applications like dynamic segmentation, adaptive data analysis, and tailored suggestions, (Li, Zhou, & Cao, 2021).
- **DBSCAN:** Database management systems (DBMS) use the potent clustering method DBSCAN (Density-Based Spatial Clustering of Applications with Noise) to find clusters of various sizes and forms, particularly in noisy datasets. DBSCAN is perfect for finding patterns in high-dimensional or spatial data because, unlike K-means, it organizes data points according to their density rather than requiring a predetermined number of clusters. DBSCAN is frequently used in DBMS

for tasks like fraud detection, anomaly detection, and geospatial data analysis. It works especially well in real-world applications because of its capacity to manage outliers and uneven cluster forms. When combined with AI, DBSCAN improves DBMS's analytical power by facilitating reliable, automated grouping and offering more in-depth understanding of intricate datasets, (Wu et al., 2022). DBSCAN is useful for applications such as trend analysis and predictive maintenance in database management systems (DBMS) since it is also very good at clustering time-series data. It can reveal hidden patterns in complicated datasets without requiring prior knowledge of the number of clusters because it can locate core points and grow clusters depending on density thresholds. DBSCAN can be used to optimize search operations for location-based queries and index spatial datasets efficiently. It also performs exceptionally well in dynamic data contexts, allowing for real-time analytics and adjusting to variations in data distribution. DBMS can use DBSCAN's noise-handling features to enhance the quality of insights obtained from unstructured or semi-structured data by merging it with AI. DBSCAN is a flexible tool for contemporary database systems because of this combination, which improves decision-making procedures, promotes anomaly detection in crucial applications like network security, and enables more reliable data presentation.

b) **Deep Learning:** Deep learning encompasses ML models based on artificial neural networks (ANNs), inspired by the human brain's structure. These models use multiple layers, such as fully connected or ReLU layers, to learn hierarchical features. Training involves backpropagation, which requires substantial computational resources, extensive labelled datasets, and meticulous hyperparameter tuning. Despite these challenges, DL methods have achieved remarkable success, often surpassing traditional ML techniques in areas such as computer vision and natural language processing—and, in some cases, even outperforming humans. Database management systems (DBMS) are increasingly using deep learning techniques to improve their capabilities and performance. By using these models to automate indexing algorithms, forecast query performance, and improve query execution plans, system efficiency can be increased. Furthermore, by seeing odd patterns in real time, deep learning helps detect anomalies in databases while maintaining data security and integrity. Natural language interfaces for databases, which allow users to query systems using conversational language, are another important application. Databases can also support advanced predictive analytics by utilizing DL, which helps businesses quickly and accurately extract meaningful insights from their data. Deep learning's revolutionary potential to make databases more intelligent, adaptable, and user-friendly is demonstrated by this integration of deep learning into DBMS, (Wang et al., 2016).

i) **Convolutional Neural Network:** Deep learning techniques are applied to improve data analysis through Convolutional Neural Networks (CNNs) for databases, especially for complicated tasks like image recognition, classification, and pattern discovery in database systems. The concepts of CNNs can be applied to databases for tasks including anomaly detection, query optimization, and predictive analytics, even though they are typically utilized for computer vision tasks. CNNs may learn hierarchical patterns by examining the structure of data, which enhances the effectiveness of data classification and retrieval, particularly in systems that contain unstructured or semi-structured data. Their capacity to handle big datasets and spot complex relationships among them can enable real-time decision making, automate data cleansing, and improve indexing tactics. Thus, by incorporating CNNs into database management systems, intelligent, automated data management solutions can be developed, improving the overall functionality of AI-driven applications. Convolutional Neural Networks (CNNs) are incredibly useful for applications like time-series forecasting and geospatial data analysis since they can also be used to process spatial and temporal data in databases. More accurate modelling of complicated data structures is made possible by their capacity to capture spatial hierarchies and linkages. CNNs can also help with feature extraction for unstructured data sources, such text or multimedia information, which makes it easier to integrate and query a variety of datasets. Pre-trained CNN models can be modified for domain-specific database applications by utilizing transfer learning, which lowers the training time and computing cost. Additionally, CNNs can improve data visualization by producing clear visual depictions of intricate relationships, which will help users comprehend and interpret their data more effectively. In addition to streamlining processes, integrating CNNs into database management systems opens the door for more reliable and expandable AI-driven database solutions, (Munappy et al., 2019) (Shen et al., 2022).

ii) **Recurrent Neural Network:** For tasks involving time-series data, such trend forecasting, anomaly detection, and predictive analytics, recurrent neural networks (RNNs) are very helpful since they provide a potent method for managing sequential data in database systems. RNNs can assess data sequences across time because, in contrast to typical neural networks, they may remember information from prior inputs through feedback loops. RNNs can be used in database contexts for tasks such as forecasting future data values, seeing trends in log files, or refining queries based on past performance. RNNs can increase forecast accuracy and identify trends that might not be seen in static, non-sequential datasets because of their capacity to represent temporal connections in data. Organizations can improve real-time data processing, automate decision-making, and extract more insightful information from time-dependent data by incorporating RNNs into database management systems, (Miao et al., 2017).

iii) **Artificial Neural Network:** Artificial Neural Networks (ANNs), which offer sophisticated capabilities for data analysis, pattern recognition, and decision-making, can greatly improve database administration systems. Complex tasks like anomaly detection, classification, and regression are especially well-suited for artificial neural networks (ANNs), which are made up of interconnected nodes that are intended to replicate the way the human brain processes information. Artificial Neural Networks (ANNs) can be used in databases to find hidden patterns in big datasets, improve data classification for effective storage and retrieval, and increase query performance by learning from past queries. Artificial Neural Networks (ANNs) facilitate automated decision-making, more accurate forecasts, and dynamic adaptability to shifting data trends by digesting vast amounts of data and adapting to new information. Thus, ANN integration with database systems can improve data quality, streamline data management, and generate insightful, data-driven insights for a range of commercial applications, (Cebi et al., 2020).

5. **Model output/ Evaluation Matrix:** When machine learning or data mining models are applied to data stored in a DBMS, we use evaluation metrics to measure how well the models are performing. These metrics help assess the accuracy, efficiency, and reliability of predictions or classifications.
6. **Query optimization:** In DBMS is the process of improving the efficiency of SQL queries so they execute faster and use fewer resources. The database system analyzes different ways to execute a query and chooses the most efficient plan using the query optimizer. This involves techniques like choosing the right indexes, reordering joins, minimizing disk I/O, and avoiding unnecessary

computations. Query optimization is crucial for large databases where poorly written queries can slow down performance. Modern systems may also use AI/ML to learn query patterns and suggest or apply automatic optimizations.

7. **Intelligent decision:** Refers to the use of AI or rule-based systems to make smart, data-driven choices. In DBMS, it helps optimize tasks like query tuning, indexing, and resource allocation automatically. These decisions are based on past data, patterns, and performance metrics. It reduces manual intervention and improves system efficiency and response time.

Recent advancements in AI and ML algorithms have significantly influenced the evolution of database management systems (DBMS), especially in areas like query optimization, indexing, workload prediction, and autonomous tuning. Fahima et al. (2024) provide a foundational overview of how machine learning enhances database operations, while Oloruntoba (2025) explores AI-driven self-tuning and intelligent indexing in enterprise environments. Enyejo et al. (2024) highlight the role of federated learning and model explainability in edge-based DBMS applications. Studies like Islam (2024) emphasize the integration of AI in SQL databases and its growing role in big data analytics. Reinforcement learning approaches, as demonstrated by Wang et al. (2024), enable improved multimodal query suggestions through human feedback. Zhang et al. (2024) introduce conflict prediction for intelligent transaction scheduling in OLTP systems, and Siddiqui and Wu (2024) review recent progress in ML-powered index tuning, noting both achievements and open challenges. Additional works by Rafique et al. (2024) and Lee et al. (2024) discuss workload-aware management and configuration tuning, respectively, further showcasing the expanding influence of AI/ML across DBMS components [AR 1-9].

SOLUTIONS AND RECOMMENDATIONS

We outline three key design approaches for embedding machine learning components within database management systems (DBMSs): 1) mode of integration, 2) source of learning, and 3) selection of the ML paradigm is shown in Figure 4.

- **Mode of Integration**

Two primary approaches for integrating ML components into DBMSs are external and Internal integration, (Al-Khassawneh, 2023).

- **Source of Learning**

Modern DBMSs offer flexibility for database administrators to control query execution performance through optimization techniques. Externally integrated ML components aim to provide recommendations to these administrators or automate tasks via standard configuration endpoints.

Figure 4. Designing model of DBMS with help of machine learning model

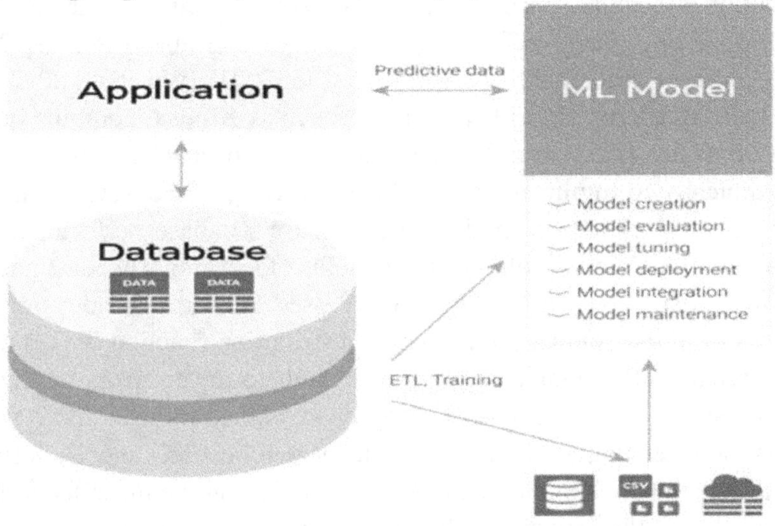

This approach allows ML components to function independently, minimizing disruptions to the existing system architecture. However, external integration can lead to interference among different components, complicating decision-making and requiring careful coordination. Additionally, external components often require iterative testing for knob tuning, which may necessitate system downtime, impeding rapid experimentation, (Rosa et al., 2024) (Ding et al., 2019) (Pulivarthy, 2024) (Kandolo, 2024). The effectiveness of ML in DBMS components largely hinges on the learning source, which can be derived from query workloads or directly from the underlying data.

o **Learning from Queries**

This approach enables ML models to focus on narrows coped problems, enhancing performance. However, it presents challenges such as the high cost of data collection and poor generalization for unseen queries. Furthermore, changes in workload patterns necessitate retraining, which can lead to system downtime.

- **Learning from Data:** Recent systems have shifted focus towards learning from DB-resident data, which improves robustness to changes in workload patterns. Techniques like cumulative distribution function (CDF) modelling, used in systems such as DBEst and DeepDB, enable effective query estimation. These models can be reused despite workload changes, though they require substantial training time and capacity to handle complex data distributions, (Nanda, Bajaj, & Gupta, 2020) (Nihalani, Silakari, & Motwani, 2009) (Huang, Gao, & Chen, 2024) (Cao et al., 2022) (Bai, 2023) (Hao, 2021) (Zhou et al., 2020) (Li, Zhou, & Cao, 2021) (Wu et al., 2022).
- **Hybrid Methods:** Hybrid approaches, such as XIndex, combine both learning from queries and data. XIndex learns the empirical CDF of keys, adapting dynamically to minimize error on frequently accessed keys, demonstrating the potential of hybrid models. To increase database performance, hybrid strategies like XIndex combine the benefits of learning from data and queries. To understand how various keys are accessed over time, XIndex, for instance, learns from the empirical cumulative distribution function (CDF) of keys. It can dynamically modify and optimize itself to lower errors by continuously adjusting to this data, particularly on keys that are used more frequently. This indicates that as time passes, the system becomes more intelligent, increasing the precision of query results. Combining the finest features of both approaches—the capacity to learn from both historical queries and present data patterns—is the concept underlying hybrid models.

- **Selection of the ML paradigm**

Internal integration entails redesigning the DBMS to incorporate ML components as core, primary elements of its architecture. This approach allows ML components greater access to low-level information and promotes coherence in decision-making. Systems like Noise Page demonstrate this model, optimizing query execution without human intervention. The integration of ML in this manner can enhance performance but may also lead to degradation during model training. Internal integration is best suited for new DBMS developments, (Chaudhuri, 1998) (Abbasi et al., 2024) (Van Aken et al., 2017) (Nookala, 2021) (Tsesmelis & Simitsis, 2022) (Gadde, 2024) (Kumar, Boehm, & Yang, 2017) (Ma, 2022) (Ramakrishnan & Gehreke, 2002) (Wang et al., 2016) (Munappy et al., 2019) (Shen et al., 2022) (Miao et al., 2017) (Cebi et al., 2020) (Paganelli et al., 2023) (Nanda, Bajaj, & Gupta, 2020) (Nihalani, Silakari, & Motwani, 2009) (Huang, Gao, & Chen, 2024) (Xuan et al., 2022) (Bai, 2023) (Hao, 2021) (Zhou et al., 2020) (Li, Zhou, & Cao, 2021) (Wu et al., 2022) (Khan et al., 2024).

Real-World Case Studies and Applications

The "Learned Index Structures" case study by Tim Kraska and his team proposes replacing traditional database indexes like B-Trees with machine learning models to improve data access efficiency. In conventional DBMS, indexes are static structures that can become inefficient when data scales or exhibits skewed distributions. The researchers introduced a method where machine learning models, such as neural networks or regression trees, learn the distribution of keys in a sorted array and predict the position of a record directly. This approach treats indexing as a prediction problem, significantly reducing memory usage and lookup times under favorable conditions. Experimental results showed that learned indexes could outperform traditional methods in speed and space efficiency, particularly when the data is relatively stable. However, challenges such as the need for retraining when data changes, handling dynamic workloads, and ensuring model reliability in all scenarios limit its immediate adoption. Despite these issues, this study opens up promising directions for integrating AI into core DBMS functions, showing how learned behavior can enhance traditional systems when applied carefully.

Application of ML and AI in Database

The integration of AI and ML into database management systems (DBMS) has revolutionized how data is stored, processed, and utilized. These technologies enhance efficiency, adaptability, and intelligence in managing vast and complex datasets.

- **Query Optimization:** ML algorithms analyze historical data to predict efficient execution plans for database queries. This reduces processing time and resource consumption, ensuring faster and more accurate query results, (Al-Khassawneh, 2023).
- **Data Cleaning and Integration:** Handling incomplete, inconsistent, or redundant data is a persistent challenge. ML models automate the identification and rectification of errors, ensuring higher data quality. AI facilitates seamless integration of data from diverse sources, reducing the need for manual intervention, (Nanda, Bajaj, & Gupta, 2020) (Nihalani, Silakari, & Motwani, 2009) (Huang, Gao, & Chen, 2024) (Cao et al., 2022).
- **Predictive Analytics:** AI-powered systems analyze patterns in historical data to forecast trends, detect anomalies, and support proactive decision-making. This application is particularly useful in industries like finance, healthcare, and retail, where data-driven predictions can drive business strategies, ((Nanda, Bajaj, & Gupta, 2020) (Nihalani, Silakari, & Motwani, 2009)

(Huang, Gao, & Chen, 2024) (Xuan et al., 2022) (Bai, 2023) (Hao, 2021) (Zhou et al., 2020) (Li, Zhou, & Cao, 2021) (Wu et al., 2022).

- **Enhanced Security:** By leveraging ML, databases can identify and respond to suspicious activities in real time. AI-based anomaly detection models monitor access patterns and flag unusual behaviour, enhancing overall security, (Rosa et al., 2024).
- **Automated Maintenance:** AI-driven systems optimize database indexing, query execution, and tuning without human intervention. These self-managing databases reduce downtime and operational costs, (Ding et al., 2019).
- **Personalized Recommendations:** ML models analyze user interactions within the database to offer tailored recommendations, such as product suggestions or content preferences. This capability is widely used in e-commerce and streaming platforms, (Pulivarthy, 2024).
- **Scalability and Performance Tuning:** ML adapts to workload changes by dynamically adjusting database configurations, ensuring consistent performance as data volumes grow. These advancements demonstrate the transformative potential of ML and AI, making databases more intelligent, reliable, and efficient for modern applications, (Kandolo, 2024).

In order to offer tailored suggestions, machine learning (ML) algorithms can examine user interactions within databases. For instance, the system may recommend goods or entertainment that a user could find entertaining based on their previous usage. E-commerce websites frequently utilize this technology to suggest products based on past searches or purchases. In a similar vein, streaming services like Netflix and Spotify use it to make personalized movie, TV show, or music recommendations. These systems improve the user experience by continuously learning from new encounters and become more adept at anticipating what users might want next. Personalized recommendations assist organizations boost user engagement and sales in addition to improving user satisfaction.

Current State of Research / Drawbacks

Current research in applying AI and ML to DBMS focuses on creating intelligent systems that can automate and optimize database operations like query planning, indexing, tuning, and resource management. Projects such as autonomous databases (e.g., Oracle Autonomous DB), learned query optimizers (like Bao and SkinnerDB), and ML-based indexing systems demonstrate the potential of these technologies to improve performance, reduce human intervention, and adapt to dynamic workloads. Research is also exploring how reinforcement learning, deep learning, and workload prediction models can help databases self-adjust in real time based on usage patterns and data changes.

Despite these advancements, several areas still require deeper investigation. One major challenge is the generalizability of ML models across different types of queries, data distributions, and workloads. Many current solutions are tailored to specific environments and may fail in broader, real-world settings. Another area needing attention is the explainability and transparency of AI decisions within DBMS, especially in critical systems where incorrect predictions can lead to performance issues or data loss. Additionally, integrating AI into DBMS introduces computational overhead and complexity, demanding further research into lightweight, efficient, and adaptive models that can operate in real-time with minimal retraining.

Challenges and Limitations

Despite the significant potential of AI and ML in transforming database management systems (DBMS), their integration and application come with a range of challenges and limitations, (Chaudhuri, 1998). These issues need to be addressed for AI-driven databases to reach their full potential in real-world environments.

- **Scalability and Computational Demands:** One of the primary concerns with implementing ML and AI in databases is the substantial computational power required to process large volumes of data. As data grows exponentially in modern applications, training AI models on such datasets becomes increasingly resource intensive. This high computational demand can lead to performance bottlenecks, making real-time data processing and analysis difficult. Scaling AI models to handle big data without compromising performance remains a significant challenge.
- **Data Privacy and Security:** Integrating AI into databases often necessitates the use of sensitive data to train models. This raises privacy concerns, particularly when dealing with personally identifiable information (PII) or confidential business data. The ability of AI models to learn from large amounts of data makes them vulnerable to data breaches or misuse. In addition, ensuring compliance with regulations such as GDPR or HIPAA becomes increasingly complex, requiring stringent data protection measures, (Cao et al., 2022). Furthermore, it gets harder to guarantee adherence to stringent data protection laws, such the Health Insurance Portability and Accountability Act (HIPAA) in the US or the General Data Protection Regulation (GDPR) in Europe, as the usage of AI in databases increases. These laws mandate that companies safeguard customer information and give explicit instructions on how to do so. As AI systems develop further, protecting data security and

privacy will become ever more crucial. To safeguard data and prevent legal or reputational concerns, businesses need to put strong security measures in place, such as encryption and access limits. To make sure these systems are safe and in compliance with the law, regular audits and modifications will be required.

- **Lack of Interpretability:** Many ML models, especially deep learning and neural networks, are often considered "black-box" models. These models can provide highly accurate results, but their decision-making process is opaque, making it difficult to understand how a model arrives at a particular conclusion. This lack of transparency can be a significant barrier to the adoption of AI in critical systems, especially in sectors where accountability and interpretability are necessary, such as healthcare, finance, or legal fields.
- **Data Quality and Bias:** AI models are highly dependent on the quality of data used for training. If the input data is incomplete, inaccurate, or biased, the performance of the model will be compromised. Poor data quality can lead to incorrect or misleading predictions, undermining the credibility of AI-driven databases. Moreover, biased data can perpetuate existing stereotypes or inequalities, leading to unfair or unethical outcomes. Ensuring that the data used for training models is representative, balanced, and clean is crucial for the success of AI in databases. The calibre of the data utilized to train AI algorithms is crucial. The AI model's performance will suffer when the input data is biased, erroneous, or incomplete. For instance, the AI could produce inaccurate or deceptive predictions if the data is incomplete or contains mistakes. This can reduce the overall efficacy of AI-driven systems and produce incorrect outcomes. Furthermore, skewed data used to train the models may produce unfair or immoral results. This is especially problematic if the data shows societal inequities or prejudices, since the AI system can inadvertently perpetuate these biases. Biased data in a hiring system, for example, can unjustly give preference to one group over another.
- **High Implementation and Maintenance Costs:** Implementing AI in database systems often involves significant financial investments. The initial costs include purchasing specialized hardware, developing or integrating AI algorithms, and training staff with expertise in both AI and database management. Ongoing maintenance costs can also be high, as AI models need continuous retraining, monitoring, and fine-tuning to remain effective. Small and medium-sized enterprises (SMEs) may find these costs prohibitive, limiting their access to AI-powered database technologies.
- **Integration with Legacy Systems:** Many organizations rely on legacy database systems that were not designed with AI in mind. Integrating modern AI techniques with these outdated systems can be complex and costly. It may

require overhauling existing database architectures, migrating data, or even replacing old systems with new, AI-enabled platforms. The compatibility issues and the need for specialized expertise to integrate AI with legacy systems can be a significant barrier to adoption.

- **Algorithmic Bias and Ethical Concerns:** AI models can unintentionally perpetuate biases embedded within the data used for training. This is particularly problematic in applications such as hiring, lending, or criminal justice, where biased AI decisions could have severe ethical and legal implications. For instance, if a database is trained on historical hiring data that reflects gender or racial bias, the AI system might perpetuate or even amplify these biases. Addressing algorithmic bias and ensuring fairness is a critical challenge in the responsible implementation of AI in databases. Biases that are already present in the training data may be inadvertently reinforced by AI models. This is a big problem, particularly in fields where AI system decisions can have major ethical and legal repercussions, like hiring, lending, and criminal justice. For instance, even while an AI system may not be purposefully biased; it may still favour certain groups when making judgments if it is educated on recruiting data from the past that indicates a preference for one gender or race over another. In certain instances, the AI might potentially exacerbate existing prejudices by promoting negative stereotypes or discriminating behaviours.
- **Continuous Learning and Adaptation:** Unlike traditional database systems, AI models require continuous learning and adaptation to stay relevant as data evolves over time. This means that AI-powered databases must be regularly updated with new data and retrained to improve accuracy. The process of continuous learning can be resource-intensive, requiring ongoing monitoring and adjustment of models. In fast-changing environments, failure to update models promptly can result in outdated predictions, making the system less effective and reliable.
- **Reliability and Stability:** AI systems, particularly those that operate in dynamic environments with large and complex datasets, can sometimes behave unpredictably. For instance, an AI model might produce inaccurate results if it encounters new patterns or anomalies not present in the training data. This lack of reliability can lead to system failures or operational disruptions, which are especially critical in applications that rely on real-time data processing, such as financial systems or autonomous vehicles. Similar to this, an AI system in an autonomous car could make a mistake if it misinterprets novel circumstances, such as an unforeseen roadblock. This unreliability can lead to delays, accidents, or system breakdowns, which are especially risky in real-time applications where every second counts. Significant operational

disruptions that impact not only the current work but also the system's or companies overall operation may result from an unstable and unreliable AI model. Therefore, it is crucial to make sure AI systems are well tested, regularly observed, and updated with fresh data. These steps can help increase the system's dependability and lower the possibility of mistakes, guaranteeing that AI operates precisely and reliably even in erratic circumstances.

- **Skill and Knowledge Gaps**: Developing, implementing, and maintaining AI powered database systems requires specialized knowledge in both database management and machine learning. There is a shortage of professionals who possess expertise in both fields, and the complexity of AI models further exacerbates this skill gap. This shortage can hinder the adoption of AI in databases and limit the ability of organizations to fully leverage these technologies.

Looking ahead, the integration of AI and DBMS holds transformative potential across industries, revolutionizing data management, decision-making, and customer interactions. In educational settings, modular and hierarchical management can enhance the quality of practical courses and talent development. Moreover, the combination of machine learning (ML) and DBMS offers opportunities to extract valuable insights from vast datasets. While the field presents challenges, continued innovation in AI-DBMS integration is essential for driving competitiveness and creating a more data-driven world. NoSQL databases play a crucial role by overcoming the limitations of traditional relational systems, offering scalability and efficient handling of unstructured data. Ajax technology also improves user experience by facilitating real-time data transmission and seamless interactions. Together, AI and big data analytics allow for intelligent processing, uncovering hidden insights, and supporting decision-making. Despite these advancements, challenges related to data privacy, security, and the need for skilled AI professionals remain. By enhancing the user experience, technologies like Ajax help these systems operate more efficiently. Because Ajax facilitates real-time data transmission, users can engage with databases without interruptions and in a smooth and effective manner.

Ethical Considerations

When integrating AI/ML techniques into database management systems, several ethical issues must be carefully addressed. **Data privacy** is a major concern, as sensitive user information may be used for training or optimization, requiring strict protection measures. **Bias and fairness** must also be ensured, as machine learning models can unintentionally favor certain types of queries, users, or workloads. The **transparency** of AI decisions is crucial—users and administrators should be able to understand why certain queries are prioritized or why specific configurations are applied. Finally, **accountability** is essential; clear responsibility must be assigned when automated decisions lead to failures, inefficiencies, or data breaches in the system.

FUTURE RESEARCH DIRECTIONS

As machine learning (ML) and artificial intelligence (AI) continue to evolve, the future of AI-driven database management systems (DBMS) promises even greater advancements in automation, efficiency, and intelligence. Several emerging trends suggest the next phase of innovation in this area.

1. **Autonomous Databases:** One of the most anticipated developments is the rise of autonomous databases, which use AI to fully manage tasks such as tuning, scaling, backups, and security. These databases would eliminate the need for human intervention in many maintenance tasks, making them more efficient, error-free, and cost-effective. With the increasing complexity of data management, autonomous systems can enable real-time performance optimization and fault detection without manual input. In addition to automating repetitive processes, autonomous databases use AI and machine learning to improve prediction capabilities, allowing for proactive resource allocation and problem solving. These systems guarantee smooth operation even with varying workloads by continually monitoring database performance, locating bottlenecks, and implementing optimizations in real-time. Autonomous databases greatly lower risks and improve data safety by including cutting-edge security features like anomaly detection and automated patching. They also enable self-service analytics, which gives consumers the ability to query and examine data without the assistance of database administrators. Autonomous databases are also essential for streamlining migrations, dynamically expanding resources, and guaranteeing high availability as more and more businesses use cloud-based solutions. This development represents a revolutionary change in database administration, offering unmatched dependability and efficiency in managing intricate data ecosystems while lowering operating expenses, (Al-Khassawneh, 2023)
2. **Integration of Natural Language Processing (NLP):** Future database systems could incorporate NLP techniques to allow users to interact with databases using natural language queries. This would significantly lower the barrier for nontechnical users, enabling them to retrieve complex data insights without needing to know query languages like SQL. Combining NLP with AI would

lead to more intuitive, user-friendly interfaces for data querying and management. By providing conversational interfaces, where users may ask questions in plain English and receive accurate responses or visualizations, the integration of Natural English Processing (NLP) into database systems has the potential to completely transform user interaction. This development will promote a more inclusive data-driven culture by opening databases to a wider audience, including stakeholders who are not technically inclined. Contextual knowledge could potentially be used by NLP-powered databases to improve query interpretations, guaranteeing more precise and pertinent results. These systems could learn user preferences and adjust over time by integrating machine learning, providing tailored recommendations and automating repetitive inquiries. NLP may also make multilingual help possible, removing linguistic obstacles and promoting accessibility on a worldwide scale. NLP-driven databases may offer sophisticated functions like entity recognition, sentiment analysis, and summarization when paired with AI, which would improve data analysis and decision-making even further. A major step toward developing intelligent, user-centric database systems that accommodate a range of requirements and skill levels has been taken with this integration, (Chaudhuri, 1998) (Abbasi et al., 2024) (Van Aken et al., 2017) (Nookala, 2021) (Tsesmelis & Simitsis, 2022).

3. **Self-Healing Databases:** AI-driven systems may eventually enable self-healing databases, where the system can automatically detect issues such as data corruption, system failures, or inefficiencies and take corrective actions. This would improve database reliability and reduce downtime, allowing businesses to maintain continuous operations. Self-healing databases could potentially be made possible by AI-driven systems, which would allow the system to identify issues like data corruption, system malfunctions, or inefficiencies on its own without the need for human assistance. For instance, the AI might detect and eliminate the need for human corrections if there is a problem with the way data is stored or if a portion of the database becomes faulty. Because fewer errors would likely lie undiscovered or unfixed for extended periods of time, databases would be far more reliable. Furthermore, self-healing databases can lessen downtime—the period of time when a system malfunctions and is not accessible to users, (Gadde, 2024) (Kumar, Boehm, & Yang, 2017).
4. **Explainable AI (XAI):** Improving openness and confidence in data-driven decision-making processes is the key to Explainable AI's (XAI) future in database systems. By incorporating XAI, databases could make sophisticated AI models easier for users to understand by offering concise, human-readable explanations for query results, forecasts, and suggestions. In delicate fields like finance, healthcare, and the legal system, where comprehending the reasoning behind AI-driven results is essential, this skill would be especially helpful. Future

developments might include interactive visualization tools to examine decision paths, real-time feedback systems to improve AI behaviour, and dynamic explanation production based on user expertise. Furthermore, by providing traceable and accountable insights into database processes, XAI may be crucial to auditing and compliance. Using XAI will be crucial to ensuring the ethical, equitable, and trustworthy use of AI in data management and analysis as databases get more autonomous and AI-driven, (Ma, 2022) (Ramakrishnan & Gehrke, 2002) (Wang et al., 2016).

5. **AI-Optimized Query and Indexing:** The future will see further development of AI algorithms that dynamically adapt indexing and query execution strategies. By leveraging real-time data patterns, AI can automatically optimize database indexing, query processing, and resource allocation, leading to more efficient database management at scale. In a similar vein, AI can optimize database resource usage, guaranteeing that processing power is distributed where it is most needed, preventing needless delays or resource overuse. The management of huge databases, where the amount of data is always increasing, would benefit greatly from these enhancements. In addition to saving database managers time, AI-optimized query and indexing will guarantee that the system can seamlessly manage increasingly complicated procedures by automating these duties. All things considered, this advancement will result in quicker, more effective database administration, enabling companies to make better judgments in less time and with less effort, (Al-Khassawneh, 2023) (Rosa et al., 2024) (Ding et al., 2019) (Pulivarthy, 2024) (Kandolo, 2024).
6. **Advanced Predictive Analytics:** As AI models become more sophisticated, they will offer even more advanced predictive analytics capabilities. These systems will not only provide insights based on historical data but will also predict future trends and behaviours with higher accuracy, enabling proactive decision-making in industries such as finance, healthcare, and e-commerce. In conclusion, the future of AI in database management is filled with opportunities to increase automation, enhance usability, and improve performance. By addressing current challenges and embracing these innovations, AI-driven databases will continue to transform data management, making it more intelligent and adaptive to the needs of modern enterprises, (Chaudhuri, 1998) (Abbasi et al., 2024) (Van Aken et al., 2017) (Nookala, 2021) (Tsesmelis & Simitsis, 2022) (Gadde, 2024) (Kumar, Boehm, & Yang, 2017) (Ma, 2022) (Ramakrishnan & Gehreke, 2002) (Wang et al., 2016) (Munappy et al., 2019) (Shen et al., 2022) (Miao et al., 2017) (Cebi et al., 2020) (Paganelli et al., 2023) (Nanda, Bajaj, & Gupta, 2020) (Nihalani, Silakari, & Motwani, 2009) (Huang, Gao, & Chen, 2024) (Xuan et al., 2022) (Bai, 2023) (Hao, 2021) (Zhou et al., 2020) (Li, Zhou, & Cao, 2021) (Wu et al., 2022) (Khan et al., 2024). In summary, there are a lot

of chances to boost automation, improve usability, and boost performance with AI in database administration in the future. AI-driven databases will continue to revolutionize data management by tackling present issues and adopting these advancements, making it more intelligent and responsive to the demands of contemporary businesses. As these technologies develop, they will be essential for stimulating creativity, propelling corporate expansion, and opening up new avenues in the big data era. In the era of big data, these technologies will be essential for stimulating innovation, propelling corporate expansion, and opening up new avenues for exploration. As these systems advance, they will assist companies in improving decision-making, streamlining processes, and maintaining their competitiveness in a world that is becoming more and more data-driven.

CONCLUSION

The integration of artificial intelligence (AI) and database management systems (DBMS) is pivotal for next-generation computing and the sustained advancement of data technologies. This research proposes a structured approach to developing intelligent databases by incorporating AI processes that enhance performance, particularly in managing large datasets. The study's research model is organized into three stages—knowledge model, conceptual model, and relational model—and includes a case study on integrating research data collection with databases, demonstrating that AI-enhanced systems outperform traditional ones in terms of efficiency. AI-based forecasting models, used to analyze historical data, further expand the capabilities of these systems by enhancing predictive accuracy and developing intellectual databases capable of advanced decision-making. A key focus of this research is the design of AI-driven information systems, especially those utilizing big data. AI and big data analytics work well together to process data more intelligently, uncover hidden insights, and enhance decision-making in general. But even with these developments, there are still issues to be resolved, like protecting data privacy, bolstering security protocols, and the continuous requirement for highly qualified AI specialists to oversee and apply these technologies.

REFERENCES

Abbasi, M., Bernardo, M. V., Váz, P., Silva, J., & Martins, P. (2024). Adaptive and Scalable Database Management with Machine Learning Integration: A PostgreSQL Case Study. *Information (Basel), 15*(9), 574.

Al-Khassawneh, Y. A. (2023). A review of artificial intelligence in security and privacy: Research advances, applications, opportunities, and challenges. *Indonesian Journal of Science and Technology, 8*(1), 79–96. DOI: 10.17509/ijost.v8i1.52709

Bai, D. (2023, December). Design of Artificial Intelligence Information System Using NoSQL Database and Ajax Technology. In *2023 International Conference on Applied Physics and Computing (ICAPC)* (pp. 678-683). IEEE.

Cao, X., Ge, B., Li, M., Wang, H., & Ren, J. (2022, November). Database Protection Techniques for Electromagnetic Radiation Based on Machine Learning. In 2022 IEEE 10th Asia-Pacific Conference on Antennas and Propagation (APCAP) (pp. 1-2). IEEE.

Cebi, C. B., Bulut, F. S., Firat, H., Sahingoz, O. K., & Karatas, G. (2020). Deep learning based security management of information systems: A comparative study. *Journal of Advances in Information Technology, 11*, 3. DOI: 10.12720/jait.11.3.135-142

Chaudhuri, S. (1998). Data mining and database systems: Where is the intersection? *IEEE Data Eng. Bull., 21*(1), 4–8.

Ding, B., Das, S., Marcus, R., Wu, W., Chaudhuri, S., & Narasayya, V. R. (2019, June). Ai meets ai: Leveraging query executions to improve index recommendations. In *Proceedings of the 2019 International Conference on Management of Data* (pp. 1241-1258).

Gadde, H. (2024). AI-Augmented Database Management Systems for Real-Time Data Analytics. *Revista de Inteligencia Artificial en Medicina, 15*(1), 616–649.

Hao, H. (2021, October). Database Mining Information System Based on Artificial Intelligence Algorithm. In *2021 IEEE International Conference on Data Science and Computer Application (ICDSCA)* (pp. 181-185). IEEE.

Huang, X., Gao, X., & Chen, G. (2024, January). Ditune: A reinforcement learning based framework for automated database index selection. In 2024 18th International Conference on Ubiquitous Information Management and Communication (IMCOM) (pp. 1-8). IEEE.

Kandolo, W. (2024). Ensuring ai data access control in rdbms: A comprehensive review. In *Proceedings of the IEEE/CVF Conference on Computer Vision and Pattern Recognition* (pp. 8400-8407).

Kumar, A., Boehm, M., & Yang, J. (2017, May). Data management in machine learning: Challenges, techniques, and systems. In *Proceedings of the 2017 ACM International Conference on Management of Data* (pp. 1717-1722).

Li, G., Zhou, X., & Cao, L. (2021, October). Machine learning for databases. In *Proceedings of the First International Conference on AI-ML Systems* (pp. 1-2).

Ma, J. (2022, July). Research on Intelligent Management System of Practical Courses Based on Artificial Intelligence Technology. In *2022 International Conference on Artificial Intelligence and Autonomous Robot Systems (AIARS)* (pp. 315-318). IEEE.

Miao, H., Li, A., Davis, L. S., & Deshpande, A. (2017, April). Towards unified data and lifecycle management for deep learning. In 2017 IEEE 33rd International Conference on Data Engineering (ICDE) (pp. 571-582). IEEE.

Munappy, A., Bosch, J., Olsson, H. H., Arpteg, A., & Brinne, B. (2019, August). Data management challenges for deep learning. In 2019 45th Euromicro conference on software engineering and advanced applications (SEAA) (pp. 140-147). IEEE.

Nanda, A., Bajaj, S. B., & Gupta, S. (2020, June). A Comprehensive Survey of Machine Learning in Scheduling of Transactions. In 2020 4th International Conference on Trends in Electronics and Informatics (ICOEI)(48184) (pp. 740-745). IEEE.

Nihalani, N., Silakari, S., & Motwani, M. (2009, July). Integration of artificial intelligence and database management system: an inventive approach for intelligent databases. In *2009 First International Conference on Computational Intelligence, Communication Systems and Networks* (pp. 35-40). IEEE.

Nookala, G. (2021). Automated Data Warehouse Optimization Using Machine Learning Algorithms. *Journal of Computational Innovation, 1*, 1.

Openko, P. V., Hohoniants, S. Y., Starkova, O. V., Herasymenko, K. V., Yastrebov, M. I., & Prudchenko, A. O. (2019, December). Problem of choosing a dbms in modern information system. In *2019 IEEE International Conference on Advanced Trends in Information Theory (ATIT)* (pp. 171-174). IEEE.

Paganelli, M., Sottovia, P., Park, K., Interlandi, M., & Guerra, F. (2023). Pushing ML Predictions Into DBMSs. *IEEE Transactions on Knowledge and Data Engineering*, *35*(10), 10295–10308. DOI: 10.1109/TKDE.2023.3269592 PMID: 37954972

Pulivarthy, P. (2024). Gen AI Impact on the Database Industry Innovations. *International Journal of Advances in Engineering Research, 28*(3), 1–10.

Ramakrishnan, R., & Gehrke, J. (2002). *Database management systems*. McGraw-Hill, Inc.

Rosa, C.. (2024). Integrating Novel Machine Learning for Big Data Analytics and IoT Technology in Intelligent Database Management Systems. *Journal of Internet Services and Information Security, 14*(1), 206–218. DOI: 10.58346/JISIS.2024.I1.014

Sanca, V., & Ailamaki, A. (2024). Efficient Model-Relational Data Management: Challenges and Opportunities. *IEEE Transactions on Knowledge and Data Engineering, 36*(12), 7399–7409. DOI: 10.1109/TKDE.2024.3384276

Shen, H., Li, Y., Tian, X., Chen, X., Li, C., Bian, Q., Wang, Z., & Wang, W. (2022). Mass data processing and multidimensional database management based on deep learning. *Open Computer Science, 12*(1), 300–313. DOI: 10.1515/comp-2022-0251

Tsesmelis, D., & Simitsis, A. (2022, May). Database optimizers in the era of learning. In 2022 IEEE 38th International Conference on Data Engineering (ICDE) (pp. 3213-3216). IEEE.

Unuriode, A., Durojaiye, O., Yusuf, B., & Okunade, L. (2023). The Integration of Artificial I Intelligence Into D Database Systems (Ai-Db Integration Review). Available at *SSRN* 4744549.

Van Aken, D., Pavlo, A., Gordon, G. J., & Zhang, B. (2017, May). Automatic database management system tuning through large-scale machine learning. In *Proceedings of the 2017 ACM international conference on management of data* (pp. 1009-1024).

Wang, W., Zhang, M., Chen, G., Jagadish, H. V., Ooi, B. C., & Tan, K.-L. (2016). Database meets deep learning: Challenges and opportunities. *SIGMOD Record, 45*(2), 17–22. DOI: 10.1145/3003665.3003669

Wang, Y., Bourhis, P., Rouvoy, R., & Royer, P. (2024, October). Challenges & Opportunities in Automating DBMS: A Qualitative Study. In *Proceedings of the 39th IEEE/ACM International Conference on Automated Software Engineering* (pp. 2013-2023).

Wannalai, N., & Mekruksavanich, S. (2019, January). The application of intelligent database for modern information management. In 2019 Joint International Conference on Digital Arts, Media and Technology with ECTI Northern Section Conference on Electrical, Electronics, Computer and Telecommunications Engineering (ECTI DAMT-NCON) (pp. 105-108). IEEE.

Li, J., Miao, B., Wang, S., Dong, W., Xu, H., & Si, C.Hiplot Consortium. (2022). Hiplot: A comprehensive and easy-to-use web service for boosting publication-ready biomedical data visualization. *Briefings in Bioinformatics*, *23*(4), bbac261.

Zhou, X., Chai, C., Li, G., & Sun, J. (2020). Database meets artificial intelligence: A survey. *IEEE Transactions on Knowledge and Data Engineering*, *34*(3), 1096–1116. DOI: 10.1109/TKDE.2020.2994641

ADDITIONAL READING

Enyejo, L. A., Adewoye, M. B., & Ugochukwu, U. N. (2024). Interpreting Federated Learning (FL) Models on Edge Devices by Enhancing Model Explainability with Computational Geometry and Advanced Database Architectures. *International Journal of Scientific Research in Computer Science, Engineering and Information Technology*, *10*, 6.

Fahima, M. M. F.. (2024). Machine Learning for Database Management and Query Optimization. *Elementaria: Journal of Educational Research*, *2*(1), 96–108.

Islam, S. (2024). Future Trends In SQL Databases And Big Data Analytics: Impact of Machine Learning and Artificial Intelligence. Available at *SSRN* 5064781.

Oloruntoba, N. O. (2025). AI-Driven autonomous database management: Self-tuning, predictive query optimization, and intelligent indexing in enterprise it environments. *World Journal of Advanced Research and Reviews*, *25*(2), 1558–1580. DOI: 10.30574/wjarr.2025.25.2.0534

Rafique, S.. (2024). Analytical Study of OLTP Workload Management in Database Management System. *Journal of Computing & Biomedical Informatics*, *6*(02), 384–401.

Siddiqui, T., & Wu, W. (2024). ML-powered index tuning: An overview of recent progress and open challenges. *SIGMOD Record*, *52*(4), 19–30. DOI: 10.1145/3641832.3641836

Wang, Z., Gan, B., & Shi, W. (2024, May). Multimodal query suggestion with multi-agent reinforcement learning from human feedback. In *Proceedings of the ACM Web Conference 2024* (pp. 1374-1385).

Zhang, T., Tomasic, A., & Pavlo, A. (2024). Intelligent Transaction Scheduling via Conflict Prediction in OLTP DBMS. arXiv preprint arXiv:2409.01675.

KEY TERMS AND DEFINITIONS

Supervised Learning: Training a model using labeled data to predict outcomes.

Reinforcement Learning: Teaching an agent to make decisions by rewarding good actions.

Query Optimization: Finding the fastest way to run database queries.

Indexing: Creating quick lookup structures to speed up data searches.

Automated Database Configuration: Using AI to adjust database settings automatically for best performance.

Chapter 4
Artificial Intelligence and the Performance of Students

Monica Chaudhary
https://orcid.org/0000-0002-8344-1447
Melbourne Institute of Technology, Sydney, Australia

Mukhammaddiyor Kurbonov
SP Jain School of Global Management, Australia

Emrana Masoud
SP Jain School of Global Management, Australia

Bahauddin Atiq Khatib
SP Jain School of Global Management, Australia

ABSTRACT

AI technologies have impacted the academic performance and skill development of marketing students. This study investigates how AI technologies affected the academic performance and the skills in marketing students. The research paper provides insight about AI technologies' role in changing marketing education for students. The research aims to identify the usage patterns of AI in marketing students, evaluating the impact of AI education on marketing students' performance and the impact on the non-academic skill developments. To investigate the changes in the skills and academics primary and secondary data has been used. The primary data includes the survey which was done using convenient and snow-ball sampling. The secondary data was collected using the research papers and studies done earlier by researchers. There were three main aims, while collecting the secondary data,

DOI: 10.4018/979-8-3373-1210-1.ch004

which are understanding consumer sentiments, improving market performance with AI and AI's influence on non-academic skill development.

INTRODUCTION

The pedagogical landscape has seen a transformation in recent years with the introduction of Artificial Intelligence (AI) technology, especially in the area of marketing education. As of 2024, the integration of AI tools and instructional strategies has changed how marketing concepts are taught as well as how students learn, hone, and apply their talents in practical settings. The purpose of this study is to methodically investigate how AI technologies affect marketing students' academic achievement and skill development. This study aims to present a detailed knowledge of AI's role in enhancing marketing education by analysing its educational affordances and data-driven insights into student performance.

The induction of AI technologies into education, especially in marketing disciplines, is indicative of the wider digital transformation occurring in academia. Researching AI's influence on education is more vital because marketing field is at the forefront of integrating digital technology. This study is crucial because of the growing pace at which AI tools—from digital marketing analytics to consumer behaviour simulation models—are being integrated into marketing curricula. Not just the academic performance of students but also their preparedness for a rapidly evolving digital economy is greatly impacted by this kind of AI integration. Since the marketing industry depends more and more on AI for customer interaction, predictive analytics, and decision-making, marketing graduates must be proficient in both traditional marketing principles and AI technologies. This modification necessitates evaluating how well the current AI-supported teaching strategies are equipping students with the necessary abilities. Furthermore, because AI can create customised learning experiences, adapt to the unique demands of each student, and provide real-time feedback, it presents an unmatched opportunity to improve learning results. However, using AI into marketing education raises additional concerns regarding which pedagogies are most suited for this new era, whether educators are ready to employ these resources, and what moral dilemmas arise when utilising AI in the classroom.

The global COVID-19 pandemic had ushered in an unprecedented era of physical distancing and the impact was felt throughout all industries, including the education sector (Chaudhary & Bhotta, 2024). This current study is especially relevant now, as the education sector continues to navigate the advantages and difficulties brought about by technological advancements. This study aims to offer significant insights into how AI technologies could be successfully incorporated into education to better prepare students for the needs of the workforce in the future by studying how AI influences marketing students' academic performance and skill development.

STUDY OBJECTIVES

This study presents an integrated research methodology, involving a literature review, quantitative study through survey (questionnaires), aimed at addressing three main objectives:

1. To identify the AI usage pattern of marketing students.
2. To evaluate the impact of AI education on academic performance of marketing students.
3. To examine the impact of AI on skill development (non-academic).

Through mixed method approach, the study utilized both quantitative and qualitative insights from a wide range of sources and perspectives to present an exhaustive picture of AI's impact on the academic and non-academic skillset for students studying marketing.

REVIEW OF LITERATURE

Artificial intelligence (AI) has emerged as a central focus across various sectors, reshaping businesses and societal landscapes (Ghouse & Chaudhary, 2024). The intersection of artificial intelligence (AI) and consumer attitudes has emerged as a key area of research in the quickly changing marketing landscape. Companies are using AI's developments to their advantage more and more to study and influence customer behaviour in previously unheard-of ways. AI-powered recommendation systems are one prominent example of the use of AI tools for personalised marketing techniques. By providing personalised product recommendations based on each user's unique browsing preferences and past purchases, these systems have been shown to increase consumer happiness and engagement (Jain et al., 2024). According to (Jain et al. (2024) extensive analysis on consumer sentiments regarding marketing tactics in the Indian context, 75% of respondents preferred personalised marketing messages that were tailored to their interests and preferences. This emphasises how important it is to use AI technologies in order to successfully understand and address customer sentiment in the Indian market.

New research has investigated into enhancing sentiment detection in online customer reviews through complex AI techniques. Utilizing machine learning algorithms like Support Vector Machines (SVM) and Recurrent Neural Networks (RNN), a latest study reported a remarkable 85% accuracy in sentiment classification, surpassing traditional methods (Singh et al., 2022). The study emphasized the importance of refining AI models with domain-specific data, such as incorporating lexicons and features tailored to the e-commerce domain, to enhance sentiment analysis outcomes (Singh et al., 2022). Furthermore, AI-driven sentiment analysis tools have markedly improved, as evidenced by research evaluating the utility of consumer sentiment as a construct and its measurement methods. Comparative experiments revealed that AI-powered sentiment analysis tools attained higher accuracy rates, reaching up to 90%, compared to conventional surveys (Kellstedt et. al., 2015). Additionally, these tools provided real-time insights into consumer opinions and preferences, enabling businesses to make prompt adjustments to their marketing strategies (Kellstedt et. al., 2015). Finally, a great amount research was done in the hospitality and tourism sector on the integration of machine learning for customer sentiment analysis in online reviews. In an analysis of internet reviews from hotels, restaurants, and tourist destinations, this evaluation combined the results of other research to determine that Neural Network-based techniques outperformed them in sentiment classification tasks, with accuracy rates surpassing 80% (Jain et al., 2021). Additionally, the review emphasised how crucial feature engineering and data pretreatment methods are to improving machine learning models' efficacy for sentiment analysis in this field (Jain et al., 2021).

AI's Influence on Skill Development (Non-Academic)

AI is a boon for marketing students as it can create new cases and situations by which various consumer behaviours can be analysed and processes and techniques can be used to develop various non-academic skills for marketing students. According to Niemi (2021) artificial intelligence simulates real word scenarios and situations based on recent cases and issues based on which students are made to analyse the cases and design solutions which is further been supported by AI. Students can effectively engage with AI to have tools to process information, analyse and interpret the same. Saputra et al. (2023) further supported the views of Pedro and adds that AI also enhance other skills such as creativity and innovation. AI provide them with creative and unique ideas, practices customised to customer needs and this leads to creativity for students to think in new manner. Marketing students become tech savvy with creation of new tools and technologies by AI, this is an important skill to be developed. In contrast to views of Ivanov (2023) stated the negative impact of AI where marketing students uses AI technology to complete their assignments, use AI based ideas complete practical projects. Bates et al. (2020) in his research stated that AI leads to development of various non-academic skills such as critical thinking. AI provide the marketing students with opportunities to analyse and interpret data. The case studies are provided to the students which they need to analyse and evaluate and criticise the recommendations made, and this developed critical thinking skills. Yilmaz and Yilmaz (2023) further added that AI also enhances problem solving skills, where based on past data future trends and consumer behaviour is forecasted, and based on this on issues and factors are analysed and students are made to identify potential challenges and solutions related to them.

Data analysis is made simple by the use of efficient data analytical tools, and marketing students can then address these particular challenges based on hypothetical situations. According to Hashim et al. (2022), AI helps kids become more adaptive and collaborative—two critical non-academic abilities. AI helps students learn how to use a variety of cutting-edge tools and technology, encouraging them to do so and become more adaptive. AI makes sure that professionals and peers from different places can collaborate remotely and use collaboration tools to work together. According to Huang et al. (2021), AI is important for enhancing people's creativity. AI helps students come up with fresh concepts based on subjects and keywords or customer demands, and it shows them that original ideas can be developed. AI develops knowledge on how to personalise services.

There are various theories are there that shows how AI can be benefitting the development of non-academic skills among marketing students. Crompton & Burke (2023) stated some theories that supports that AI can develop various non-academic skills. Cognitive apprenticeship theory states that individual learns when they gain knowledge from experts, and in case of AI, its tools, guides, and online supports act as expert and this create knowledge and develop skills. Igbokwe (2023) has proposed some more theories which support AI to develop skills. Social learning theory states that social interactions lead to knowledge, and IA act as the social environment with its peer collaboration and communication, providing consumer behaviour analysis, data and new cases related to marketing, and this ensures gaining skills. Guan et al. (2020) focuses on some empirical evidence to develop skills via AI. AI improved problem solving where use of new case studies, data analysis learning via tools leads to development of problem solving. Digital literacy is improved by use of AI where learner can use tools, computer, analyse data and have online communication and more.

Predictive analytics using artificial intelligence (AI) has greatly improved market performance in a number of industries. Supply chain efficiency has grown thanks to AI-driven decision support systems that use machine learning algorithms for performance optimisation and predictive analytics (Ivanov & Dolgui, 2020). One notable example, according to a comparative study (Ma & Sun., 2020), is the application of cluster analysis for customer segmentation, which has effectively enabled companies to tailor their strategies to certain client clusters. Support Vector Machine (SVM) algorithms have a significant competitive edge in the financial markets due to their superior performance over traditional financial prediction methods. A meta-study by Basak et al. (2019) found that SVM performed better for stock price prediction than time series analysis, enhancing the use of AI for precision and speed in market-related decision-making.

Moreover, the implementation of AI and machine learning for business performance indicators has resulted in organisational changes that foster an environment conducive to dynamic decision-making (Trunk et al., 2020). These technological developments have been associated with increased consumer satisfaction and loyalty. This is exemplified by a survey study (Ma & Sun, 2020) wherein the application of AI and ML models enhanced targeted marketing techniques, hence directly influencing market performance.

Demand forecasting, pricing optimisation, and sales forecasting have all been significantly impacted by applications of artificial intelligence. Sarkar et al. (2023) have presented an AI-driven technique that uses k-means clustering to categorise clients in order to improve demand forecasting. As a consequence, there is an 83% clear cluster variation (Sarkar et al., 2023, p. 190). The unique purchasing patterns exhibited by each clientele group are further investigated in order to determine dynamic pricing. Regression models provide pricing ranges in which consumers' sensitivity to price fluctuations varies. For instance, clients are very responsive to price increases in the $400–$4000 range, according to Cluster 1's price sensitivity coefficient of 0.0676 (Sarkar et al., 2023).

AI price optimisation makes use of logistic regression, which predicts customer purchases within preset price ranges, significantly enhancing sales estimates. The model's performance is displayed by the Receiver Operating Characteristic (ROC) curve, which has high Area Under the Curve (AUC) values and significant prediction abilities (Sarkar et al., 2023, p. 191). Furthermore, by enabling a customised pricing approach for different client segments, this model improves income streams and raises the precision of customer buy estimations, which benefits sales forecasts. Cluster 4, which has a higher-end price range of $2000-$25000, showed a lower price sensitivity coefficient, indicating less price-driven buying behaviour. This shows how well the model works to customise prices for diverse customer profiles (Sarkar et al., 2023). These AI-powered e-commerce apps show how a customised approach has replaced a one-size-fits-all approach by leveraging AI's computational power and predictive analytics to increase customer satisfaction and market performance.

The empirical research on the impact of AI on revenue growth and profitability provides valuable insights. The study, which looked at data from more than 50 companies employing AI in their digital marketing campaigns, found an average 37% increase in cost efficiency. Higher conversion rates and better engagement metrics served as evidence of this (Rathore, 2020). One example of AI's impact in internet advertising is the usage of real-time bidding systems, which leverage AI to improve budget utilisation and ad placements by quickly analysing consumer behaviour data. AI-powered email marketing tools are another example. These products use artificial intelligence to determine the optimal times to send emails and customise the content for each receiver. It has been demonstrated that doing this increases open and conversion rates, which increases profitability.

Use of AI has impacted earning to a great length (an average 23% increase in earnings, demonstrating AI's direct impact on revenue growth, Rathore, 2020). These figures demonstrate a notable shift from conventional marketing approaches to AI-powered personalised campaigns that offer consumers experiences that are uniquely catered to them, increasing customer engagement and conversion rates. The study highlights the relationship between financial measurements and AI adoption through the use of visual aids such as graphs and tables. A graph showing the relationship between customer engagement levels and AI integration shows a positive trend that is connected to an increase in profitability (Rathore, 2020).

Based on current empirical research in the banking sector, artificial intelligence (AI) seems to be good for revenue growth and profitability. The Turkish Journal of Computer and Mathematics Education conducted research that looked at how artificial intelligence (AI) and cloud computing are affecting banking services. The findings demonstrated the significant advantages for banks utilising these technology (Tiwari et al., 2021).

AI's Potential Detriment to Students' Education and Learning Capabilities

Though we know that overuse of internet as a medium by students may be addictive (Nain & Chaudhary (2022), AI has been considered as a game-changer in academics. It has the potential to improve student experiences and learning results. Nonetheless, several studies present contradictory opinions regarding the possible risks and disadvantages associated with the extensive incorporation of AI in educational environments. A latest study presented a few risk areas related to AI integration in K–12 education (Karan & Angadi, 2023). Concerns regarding privacy, autonomy, biases, accuracy, and functional dangers are some of these risks. According to the research, although artificial intelligence (AI) has the potential to be innovative, it also poses risks that could have a big influence on the process of teaching and learning.

The discussion by Ta & West (2023) of the incorporation of generative AI tools in the classroom poses significant difficulties. The essay draws attention to possible dangers such a rise in student plagiarism, cheating, misinformation, discriminatory bias, and a decline in critical thinking abilities. These dangers highlight how difficult it is to incorporate AI into teaching methods and emphasise the need to carefully weigh the effects. Furthermore, Ivanov (2023) illuminates the less desirable parts of AI in education by highlighting possible risks, disadvantages, and resistance to its broad implementation. The possible decline in pupils' emotional intelligence and social abilities as a result of an over dependence on AI for interpersonal communication is especially concerning. This emphasises a vital component of education that goes beyond scholastic success.

These important viewpoints highlight the necessity for legislators and educators to proceed cautiously when integrating AI into the classroom. While AI holds great promise to revolutionise education, it is crucial to critically assess its impact on students' learning skills and education. While AI offers promising opportunities for innovation, its potential risks and drawbacks must be carefully addressed to ensure that students' learning experiences are not hampered but rather enhanced by its implementation. Through careful consideration of the issues brought up in these articles and additional investigation, educators can make the most of AI's advantages while minimising any potential drawbacks.

Empirical research shows that artificial intelligence (AI) has the ability to improve market performance despite these obstacles by means of demand forecasting, pricing optimisation, revenue growth, and predictive analytics. Sarkar et al. (2023), for instance, demonstrated how the application of clustering approaches by AI-driven methodologies enhanced demand forecasting, producing a clear cluster variation of 83%. Furthermore, Support Vector Machine algorithms beat conventional methods for stock price prediction, according to a meta-analysis by Kar et al. (2019), demonstrating the effectiveness of AI in market-related decision-making.

In terms of analysis, AI has the potential to completely transform a number of industries, including marketing and education. However, in order to guarantee successful adoption, ethical, social, and pedagogical ramifications must be carefully considered. The results highlight the necessity for educators, legislators, and companies to proceed cautiously when integrating AI, taking into account issues like privacy, prejudices, and the possible effects on students' social and critical thinking abilities. In addition, more investigation and the thoughtful application of AI technologies are necessary to optimise advantages and minimise possible obstacles to meeting business and educational goals. Stakeholders may effectively leverage the revolutionary potential of AI to improve market performance, accelerate innovation, and enhance learning experiences by employing it responsibly and ethically.

RESEARCH METHODOLOGY

The research involves usage of primary and secondary research. Talking about the primary data, it was collected by conducting an online questionnaire. The questionnaire was constructed in a way that aimed three major areas, which are identifying the usage patterns of AI in marketing students; evaluating the impact of AI education on marketing student's academic performance and the impact of AI on skill development (Non-Academic).

The questionnaire was constructed via google forms and it included questions which likert scale and multiple-choice questions. The target respondents were marketing students and because of time constraints the target for response were between 100 to 125. Due to time restrictions and convenience, convenient and snow-ball sampling is used for the study. The survey was sent to Australia, specifically Sydney's marketing students. The reason for convenient sampling is due to time constraints. This may create biases as the respondents might have similar characteristics and opinions. Research papers have been used to gather secondary data. The secondary data involves current and past studies which have been done in the research papers. The references are clearly stated in the paper.

The piloting of the survey was done using first 30 responses and the question taken for piloting were likert scale questions. The Cronbach's alpha score of the pilot data was 0.894 which illustrates that the survey questions are good enough to progress with the survey. Once the data collection done. In total, 143 completed questionnaires were used for analysis. The reliability check was carried out which included the total amount of responses we received. The Cronbach's alpha score is 0.859 indicating high reliability.

DATA ANALYSIS & FINDINGS

After analyzing the secondary data extracted from the literature encompassing various domains including marketing education, skills, strategies, and decision-making, the analysis of the survey data further enriched the understanding. This comprehensive approach sheds light on the multifaceted impact of AI across diverse realms, offering insights into its influence on skill development, strategic formulation, and decision-making processes. After conducting survey, it was found that 66% of marketing students have used AI in their marketing education journey in university and college (Figure 1).

Figure 1. Exposure to AI for studying marketing

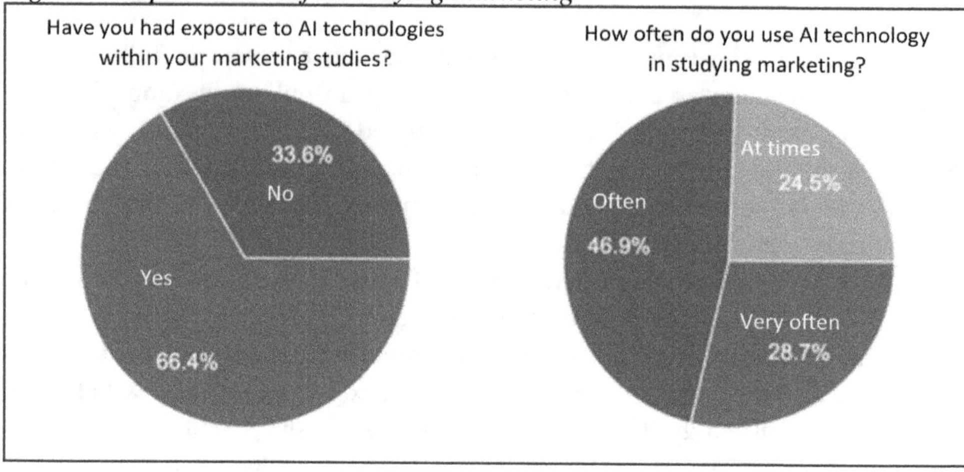

About the familiarity with AI technology, the survey reported that only 19% are very familiar with AI technology and many have commented that is because they find it difficult to ask the right questions using the right keywords and some believe that some of the AI technologies are "complicated to understand ". Forty-seven percentage of the marketing students reported that they often use AI technologies to help in their marketing studies. Almost 30% use AI very frequently and only 24.5% do not really incorporate AI in their marketing studies.

Although, through our secondary research findings we found out AI is very necessary in the dynamic world of marketing, similarly there is a strong belief among respondents that AI is necessary for marketing students, with an average rating of around 7.6 out of 10. Moreover, eighty-three percentage of the respondent students generally believe that AI education has helped them better understand marketing concepts and theories and only 16.8% believe it did not help improve their understanding. Another interesting finding about how much time students save (in hours per week) by using AI for their assignments (Figure 2), the findings are insightful. Almost forty-five percent of the student respondents were able to save on an average between 4-6 hours (per week) and forty percent saved 1-3 hours (per week) and seven percent showed significant reduction of over 16 hours (per week).

Figure 2. AI helps marketing students

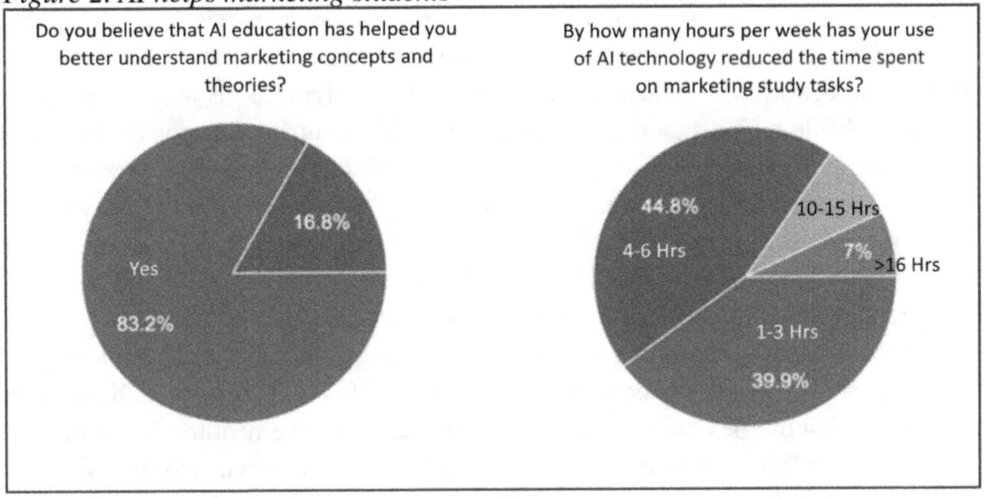

The incorporation of AI technologies has led to improvements in academic performance in marketing courses for many students. 50% believe it improved just slightly while 27% believe it improved significantly. 17.5% believe it did not affect their academic performance and only 5% believed their performance declined. Based on the survey the AI exposure is perceived to provide a competitive advantage in marketing courses compared to peers who haven't received similar exposure with 41% strongly agreeing to the statement and 14% are not sure or the believe it did not provide them with competitive advantage. Almost fifty percent of the respondents believe the AI somewhat influenced their ability to analyse marketing data and making decisions while 30% believed it significantly influenced it. On the other hand, 14% think it did not make any difference.

Based on the survey findings, over 60% of the respondents reported experiencing enhancements not only in their academic performance and educational progression but also expressed confidence in their ability to enhance presentation and communication skills, rating their 24 improvements above 5 on a scale of 1 to 10, attributed to the assistance of AI technologies. This suggests that AI technologies likely aid individuals across various educational levels and disciplines in refining their communication and presentation abilities. The survey also found that 84% of respondents credited AI-driven simulations for enhancing their teamwork in marketing projects, with only 16% rating their experience below 5 on a scale of 1 to 10. This suggests a strong link between AI simulations and effective collaboration, while the lower rating from a minority may stem from varying learning preferences or prior exposure to such technologies.

Respondents were also asked to rate (on rating scale of 1-10) the usefulness of AI in developing your problem-solving skills through personalized learning paths and case study analysis in marketing. The ratings suggest a dynamic landscape in perceptions towards AI's role in sharpening problem-solving skills within marketing contexts. While a significant portion perceives AI's contribution positively, those rating below 5 might point to nuances in personal learning preferences or areas where AI interventions could be tailored for enhanced efficacy. The majority (46%) highly rate AI's impact on adaptability and creativity in marketing, while a significant portion (53.1%) remains below this threshold (below 8), possibly indicating varying perspectives on its effectiveness or awareness of its limitations.

It's clear that AI is changing the face of marketing education, as a sizable majority recognises its beneficial educational influence. This is consistent with data that shows AI technologies have been widely adopted and have resulted in significant time savings. While there are obvious benefits to AI, the research also shows that its integration must be done carefully. The poor familiarity rates and worries about the development of social skills emphasise how crucial it is to strike a balance between human-centric learning approaches and technological improvements.

Students' significant time savings highlights AI's revolutionary impact on time management in marketing courses. This indicates that AI can improve productivity and streamline processes, which is consistent with research that highlights AI's ability to save time. The varying experiences with AI-powered role-playing games and simulations point to a complex influence on creativity. Although most people see improvements, a sizable minority thinks they have improved less, suggesting that different pupils may be affected differently by AI's impact on creativity. All things considered, the combination of survey results and previously published works presents a nuanced picture of AI's application in marketing education. Although AI has clear advantages in terms of productivity and efficiency, care must be taken to prevent the adoption of AI from overshadowing the development of crucial creative and interpersonal skills that are necessary for success in the area.

CONCLUSION & IMPLICATIONS

To sum up, this research offers a comprehensive examination of the ways in which artificial intelligence (AI) is influencing marketing education, with an emphasis on the ways in which AI impacts students' academic achievement and skill development. Through an integrated research methodology that combined literature reviews, surveys, and questionnaires, we were able to gather both quantitative and qualitative insights into the usage patterns of AI among marketing students, its impact on their academic performance, and its impact on the development of non-academic skills.

The findings indicate that marketing education is increasingly using artificial intelligence (AI). This is due to AI's ability to deliver personalised learning settings, offer data-driven insights into student performance, and simplify the usage of interactive simulation tools. This integration, which reflects the wider digital transformation taking place across industries, emphasises how important it is to provide marketing graduates with the capabilities they need to employ both traditional marketing concepts and AI technology. But the study also emphasises the risks and challenges associated with implementing AI in the classroom. Concerns concerning privacy, biases, accuracy, and the potential for an over-reliance on AI to degrade students' social and emotional development underscore the need for a balanced approach to incorporating AI technologies in educational settings.

The research delves into empirical examples that demonstrate AI's capacity to improve market performance by means of predictive analytics, demand forecasting, pricing optimization, and its influence on revenue growth and profitability. AI's ability to transform market strategies and decision-making procedures and enhance organizational outcomes is demonstrated by its implementation in various domains. This study emphasizes the significance of addressing the ethical, social, and pedagogical aspects of AI integration despite the clear benefits of AI in improving educational and market performance. The results indicate that although artificial intelligence (AI) presents encouraging prospects for innovation in marketing education and practice, its application needs to be handled carefully to guarantee favourable results for practitioners and students alike.

In light of these insights, it is imperative that influential figures in business, academia, and government keep debating and researching the most effective ways to address the difficulties associated with incorporating AI. By doing this, teachers can harness the revolutionary potential of AI to build a learning environment that enhances student performance academically and helps them develop their skills, all while preparing them for the always evolving demands of the digital economy. In order to teach students, the skills and competencies they need to flourish in an increasingly AI-driven society, this study ultimately highlights how crucial it is to strategically and ethically integrate AI technology into marketing education. As we explore AI's potential in the workplace, we must continue to take into account how it can impact human-centric skills and the overall standard of learning experiences.

The study text as it will appear in the book then begins here. Note that the purpose of this sample is to show how to include the various aspects outline above including abstracts, keywords, tables, figure callouts and special characters. The actual formatting in terms of line spacing and font size etc. only needs to be clear and consistent rather than following any requirements.

REFERENCES

Basak, S., Kar, S., Saha, S., Khaidem, L., & Dey, S. R. (2019). Predicting the direction of stock market prices using tree-based classifiers. *The North American Journal of Economics and Finance, 47*, 552–567. DOI: 10.1016/j.najef.2018.06.013

Bates, T., Cobo, C., Mariño, O., & Wheeler, S. (2020). Can artificial intelligence transform higher education? *International Journal of Educational Technology in Higher Education, 17*(1), 1–12. DOI: 10.1186/s41239-020-00218-x

Chaudhary, M., & Bhotta, D. (2023). Online student engagement and innovative teaching strategies post COVID-19. *International Journal of Innovation in Education, 8*(2-4), 96–111. DOI: 10.1504/IJIIE.2023.136160

Crompton, H., & Burke, D. (2023). Artificial intelligence in higher education: The state of the field. *International Journal of Educational Technology in Higher Education, 20*(1), 22. DOI: 10.1186/s41239-023-00392-8

Ghouse, S. M., & Chaudhary, M. (2024). Artificial Intelligence (AI) for Tourism Start-Ups. In *Innovative Technologies for Increasing Service Productivity* (pp. 161-178). IGI Global.

Guan, C., Mou, J., & Jiang, Z. (2020). Artificial intelligence innovation in education: A twenty-year data-driven historical analysis. *International Journal of Innovation Studies, 4*(4), 134–147. DOI: 10.1016/j.ijis.2020.09.001

Hashim, S., Omar, M. K., Ab Jalil, H., & Sharef, N. M. (2022). Trends on technologies and artificial intelligence in education for personalized learning: Systematic literature. *Journal of Academic Research in Progressive Education and Development, 12*(1), 884–903. DOI: 10.6007/IJARPED/v11-i1/12230

Huang, J., Saleh, S., & Liu, Y. (2021). A review on artificial intelligence in education. *Academic Journal of Interdisciplinary Studies, 10*(3).

Igbokwe, I. C. (2023). Application of artificial intelligence (AI) in educational management. *International Journal of Scientific and Research Publications, 13*(3), 300–307. DOI: 10.29322/IJSRP.13.03.2023.p13536

Ivanov, D., & Dolgui, A. (2020). Viability of intertwined supply networks: Extending the supply chain resilience angles towards survivability. A position paper motivated by COVID-19 outbreak. *International Journal of Production Research, 58*(10), 2904–2915. DOI: 10.1080/00207543.2020.1750727

Ivanov, S. (2023). The dark side of artificial intelligence in higher education. *Service Industries Journal, 43*(15-16), 1055–1082. DOI: 10.1080/02642069.2023.2258799

Jain, P. K., Pamula, R., & Srivastava, G. (2021). A systematic literature review on machine learning applications for consumer sentiment analysis using online reviews. *Computer Science Review, 41*, 100413. DOI: 10.1016/j.cosrev.2021.100413

Jain, S. K., Goel, P., & Jain, S. (2024). Understanding Consumer Sentiments Towards Marketing: An Investigation in Indian Context. *Vision (Basel), 28*(2), 210–224. DOI: 10.1177/09722629211027327

Karan, B., & Angadi, G. R. (2023). Potential Risks of Artificial Intelligence Integration into School Education: A Systematic Review. *Bulletin of Science, Technology & Society, 43*(3-4), 67–85. DOI: 10.1177/02704676231224705

Kellstedt, P. M., Linn, S., & Hannah, A. L. (2015). The usefulness of consumer sentiment: Assessing construct and measurement. *Public Opinion Quarterly, 79*(1), 181–203. DOI: 10.1093/poq/nfu056

Ma, L., & Sun, B. (2020). Machine learning and AI in marketing–Connecting computing power to human insights. *International Journal of Research in Marketing, 37*(3), 481–504. DOI: 10.1016/j.ijresmar.2020.04.005

Nain, H., & Chaudhary, M. (2022). Internet Usage by Young Kids in India. *Fwu Journal of Social Sciences, 16*(3).

Niemi, H. (2021). AI in learning: Preparing grounds for future learning. *Journal of Pacific Rim Psychology, 15*, 18344909211038105. DOI: 10.1177/18344909211038105

Rathore, B. (2020). Personalization and Profits: The Impact of AI on Targeted Digital Marketing. *International Journal of Transcontinental Discoveries, 7*(1), 1–14.

Saputra, Y. M., Ali, E. Y., & Fadhli, R. (2023). Implementation of Artificial Intelligence (AI) Technology in Students' Academic and Non-Academic Activities in Higher Education: A Wright Map Analysis. *Journal for ReAttach Therapy and Developmental Diversities, 6*(10s), 1183–1193.

Sarkar, M., Ayon, E. H., Mia, M. T., Ray, R. K., Chowdhury, M. S., Ghosh, B. P., & Puja, A. R. (2023). Optimizing E-Commerce Profits: A Comprehensive Machine Learning Framework for Dynamic Pricing and Predicting Online Purchases. *Journal of Computer Science and Technology Studies, 5*(4), 186–193. DOI: 10.32996/jcsts.2023.5.4.19

Singh, U., Saraswat, A., Azad, H. K., Abhishek, K., & Shitharth, S. (2022). Towards improving e-commerce customer review analysis for sentiment detection. *Scientific Reports, 12*(1), 21983. DOI: 10.1038/s41598-022-26432-3 PMID: 36539524

Ta, R., & West, D. M. (2023). Should schools ban or integrate generative AI in the classroom?.

Tiwari, S., Bharadwaj, S., & Joshi, S. (2021). A study of impact of cloud computing and artificial intelligence on banking services, profitability and operational benefits. [TURCOMAT]. *Turkish Journal of Computer and Mathematics Education, 12*(6), 1617–1627.

Trunk, A., Birkel, H., & Hartmann, E. (2020). On the current state of combining human and artificial intelligence for strategic organizational decision making. *Business Research, 13*(3), 875–919. DOI: 10.1007/s40685-020-00133-x

Yilmaz, R., & Yilmaz, F. G. K. (2023). The effect of generative artificial intelligence (AI)-based tool use on students' computational thinking skills, programming self-efficacy and motivation. *Computers and Education: Artificial Intelligence, 4*, 100147. DOI: 10.1016/j.caeai.2023.100147

Chapter 5
Designing the Future With Generative AI by Overcoming Challenges and Maximizing Opportunities:
The Current State of Generative AI Technologies

Hatice Kübra Kılınç
https://orcid.org/0000-0003-3040-6776
Kahramanmaraş Sütçü İmam University, Turkey

Ökkeş Fatih Keçecioğlu
Kahramanmaraş Sütçü İmam University, Turkey

ABSTRACT

This chapter explores the future potential of generative AI (GenAI) and the key challenges it presents. It highlights opportunities in creativity, education, healthcare, and industry, while also addressing major risks such as fake content, privacy issues, and algorithmic bias. The chapter emphasizes the need for clear communication with non-expert audiences and examines evolving AI policy-making processes. It offers insights into managing risks and maximizing benefits, helping stakeholders better navigate GenAI's complexities. With practical recommendations for transparency and responsible use, this chapter serves as a valuable guide for academics, policymakers, industry leaders, and educators working to understand and manage the societal impact of generative AI.

DOI: 10.4018/979-8-3373-1210-1.ch005

INTRODUCTİON

The Current State of Generative AI Technologies

The advent of artificial intelligence has led to transformative changes in technology and has brought about new needs. Many individuals and institutions have tried to adapt technologies such as machine learning and deep learning to their own fields, while some institutions have continued to remain distant from these developments. However, the emergence of generative artificial intelligence has created a deep and widespread impact across all sectors. Questions such as whether artificial intelligence should be used, whether it is dangerous, or how it should be used have been replaced by the emergence of high-level projects that even technology giants compete in. This change has happened so quickly that many governments were caught unprepared. In this section, we will examine the effects, current state, and trends of this rapidly developing field, and aim to help readers better understand the professions affected by generative artificial intelligence.

Generative AI initially emerged in the form of newly created images, sounds, and texts generated by artificial intelligence; this may not have clearly reflected to many how diverse its application areas could be and how it could be used. Today, generative AI is used in areas such as personal assistants, company-specific CEO like agents, financial advisors, university-level instructors, and even in medical diagnostics like doctors. More detailed examples and categories of these use cases will be presented in the following parts of the text(Broussard, 2019; Brown et al., 2020; Mahsun et al., 2024). Thanks to generative AI, it is now possible to produce videos, code, 3D models, and even proteins. Algorithms capable of generating molecules and decoding protein structures in a highly complex field are receiving increasing attention every day(Ramesh et al., 2022; Saharia et al., 2022).

Training a language model is a complex process. It involves adjusting the weight and bias values in the neural network to minimize the loss function by measuring the difference between the predicted outputs and the actual data. These models are typically developed using statistical methods such as Markov chains or artificial neural networks(Ian. Goodfellow et al., 2017). Core components include extensive text data, architectures like Markov models, neural networks, and transformers, along with training algorithms that fine-tune the model's parameters and weights to learn the structure of language (Brown et al., 2020; I. J. Goodfellow et al., 2014).

The richness and breadth of the corpus enable models to learn various language structures, meanings, and contextual subtleties. Language models, trained on massive text datasets, learn the structure and usage of language, enabling them to interpret human language and generate coherent text. Language models fundamentally rely on large and diverse datasets to be trained effectively. These datasets typically include books, articles, websites, and other types of text available on the internet. Data volume is critical; for example, models like GPT-3 have shown performance improvements in various language tasks by accessing 570 GB of text (Brown et al., 2020; Kaplan et al., 2020). Language models have been integrated into various applications such as content generation, machine translation, sentiment analysis, and dialogue systems. Similarly, image generation tools like DALL·E democratize access to high-quality visual content by being used in marketing, product design, and creative arts(Dan Jurafsky and James H. Martin, 2025).

Image generation systems like DALL·E and Stable Diffusion leverage large-scale image datasets paired with text. This dual structure enables models to understand and generate images based on textual inputs. Both models use variations of generative adversarial networks (GANs) or diffusion models that iteratively work to improve the generated image in terms of realism and consistency(I. J. Goodfellow et al., 2014a; Ho et al., 2020; Ramesh et al., 2022).

Transformer models have also made it possible to train on large datasets without the need for prior labeling. Their ability to make inferences across pages and sections has significantly contributed to the growth of this field. The attention mechanism within the transformer architecture enables the model to establish these meaningful connections across textual elements (Ramesh et al., 2022; Schuhmann et al., 2022) With the development of powerful language models by companies, striking results have begun to emerge, triggering a wave of intense competition. We have now reached a point where it can be said that companies have become more influential than governments in certain areas. This field is evolving with remarkable rapidity.

Generative models represent a specialized type of artificial neural network, designed for tasks such as generating, synthesizing, or completely transforming data.

Some of the main tasks made possible by language models include:

- Text generation
- Text understanding
- Question-answering systems
- Language translation
- Text classification

Increased accessibility of generative AI platforms and APIs has allowed broader public use, enabling the rapid emergence of small-scale ventures. Many companies initially released their tools as open-source but transitioned to closed-source once they gained a certain level of growth and user base(Charles Owen-Jackson, 2024).

Before diving deeper, it is useful to distinguish between traditional AI and generative AI. These differences can be summarized under several subheadings:

- **Content Creation and Flexibility:** Traditional AI operates within predefined rules and can derive meaning from existing data, but it cannot generate entirely new content. Generative AI, on the other hand, offers much more flexibility. It can create novel content from scratch.
- **Problem-Solving Approach:** While traditional AI tends to approach problems holistically, generative AI adopts a more modular approach, breaking down complex problems into smaller components. This fosters more innovative and diverse solutions.
- **Learning Process and Data Requirements:** Traditional AI often requires labeled data and supervised learning. Generative AI, however, learns from large and diverse datasets through unsupervised learning methods, which also necessitate large-scale data availability.
- **Application Domains and Use Cases:** Traditional AI has been applied in areas such as data analytics, manufacturing, and sentiment analysis. While these applications brought innovation, generative AI has an even broader scope, providing powerful solutions in art, design, natural language processing, text generation, coding, 3D modeling, and process planning.
- **Strengths and Weaknesses:** Traditional AI is quite successful at solving specific and well-defined problems, yet it struggles to adapt to real-world conditions. While generative AI offers more creative and flexible solutions, it may face challenges in evaluating the quality of the generated content and preventing biases.

Although traditional AI performs well on clearly defined tasks, it tends to be weak in adapting to dynamic, real-world situations or producing instant responses. On the other hand, generative AI models that we can converse with in real time or even have them select our flight tickets provide more flexible solutions. However, their outputs still require quality control. Moreover, the likelihood of biased responses remains high, and evidence supporting this concern continues to grow day by day. This issue will be explored in greater depth in the section where we discuss the risks of artificial intelligence (Stuart Russell and Peter Norvig, 2011).

Milestones in AI

This section highlights how generative AI has transformed various sectors between 2020 and 2030(Kılınç & Keçecioğlu, 2024). These models are predicted to outperform human professionals in many areas within just a few years:

1. Text

- **Pre-2020**: Applications like fake news detection, basic translation, and QA systems.
- **2020**: Basic drafts and copywriting.
- **2022**: Enhanced draft writing and better text generation.
- **2023**: Domain-specific fine-tuning (e.g., scientific writing).
- **2025**: AI-generated drafts slightly outperform human-written ones.
- **2030+**: AI-generated texts surpass those written by professional authors.

2. Code
   - **Pre-2020**: Auto-completion of single lines.
   - **2020**: Multi-line code generation.
   - **2022**: Generation of longer and more complex code blocks.
   - **2023**: Multilingual code support.
   - **2025**: Text-to-image coding.
   - **2030+**: Text-to-product models will outperform full-time developers.
3. Image
   - **Pre-2020**: Very limited image generation capabilities.
   - **2020**: AI-generated art, logos, and photography.
   - **2022**: Applications in model design, product design, and architecture.
   - **2025**: Full design processes handled end-to-end by AI.
   - **2030+**: AI-generated designs outperform professional designers.
4. Video and 3D Games
   - **Pre-2020**: Little to no use of AI in this domain.
   - **2020**: First drafts of 3D/video content.
   - **2022**: Simple video and 3D file generation (first versions).
   - **2025**: Improved second versions.
   - **2030+**: Personalized video games and films created by AI.

Generative AI has made an impact across various industries. In the upcoming sections, we aim to offer readers informed perspectives through concrete examples.

- **In the arts**: Generating music, scripts, and design assets
- **In marketing and advertising**: Creating personalized campaigns and ads
- **In software development**: Generating code, debugging, and building new applications from scratch
- **In scientific research**: Simulating molecules, analyzing data, and designing new materials
- **In education**: Enabling personalized learning materials

While the current landscape of generative AI demonstrates remarkable capabilities across various sectors, it is equally important to examine the potential risks these systems pose to individuals, institutions, and society at large.

POTENTİAL RİSK OF GENAI

The rapid expansion of the application areas and capacities of artificial intelligence technologies, along with the high speed of these developments, has left many sectors unprepared. Just as opportunities must be assessed, it is also of great importance to carefully evaluate the potential risks and threats in this field. Threats such as the generation of fake content, privacy violations, misleading the public, perception manipulation, and the undermining of factual information just to name a few can pose truly frightening risks. Alongside these challenges, there is also the potential to offer innovative and personalized solutions in various sectors, especially in education and healthcare services. In this section, you will read about both the existing work in this field and the possible risks it may bring, including issues such as patient rights. As AI solutions become integrated into every area of society, it is essential to develop proactive strategies to minimize their negative impacts and maximize their benefits.

The Ability to Generate Realistic Fake Content

In the World Economic Forum's Global Risks Perception Survey 2024–2025, several charts were shared as projections regarding the current and future risks facing our world. In these studies, "misinformation and disinformation" appeared on the list of the world's greatest risks with a rate of 7%. The fact that this issue, which participants identified as one of the most serious threats, accounted for 7% is truly striking and significant (*World Economic Forum-The Global Risks Report 2024*, 2024). The ability to generate realistic fake content, the capacity to spread misinformation, and the emergence of deepfakes pose significant risks. There are numerous examples of deepfakes. One of the most sensational incidents occurred in the early months of 2025: a deepfake video showing U.S. President Donald Trump kissing Elon Musk's feet, accompanied by the phrase "Long Live the Real King," was played on a screen at the headquarters of the U.S. Department of Housing and Urban Development in Washington. This cyberattack, carried out by hackers, demonstrated that individuals can be threatened regardless of their rank or position. While such deepfake productions may begin as simple reputation attacks, they have the potential to cause harm on much larger scales(*BBC Verify: Viral Donald Trump*

Jr Audio Highly Likely AI Fake, 2025; *TVs at US Government Building Show AI Video of Trump Kissing Musk's Feet*, 2025; reuters, 2025).

Deepfake attacks can cause not only reputational damage to individuals but also significant financial losses. In Hong Kong, a finance employee was deceived during a fake video meeting organized by hackers using deepfake technology. The hackers impersonated the company's CFO and several other employees, and the convincing nature of the video conference led to a financial loss of $25.6 million for the company (Heather Chen and Kathleen Magramo, 2024; *Multinational Loses HK$200 Million to Deepfake Video Conference Scam, Hong Kong Police Say*, 2024).

In a similar incident, the CEO of a UK-based energy company was defrauded using voice-mimicking deepfake technology. By imitating the voice of an executive from the parent company, the attackers deceived the CEO into authorizing a large fund transfer, resulting in a loss of $243,000. Such incidents highlight the seriousness of the threats that deepfake technology poses to companies and senior executives(*Deepfakes Are Coming for the Financial Sector*, 2024; *Unusual CEO Fraud via Deepfake Audio Steals US$243,000 From UK Company*, 2019).

Algorithmic Bias

Unfortunately, generative artificial intelligence has become a technology capable of influencing even matters as critical as warfare. In 2022, a fake video circulated online showing Ukrainian President Zelensky allegedly ordering Ukrainian soldiers to surrender. Although the deepfake was of low quality, it demonstrated just how rapidly disinformation can spread (*Deepfake Footage Purports to Show Ukrainian President Capitulating*, 2022).

These examples illustrate the dangers of malicious uses of this technology, but there are also significant issues arising during the development of these systems. Large language models developed by companies or governments can unfortunately be biased. By positioning themselves as arbiters of truth deciding what is accurate, who is right or wrong, who is the oppressor and who is the oppressed these developers essentially appoint themselves as judges. Although such implications may seem alarming for the future, recent incidents have shown that these are no longer just hypothetical concerns. Generative AI models can exhibit biased and discriminatory behavior depending on the datasets they are trained on. This was evident in both OpenAI's GPT and China-based researchers' DeepSeek model.

The International Court of Justice ruled that Israel's presence in Palestinian territories is unlawful, and called for an immediate end to such actions and compensation for the damages caused to individuals and entities in Palestinian lands. Despite this ruling, when GPT was asked whether Israel and Palestine deserve justice, it provided a biased response. While defending Israel's actions as its "right to self-defense" despite accusations of genocide, it described the issue in vague terms when referring to Palestine, calling it "a complex matter." After a user shared this response and it sparked backlash, the system administrators intervened. Later, similar questions were left unanswered (*ChatGPT on Palestine and Israel - What Do You Make of This?*, 2023; ian bremme, 2023; Mazen Baroudi, 2023; Mona Chalabi, 2023). A similar incident occurred with the product of a China based artificial intelligence company, DeepSeek, which quickly made headlines after its release. As a large language model, DeepSeek gained attention for its lower development cost compared to GPT and its use of reinforcement learning to optimize decision making. However, it also drew criticism for censoring information regarding the inhumane treatment of Uyghur Turks in China. The model's lack of neutrality in its responses sparked public backlash (DeepSeek's Answers Include Chinese Propaganda, Researchers Say, 2025). Although its open-source nature attracted the interest of developers, this situation once again highlights the critical need for caution in the development of such technologies, as well as the necessity for robust new policies.Today, information is no longer primarily learned from books, but from AI tools. If the source of that information is false or misleading, it can lead to extremely harmful consequences.

Privacy Violations and Unethical Use

Large language models and generative AI products are generally developed through the training of massive datasets. However, the data collection processes involved in building these models do not always adhere to ethical standards. This can lead to violations of personal rights and the unauthorized use of institutional data(International Science Council, 2023, 2025; REPUBLIC OF TÜRKİYE COUNCIL OF HIGHER EDUCATION, n.d.). When we talk about privacy violations, unfortunately, many scenarios are possible. To make this issue more tangible, we would like to provide a few examples. Personal data such as health records, financial information, location data, and details related to an individual's physical appearance can be accessed and exploited without proper authorization. The unauthorized use and sharing of such data is illegal. Technologies like facial recognition have made it increasingly feasible to track individuals, raising serious concerns about surveillance and the erosion of privacy (G R Mukesh, 2024). Various risks of violation are also possible with the use of biometric data. Biometric data may include fingerprints, retina scans, and similar information. Sam Altman recently invested in an initiative that performs retina scans and encrypts individuals' personal information using blockchain technology, turning it into a non-replicable identity. The advantages of such technologies will be discussed in the next section, under the heading Opportunities Brought by These Technologies (Cooper & Yon, 2019; Wenhua et al., 2023). Large language models are trained on texts, images, and other content collected from the internet.

The unauthorized use of this internet sourced data as training material can lead to copyright violations. Such infringements include the replication of artists' works and the use of authors' writings, which have resulted in various legal cases(Surden, 2019). It is certain that these rapidly advancing and large scale technologies will impact various sectors and lead to job losses. As can be clearly seen in the table we provided, in many industries, AI systems can already outperform human professionals. By 2030, it is highly likely that we will see models capable of producing architectural designs superior to those created by professional architects. Even today, the foundational examples of such capabilities are quite exciting.

On the other hand, this transformation carries potential societal impacts in terms of the labor force. These potential effects can be summarized as follows:

- Job losses in fields like manufacturing, customer service, call centers, and cashier roles, where automation can replace human labor
- The need to retrain the existing workforce to adapt to new and emerging areas of expertise
- An increasing demand for human workers who can collaborate with AI powered systems
- A rise in unemployment rates and a deepening of social inequality

While these are the predicted potential outcomes, it's important to remember that the adoption of traditional and generative AI models in the industry is not easy, as they are not entirely separate but complementary technologies. Humans are emotional beings, and there will naturally be resistance especially within organizations toward replacing people with automated systems. Additionally, we must consider the inherent limitations of automation itself. For instance, OpenAI's GPT models generate realistic outputs by essentially reproducing what they have been trained on. Even when we ask them to generate something from scratch, it's important to remember that they are still referencing existing patterns. This reflects the difficulty of transferring human traits such as creativity, empathy, and complex problem solving into automated systems.

DeepSeek, on the other hand, appears to have somewhat overcome these limitations by using reinforcement learning, allowing it to go beyond simply copying or mimicking information. This suggests that new training approaches may help overcome these existing challenges. Training AI models is also extremely costly. According to Stanford University's AI Index Report, OpenAI's GPT-3 model cost $4.3 billion to train in 2020, while Gemini Ultra was trained for $19.4 billion in 2023. These massive figures demonstrate that such developments require significant resources and cannot be undertaken by every team. At the same time, this raises concerns about the monopolization of the industry (Artificial Intelligence Index Report 2023

Introduction to the AI Index Report 2023, n.d.; The Risk of Automation for Jobs in OECD Countries, 2016; Cao et al., 2022). According to a report published by Stanford University, Table 1 presents a comparative analysis of the training costs of artificial intelligence models.

Table 1. Comparison of AI model training costs

Model / Company	Release Year	Training Cost
Gemini Ultra (Google)	2023	$191.4M
GPT-4 (OpenAI)	2023	$78.3M
PaLM 540B (Google)	2022	$12.3M
Megatron-Turing NLG 530B (Microsoft - Nvidia)	2021	$6.4M
GPT-3 175B Davinci (OpenAI)	2020	$4.3M

Note. Estimated training costs are reported in millions of USD and reflect publicly available information as of 2024.

Effects on Non-Expert Audiences

The emergence of new areas of expertise will create a demand for new employees in the sector. The existing workforce will need to acquire new technical skills in order to work in coordination with AI tools integrated into companies.

At the same time, a growing sense of fear and distrust toward AI technologies among the general public is likely in the coming years. To overcome this within companies, it will be important to create environments where employees can freely express their concerns and thoughts. This will contribute positively to the successful adaptation and full efficiency of AI systems within organizations(Harvard Business Review, 2019).

Another potential consequence is the confusion caused by AI generated outputs such as realistic images, voices, and texts. The difficulty in distinguishing accurate information can pose a serious threat, particularly for individuals who are unfamiliar with the technology.

Raising public awareness about the ethics and risks of AI technologies appears to be a critical area for promoting social consciousness, guiding government actions, and protecting communities. The importance of public education has not diminished in the age of AI.

Challenges in AI Integration and Simple Solutions

One of the most important points that companies, managers, institutions, and even governments need to understand is that machines are no longer just tools they are becoming active members of our teams. We must prepare accordingly and accelerate the adoption process. Instead of avoiding or fearing algorithms, we should seek to understand them correctly, identify our needs accurately, and build teams to develop appropriate solutions. We are living in an era where investing in the training of experts is essential.

The selection of appropriate data inputs is critical for AI systems to make healthy and reliable decisions. For instance, in municipal auditing processes, the data selected for analysis can directly influence the accuracy of AI generated decisions. Therefore, the teams developing AI systems must fully understand the diversity of data and its impact on decision making processes and reflect this awareness in system design.

Additionally, for AI to be effectively implemented within organizations, data selection processes must be handled meticulously, and development teams must be educated on the importance of these processes. AI models fed with high quality and relevant data can produce more trustworthy and transparent outcomes in decision making, ultimately enabling more effective organizational integration of AI.

Teaming Up with AI: Rethinking Institutional Roles in the AI Era

Today, one of the most important realizations for companies, managers, institutions, and even governments is that machines are no longer just tools, they are becoming active members of working teams. We briefly addressed this necessity in the previous section, and now we would like to summarize it in bullet points. AI and automation systems have evolved from merely supporting business processes to becoming key contributors to decision-making mechanisms. Accepting this transformation and preparing institutional structures accordingly has become critical for gaining a competitive edge.

Instead of avoiding or fearing AI and algorithms, organizations must focus on understanding and properly integrating them. When the role of algorithms in business processes is well understood, it can enhance both operational efficiency and innovation capacity. Working with algorithms can be seen as a form of strategic nourishment. To achieve this, the following steps should be taken:

- **Accurately identifying needs:** Determining which areas of the business can benefit most from AI.
- **Effective strategic integration:** Adapting AI systems to existing workflows for efficient use.

- **Training expert personnel:** Investing in technical and managerial human resources to ensure the successful implementation of algorithm and AI based solutions.
- **Encouraging collaboration between employees and AI:** Promoting the understanding that AI powered systems are meant to complement not replace human labor.

Accelerating AI Adoption by Governments and Institutions

Integrating AI into the workforce is not solely the responsibility of private companies; it must also be supported by public policies and regulations. Countries such as the United States, the European Union, and China have developed national strategies to accelerate AI-driven digital transformation. In this context, several responsibilities fall upon governments and institutions, including:

- Investing in education and reskilling programs.
- Establishing regulations that support AI initiatives and innovation.
- Offering incentives to ease companies' transition into AI transformation.

The era we live in requires us to view AI not merely as a technology, but as an integral part of both the business world and society. The integration of AI into the workforce presents great opportunities for organizations willing to embrace it, while posing serious competitive disadvantages for those that fail to adapt. Therefore, companies, managers, and governments must understand how to collaborate with AI and algorithms, and take strategic steps in this direction.

Despite the significant risks and ethical concerns surrounding generative AI, it is equally important to acknowledge the transformative opportunities it offers across various domains such as creativity, education, healthcare, and innovation-driven industries. In the following section, we will explore these opportunities in greater depth.

OPPORTUNİTİES OFFERED BY GENERATİVE AI

Generative AI has introduced innovations and personalized solutions across various sectors. It is applicable in many fields such as manufacturing, art, finance, entertainment, and robotics, producing tailored solutions to meet specific needs. This technology stands out by its capability to generate new content rather than just performing data analysis and predictions, resulting in striking impacts across multiple industries. In this section, we examine the advantages this field offers, presenting new opportunities for both individuals and institutions (Boscardin et al., 2024; Chuma & De Oliveira, 2023; Eman A. Alasadi and Carlos R. Baiz*, 2023).

Innovations and Personalized Solutions in Various Sectors

Generative AI can produce very fast solutions in areas requiring personalization. In the fashion and design sectors, it is now significantly easier to create personalized clothing and accessories using AI-supported tools, eliminating the need for a professional designer. A company called Stitch Fix has started providing fashion recommendations tailored specifically to their customers' individual styles by analyzing their preferences (Stitch Fix, 2023).

These examples offer new insights into how widely this technology can be applied. Unique and personal designs, in particular, can attract specific audiences more effectively(Farrelly & Baker, 2023; *International Journal of Arts, Humanities & Social Science*, 2020).

Similarly, tools developed in the marketing sector for analyzing customer preferences and delivering personalized advertisements have become increasingly common. Prominent international shopping platforms have been employing these methods for years, and companies such as Netflix also utilize them to offer customized movie and series recommendations based on user behavior. Netflix highlights the significance of personalized content delivery by reporting that more than 80% of the content viewed on their platform results directly from personalized recommendations (Zohuri, 2023). These personalized solutions not only enhance customer satisfaction but also intensify competition among companies that adopt AI-supported tools.

There are numerous online business and shopping websites where people purchase goods from various sellers or pay for online services provided by others. Sometimes, disruptions or issues may arise during these processes. When such problems occur, having quick access to a customer representative who can promptly provide solutions is crucial for keeping customers engaged and satisfied. To address this, some companies have implemented AI-driven systems capable of delivering human-like responses to customers. For instance, the customer service representative on Upwork is an AI that responds in less than 1 or 2 seconds, regardless of how long or complicated the query is. This response time is remarkably fast, and AI solutions like these, capable of replacing traditional customer service representatives, are expected to become even more widespread in the future (Upwork, 2024).

Generative AI has also opened new doors in the gaming industry. Creating game characters and designing game worlds are highly challenging tasks. With these technologies, new characters can now be developed much more easily. Additionally, an AI algorithm can analyze a player's gaming style and dynamically adjust the game's difficulty level and in-game events to suit the player best (Hare & Tang, 2023; Liapis et al., 2019).

Utilizing Nvidia Canvas to transform simple sketches into realistic landscapes offers substantial benefits to game developers, facilitating the rapid creation of immersive virtual worlds (NVDIA, 2024; QuantumFind, 2024).

Similarly, Ubisoft's AI-powered tool, Ghostwrite, automates the generation of in-game dialogues, significantly streamlining content creation processes(Aiden, 2023).

Although the initial development of these AI systems requires substantial investments, they ultimately provide long-term economic benefits. Furthermore, DeepMind's AlphaStar has exhibited advanced, human-like decision-making capabilities, achieving world-champion-level performance in complex and demanding games such as StarCraft II (DeepMinde, 2019).

Companies frequently subject their AI-driven tools to rigorous competitive benchmarks to evaluate their effectiveness and capabilities accurately. The Game Developers Conference (GDC), a major event where industry experts share research findings and innovative techniques, often highlights these benchmarking practices in presentations and proceedings. Recent discussions at GDC underscore the growing significance of these advancements, reflecting the ongoing expansion of generative AI applications within the gaming industry.

Artificial Intelligence in the Healthcare Sector

GenAI (Generative Artificial Intelligence) is offering very promising solutions to doctors and researchers in disease diagnosis and treatment. By analyzing medical images and data, it enables more accurate and rapid disease diagnoses (Skandarani et al., 2023). While GANs (Generative Adversarial Networks) models are used in many areas of generative AI, there are numerous examples of their use in the more accurate detection of cancer cells, in addition to generating visuals. Generative Adversarial Networks (GANs) are a type of AI model that can generate realistic images. In healthcare, GANs are being used to create synthetic medical images, which can help train AI algorithms to better detect cancer cells (Al-Rasheed et al., 2022; Baur et al., 2018). This is a very important use of AI, that is currently being researched, and developed. The ability of generative models to produce data in areas where data is lacking enables various studies to be carried out. Incredible studies that serve to generate new and personalized treatment plans by analyzing patients' past medical conditions continue to amaze many people. The startup PathAI develops artificial intelligence models to support doctors in cancer diagnosis. Additionally, the Babylon Health application provides patients with medical advice based on their symptoms(Aniruddh Alumni, 2022).

IBM Watson Health, which has been in the industry for many years, is another example of using generative AI for cancer treatment to create personalized treatment plans based on patients' genetic makeup and medical history(Zhou et al., 2019). An AI-powered scanning device capable of detecting diseases in people years before symptoms emerge has been developed by Neko Health. This initiative, founded by Spotify's founder Daniel Ek, utilizes more than 70 sensors and artificial intelligence technology to capture over 2,000 high-resolution images in just 20 seconds, effectively mapping every centimeter of the skin. Laser sensors measure the movement of blood through veins, heart rhythm, and blood flow velocity without any physical contact. This data is analyzed by artificial intelligence, enabling the detection of potential diseases even before they manifest.

Protein Folding

DeepMind, Google's artificial intelligence company, conducts numerous studies in the field of health sciences. One of its most intriguing and groundbreaking projects is AlphaFold, an AI system capable of accurately predicting how proteins fold. Determining proteins' three-dimensional structures and functions through experimental methods is both costly and time-consuming. AlphaFold predicts the structures of proteins in three dimensions by analyzing amino acid sequences, significantly speeding up this process. This innovation has revolutionized biology and medicine, enabling better understanding of diseases, facilitating the development of new treatments, and playing a crucial role in drug discovery.

AlphaFold's first version won first place in the 13th Critical Assessment of Protein Structure Prediction (CASP13) competition held in 2018. An improved version, AlphaFold 2, achieved even greater accuracy in protein structure predictions at CASP14 in 2020, marking a significant milestone. Released in 2024, AlphaFold 3 can now also predict interactions of proteins with DNA, RNA, and other molecules(The AlphaFold team, 2020). Thanks to these remarkable achievements, Demis Hassabis and John Jumper from DeepMind were awarded the Nobel Prize in Chemistry in 2024(Helen Briggs, 2020). AlphaFold has revolutionized the prediction of protein structures, opening new horizons in biology and medicine. This advancement has enabled a better understanding of diseases and facilitated the development of new treatment methods. (Kryshtafovych et al., 2019; Moult et al., 1995).

Early Detection of Eye Diseases

Google's DeepMind project also develops artificial intelligence models for the early detection of eye diseases, speeding up the diagnostic process for doctors and increasing the chances for patients to receive early treatment. In 2016, DeepMind collaborated with Moorfields Eye Hospital in London to utilize AI technology for analyzing eye scans. This partnership aimed to detect early signs of eye diseases, thus preventing conditions that could lead to blindness(BBC, 2016).

Acute Kidney Injury Management

Kidney diseases constitute a significant portion of hospitals' budgets and costs today. In collaboration with the Royal Free London NHS Foundation Trust, DeepMind developed a mobile application called "Streams." This app provides clinicians with real-time alerts about patients at risk of acute kidney injury, facilitating rapid intervention and improved patient management(Vincent, 2017)

Breast Cancer Detection

In 2017, DeepMind collaborated with the Cancer Research Centre at Imperial College London to analyze mammography images using machine learning techniques. This research has contributed to more accurate and early detection of breast cancer. Currently, various GAN algorithms are also being employed to facilitate easier detection of such cancer types(Eric David, 2017).

AI-Powered Research Assistant

Developing assistants tailored specifically for researchers or various industries significantly simplifies complex tasks. In 2025, Google announced the development of an artificial intelligence tool designed as a virtual collaboration assistant for biomedical researchers. This tool aims to help researchers synthesize extensive literature and formulate new hypotheses. reuters.com These projects demonstrate how DeepMind applies artificial intelligence technologies in health sciences, achieving significant advancements in this field (Muvija M, 2025).Numerous studies and initiatives aim to extend human lifespan. Today, we are witnessing the realization of technologies previously imagined as futuristic just a decade ago. Retro Biosciences, a startup in longevity science, has received a $180 million investment from Sam Altman. This company, aiming to extend human life by 10 years, is developing treatments to prevent and reverse age-related diseases. Collaborating with OpenAI, Retro Biosciences focuses on three primary research areas(Retro, 2025).

Figure 1. Developed treatments

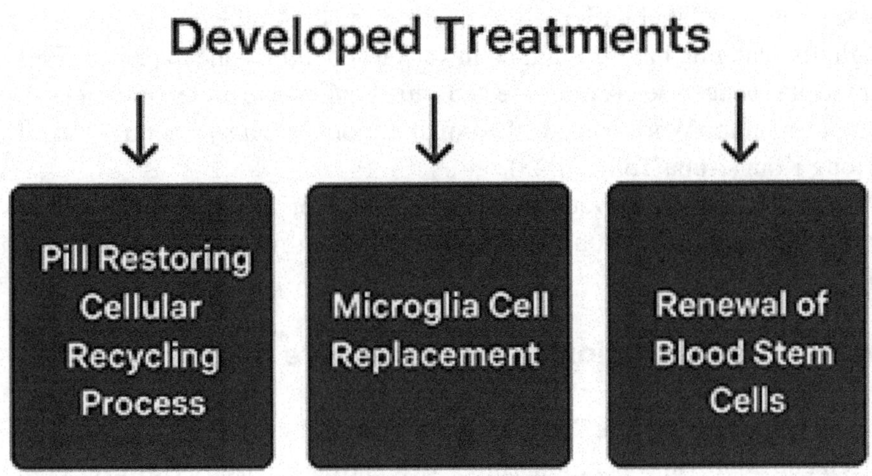

Developed Treatments:

- **Pill Restoring Cellular Recycling Process:** This drug aims to restore the internal cellular recycling process (autophagy). Disruption of autophagy is associated with diseases such as Alzheimer's.
- **Microglia Cell Replacement:** This cell therapy targets Alzheimer's by aiming to replace brain cells called microglia.
- **Renewal of Blood Stem Cells**: This treatment targets the rejuvenation of blood cells by replacing older blood stem cells with younger ones.

An artificial intelligence model has been developed that transforms normal cells into stem cells, aiming to reverse aging and facilitate cellular rejuvenation.

Interdisciplinary collaboration opportunities in health sciences not only advance healthcare technologies but also enable the development of innovative products across different technological fields. Another initiative funded by Sam Altman, named WorldCoin, scans users' eyes and creates World IDs through iris scanning(World Team, 2024) .

This cryptocurrency, developed for digital identity and financial access, stands as one of the most effective solutions against DeepFake, expected to play a significant role in combating fake bots and fake digital identities. However, there are also risks and concerns associated with these technologies. The collection of biometric data through iris scanning has been halted in various countries due to privacy concerns, with requests made to delete the collected data. Spain's data protection agency issued such a decision for Worldcoin, with similar actions taken by countries like Kenya and Hong Kong(Anna Tong, 2023).

Despite offering an innovative approach, data security and privacy concerns will determine the future adoption and success of such projects(Muhammad Zulhusni, 2025).

Human-AI Collaboration in the Healthcare Sector

In the healthcare system, AI offers great potential in medical diagnosis, patient management, improving operational processes, and data analysis. However, completely removing the human element from these processes is not possible (Topol, 2019).

AI integration into healthcare services can become more efficient when responsibilities are clearly defined, as shown below:

Cognitive Technology: Analyzes patient records and offers predictions about disease risks and possible diagnoses.
Doctors: Interpret AI-generated insights to make clinical decisions and manage direct communication with patients.
Cognitive Technology: Provides automated analysis in medical imaging systems (e.g., radiology, MRI, CT scans) for faster diagnostics.
Radiologists: Verify AI-generated findings, assess complex cases, and propose treatment plans.
Cognitive Technology: Enhances operational efficiency in hospital management by optimizing appointment systems and improving access to care.
Hospital Administrators: Use AI-generated insights to allocate resources, plan workforce management, and make strategic decisions.

As AI's role in medical diagnosis, patient care, and operational efficiency grows, projects by organizations like IBM Watson Health, Google DeepMind Health, and Mayo Clinic demonstrate how this technology can enhance healthcare services. Nevertheless, human doctors and administrators remain active in verifying AI-generated predictions, managing patient relationships, and making strategic decisions.

AI usage in both the business world and healthcare improves organizational efficiency and offers innovative solutions by strengthening collaboration between humans and technology. However, the most important aspect of this transformation is evaluating cognitive technologies as complementary tools to human capabilities and clearly defining roles and responsibilities.

In sectors like finance, healthcare, and beyond, AI supports decision-making processes by accelerating workflows and offering analytical insights. Still, final decisions must be made by human experts, and AI-generated data must be evaluated ethically, reliably, and accurately.

In conclusion, integrating AI and cognitive technologies into organizational structures—when accompanied by clearly defined roles and responsibilities—provides significant opportunities for both businesses and healthcare systems. In the future, wider adoption of AI and strengthening human-machine collaboration will be critical for leveraging the full benefits of technology.

As generative AI continues to reshape core functions in education, healthcare, and creative industries, its impact on economic structures and value creation models is becoming increasingly evident. In the next section, we turn our attention to how these technologies are enabling entirely new business models and unlocking innovative opportunities for entrepreneurship.

NEW BUSİNESS MODELS AND ENTREPRENEURSHİP OPPORTUNİTİES

The wide variety of application areas offers opportunities for developing new business models and innovative solutions. This particularly facilitates entrepreneurs' competitiveness in production and design fields. Tools such as Canva help create professional designs. Many small businesses utilize this tool themselves, thus saving additional designer costs. As a result, even individuals without design expertise can produce high-quality visual content. OpenAI's GPT models are used for text-based content generation, accelerating the content creation process for bloggers, marketers, and similar professionals. Such technologies enable entrepreneurs to achieve more with fewer resources. These new service areas can be summarized in three distinct categories.

Figure 2. Advanced digital strategies

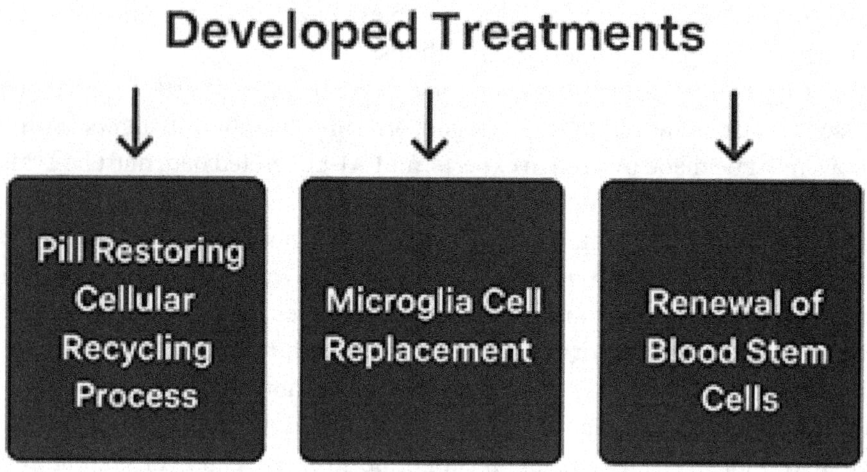

AI-Based Products and Services: Customized chatbots, content generation tools, and data analytics solutions enable entrepreneurs to differentiate themselves in the market. As previously mentioned, Jasper AI provides AI-powered content generation tools specifically for marketers. Significant competition exists among companies producing these tools, not just among users.

Digital Marketing and Content Creation: Brands can deliver more effective and authentic content to their target audiences through AI-assisted content creation. In addition to the previously mentioned example of Netflix, social media platforms such as YouTube and Instagram prominently utilize these capabilities(Smith & Hutson, 2024).

Automated Workflows: Software solutions automating business processes and enhancing efficiency across various industries stimulate the emergence of new business ideas. For instance, UiPath provides robotic process automation solutions that help companies automate routine tasks. Many factories are expected to move toward automating these workflows in the near future (Fu et al., 2021).

Effective Communication Strategies for Building Public Trust and Promoting Benefits

Societal adoption and trust in generative artificial intelligence can be effectively supported through strategic communication, enabling gradual dissemination of these technologies without causing confusion. Acceptance of the opportunities presented by generative AI primarily depends on providing accurate information and education. Effective communication strategies are also crucial. In particular, raising public awareness about how AI technologies work and their benefits is essential for building trust. Misleading information, particularly fear-triggering misinformation, is damaging. For example, the European Union promotes responsible use of AI by publishing comprehensive guidelines on AI ethics and trustworthiness.

Additionally, companies implementing communication campaigns that highlight the benefits of generative AI is another solution. For instance, Microsoft creates positive public perception by sharing success stories of AI technologies in education and healthcare. These strategies help disseminate the societal benefits of generative AI to broader audiences. This can be concisely summarized under three main points:

Transparency and Clarity: Clear and transparent information should be provided about how AI functions and the data it uses. For instance, OpenAI provides detailed reports on how the GPT-4 model is trained and its data sources. Similarly, DeepSeek, becoming notable in 2025, operates on an open-source basis(Getlago, 2025).

Ethical Usage Principles: To gain societal trust, AI must be developed following ethical guidelines. For example, IBM ensures ethical development of AI systems through its AI Ethics Board. Urgent legal regulations are needed, and such initiatives exist in Türkiye as well as many other countries worldwide. In Türkiye, the National Artificial Intelligence Strategy 2024-2025 Action Plan includes various goals such as training artificial intelligence experts and increasing employment, supporting research, entrepreneurship, and innovation, expanding access to quality data and technical infrastructure, making regulations to accelerate socioeconomic adaptation, and strengthening international cooperation (Begüm Yavuzdoğan Okumuş, 2024; EEA, 2022; IBM, 2024).

Education and Awareness: Society should be educated and informed through programs and content highlighting generative AI's benefits. Educational programs within institutions and universities are among the most effective methods, as these technologies have the potential to impact various sectors to different degrees. For instance, Google's AI for Everyone program offers education aimed at raising broad public awareness about AI (EEA, 2022).

While generative AI paves the way for groundbreaking business models and entrepreneurial ventures, its long-term success depends on how effectively risks are managed and opportunities are strategically maximized. The following section focuses on key strategies for mitigating challenges while enhancing the benefits of generative AI across domains.

RİSK MANAGEMENT AND MAXİMİZİNG OPPORTUNİTİES

While algorithms support decision-making processes for executives, if not managed properly, they can also introduce new risks. The data-driven predictions offered by algorithms help reduce uncertainties and contribute to more accurate strategic decisions. However, when the operating principles of these systems are not well understood, they can lead to unexpected errors or unforeseen outcomes.

Indeed, large-scale platforms like Netflix and Facebook have achieved high profitability and enhanced user experiences when managing their algorithms correctly. Conversely, mismanagement can result in losses amounting to millions of dollars. For instance, Facebook's algorithm-related issues highlight that overlooking data governance and ethical responsibilities can lead to serious economic and operational costs.

Algorithms are vital for personalized distribution systems. Important issues such as user interaction, satisfaction, and loyalty depend on algorithms. The Cambridge Analytica incident, which involved the unauthorized collection of user data to influence elections using Facebook's algorithms, severely affected the company. This situation demonstrates that platforms are floundering in data governance. Reports indicate that Facebook experienced a decline in user trust, leading to a financial downturn that affected its stock price and user base. The total estimated economic impact, in terms of shareholder losses and reputational damage, is measured in billions of dollars (John Gapper, 2018). To maximize the opportunities that algorithms offer, managers must understand how these systems function and proactively manage potential risks. The effective use of AI-supported decision-making mechanisms requires a multidisciplinary approach in which not only technical teams but also executives are actively involved in algorithmic processes (IBM, 2023).

According to a study by Harvard Business Review, an analysis of 152 cognitive projects revealed that AI can differ across three main categories: robotic and computer automation, cognitive insight, and cognitive engagement (Harvard Business Review, 2019). Although the use of cognitive technologies to address business problems is increasing, even the most ambitious AI projects can face setbacks and failures. To minimize such issues, AI applications should be evaluated and implemented within well-defined categories. Therefore, it is crucial for companies to approach AI transformation with a gradual and strategic mindset. Rather than replacing human capabilities entirely, the focus should be on enriching and supporting these abilities with AI. This approach not only integrates technological advancements with economic development but also plays a vital role in increasing skilled labor and minimizing unemployment risks.

Generative AI is creating significant opportunities for individuals and organizations by offering innovations and personalized solutions across various sectors. It plays a critical role in key areas like education and healthcare, while also introducing new business models and entrepreneurial opportunities. However, for society to fully embrace these opportunities, effective communication strategies are essential. Realizing the full potential of generative AI depends on both technological progress and public awareness (Holmes, 2016).

A frequently overlooked yet critical element of digital transformation is allowing human concerns to be openly expressed. While focusing on technical details is important, enabling employees and managers to voice their concerns directly impacts the success of the transformation process. Through open communication, uncertainties are reduced, problems are identified more quickly, and solution processes become more manageable. This approach is important not only for managers and employees but also for engineers developing AI technologies. Understanding real needs leads to more functional and sustainable solutions. Therefore, a sincere and transparent communication environment is one of the foundational elements of achieving success in digital transformation by focusing on both human and technological aspects.

To make the most of AI, it is essential to clearly understand which technologies serve which tasks and to structure project planning accordingly. For organizations to adopt AI solutions at the corporate level, strategic planning must be conducted across the entire organization, and these plans must be translated into concrete actions. The effective use of AI requires not only technological adaptation but also the creation of a sustainable model in terms of economic and human resource management.

In this context, it is essential for companies to handle AI transformation through a phased and strategic approach. The focus of this transformation should not be to entirely replace human talent, but rather to enhance and enrich it through AI. Such an approach integrates technological advancements with economic development and plays a key role in increasing the skilled workforce while minimizing unemployment risks.

Therefore, to benefit from AI most effectively, organizations must clearly understand which technologies fulfill which roles and structure their project planning accordingly. Strategic planning across the organization and transforming these plans into tangible actions is vital for ensuring the institutional adoption of AI solutions. Effective use of AI involves more than just technological adaptation it also requires building a sustainable model in terms of both economy and human capital management.

Organizations can integrate AI into their business processes through two primary approaches:

Short-Term Projects: Institutions can identify specific business needs with external expert support and develop AI solutions accordingly. This approach focuses on improving existing workflows and increasing operational efficiency in the short term.

Long-Term Strategic Approach: Institutions can establish their own AI ecosystems by forming internal teams with competent and skilled employees to sustain AI projects over time. This method aims to develop in-house AI expertise and create long-term competitive advantages.

Both approaches have their advantages and challenges. The organization's goals, budget, and strategic vision for AI will be the key factors in determining which method to adopt.

When companies want to implement an AI system, the first step should be identifying opportunities and selecting the appropriate technology. Although this may seem like a simple three-step process, it holds significant importance.

Projects often begin as pilot implementations. Especially before rolling out cognitive applications across the entire organization, starting with a pilot project helps lower costs and ensures the process is more manageable and effective. Senior executives can be influenced by unnecessary projects promoted by tech vendors; thus, careful consideration is needed. Whether the application truly meets a need will become clear during the process and can save the company from major financial losses.

Organizations must reconsider how workflows are designed, particularly when redistributing workload between humans and AI. Determining how to allocate responsibilities is a key step in creating an efficient workflow(Harvard Business Review, 2019).

The next phase after pilot applications is scaling up. There must be collaboration between technology experts and the process owners whose operations are being automated. It is especially important that IT teams are included in discussions about the new cognitive process or AI tool being introduced. Providing a space where they can comfortably express concerns and opinions will help improve the system and align it with the organization and its employees.

To use technologies effectively, companies must first understand them. It is necessary to grasp what types of tasks they can perform, along with their strengths and limitations. Traditional rule-based or expert systems and robotic process automation (RPA) are relatively transparent in how they operate. However, today we also have learning-based and generative AI systems. For example, you can now assign a company-specific CEO persona designed using generative AI(Alexander Sukharevsky, 2025).

AI Policy and Risk Governance

Artificial intelligence has introduced a wide range of new opportunities for society. While it brings about significant welfare gains, it also poses risks for both individuals and the environment. These risks have already begun to manifest. Some of the most evident issues include bias, discrimination, consumer manipulation, polarization of opinions, privacy violations, and widespread surveillance. This section will explore the risks associated with AI, as well as provide insights into possible solutions and policy recommendations for decision-makers.

Businesses involved in the development and deployment of AI systems are expected to adhere to international standards on human rights and responsible business conduct. This responsibility is commonly referred to as *due diligence*, and organizations are expected to operate within this framework.AI systems should promote accountability for harms caused by their use, and this issue will be addressed in more detail in the following sections.

While algorithms enhance decision-making processes for executives, if not properly managed, they can introduce new risks. The predictive capabilities of data-driven systems reduce uncertainty and support more accurate strategic planning. However, when the underlying logic and operating mechanisms of these systems are not well understood, they may lead to errors or unintended consequences.

The European Union emphasizes that the widespread adoption of AI technologies must be accompanied by systematic attention to the risks they entail. The EU AI Act and its accompanying regulatory frameworks offer comprehensive policies aimed at identifying high-risk systems, ensuring compliance with ethical principles, and making the societal impact of AI systems auditable. In this context, the risks associated with AI are not limited to technical shortcomings but are also deeply intertwined with social, psychological, and environmental consequences (Peter Slattery, 2025).

Figure 3. Typology of emerging risks in AI deployment

Indeed, large-scale platforms like Netflix and Facebook have achieved high profitability and enhanced user experiences when managing their algorithms correctly. Conversely, mismanagement can result in losses amounting to millions of dollars. For instance, Facebook's algorithm-related issues highlight that overlooking data governance and ethical responsibilities can lead to serious economic and operational costs.

According to documents published as part of the European Union's digital strategies, the risks associated with artificial intelligence can be examined under four main categories (EC Europa, n.d.).

Figure 4. Hierarchy of risk categories in artificial intelligence

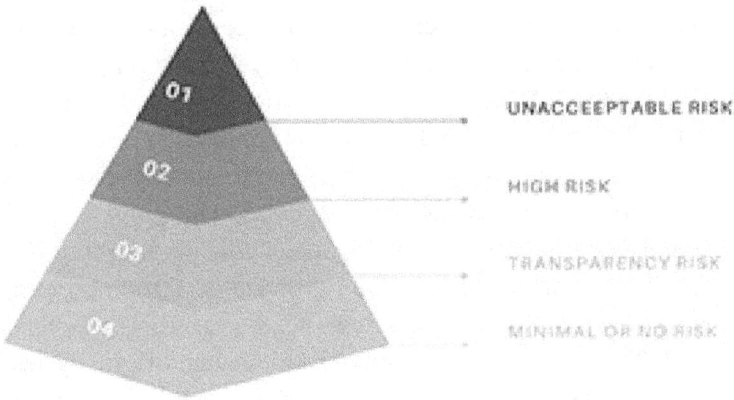

Under the European Union's digital strategies, the risks associated with artificial intelligence can be categorized into four main groups:

Unacceptable Risk: AI systems that endanger safety, human rights, or livelihoods are prohibited under current regulations, including uses such as manipulative deception, exploitation of vulnerabilities, social scoring, crime prediction, mass facial recognition, emotion detection in schools or workplaces, and biometric categorization.
High-Risk Systems: AI applications that impact health, safety, or fundamental rights—such as those used in education, healthcare, recruitment, law enforcement, and public services—are subject to strict regulatory oversight. These systems must adhere to rigorous requirements, including risk assessments, high-quality data, transparency, human oversight, and strong security measures.
Transparency-Required Risks: Users must be clearly informed when interacting with AI, particularly in cases involving chatbots, generative content, or synthetic media that could influence public opinion.
Low-Risk Applications: Most AI applications (e.g., video games, spam filters) are not subject to additional regulation. (Andrea Renda, 2023)

Trustworthy AI for the Reliable Use of Large Artificial Intelligence Models

General-purpose AI models, with their ability to perform a wide range of tasks, form the backbone of many systems across the European Union. However, when these models have high capacity or are widely deployed, they may pose systemic risks. Therefore, under the AI Act, a set of regulations—including transparency requirements and copyright provisions has been introduced for such models. Providers of models that pose systemic risks are required to conduct risk assessments and implement mitigation measures(EC Europa, n.d.). The provisions of the AI Act regarding general-purpose artificial intelligence will enter into force in August 2025. To support the compliance process, the European AI Office is developing a Code of Practice, which will serve as a key reference for ensuring adherence to the legislation._The OECD Principles on Artificial Intelligence, originally adopted in 2019, were updated in May 2024 to align with ongoing technological and policy developments. These principles provide guidance for the development of trustworthy AI systems and assist policymakers in designing effective regulations (OECD, 2019). The European Union, the United States, the United Nations, and many other countries reference the OECD's definition of artificial intelligence and its life-cycle approach in their laws and policies. This framework forms the basis for international alignment and interoperability(Andrea Renda, 2023; OECD, 2019). In this context, both regulatory frameworks and international principles offer a shared vision for ensuring the trustworthiness of AI systems. Large-scale and general-purpose AI models, in particular, have become a critical focal point where this vision is translated into concrete practices—due to their expanding areas of use and potential impact. The **Trustworthy AI** approach defines the framework for the responsible and auditable use of these models.

A Life Cycle-Based Risk Management Framework for Trustworthy Artificial Intelligence

This framework offers a comprehensive governance approach to ensure that AI systems are developed in a reliable, auditable, and ethically aligned manner. It serves as a practical guide particularly for policymakers and institutional leaders. At its core lies the principle that AI systems should not only aim for technical success but also operate with fairness, security, transparency, and accountability. The process begins with system planning, data collection and preprocessing, model development and implementation, followed by performance and safety testing, deployment, and continuous monitoring. This sequence ensures traceability and accountability across the entire lifecycle. Risks associated with AI systems must be continuously monitored and mitigated at every stage, rather than addressed in isolation. Furthermore, the integration of ethical values, corporate oversight mechanisms, and compliance practices is essential. Key components include documentation of decision-making processes, stakeholder engagement, risk treatment protocols, and embedding ethical principles throughout all phases of development and deployment. Ultimately, this structure supports the implementation of trustworthy AI systems that meet not only technological standards but also ethical, legal, and managerial obligations(Anderson et al., n.d.; EC Europa, n.d.; Simonofski et al., 2022; Spiegelhalter, 2020).

Figure 5. Integrated risk and governance model for trustworthy AI systems

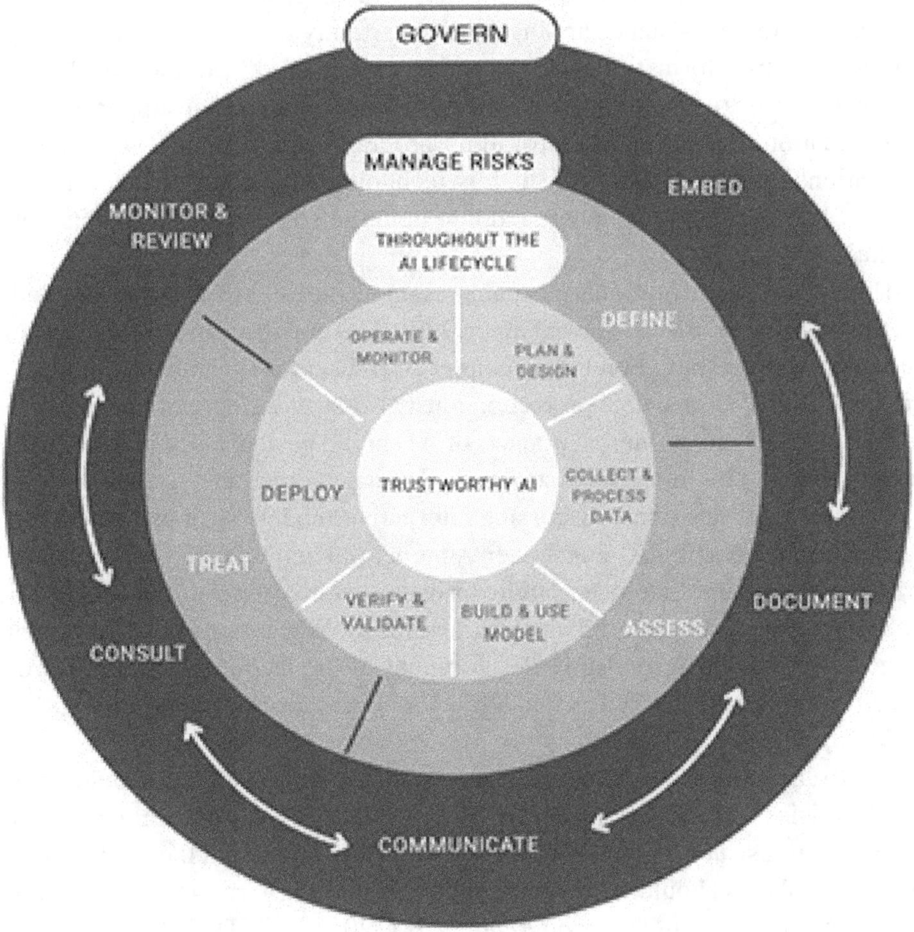

Role Allocation Between Artificial Intelligence and the Human Workforce and Strategic Priorities for Policymakers

Artificial intelligence (AI) holds significant transformative potential in areas such as decision-making, automation, and data analytics within both public and private sector processes. However, realizing the societal benefits of this transformation depends not only on technical advancements but also on the support of ethical, legal, and governance-based strategies. In this regard, policymakers must take strategic steps to promote human-centered AI applications.

First, the division of roles between AI and the human workforce must be clearly defined. This definition should be supported by guiding policy documents, particularly in high-impact sectors such as healthcare, finance, and education. Such clarity reduces workforce resistance arising from uncertainty and enables healthier participation in the transformation process(Anderson et al., n.d.; Boniface et al., 2022).

Second, priority should be given to educational policies that support workforce transformation. Reskilling and upskilling programs are of critical importance for occupational groups directly affected by technological change. At the same time, basic AI literacy should be integrated into both the educational system and public institutions.

Third, legal and institutional mechanisms should be established to promote ethical and trustworthy AI use. To prevent algorithmic bias and discrimination, regulations must be developed based on the principles of transparency, human oversight, and accountability. Personal data protection must also be at the core of these processes.

Fourth, the socio-economic impacts of AI should be addressed in a multidimensional manner. This includes restructuring social protection systems in response to occupational transitions, discussing alternative models such as universal basic income, and supporting AI-enabled entrepreneurial activities.

Fifth, it is essential to foster public–private sector collaboration. R&D projects involving universities, research centers, and technology companies will contribute to the effective and responsible development of AI technologies. Pilot projects implemented in public services will allow for observation of the technology's real-world impact.

Finally, a national AI strategy aligned with international norms should be established. Policies should be adopted in harmony with the ethical and technical principles of organizations such as the OECD, the European Union, and the United Nations, and these policies should be institutionalized with long-term goals at the national level(*Development Co-Operation Report 2021*, 2021; OECD, 2019; Spiegelhalter, 2020; Varian, 2018).

Actionable Steps for Policymakers

- **Participatory Policy Design**: Maintain ongoing consultation with representatives from academia, the private sector, and civil society.
- **Adaptive Legislation**: Develop legal frameworks that are responsive to technological advancements, allowing for revision and flexibility.
- **Impact Monitoring and Evaluation**: Regularly measure the social and economic impacts of AI policies and share this data transparently with the public.
- **Building Public Trust**: Implement clear and transparent communication strategies about AI technologies to enhance public confidence.

It is crucial for policymakers to adopt a participatory and multi-stakeholder approach in the development of artificial intelligence strategies. In this context, continuous consultation with academic institutions, private sector representatives, and civil society organizations is essential; policy processes should not be confined solely to central authorities. Furthermore, flexible and adaptable legal frameworks must be developed in response to technological advancements, ensuring that the rapidly evolving nature of AI systems is supported by revisable regulatory infrastructures.

Regular monitoring and evaluation of the social and economic impacts of implemented policies, along with the performance analysis of these measures and transparent sharing of the results with the public, will enhance the legitimacy and effectiveness of policy efforts. Finally, to build trust at the societal level, open, accessible, and understandable communication strategies regarding artificial intelligence technologies should be implemented to enhance public awareness and participation(Andrea Renda, 2023; EC Europa, n.d.; Peter Slattery, 2025).

Figure 6. Strategic roadmap for the integration of human-gentric AI into national policy

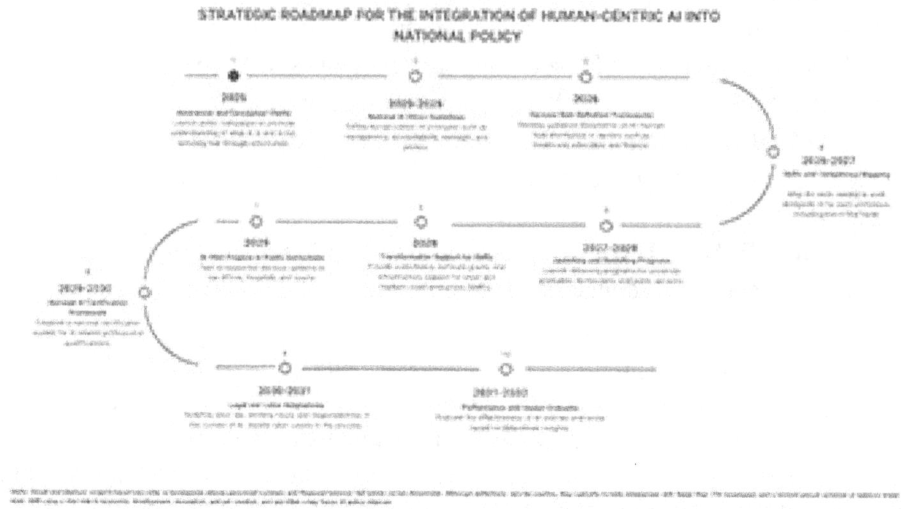

This strategic roadmap, developed as part of our comprehensive policy vision, outlines a structured and actionable path for integrating human-centric AI into national frameworks over the coming decade. By setting clear milestones from public awareness to legal reform we aim to ensure that AI technologies serve the public good while preserving ethical and social integrity. The development of this roadmap demonstrates our proactive leadership in shaping responsible AI governance.

Clarifying Roles Between AI and Humans in the Workplace

Effectively using AI in business depends on clearly defining roles and minimizing uncertainties about the future. However, this transformation process also brings certain concerns. In particular, how cognitive technologies and consulting processes will be positioned is a critical factor in successfully integrating AI systems into organizations.

While cognitive technologies can take on specific tasks, they are not meant to replace humans entirely, but rather to work alongside people and managers. Therefore, clearly defining the tasks that AI will undertake helps build a healthier organizational structure and ensures practical feasibility(Anderson et al., n.d.; EC Europa, n.d.; Henman, n.d.).

For example, in a financial firm, the division of labor between cognitive technologies and human advisors in investment consulting could be structured as follows:

- Cognitive technology can create financial plans and offer real-time, goal-oriented predictions.
- Human advisors can develop personalized implementation plans by understanding the client's investment goals.
- Technological tools can analyze data and optimize reporting processes to accelerate this workflow.
- Cognitive technology can interact with clients virtually and provide information.
- Advisors can act as behavioral coaches, guide investment decisions, and monitor spending habits.

Similarly, in hospital management or other corporate organizations, the roles that cognitive technologies can assume may vary. For instance, in a hospital setting, AI can analyze patient records, optimize treatment plans, and improve operational processes. Still, doctors and administrators will continue to play a crucial role in decision-making and human-centered services (IBM, n.d.).

In conclusion, cognitive technologies should be viewed as complementary tools to human expertise. Clearly defined divisions of labor not only enable more effective use of AI within organizations but also help employees and managers adapt to this transformation with greater confidence. We now move into the conclusion, where the implications and key takeaways of this framework will be synthesized.

CONCLUSİON AND RECOMMENDATİON

While generative artificial intelligence reshapes industries and offers unprecedented opportunities, it also brings with it a new era defined by emerging risks. The ability of this new technology to automate complex tasks and provide personalized services presents incredible potential for innovation and society. However, it simultaneously requires strategic approaches to risk management and public engagement.

Striking a delicate balance between encouraging innovation and minimizing foreseeable risks is essential, and action must be taken swiftly. Within this balance, transparency, accountability, and ethical frameworks must foster a climate of trust. Policymakers, industry leaders, and even civil society organizations must be included in this evolving process. Privacy violations and unethical use cases further highlight the urgency of establishing this balance.

To build public trust, communication strategies must be developed, and non-experts must be educated in AI literacy. As the flow of work changes, the need to develop skills compatible with these technologies becomes increasingly urgent. Effective policymaking will be facilitated through interdisciplinary collaboration and

AI-powered transformation. Policymakers must actively engage with stakeholders, encourage cross-sectoral cooperation, and establish regulatory mechanisms to foster emerging opportunities. A dynamic regulatory approach must be adopted one that evolves with technological progress and avoids becoming obsolete.

Recommendations

A Strategic Roadmap for Responsible Artificial Intelligence

Based on the analysis presented in this section, the following recommendations are proposed to manage the impact of generative AI effectively:

1.Regulatory and Ethical Frameworks

- Governments should develop clear regulatory guidelines that balance innovation with public safety.
- Clear and ethical rules must be established, addressing issues such as data privacy and transparency in a comprehensive manner. These rules should be enforceable but must not hinder technological advancement.
- AI developers should adopt responsible AI principles by ensuring transparency in training data, model biases, and decision-making processes.
- Independent auditing bodies should be established to monitor AI-generated content and implement accountability measures.
- Data protection standards must be revised to prevent unauthorized access. There is also a need to develop new international data protection frameworks concerning biometric data and encrypted personal information.

2.Risk Mitigation Strategies

- Combating misinformation: Platforms must implement robust detection systems to minimize the spread of false information generated by AI.
- Workforce adaptation: Reskilling programs led by experts should be invested in to prepare employees for AI-driven job transformations.
- Promoting collaboration: Human-machine interoperability standards should be developed to address integration challenges of AI systems more efficiently.
- Privacy safeguards: Data protection laws should be strengthened, and explicit consent should be obtained for the use of personal data by AI systems.

3.Public Awareness and Communication

- AI literacy campaigns should be launched in educational institutions and workplaces to help individuals critically evaluate AI-generated content. Increasing educational initiatives should be encouraged.
- Businesses must prioritize transparency in AI applications, allowing consumers to understand how generative AI influences services and decision-making processes.
- Media partnerships should promote responsible AI reporting to enhance public understanding and reduce fear-based narratives.

4.Innovation and Economic Growth

- Responsible AI entrepreneurship should be encouraged, with financial incentives provided for startups aligned with ethical AI principles.
- AI-driven research should be supported in areas such as education, healthcare, and climate solutions to promote growth and impact.
- Personalized learning initiatives for disadvantaged and disabled individuals should be expanded. With GenAI, establishing customized services and educational models has become easier. The use of this technology to support the development and inclusion of all members of society should be actively promoted.
- Multi-stakeholder dialogue between AI researchers, governments, businesses, and civil society must be encouraged.

With a forward-looking and inclusive approach centered on human needs and long-term societal benefits, generative AI and future technologies can continue to serve the public good. This paper has highlighted the importance of understanding current technologies, applying them to one's work, and drawing on expert support. We also addressed how interdisciplinary collaboration and division of labor can be structured. Societies can leverage the transformative power of generative AI while minimizing its risks. Guiding this technological revolution thoughtfully and fairly is a shared responsibility among policymakers, researchers, industry leaders, and the public.

REFERENCES

Al-Rasheed, A., Ksibi, A., Ayadi, M., Alzahrani, A. I. A., Zakariah, M., & Ali Hakami, N. (2022). An Ensemble of Transfer Learning Models for the Prediction of Skin Cancers with Conditional Generative Adversarial Networks. *Diagnostics (Basel), 12*(12), 3145. Advance online publication. DOI: 10.3390/diagnostics12123145 PMID: 36553152

Alumni, A. (2022). *PathAI – Can we create a better, more robust pathologist.*

Anderson, C. L., Biscaye, P. E., & Reynolds, T. W. (2017). National ID programs: A multi-country review and analysis of policy and practical challenges. In Data for Policy 2017 Conference: Government by Algorithm.

Andrea Renda, N. B. (2023). *AI Risk & Accountability.* https://oecd.ai/en/site/risk-accountability

Artificial Intelligence Index Report 2023 Introduction to the AI Index Report 2023. (n.d.).

Baur, C., Albarqouni, S., & Navab, N. (2018). *MelanoGANs: High Resolution Skin Lesion Synthesis with GANs.* http://arxiv.org/abs/1804.04338

BBC. (2016). *Google's DeepMind to peek at NHS eye scans for disease analysis.*

BBC Verify: Viral Donald Trump Jr audio highly likely AI fake. (2025).

Begüm Yavuzdoğan Okumuş, Y. U. T. S. T. (2024). *Türkiye'de Yapay Zekanın Düzenlenmesine İlişkin Gelişmeler.*

Boniface, M., Carmichael, L., Hall, W., Pickering, B., Stalla-Bourdillon, S., & Taylor, S. (2022). The Social Data Foundation model: Facilitating health and social care transformation through *datatrust services.Data & Policy, 4*, e6. DOI: 10.1017/dap.2022.1

Boscardin, C. K., Gin, B., Golde, P. B., & Hauer, K. E. (2024). ChatGPT and Generative Artificial Intelligence for Medical Education: Potential Impact and Opportunity. *Academic Medicine, 99*(1), 22–27. DOI: 10.1097/ACM.0000000000005439 PMID: 37651677

Helen Briggs. (2020). *One of biology's biggest mysteries "largely solved" by AI.*

Broussard, M. (2019). *Artificial unintelligence : how computers misunderstand the world.* The MIT Press.

Brown, T. B., Mann, B., Ryder, N., Subbiah, M., Kaplan, J., Dhariwal, P., Neelakantan, A., Shyam, P., Sastry, G., Askell, A., Agarwal, S., Herbert-Voss, A., Krueger, G., Henighan, T., Child, R., Ramesh, A., Ziegler, D. M., Wu, J., Winter, C., & Amodei, D. (2020). *Language Models are Few-Shot Learners*. http://arxiv.org/abs/2005.14165

Cao, H., Tan, C., Gao, Z., Xu, Y., Chen, G., Heng, P.-A., & Li, S. Z. (2022). *A Survey on Generative Diffusion Model*. http://arxiv.org/abs/2209.02646

Mona Chalabi. (2023, October 16). *Asking ChatGPT about israel/Palastine*.

Charles Owen-Jackson. (2024). *Open source, open risks: The growing dangers of unregulated generative AI*. IBM.

ChatGPT on Palestine and Israel - What do you make of this? (2023).

Chuma, E. L., & De Oliveira, G. G. (2023). Generative AI for Business Decision-Making: A Case of ChatGPT. *Management Science and Business Decisions*, *3*(1), 5–11. DOI: 10.52812/msbd.63

Cooper, I., & Yon, J. (2019). Ethical Issues in Biometrics. *Science Insights*, *30*(2), 63–69. DOI: 10.15354/si.19.re095

Dan Jurafsky and James H. Martin. (2025). *Speech and Language Processing: An Introduction to Natural Language Processing*. Computational Linguistics, and Speech Recognition with Language Models.

Eric David. (2017). *Google DeepMind announces new research partnership to fight breast cancer with AI*.

Deepfake footage purports to show Ukrainian president capitulating. (2022).

Deepfakes Are Coming for the Financial Sector. (2024).

DeepMinde. (2019). *AlphaStar: Mastering the real-time strategy game StarCraft II*. .

Development Co-operation Report 2021. (2021). OECD. DOI: 10.1787/ce08832f-en

EEA. (2022). *Ethical guidelines on the use of artificial intelligence and data in teaching and learning for educators*.

Eman A. Alasadi and Carlos R. Baiz*. (2023). *Generative AI in Education and Research: Opportunities, Concerns, and Solutions*.

Europa, E. C. (n.d.). *AI Act A risk-based approach The AI Act defines 4 levels of risk for AI systems*. https://ec.europa.eu/commission/presscorner/detail/en/ip_24_383

Farrelly, T., & Baker, N. (2023). Generative Artificial Intelligence: Implications and Considerations for Higher Education Practice. *Education Sciences*, *13*(11), 1109. DOI: 10.3390/educsci13111109

Stitch Fix. (2023). *How We're Revolutionizing Personal Styling with Generative AI*.

Fu, Z., Teng, Q., Wang, X., & Wu, X. (2021). Analysis for the Robotic process automation firm's future development based on the business model. *BCP Business & Management*, *14*, 208–215. DOI: 10.54691/bcpbm.v14i.146

John Gapper. (2018). *Cambridge Analytica exploited Facebook data with style*.

Getlago. (2025). *Why DeepSeek had to be open-source (and why it won't defeat OpenAI)*.

Goodfellow, I. Bengio, Yoshua., & Courville, Aaron. (2017). *Deep learning*. The MIT Press.

Goodfellow, I. J., Pouget-Abadie, J., Mirza, M., Xu, B., Warde-Farley, D., Ozair, S., Courville, A., & Bengio, Y. (2014a). Generative adversarial nets. *Advances in Neural Information Processing Systems*, *3*(January), 73–76. Advance online publication. DOI: 10.1007/978-3-658-40442-0_9

Goodfellow, I. J., Pouget-Abadie, J., Mirza, M., Xu, B., Warde-Farley, D., Ozair, S., Courville, A., & Bengio, Y. (2014b). *Generative Adversarial Networks*. http://arxiv.org/abs/1406.2661

Hare, R., & Tang, Y. (2023). Player Modeling and Adaptation Methods Within Adaptive Serious Games. *IEEE Transactions on Computational Social Systems*, *10*(4), 1939–1950. DOI: 10.1109/TCSS.2022.3203926

Harvard Business Review, M. E. P. T. H. D. P. D. H. J. W. (2019). *HBR's 10 Must Reads on AI, Analytics, and the New Machine Age*.

Heather Chen and Kathleen Magramo. (2024). *Finance worker pays out $25 million after video call with deepfake 'chief financial officer*. CNN.

Henman, P. (n.d.). *The computer says "DEBT": Towards a critical sociology of algorithms and algorithmic governance*. DOI: 10.5281/ZENODO.884117

Ho, J., Jain, A., & Abbeel, P. (2020). Denoising Diffusion Probabilistic Models. *Advances in Neural Information Processing Systems*, *33*, 6840–6851. https://proceedings.neurips.cc/paper/2020/hash/4c5bcfec8584af0d967f1ab10179ca4b-Abstract.html

Holmes, W. (2016). *Intelligence Unleashed: An argument for AI in Education*. https://www.researchgate.net/publication/299561597

ian bremme. (2023, October 16). *Asking chatgpt about justice for israel/palestine generates vastly different responses*. Https://Twitter.Com/Ianbremmer/Status/1713985163191837045

IBM. (2023). *The CEO's Guide to Generative AI.*

IBM. (2024). How to establish. *AI and Ethics*.

IBM. (n.d.). *CEO decision-making in the age of AI*.

International journal of arts, humanities & social science. (2020).

International Science Council. (2023). *A framework for evaluating rapidly developing digital and related technologies: AI, Large Language Models and beyond.*

International Science Council. (2025). *Preparing National Research Ecosystems for AI*.

Kaplan, J., McCandlish, S., Henighan, T., Brown, T. B., Chess, B., Child, R., Gray, S., Radford, A., Wu, J., & Amodei, D. (2020). *Scaling Laws for Neural Language Models*. http://arxiv.org/abs/2001.08361

Kılınç, H. K., & Keçecioğlu, Ö. F. (2024). Generative Artificial Intelligence: A Historical and Future Perspective. *Academic Platform Journal of Engineering and Smart Systems*, *12*(2), 47–58. DOI: 10.21541/apjess.1398155

Kryshtafovych, A., Schwede, T., Topf, M., Fidelis, K., & Moult, J. (2019). Critical assessment of methods of protein structure prediction (CASP)—Round XIII. *Proteins*, *87*(12), 1011–1020. DOI: 10.1002/prot.25823 PMID: 31589781

Liapis, A., Yannakakis, G. N., Nelson, M. J., Preuss, M., & Bidarra, R. (2019). Orchestrating game generation. *IEEE Transactions on Games*, *11*(1), 48–68. DOI: 10.1109/TG.2018.2870876

Mahsun, M., Ali, M., Ekaningrum, I. R., & Ibda, H. (2024). Trend of Using ChatGPT in Learning Process and Character Education: A Systematic Literature Review. *International Journal of Learning. Teaching and Educational Research*, *23*(5), 387–402. DOI: 10.26803/ijlter.23.5.20

Mazen Baroudi, S. C. F. A. W. (2023). *What happened to "All human beings are born free"? Reflections on a ChatGPT "experiment."*

Moult, J., Pedersen, J. T., Judson, R., & Fidelis, K. (1995). A large-scale experiment to assess protein structure prediction methods. *Proteins*, *23*(3). Advance online publication. DOI: 10.1002/prot.340230303 PMID: 8710822

G R Mukesh. (2024). *Are We Ready For This? Dutch Journalist Demonstrates "Real-Time AI Facial Recognition."*

Multinational loses HK$200 million to deepfake video conference scam, Hong Kong police say. (2024).

Muvija M. (2025). *Google develops AI co-scientist to aid researchers.*

NVDIA. (2024). *NVIDIA Studio | Built for Creators.*

OECD. (2019). *OECD AI Principles overview.* https://oecd.ai/en/ai-principles

QuantumFind. (2024). *NVIDIA Canvas: Astonishing Digital Art with AI in 2024.* https://quantumfind.ai/nvidia-canvas/

Ramesh, A., Dhariwal, P., Nichol, A., Chu, C., & Chen, M. (2022). *Hierarchical Text-Conditional Image Generation with CLIP Latents.* http://arxiv.org/abs/2204.06125

REPUBLIC OF TÜRKİYE COUNCIL OF HIGHER EDUCATION. (n.d.). *ETHICS GUIDE OF GENERATIVE ARTIFICIAL INTELLIGENCE USE IN THE SCIENTIFIC RESEARCH AND PUBLICATION PROCESS OF HIGHER EDUCATION INSTITUTIONS.* Retrieved April 3, 2025, from https://www.yok.gov.tr/en/Documents/2024/ethics-guide-of-generative-ai-use-in-the-scientific-research-and-publication-process.pdf

Retro. (2025). *We're Adding 10 Years to Healthy Human Lifespan.*

reuters. (2025). Bogus video of Trump and Musk briefly appears on screens at US government office. *Reuters.*

Saharia, C., Chan, W., Saxena, S., Li, L., Whang, J., Denton, E., Ghasemipour, S. K. S., Ayan, B. K., Mahdavi, S. S., Lopes, R. G., Salimans, T., Ho, J., Fleet, D. J., & Norouzi, M. (2022). *Photorealistic Text-to-Image Diffusion Models with Deep Language Understanding.* http://arxiv.org/abs/2205.11487

Schuhmann, C., Beaumont, R., Vencu, R., Gordon, C., Wightman, R., Cherti, M., Coombes, T., Katta, A., Mullis, C., Wortsman, M., Schramowski, P., Kundurthy, S., Crowson, K., Schmidt, L., Kaczmarczyk, R., & Jitsev, J. (2022). *LAION-5B: An open large-scale dataset for training next generation image-text models.* http://arxiv.org/abs/2210.08402

Simonofski, A., Tombal, T., De Terwangne, C., Willem, P., Frenay, B., & Janssen, M. (2022). Balancing fraud analytics with legal requirements: Governance practices and trade-offs in public administrations. *Data & Policy, 4*, e14. DOI: 10.1017/dap.2022.6

Skandarani, Y., Jodoin, P.-M., & Lalande, A. (2023). GANs for Medical Image Synthesis: An Empirical Study. *Journal of Imaging*, *9*(3), 69. DOI: 10.3390/jimaging9030069 PMID: 36976120

Slattery, P. (2025). *What are the risks from Artificial Intelligence*. https://airisk.mit.edu

Smith, A., & Hutson, J. (2024). From concept to creation: The role of generative artificial intelligence in the new age of digital marketing. *Design*, *1*(1), 4776. DOI: 10.36922/dp.4776

Spiegelhalter, D. (2020). Should We Trust Algorithms? *Harvard Data Science Review*. Advance online publication. DOI: 10.1162/99608f92.cb91a35a

Steven Lee Myers. (2025). *DeepSeek's Answers Include Chinese Propaganda, Researchers Say*. https://www.nytimes.com/2025/01/31/technology/deepseek-chinese-propaganda.html

Stuart Russell and Peter Norvig. (2011). *Artificial Intelligence A Modern Approach* (3rd ed.).

Alexander Sukharevsky. (2025). *The state of AI: How organizations are rewiring to capture value.*

Surden, H. (2019). *Artificial Intelligence and Law: An Overview, 35 GA*. https://scholar.law.colorado.edu/faculty-articles

The AlphaFold team. (2020). *AlphaFold: a solution to a 50-year-old grand challenge in biology.*

The Risk of Automation for Jobs in OECD Countries (OECD Social, Employment and Migration Working Papers, Vol. 189). (2016). DOI: 10.1787/1815199X

Anna Tong. (2023). *OpenAI's Sam Altman launches Worldcoin crypto project.*

Topol, E. J. (2019). *Deep Medicine: How Artificial Intelligence Can Make Healthcare Human Again.*

TVs at US government building show AI video of Trump kissing Musk's feet. (2025).

Unusual CEO Fraud via Deepfake Audio Steals US$243,000 From UK Company. (2019).

Upwork. (2024). *Using the Upwork chatbot.*

Varian, H. (2018). Artificial Intelligence, Economics, and Industrial Organization. *NBER Chapters*, 399–419. https://ideas.repec.org/h/nbr/nberch/14017.html

Vincent, J. (2017). *DeepMind's Go-playing AI doesn't need human help to beat us anymore*.

Wenhua, Z., Qamar, F., Abdali, T. A. N., Hassan, R., Jafri, S. T. A., & Nguyen, Q. N. (2023). Blockchain Technology: Security Issues, Healthcare Applications, Challenges and Future Trends. In *Electronics (Switzerland)* (Vol. 12, Issue 3). MDPI. DOI: 10.3390/electronics12030546

World Economic Forum-The Global Risks Report 2024. (2024). www.weforum.org

World Team. (2024). *World ID is a privacy-preserving proof of human for age of AI.*

Zhou, N., Zhang, C.-T., Lv, H.-Y., Hao, C.-X., Li, T.-J., Zhu, J.-J., Zhu, H., Jiang, M., Liu, K.-W., Hou, H.-L., Liu, D., Li, A.-Q., Zhang, G.-Q., Tian, Z.-B., & Zhang, X.-C. (2019). Concordance Study Between IBM Watson for Oncology and Clinical Practice for Patients with Cancer in China. *The Oncologist*, *24*(6), 812–819. DOI: 10.1634/theoncologist.2018-0255 PMID: 30181315

Zohuri, B. (2023). Charting the Future The Synergy of Generative AI, Quantum Computing, and the Transformative Impact on Economy, Society, Jobs Market, and the Emergence of Artificial Super Intelligence. [CTES]. *Current Trends in Engineering Science*, *3*(7), 1–4. DOI: 10.54026/CTES/1050

Muhammad Zulhusni. (2025). *Sam Altman's World Network introduces messaging feature with identity verification*.

Chapter 6
Green AI:
Balancing Innovation With Environmental Sustainability

Ziyi Wang
https://orcid.org/0000-0003-3414-3467
Cornell University, USA

ABSTRACT

This chapter examines the environmental impact of artificial intelligence (AI) and explores strategies to align AI development with sustainability goals. As AI-driven technologies expand, their energy consumption and carbon footprint present significant challenges, particularly in the operation of data centers and high-performance computing infrastructure. This chapter analyzes AI's dual role as both a contributor to environmental challenges and a tool for sustainability. It discusses AI's carbon footprint and AI's potential to drive climate action. Policy interventions, such as financial incentives, regulations for data centers, and carbon offset initiatives, are also examined. By integrating sustainability into AI development, this chapter provides a framework for fostering Green AI that minimizes ecological impact while leveraging AI's capabilities for global sustainability efforts.

INTRODUCTION: AI AND SUSTAINABILITY IN THE DIGITAL AGE

Artificial intelligence (AI) is transforming industries, economies, and societies by driving innovation, optimizing operations, and enhancing decision-making across various domains. From automating complex tasks to enabling personalized consumer experiences, AI has become an essential driver of technological advancement, reshaping sectors such as healthcare, finance, manufacturing, and

DOI: 10.4018/979-8-3373-1210-1.ch006

transportation (Abduljabbar et al., 2019; Cao, 2023; Saraswat et al., 2022; Shaheen, 2021). Its ability to process vast amounts of data and generate insights with unprecedented speed and accuracy has unlocked new frontiers in scientific discovery, business intelligence, and public policy (Gupta et al., 2023). However, alongside its transformative potential, AI's rapid expansion raises critical concerns about its environmental sustainability, particularly regarding energy consumption and carbon emissions (Nishant et al., 2020).

The development and deployment of AI technologies, particularly deep learning models, require substantial computational resources. Training state-of-the-art machine learning models demands immense processing power, often necessitating high-performance computing infrastructure housed within energy-intensive data centers. These facilities operate continuously, consuming vast amounts of electricity, much of which is still generated from fossil fuels, thereby contributing significantly to global carbon emissions. Additionally, AI-driven applications such as cloud computing, real-time data processing, and autonomous systems further exacerbate the environmental footprint, intensifying concerns about resource efficiency and long-term sustainability.

As the world faces escalating climate challenges, ensuring that AI advances align with sustainability goals has become an urgent priority. Addressing AI's carbon footprint requires a comprehensive approach that includes optimizing algorithms for energy efficiency, integrating AI with renewable energy solutions, and implementing policies that promote responsible AI development (Olatunde et al., 2024). At the same time, AI holds immense potential to aid in climate change mitigation and adaptation. From enhancing climate modeling and optimizing energy grids to improving resource management and enabling smart cities, AI-driven solutions can play a crucial role in advancing global sustainability efforts.

This chapter explores the dual role of AI as both a contributor to environmental challenges and a potential solution for mitigating climate change. It examines the carbon footprint of AI, the opportunities for leveraging AI to address environmental issues, and the policy interventions necessary to foster green AI development. By examining these themes, this chapter aims to provide a comprehensive understanding of AI's environmental impact while outlining a roadmap for integrating sustainability into its design, deployment, and governance.

THE CARBON FOOTPRINT OF AI

To understand how AI is impacting sustainability, we must first examine the carbon footprint of AI. AI's rapid development and deployment come with significant energy demands, primarily due to the high computational power required to train, run, and maintain complex machine learning models. While AI holds great promise in revolutionizing sectors ranging from healthcare to finance, the energy-intensive nature of its infrastructure raises serious concerns about its sustainability.

The environmental impact of AI is largely driven by the energy demands of its underlying infrastructure. The energy consumption of AI stems largely from two sources: the training phase and the inference phase. The training phase involves feeding vast amounts of data into machine learning models and running multiple iterations of optimization algorithms until the model achieves an acceptable level of accuracy. This process requires vast computational power and extended processing time. It takes thousands of graphical processing units (GPUs) or tensor processing units (TPUs) running in parallel, often for days, weeks, or even months. In contrast, the inference phase involves using trained models to process new data, make predictions, and generate responses in real time, which, while generally less energy-intensive than training, still contributes significantly to overall power consumption—especially at scale.

Several studies and real-world examples highlight the substantial carbon footprint of AI. For instance, research by Strubell et al. (2019) showed that training a single large NLP model generates approximately 626,000 pounds of carbon dioxide. This figure is equivalent to the carbon footprint of five average American cars throughout their entire lifespan. The study specifically analyzed the environmental impact of training deep learning models for NLP tasks, revealing that the energy consumption required for just one training cycle of a large transformer-based model could exceed that of a commercial transatlantic flight.

The environmental toll of AI is particularly evident in state-of-the-art language models such as BERT, GPT-3, and their successors. OpenAI's GPT-3, with its 175 billion parameters, required an estimated 1,287 megawatt-hours (MWh) of electricity during training—enough to power hundreds of households for an entire year. The emissions associated with such training cycles are amplified when AI research institutions and tech companies rely on non-renewable energy sources to power their data centers.

Beyond language models, AI-powered recommendation systems deployed by tech giants such as Google, Amazon, and Netflix consume substantial computational resources. These systems analyze vast amounts of user data in real time, continuously refining their recommendations based on evolving preferences and behaviors. While they enhance user experiences and drive revenue for businesses, the computational workload associated with personalized content delivery translates into massive electricity usage and, consequently, higher carbon emissions.

Besides, the increasing reliance on AI-driven technologies is fueling the expansion of data centers, which serve as the backbone of AI operations. Data centers house the servers, networking equipment, and storage infrastructure necessary to process and store the enormous volumes of data required for machine learning and AI applications. However, their energy consumption has become a growing concern. According to estimates by the International Energy Agency (IEA), global data center electricity consumption is 240–340TWh, or around 1–1.3 percent of global final electricity demand (approximately 25,000TWh). This figure is projected to rise as AI adoption accelerates, with some estimates suggesting that data centers could account for as much as 8% of global electricity consumption by 2030 if energy efficiency measures do not keep pace.

For another example, the environmental impact of AI-driven data centers can be seen through the case of Google. The company's greenhouse gas emissions increased by nearly 50% over five years due to the growing energy demands of AI workloads. Despite Google's commitment to sustainability—including its pledge to operate entirely on carbon-free energy by 2030—the energy-intensive nature of AI computations remains a significant challenge.

High-performance computing (HPC) systems used in AI model training often rely on non-renewable energy sources, exacerbating their environmental footprint. The carbon emissions associated with AI data centers are particularly concerning in regions where electricity grids are still heavily dependent on coal and other fossil fuels. Without systemic shifts toward cleaner energy sources, the rapid expansion of AI could undermine global efforts to reduce carbon emissions.

While AI undoubtedly contributes to increased energy demand, it also plays a role in optimizing efficiency across various industries. AI-powered solutions have demonstrated their ability to enhance energy management, streamline logistics, and reduce resource wastage. For instance, AI is used in predictive maintenance for industrial equipment, which helps reduce unnecessary replacements and extends the lifespan of machinery, thereby decreasing material and energy waste.

In supply chain management, AI-driven analytics optimize delivery routes and inventory planning, leading to lower fuel consumption and reduced carbon emissions. Similarly, AI applications in smart grids help balance electricity supply and demand, improving the integration of renewable energy sources such as solar and wind power. These examples illustrate how AI, when applied strategically, can offset some of the negative environmental impacts associated with its energy use.

However, there are instances where traditional computational methods might be more sustainable than AI-driven solutions. In cases where simpler statistical models or rule-based systems can achieve comparable results with significantly lower computational costs, the adoption of AI should be carefully evaluated. The challenge, therefore, lies in striking a balance between leveraging AI's capabilities and minimizing its environmental footprint.

Emerging solutions are beginning to address this challenge. One of the most effective ways to reduce AI's carbon footprint is through the development of energy-efficient hardware. Traditional AI processing relies on general-purpose chips, such as CPUs and GPUs, which are not optimized for the specific computational needs of machine learning tasks. To improve efficiency, companies are now investing in specialized AI accelerators, such as Tensor Processing Units (TPUs) and neuromorphic chips, which are designed to execute AI workloads with significantly lower power consumption. For instance, Amazon has been developing its own AI processing chips at a facility in Texas, which it claims offer higher performance while consuming less energy than traditional processors. Similarly, Google has been refining its TPUs, which are specifically optimized for machine learning tasks, enabling faster computations with reduced energy requirements. These advancements in AI hardware allow models to be trained and deployed more efficiently, decreasing the overall energy demand of AI applications.

Beyond chip-level optimizations, major technology companies are making sustainable advancements in data center infrastructure to reduce energy consumption and greenhouse gas emissions. Microsoft, for example, is investing in energy-efficient data centers that leverage advanced cooling techniques, modular architectures, and AI-driven resource management systems to minimize power usage. The company is also experimenting with underwater data centers, which use the surrounding water for natural cooling, significantly reducing the need for energy-intensive air conditioning systems. In addition, Google has committed to operating its data centers on 100% carbon-free energy by 2030, a move that sets a precedent for the rest of the industry. While large corporations have the resources to invest in greener infrastructure, a broader industry-wide transition to renewable energy and sustainable data center design is necessary to achieve significant environmental benefits.

Advancements in machine learning algorithms are also playing a crucial role in improving AI's energy efficiency. The traditional approach to training AI models involves running thousands of iterations over massive datasets, requiring extensive computational power. However, researchers are developing techniques that allow AI models to achieve similar levels of accuracy with significantly fewer computations. One such technique is model pruning, which removes unnecessary parameters from neural networks, reducing the number of calculations needed to process data. Another approach, knowledge distillation, involves training a smaller model to mimic the behavior of a larger one, effectively compressing complex AI models into more efficient versions without sacrificing performance. Additionally, quantization reduces the precision of numerical computations, allowing AI models to run with lower memory requirements and reduced energy consumption. These algorithmic innovations help AI developers build models that require less computing power while maintaining high accuracy and functionality.

A promising approach to reducing the energy demands of AI training is federated learning, a decentralized method that allows AI models to be trained across multiple devices instead of relying solely on centralized data centers. Traditional machine learning models require massive amounts of data to be uploaded to cloud servers for centralized processing, a process that is both energy-intensive and resource-consuming. Federated learning, on the other hand, enables devices such as smartphones, edge servers, and IoT sensors to process data locally while periodically sharing updates with a central model. This distributed computing approach not only enhances data privacy and security but also significantly reduces the computational burden on data centers, leading to lower energy consumption. By leveraging federated learning, AI developers can train models in a more environmentally sustainable manner while still achieving high levels of performance.

Despite advancements in hardware, infrastructure, and algorithm efficiency, AI technologies will still have a residual carbon footprint. To counteract emissions generated by AI computing, some companies are investing in carbon offset programs as a complementary strategy to direct emissions reductions. Carbon offsetting involves funding initiatives that remove or reduce greenhouse gas emissions, such as reforestation projects, renewable energy investments, and carbon capture technologies. For instance, Microsoft has pledged to become carbon-negative by 2030, meaning it will remove more carbon from the atmosphere than it emits. The company is actively investing in carbon sequestration projects that capture CO_2 emissions and store them in geological formations or repurpose them for industrial applications. Similarly, AI companies are funding projects that support sustainable energy production, such as solar and wind farms, to offset their energy-intensive AI operations. While carbon offsetting is not a long-term solution to AI's environmental impact, it serves as an important interim measure while more sustainable computing technologies continue to be developed.

Another promising area of research focuses on AI-driven optimization of energy use. AI itself can be used to enhance energy efficiency in data centers by predicting workloads, dynamically adjusting power allocation, and optimizing server utilization. Companies such as Google and IBM have deployed AI-driven cooling systems that analyze environmental factors and adjust air conditioning settings in real-time, reducing energy consumption without compromising performance. These intelligent cooling systems can lower a data center's energy use by up to 40%, demonstrating how AI can be both a cause of and a solution to energy-related challenges. AI is also being applied to smart grids, where machine learning models predict energy demand fluctuations and improve the distribution of renewable energy, helping to maximize the efficiency of power grids and reduce reliance on fossil fuels.

While these emerging solutions are promising, their effectiveness depends on widespread adoption and continuous improvements in AI sustainability strategies. Many of the current innovations in energy-efficient AI hardware, green data center design, and low-energy machine learning models remain concentrated within a handful of major technology firms. To achieve meaningful environmental impact, policymakers and industry leaders must work together to create incentive structures, regulations, and collaborative frameworks that encourage AI developers across all sectors to prioritize sustainability. Government grants, tax incentives, and mandatory emissions reporting for AI companies can play a crucial role in accelerating the adoption of green AI practices. Additionally, greater investment in academic research on energy-efficient AI algorithms will help ensure that sustainability considerations are embedded in future AI developments.

The path toward sustainable AI requires a holistic approach that combines hardware advancements, software innovations, data center optimizations, decentralized computing strategies, and carbon offset initiatives. While progress is being made, AI developers and policymakers must recognize that addressing AI's environmental impact is an ongoing challenge that requires continuous adaptation and innovation. By scaling these emerging solutions and integrating sustainability into every stage of AI's lifecycle, the technology can continue to drive innovation and economic growth while minimizing its ecological footprint. The success of AI as a transformative force should not be measured solely by its intelligence or capabilities but also by its ability to operate in a manner that aligns with long-term environmental sustainability.

LEVERAGING AI FOR CLIMATE ACTION

While AI contributes to environmental challenges through its significant energy consumption and carbon emissions, it also holds immense potential as a tool to combat climate change and promote sustainability. AI-driven innovations are already being deployed across various sectors, demonstrating their ability to optimize resource use, enhance energy efficiency, and accelerate the transition toward a more sustainable economy. By leveraging machine learning, data analytics, and intelligent automation, AI has the capacity to drive environmental innovation at an unprecedented scale.

Predictive Climate Modeling

One of the most impactful applications of AI lies in predictive climate modeling. Climate change is a complex and dynamic phenomenon influenced by numerous factors, including greenhouse gas emissions, oceanic currents, atmospheric circulation, and human activity. Accurately predicting climate patterns and extreme weather events is essential for disaster preparedness, resource management, and policymaking. Traditional climate models rely on physics-based simulations, which, while effective, are computationally intensive and sometimes lack the precision needed for localized forecasts.

AI enhances climate modeling by processing vast datasets from satellites, weather stations, and historical records, identifying patterns and correlations that may be difficult to detect using traditional methods. Machine learning algorithms, particularly deep learning models, can analyze terabytes of environmental data in real time, enabling more accurate and granular predictions of climate trends.

For example, Google's DeepMind has collaborated with meteorological institutions to develop AI models that predict extreme weather events, such as hurricanes, floods, and heatwaves, with greater accuracy. These AI-powered forecasts allow governments and disaster response teams to implement early warning systems, allocate resources effectively, and minimize loss of life and property.

Moreover, AI can improve climate risk assessment for businesses and policymakers by modeling the long-term impacts of climate change on infrastructure, agriculture, and human populations. This information is crucial for designing climate-resilient cities, developing adaptive agricultural strategies, and implementing policies that mitigate environmental risks.

AI in Renewable Energy Optimization

The transition to renewable energy is a key component of global efforts to combat climate change. However, one of the biggest challenges in scaling renewable energy sources such as solar and wind power is their intermittency—the fact that energy generation fluctuates based on weather conditions. AI is playing a crucial role in addressing this challenge by optimizing the integration of renewable energy into existing power grids.

Machine learning algorithms can predict fluctuations in solar and wind energy production by analyzing meteorological data and historical trends. By forecasting energy output, AI enables grid operators to balance supply and demand more efficiently, reducing reliance on fossil fuels and enhancing the stability of renewable energy grids.

Companies like IBM and Google have developed AI-driven energy management systems that use real-time data to optimize the operation of wind farms and solar power plants. Google's AI-powered wind energy forecasting system has improved wind farm efficiency by 20%, allowing operators to make better-informed decisions about energy storage and distribution.

AI is also being used to enhance energy storage solutions, such as battery management systems. Advanced algorithms can predict energy demand, optimize charging and discharging cycles, and extend the lifespan of battery storage units. These innovations help stabilize renewable energy supply, making clean energy sources more reliable and economically viable.

Furthermore, AI-powered smart grids are revolutionizing the way electricity is distributed. Smart grids use real-time data analytics to dynamically adjust energy distribution, reduce transmission losses, and prevent blackouts. By integrating AI with Internet of Things (IoT) devices, utility companies can enhance efficiency, lower energy costs, and facilitate the widespread adoption of renewable energy.

AI in Sustainable Agriculture and Food Security

AI is also revolutionizing agriculture by enabling precision farming techniques, which optimize the use of water, fertilizers, and pesticides while maximizing crop yields. Agriculture is a major contributor to greenhouse gas emissions, with deforestation, fertilizer use, and livestock production releasing significant amounts of carbon dioxide and methane into the atmosphere. AI-driven solutions are helping farmers adopt more sustainable practices that reduce environmental impact while ensuring food security.

Through real-time analysis of soil conditions, weather patterns, and crop health, AI systems assist farmers in making data-driven decisions. For instance, machine learning models can analyze satellite imagery to detect signs of drought, pest infestations, or nutrient deficiencies in crops, allowing farmers to take proactive measures before problems escalate.

Startups like Blue River Technology, a subsidiary of John Deere, have developed AI-powered robotic systems that use computer vision to precisely apply herbicides only where needed, reducing chemical usage by up to 90%. Similarly, AI-powered irrigation systems optimize water distribution by predicting soil moisture levels and adjusting watering schedules accordingly. This reduces water waste and improves efficiency in regions prone to drought.

AI is also being applied to livestock management to monitor animal health, detect diseases early, and optimize feed consumption. By analyzing data from wearable sensors attached to livestock, AI can identify patterns in animal behavior and alert farmers to potential health issues, reducing the need for antibiotics and improving overall farm sustainability.

Additionally, AI is helping to address food waste, which accounts for nearly 8-10% of global greenhouse gas emissions. AI-driven supply chain optimization tools help retailers, distributors, and restaurants predict demand more accurately, reducing food spoilage and minimizing waste.

AI in Carbon Capture and Climate Mitigation

Innovative AI applications extend to carbon capture technologies, which are essential for reducing atmospheric CO_2 levels. While reducing emissions at the source is the most effective way to combat climate change, carbon capture and storage (CCS) technologies play a crucial role in mitigating existing emissions from industrial processes.

Machine learning models are being used to enhance the efficiency of carbon capture processes by identifying optimal materials and designs for carbon-absorbing systems. For example, AI is helping researchers discover new nanomaterials and chemical compounds that can absorb CO_2 more effectively than traditional methods.

AI also optimizes the operation of direct air capture (DAC) plants, which remove CO_2 directly from the atmosphere. By analyzing factors such as temperature, air pressure, and energy consumption, AI systems can improve the efficiency of these plants and reduce their operational costs.

In addition to carbon capture, AI is being used to develop climate engineering solutions, such as afforestation and ocean-based carbon sequestration projects. AI-driven modeling tools help identify the best locations for reforestation efforts, predict the long-term carbon storage potential of forests, and monitor deforestation in real time through satellite imagery.

AI-Powered Environmental Monitoring and Conservation

AI is also playing a crucial role in environmental monitoring and conservation efforts. Remote sensing technologies, combined with AI, allow scientists to track deforestation, biodiversity loss, and pollution levels more accurately than ever before.

For instance, AI-powered satellite imagery analysis helps conservationists detect illegal logging activities in rainforests, enabling authorities to take action before extensive damage occurs. Organizations like Rainforest Connection use AI-powered acoustic monitoring systems to detect chainsaw noises in real time, alerting law enforcement to deforestation activities.

AI is also being used to monitor ocean health by analyzing data from underwater sensors, drones, and satellites. Machine learning models can detect changes in ocean temperature, acidification levels, and coral reef health, helping researchers better understand the impacts of climate change on marine ecosystems.

In urban areas, AI is being applied to air quality monitoring, predicting pollution levels and identifying sources of emissions. Cities like London and Los Angeles use AI-powered air quality sensors to develop targeted policies for reducing pollution hotspots.

Conclusion

As the world faces mounting environmental challenges, AI's ability to analyze complex datasets, optimize resource usage, and enhance decision-making presents a powerful opportunity to drive sustainability. However, while AI offers transformative solutions for climate change mitigation, its deployment must be carefully managed to ensure that it does not exacerbate existing environmental problems through excessive energy consumption.

A sustainable AI future requires continued investment in energy-efficient AI models, renewable energy-powered data centers, and green infrastructure. Policymakers, businesses, and researchers must collaborate to establish ethical and environmental guidelines that ensure AI technologies contribute positively to global sustainability efforts.

POLICIES FOR GREEN AI DEVELOPMENT

As artificial intelligence (AI) continues to revolutionize industries and drive economic growth, its environmental impact is becoming a growing concern. The rapid expansion of AI applications, coupled with the increasing computational power required to train and deploy large-scale models, has led to rising energy consumption and carbon emissions. To ensure that AI development aligns with sustainability goals, robust policy frameworks at both national and international levels are essential. Governments, private companies, and academic institutions must work together to create regulatory and incentive structures that promote energy-efficient AI technologies, encourage responsible data center operations, and foster innovation in sustainable computing.

The successful integration of sustainability into AI development requires a multifaceted approach. Policies must address key areas, including financial incentives for green AI research, regulations for energy-efficient data centers, carbon offset programs for AI-driven companies, and collaboration between public and private stakeholders. By implementing well-designed policies, it is possible to minimize AI's environmental footprint while maximizing its potential to support global sustainability efforts.

Incentives for Energy-efficient AI Research

One of the most effective ways to promote the development of sustainable AI is through financial incentives for energy-efficient research and innovation. Governments and international organizations have recognized the need to support

AI researchers and developers in creating environmentally responsible solutions. Financial incentives such as grants, tax credits, and funding for low-carbon AI research encourage companies, universities, and startups to prioritize sustainability in AI development.

The European Commission has taken a leading role in implementing policies that support green AI development. In 2022, the European Green Deal introduced funding initiatives to promote AI models with lower energy consumption and carbon footprints. Similarly, the U.S. Department of Energy (DOE) has launched research grants to develop AI-driven solutions for optimizing energy use in various industries. By financially supporting sustainable AI innovations, these policies incentivize companies to develop new energy-efficient algorithms and hardware.

A promising area of research benefiting from such incentives is neuromorphic computing, which mimics the energy-efficient processing mechanisms of the human brain. Unlike conventional machine learning models that require vast computational resources, neuromorphic processors use event-driven computations, significantly reducing energy consumption. Public funding and subsidies for research into neuromorphic chips and edge AI solutions can play a crucial role in making AI more sustainable.

In addition to direct financial incentives, governments can implement green AI certification programs that reward companies for meeting sustainability benchmarks in AI development. AI systems that meet specific energy efficiency and carbon neutrality criteria could receive eco-labels or be given priority in government procurement contracts, providing further motivation for companies to invest in green AI.

Regulations for Sustainable Data Centers

The increasing demand for AI has led to a surge in data center expansion. Since AI applications, particularly large-scale models like GPT-4 and BERT, require massive computational power, they are major contributors to data center energy use. Without effective regulatory measures, the continued expansion of AI-driven data centers could significantly increase global carbon emissions.

Governments are introducing policies to mandate the integration of renewable energy sources into data center operations. Countries such as Denmark and the Netherlands have already implemented strict energy efficiency requirements for data centers, compelling operators to use renewable energy and implement advanced cooling technologies. The European Union's Green Data Center Initiative requires new data centers to comply with strict energy efficiency and sustainability standards, encouraging the tech industry to reduce its reliance on fossil fuels.

Several major technology companies have already committed to carbon-neutral data center operations. Google, for example, has pledged to run its data centers on 100% carbon-free energy by 2030, while Microsoft has set a goal of being carbon-negative by the same year. However, smaller firms often lack the financial resources to transition to renewable energy on their own. Public-private partnerships and government subsidies for renewable energy adoption in data centers can help level the playing field, ensuring that businesses of all sizes can invest in sustainable infrastructure.

In addition to mandating renewable energy usage, regulations should also promote energy-efficient cooling solutions. Traditional data centers use vast amounts of electricity for air conditioning and cooling systems, leading to unnecessary energy waste. Governments can encourage the adoption of liquid cooling, free-air cooling, and heat recycling technologies, significantly reducing overall energy consumption. Some policies in Germany and Sweden already provide tax incentives for companies that invest in waste heat recovery systems, allowing excess heat from data centers to be redirected to residential heating systems.

Furthermore, mandatory sustainability reporting for data centers can increase transparency and accountability. By requiring AI companies to disclose their energy consumption, carbon emissions, and sustainability efforts, governments can create incentives for businesses to adopt cleaner energy practices and set measurable targets for reducing their environmental impact.

Carbon Offset Programs for AI Companies

Carbon offset programs are another crucial policy mechanism for reducing AI's environmental footprint. While transitioning to energy-efficient AI models and renewable energy sources is the ultimate goal, carbon offset programs provide an interim solution for mitigating emissions generated by existing AI operations.

AI-driven companies can participate in carbon offset markets, investing in projects that remove or reduce carbon dioxide emissions from the atmosphere. These projects include reforestation initiatives, renewable energy developments, and carbon capture technologies. Several tech companies have already incorporated carbon offsetting into their sustainability strategies. Microsoft has been actively investing in carbon sequestration projects and aims to remove all the carbon it has ever emitted since its founding. Amazon's Climate Pledge Fund supports carbon offset projects while funding startups that develop low-carbon technologies. Google purchases carbon offsets to neutralize emissions from its AI-driven services, though the company is also working toward eliminating the need for offsets by achieving total carbon-free energy usage.

Governments can expand carbon offset opportunities by creating regulatory frameworks that standardize and certify offset projects, ensuring their credibility and effectiveness. Transparency and third-party verification can prevent companies from engaging in "greenwashing"—a practice where businesses make misleading claims about their environmental impact. Greenwashing has significant negative impact on s=consumer confidence and trust, hence these measures will address this severe problem.

Another innovative approach is the integration of AI in carbon tracking and trading systems. AI can enhance carbon offset programs by accurately monitoring emissions, verifying offset credits, and optimizing investment in environmental projects. Policymakers can leverage AI itself to ensure the effectiveness of carbon markets, enhancing their credibility and impact.

Collaboration for Green AI

The transition to sustainable AI cannot be achieved by governments or corporations alone. It requires collaboration between governments, private sector companies, and academic institutions to advance research and development in energy-efficient AI technologies and establish global standards for sustainability.

Public-private partnerships are essential in fostering innovation and investment in green AI research. Governments can partner with AI companies, universities, and nonprofit organizations to fund research initiatives focused on developing energy-efficient AI algorithms, sustainable hardware, and low-carbon data centers. For example, the European Union's Horizon 2020 program has allocated funding for AI-driven sustainability projects, encouraging collaboration between public and private entities. Similarly, the U.S. National Science Foundation (NSF) has established grant programs that incentivize researchers and businesses to develop AI solutions with lower carbon footprints. Encouraging corporate responsibility through sustainability pledges and commitments can also drive progress. Tech giants like Google, Apple, and IBM have already committed to carbon neutrality and energy efficiency goals, but policies should extend to smaller AI firms and startups, ensuring they have the financial and technological resources to adopt greener practices.

Global cooperation is also key to the AI governance. AI's impact is not confined to national borders, making international cooperation crucial in establishing standardized sustainability frameworks. Organizations like the United Nations (UN), the European Commission, and the OECD should work toward global AI sustainability guidelines, ensuring that AI regulations and energy efficiency benchmarks are universally aligned.

A Global Green AI Framework could define best practices for energy-efficient AI development, ethical AI research, and carbon-neutral computing, providing governments and businesses with a roadmap for achieving sustainable AI operations.

Finally, governments and research institutions should actively support AI-driven climate research. AI can play a crucial role in climate modeling, emissions tracking, and conservation efforts, but its full potential remains untapped. Increased investment in AI applications for environmental monitoring, smart grid optimization, and carbon capture research can accelerate climate action, turning AI from an environmental challenge into a powerful tool for sustainability.

Conclusion

The policies outlined above provide a roadmap for integrating sustainability into AI development, ensuring that technological advancements align with environmental goals. By incentivizing green AI research, regulating data centers, promoting carbon offset programs, and fostering collaboration between public and private sectors, policymakers can minimize AI's carbon footprint while maximizing its potential for climate solutions.

As AI continues to shape the future of industries and societies, ensuring that it is developed responsibly and sustainably is critical. A global effort—involving policymakers, researchers, businesses, and civil society—is required to achieve a green AI revolution, where innovation and environmental responsibility go hand in hand.

ECONOMIC AND SOCIETAL IMPLICATIONS

The transition to sustainable AI practices has profound economic and societal implications. As AI continues to reshape industries and drive technological advancements, integrating sustainability into its development presents both opportunities and challenges. The economic implications of Green AI extend beyond direct financial benefits, influencing job creation, industry competitiveness, and the evolution of markets focused on environmental sustainability. At the same time, the societal impacts of Green AI touch on equity concerns, accessibility, and the broader relationship between technology and social well-being.

This section explores the economic opportunities presented by Green AI, the importance of equitable access to sustainable AI technologies, and how Green AI can foster inclusive economic growth. Additionally, it highlights the social responsibilities associated with Green AI adoption, emphasizing the need for international cooperation and ethical frameworks to ensure that sustainability efforts benefit all nations and communities.

Economic Opportunities in Green AI

The development of Green AI is expected to generate substantial economic value, creating new business opportunities, increasing efficiency, and driving sustainable growth. AI-driven sustainability solutions enable organizations to reduce operational costs while simultaneously improving their environmental performance. As industries worldwide strive to meet ambitious carbon reduction targets, AI-powered sustainability tools are playing an increasingly vital role in shaping the future economy.

AI-Driven Growth in Renewable Energy

One of the most promising economic opportunities lies in renewable energy optimization. AI technologies are already being deployed to enhance the efficiency of solar, wind, and hydroelectric power generation. Machine learning models analyze weather patterns, energy demand fluctuations, and grid performance, allowing for more reliable integration of intermittent renewable energy sources into power grids.

For example, Google's AI-powered energy management system has increased the efficiency of wind farms by 20%, demonstrating the potential economic gains associated with AI-driven renewable energy optimization. Similarly, DeepMind, in partnership with National Grid, has developed predictive AI models that help manage electricity distribution, reducing reliance on fossil fuels and improving overall system efficiency.

AI applications in energy management alone could contribute trillions of dollars to global GDP by 2030. The economic benefits of AI in renewable energy include: lowering energy production costs through optimized generation and storage, reduced carbon pricing liabilities for companies subject to emissions regulations; and increased investment in clean technology startups and sustainable AI-driven innovation hubs.

Governments and private investors are increasingly recognizing these economic opportunities, allocating billions of dollars toward AI-driven climate solutions. Companies investing in Green AI not only enhance their profitability but also strengthen their brand reputation by aligning with sustainability and ESG (Environmental, Social, and Governance) goals.

AI and the Circular Economy

Beyond energy efficiency, AI is also driving growth in the circular economy. The circular economy is an emerging economic model designed to eliminate waste, optimize resource efficiency, and promote sustainability by reusing, repairing, refurbishing, and recycling materials. Unlike the traditional linear economy, which follows a "take-make-dispose" model, the circular economy aims to extend the lifecycle of products, minimize environmental impact, and create sustainable business opportunities. AI plays a transformative role in this transition by enhancing material efficiency, optimizing waste management, and fostering innovative business models that reduce ecological footprints.

One of the most significant applications of AI in the circular economy is its ability to improve waste management and recycling processes. Traditional waste management systems often struggle with inefficient sorting methods, leading to high contamination rates in recycling streams and reduced material recovery. AI-powered computer vision and robotic sorting systems are revolutionizing this process by identifying, classifying, and sorting waste more accurately and efficiently. AI-driven waste sorting systems use machine learning algorithms and robotic arms equipped with cameras and sensors to detect materials in real time. Companies such as AMP Robotics and ZenRobotics have developed AI-powered robotic sorting solutions capable of identifying different types of plastics, metals, and paper, dramatically improving recycling efficiency. Traditional recycling plants often rely on manual sorting, which is labor-intensive and prone to human error. AI-powered sorting machines increase speed and accuracy, improving recovery rates and reducing operational costs. For example, AI algorithms can distinguish between biodegradable, non-recyclable, and high-value recyclable materials, ensuring that resources are directed to the appropriate recycling streams. Additionally, AI can be applied in waste reduction strategies by predicting waste generation patterns and providing data-driven insights to policymakers and businesses. Municipalities and industries can use AI-driven analytics to optimize collection schedules, reduce landfill waste, and increase recycling efficiency.

Another area where AI contributes to the circular economy is in predictive maintenance, which reduces waste and extends the lifespan of industrial equipment and consumer goods. Machine learning algorithms can analyze data from IoT sensors embedded in machinery to predict failures before they occur, minimizing downtime and unnecessary replacements. AI-driven predictive maintenance is widely used in industrial production, where equipment failures can lead to costly repairs and wasted materials. Companies implementing AI-based failure detection models have reported a 20–40% reduction in maintenance costs and significantly lower material waste. AI-powered diagnostics allow manufacturers to perform targeted repairs rather than replacing entire components, leading to longer-lasting products and reduced environmental impact. AI is also enabling remanufacturing strategies, where used products are refurbished and resold, further supporting circular economy goals. Predictive maintenance not only improves cost efficiency for businesses but also significantly reduces industrial waste, contributing to a more sustainable economy.

AI also plays a key role in optimizing supply chains, ensuring that materials are used efficiently and waste is minimized. Traditional supply chains often suffer from excess inventory, inefficient logistics, and high levels of material waste. AI-driven solutions provide real-time insights into demand forecasting, inventory optimization, and transportation efficiency, reducing both costs and environmental impact. AI-powered analytics predict fluctuations in consumer demand, allowing companies to adjust production levels accordingly. By preventing overproduction and surplus inventory, businesses can significantly reduce waste and resource depletion. AI also enhances reverse logistics, which involves the collection, repair, and redistribution of used products. Companies like Dell and HP leverage AI to track used electronics, ensuring they are properly recycled or refurbished rather than discarded in landfills. AI-powered logistics platforms optimize delivery routes to minimize fuel consumption and carbon emissions. By analyzing traffic patterns, weather conditions, and delivery schedules, AI systems can reduce inefficiencies in transportation networks, supporting circular economy principles. By improving supply chain transparency and real-time tracking of materials, AI is enabling businesses to make data-driven decisions that align with sustainability goals.

Beyond optimizing waste management and supply chains, AI is fostering new circular business models that redefine how products and services are consumed. Companies are increasingly shifting towards service-based models that prioritize access over ownership, extending the useful life of products and reducing environmental impact. AI provides Product-as-a-Service (PaaS) and AI-Enabled Sharing Economy. AI is helping companies transition from selling products to offering services. Instead of purchasing new equipment, consumers and businesses can lease products while AI-powered monitoring systems ensure optimal usage and predictive maintenance. Examples include Schneider Electric's energy management services and Michelin's tire subscription model, both of which use AI to maximize product efficiency while minimizing waste. Moreover, platforms like Uber, Airbnb, and Rent the Runway leverage AI to optimize resource sharing, reducing the need for excessive consumption. AI-driven demand forecasting and pricing algorithms ensure efficient utilization of shared assets, promoting sustainability through shared access rather than individual ownership. AI-powered circular business models are not only environmentally sustainable but also provide economic advantages, reducing costs for both businesses and consumers.

By enhancing resource efficiency, AI contributes to the global shift away from a linear economy (take-make-waste) toward a circular model that prioritizes sustainability and economic resilience.

Equity Concerns and Access to Green AI

As artificial intelligence (AI) continues to advance and integrate into sustainability initiatives, a significant challenge arises in ensuring equitable access to green AI technologies. While developed nations and large corporations are making strides in implementing AI-driven sustainability solutions, many developing countries and under-resourced communities face barriers to participation. Without deliberate efforts to close this gap, the benefits of green AI may remain concentrated among a select group of nations and organizations, exacerbating existing inequalities in economic development, environmental protection, and technological access. Addressing these disparities requires targeted policies, international cooperation, and investments in infrastructure, education, and knowledge-sharing mechanisms to ensure that all regions can harness the power of AI for sustainability.

One of the primary barriers to equitable access to green AI is the digital divide. Many developing nations lack the high-performance computing infrastructure necessary for AI research and deployment. While developed countries benefit from extensive cloud computing services, data centers, and AI research institutions, lower-income nations often struggle with unreliable internet connectivity, limited access to cloud-based resources, and outdated technological infrastructure. These constraints make it difficult for researchers, policymakers, and businesses in these regions to leverage AI-driven climate solutions. To bridge this gap, governments and international organizations must invest in expanding technological infrastructure, providing affordable access to AI tools, and fostering regional research collaborations that enable local innovation in AI-driven sustainability.

Financial constraints present another major obstacle to the widespread adoption of green AI in developing nations. The cost of AI development, including the computational power required to train models, the acquisition of high-quality datasets, and the integration of AI into existing systems, can be prohibitively high for countries with limited budgets. Additionally, many sustainability projects rely on external funding, and without targeted financial mechanisms, such as grants, subsidies, or low-interest loans, it is unlikely that AI-driven climate solutions will be accessible to all. Multilateral organizations such as the World Bank, the International Monetary Fund, and regional development banks can play a crucial role in providing financial support for AI-based environmental initiatives in lower-income countries. Such funding can be directed toward developing AI-powered early warning systems for climate-related disasters, optimizing energy efficiency in infrastructure projects, and enhancing resource management in agriculture.

Beyond infrastructure and financial limitations, the lack of technical expertise and AI education in many regions further widens the divide in green AI adoption. AI-driven sustainability solutions require skilled professionals who understand both machine learning and environmental science, yet many developing countries struggle to provide adequate training in these fields. Universities and technical institutions in low-income nations often lack access to AI research funding, computational resources, and faculty with expertise in AI applications for sustainability. Addressing this challenge requires greater investment in education, workforce training, and knowledge-sharing initiatives. Expanding AI-related curricula in universities, launching online educational programs, and establishing international collaborations between research institutions can empower a broader pool of talent to contribute to AI-driven sustainability solutions.

International cooperation is crucial to ensuring that green AI benefits are shared equitably. Wealthier nations and technology firms that have developed advanced AI tools for sustainability should commit to technology transfer programs that enable developing countries to implement these solutions. Open-source AI models, which allow researchers and organizations to access and modify algorithms without incurring high costs, can serve as an effective means of democratizing AI. Organizations like the United Nations and regional alliances can facilitate partnerships that encourage the sharing of AI-driven sustainability technologies while ensuring that intellectual property rights do not become a barrier to implementation.

Another important factor in achieving equitable access to green AI is addressing environmental justice concerns. The impacts of climate change disproportionately affect marginalized and low-income communities, which often bear the brunt of environmental degradation while having the least access to technological resources. AI-driven sustainability initiatives should prioritize these communities, ensuring that they benefit from climate adaptation strategies, resource optimization, and environmental monitoring tools. AI-powered climate modeling can be used to predict and mitigate the effects of extreme weather events, while AI-driven agricultural optimization can help small-scale farmers in developing regions improve yields and reduce resource waste. Governments and international organizations should actively involve local communities in the development and deployment of AI solutions to ensure that they align with local needs and priorities.

Ensuring equitable access to green AI also requires addressing ethical considerations related to AI governance and data accessibility. Many AI models rely on large datasets to train and refine their algorithms, yet data collection in developing regions can be inconsistent or biased. AI models trained primarily on data from wealthier nations may not be well-suited to the environmental and economic conditions of lower-income countries, leading to ineffective or even harmful applications. Establishing global standards for AI fairness, transparency, and data inclusivity can help mitigate these risks. Efforts should be made to create diverse, representative datasets that capture environmental patterns across different regions, ensuring that AI models function effectively for a global audience.

Policymakers must also consider the potential for green AI to reinforce existing economic inequalities if access to AI-driven sustainability solutions remains restricted to wealthy corporations and developed nations. There is a risk that AI will become a tool primarily used by powerful entities to further their competitive advantage, while smaller businesses, rural communities, and underdeveloped regions are left behind. Regulatory frameworks should encourage AI development that prioritizes accessibility, affordability, and sustainability over purely profit-driven motives. Governments can establish policies that require companies to contribute to AI knowledge-sharing initiatives or mandate that AI-driven climate solutions be made available to public-sector agencies, non-profit organizations, and local governments in lower-income regions.

Achieving equitable access to green AI is not only a matter of ethical responsibility but also an essential strategy for global climate action. Climate change is a shared challenge that requires collective solutions, and ensuring that all nations have access to AI-driven sustainability tools enhances the effectiveness of these solutions on a worldwide scale. If only a fraction of the global population can leverage AI for environmental management, mitigation efforts will be insufficient to address the full scope of the climate crisis. A truly sustainable future requires inclusive AI development that empowers all regions, especially those most vulnerable to climate change.

A comprehensive strategy for achieving equity in green AI should incorporate a combination of infrastructure development, financial support, education and capacity-building, international technology-sharing agreements, and ethical AI governance frameworks. By fostering an inclusive approach, the world can ensure that AI serves as a force for sustainable progress rather than a mechanism that deepens existing disparities. Green AI has the potential to revolutionize the fight against climate change, but for it to be truly effective, it must be accessible to all, not just a privileged few.

Green AI and Inclusive Economic Growth

Green AI has the potential to drive inclusive economic growth by aligning technological innovation with environmental sustainability. As AI-powered solutions become increasingly integrated into sectors such as energy, manufacturing, agriculture, and urban development, they can create new economic opportunities while promoting responsible resource management. However, for Green AI to contribute to broad-based economic development, it must be designed and implemented in a way that fosters equitable access to its benefits, ensuring that both developed and developing economies can participate in and benefit from its transformative potential.

The intersection of AI and sustainability presents opportunities for economic expansion, particularly in industries that are critical to achieving a low-carbon future. AI-driven tools can optimize energy efficiency, reduce material waste, and improve supply chain logistics, leading to lower operational costs and increased productivity. As companies and governments invest in sustainable AI solutions, new markets for green technologies emerge, creating millions of new jobs in AI-driven sectors. The economic advantages of Green AI, however, must extend beyond high-income countries and large corporations to reach smaller businesses, local economies, and marginalized communities that stand to gain the most from sustainable growth.

Job Creation in the Green AI Economy

One of the most significant contributions of Green AI to economic growth is its role in job creation. Contrary to fears that AI and automation will displace large numbers of workers, Green AI is expected to generate employment in emerging industries focused on sustainability and digital transformation. The shift toward AI-driven renewable energy, sustainable manufacturing, and climate-conscious urban planning is creating demand for new skill sets, leading to the rise of employment opportunities in fields such as AI-powered energy management, smart infrastructure design, and environmental monitoring.

In the renewable energy sector, AI is optimizing solar and wind energy generation, making these sources more cost-effective and widely accessible. As countries ramp up investments in smart grids, battery storage, and AI-driven energy forecasting, employment opportunities arise in software development, engineering, and AI-driven system maintenance. The International Renewable Energy Agency estimates that transitioning to a clean energy economy will create over forty million new jobs worldwide by 2050, many of which will involve AI-powered optimization systems.

Similarly, AI-powered circular economy models, which focus on reducing waste and improving material efficiency, are generating new employment in areas such as recycling automation, predictive maintenance, and remanufacturing. AI-driven sorting systems in waste management facilities are improving the efficiency of recycling operations, while machine learning algorithms help manufacturers reduce raw material consumption and extend product lifespans. These developments contribute to sustainable economic expansion while simultaneously addressing environmental concerns.

The growth of AI-powered precision agriculture also provides an opportunity for inclusive economic development, particularly in rural and agricultural economies. AI models that analyze soil health, weather patterns, and crop conditions are helping farmers maximize yields with minimal resource input, reducing water consumption and pesticide use. Smallholder farmers, who often lack access to advanced agricultural technologies, can benefit significantly from AI-powered advisory tools that offer real-time insights on crop management, improving both productivity and resilience to climate change.

While AI is contributing to job creation in the green economy, workforce development must be prioritized to ensure that workers acquire the skills necessary to participate in these emerging fields. Governments, educational institutions, and businesses must collaborate to provide training programs, reskilling initiatives, and technical education that equip workers with competencies in AI applications, environmental science, and sustainable engineering. Without proactive investments in workforce development, there is a risk that AI-driven economic growth will be concentrated in regions with high levels of digital literacy and technological expertise, leaving other areas behind.

AI and Climate-Resilient Infrastructure

AI is playing an essential role in climate-resilient infrastructure and sustainable urban development, both of which contribute to long-term economic stability and growth. As climate change intensifies, cities and governments must invest in resilient infrastructure that can withstand extreme weather events, reduce energy consumption, and support growing urban populations. AI-powered solutions are helping urban planners design energy-efficient buildings, optimize transportation networks, and enhance climate adaptation strategies.

Smart cities powered by AI are transforming urban environments into hubs of sustainability and innovation. AI-driven traffic management systems optimize traffic flow, reducing fuel consumption and emissions, while AI-enabled public transportation systems improve efficiency and accessibility. AI-powered building management systems use real-time energy monitoring to reduce heating, cooling, and electricity waste, leading to lower costs and environmental impact.

By investing in AI-driven smart infrastructure, cities can drive economic productivity while promoting sustainability, creating new employment opportunities in urban planning, environmental engineering, and AI-based monitoring systems. The adoption of AI in infrastructure projects also fosters economic inclusivity, as improved public transportation, energy-efficient housing, and climate adaptation strategies benefit low-income and marginalized communities that are disproportionately affected by environmental degradation.

The potential of Green AI to contribute to economic resilience is particularly significant in climate-vulnerable regions. AI-powered climate modeling enables governments to anticipate and mitigate natural disasters, reducing economic losses from extreme weather events such as floods, droughts, and hurricanes. By leveraging AI for early warning systems, resource allocation, and emergency response coordination, governments can minimize economic disruptions caused by climate-related disasters. These AI-driven solutions not only protect vulnerable populations but also enhance long-term economic stability by preventing large-scale economic losses and infrastructure damage.

AI and Sustainable Business Models

The benefits of Green AI must extend beyond major corporations and wealthy nations to support small businesses, local economies, and emerging markets. Many small and medium-sized enterprises face barriers to adopting AI-driven sustainability solutions due to limited financial resources, lack of technical expertise, and difficulty accessing AI-driven tools. However, if AI-powered sustainability technologies become more affordable and accessible, SMEs can reduce operational costs, improve efficiency, and participate in the global green economy.

One promising avenue for inclusive economic growth is the development of AI-driven sustainability platforms that offer cloud-based services for SMEs. These platforms allow small businesses to track their carbon footprint, optimize energy consumption, and implement AI-powered supply chain management without requiring extensive in-house expertise. By providing affordable and user-friendly AI solutions, technology companies can help SMEs transition to more sustainable business models while remaining competitive in a rapidly evolving marketplace.

For developing nations, Green AI represents an opportunity to leapfrog traditional industrialization models and transition directly into sustainable economic development. AI-powered solutions in renewable energy, agriculture, and smart infrastructure can drive economic growth while avoiding the environmental degradation associated with conventional industrialization. Countries that invest in AI-driven sustainability initiatives can attract foreign investment, create jobs, and strengthen their global competitiveness in emerging industries.

International cooperation and policy support are essential to ensuring that AI-driven economic growth benefits all nations equitably. Governments and international organizations must implement technology-sharing initiatives, funding programs, and AI capacity-building projects that enable low-income nations to adopt Green AI solutions. Without these efforts, there is a risk that the benefits of AI-driven sustainability will remain concentrated among high-income nations, reinforcing global economic inequalities.

Challenges and Policy Considerations for Equitable AI-Driven Growth

Despite its vast potential, the widespread adoption of Green AI faces several challenges that must be addressed to ensure inclusive and sustainable economic growth. One of the key concerns is the high computational cost of AI models, which can limit accessibility for small businesses and developing economies. Governments and private-sector leaders must work toward energy-efficient AI models, open-source AI tools, and cloud-based AI platforms that make sustainable AI solutions available to a wider range of users.

Another challenge is the regulatory landscape surrounding AI and sustainability. Policymakers must develop clear guidelines, incentives, and ethical frameworks that encourage the development of responsible AI-driven sustainability solutions. Tax incentives for green AI research, subsidies for AI-powered clean energy projects, and regulatory support for AI-driven climate initiatives can accelerate the adoption of Green AI while ensuring economic inclusivity.

To maximize the economic benefits of Green AI, governments, businesses, and international organizations must work together to foster an ecosystem of innovation, education, and investment that ensures AI contributes to both sustainability and equitable economic development.

Conclusion: A Path to Sustainable and Inclusive AI Development

Green AI has the potential to drive economic growth, create jobs, and foster inclusive development while simultaneously addressing the pressing challenges of climate change and environmental degradation. By ensuring that AI-driven sustainability solutions are accessible, affordable, and equitably distributed, policymakers and industry leaders can create a future where AI-powered economic progress aligns with sustainability goals. The transition to Green AI must be inclusive, ensuring that all economies, regardless of size or wealth, can participate in the benefits of sustainable technological advancement.

CONCLUSION: TOWARD A SUSTAINABLE AI ECOSYSTEM

Artificial intelligence has rapidly emerged as a transformative force across industries, driving innovation and efficiency in ways that were once unimaginable. However, as AI's influence expands, so does its environmental footprint. The very technologies that promise to optimize energy use, enhance climate modeling, and streamline resource management are themselves major contributors to energy consumption and carbon emissions. AI's dual role as both a contributor to environmental challenges and a potential solution for sustainability highlights the urgency of integrating green practices into AI development, deployment, and governance.

The carbon footprint of AI is primarily driven by the energy demands of data centers and high-performance computing infrastructures required for training and running complex machine learning models. Large-scale AI systems, such as deep learning models, demand extensive computational resources, often requiring the use of thousands of GPUs or TPUs operating in parallel. These energy-intensive processes place significant strain on global electricity grids, much of which is still derived from fossil fuels, contributing to greenhouse gas emissions. Without targeted efforts to mitigate this impact, the expansion of AI technologies could exacerbate climate change rather than help address it.

Despite these challenges, AI's potential as a tool for sustainability remains undeniable. AI-driven climate modeling enhances our ability to predict and mitigate climate change effects, providing governments and organizations with real-time insights for disaster preparedness and resource allocation. AI-powered energy management systems are revolutionizing the way electricity grids function, allowing for the seamless integration of renewable energy sources while reducing reliance on fossil fuels. In agriculture, AI is optimizing irrigation, monitoring crop health, and minimizing waste, thereby contributing to food security and sustainability. AI is also being deployed in smart cities to improve transportation efficiency, optimize waste management, and reduce energy consumption in buildings, leading to lower emissions and more sustainable urban development.

To fully harness AI's sustainability potential while mitigating its environmental impact, a multifaceted approach is required. The development of energy-efficient AI models must become a top priority. Researchers and engineers are already exploring ways to reduce the computational demands of AI by optimizing algorithms, employing neuromorphic computing techniques, and using federated learning approaches that reduce the need for large-scale centralized training. Investments in specialized AI chips that consume less power while maintaining performance standards will also play a crucial role in minimizing AI's carbon footprint.

At the same time, the infrastructure supporting AI must be reimagined with sustainability in mind. Data centers, which consume a significant share of global electricity, must transition to renewable energy sources to offset their environmental impact. Leading technology companies such as Google, Microsoft, and Amazon have made commitments to power their data centers with 100 percent renewable energy, setting an example for the industry. However, smaller firms and research institutions often lack the resources to make such transitions independently. Public-private partnerships, government subsidies, and financial incentives will be essential in facilitating the shift toward green data infrastructure on a global scale.

Beyond technological advancements, regulatory frameworks must be established to guide the sustainable development of AI. Governments and international organizations must collaborate to implement policies that promote transparency in AI energy consumption, encourage investments in low-carbon AI research, and enforce sustainability standards in AI-driven industries. Carbon pricing mechanisms and tax incentives for AI companies that prioritize energy efficiency could accelerate the adoption of greener practices. Additionally, global sustainability benchmarks for AI should be developed, ensuring that organizations measure and report their environmental impact in a standardized manner.

Ensuring equitable access to sustainable AI technologies is also a critical component of this transition. Many developing countries lack the infrastructure, financial resources, and technical expertise to deploy AI-driven sustainability solutions, creating disparities in technological benefits. While wealthier nations and corporations leverage AI for climate resilience, developing regions continue to bear the brunt of climate change with limited access to technological tools that could aid in adaptation. Addressing this gap requires international cooperation, technology transfer initiatives, and investment in AI capacity-building programs for low-income nations. By fostering knowledge-sharing and collaboration, the global community can ensure that AI's sustainability potential is realized in all regions, not just in technologically advanced economies.

In addition to promoting environmental sustainability, AI's integration into green initiatives must align with inclusive economic growth. The shift toward sustainable AI practices has the potential to create millions of new jobs in emerging industries such as renewable energy, smart infrastructure, and circular economy solutions. However, workforce development programs must be prioritized to equip individuals with the necessary skills to participate in the AI-driven green economy. Governments, universities, and private companies must work together to establish training programs, reskilling initiatives, and technical education curricula that prepare workers for the evolving job market. Without such efforts, there is a risk that the benefits of Green AI will be concentrated among a select group of highly skilled professionals, further widening economic disparities.

Collaboration between policymakers, industry leaders, researchers, and civil society will be essential in driving the transition to a sustainable AI ecosystem. No single entity can address the environmental challenges associated with AI alone. Governments must enforce regulations that incentivize green AI development while fostering innovation and economic progress. Businesses must integrate sustainability into their AI strategies, investing in energy-efficient models and responsible data center management. Research institutions must continue exploring breakthroughs in low-energy AI computation, ensuring that sustainability remains a central focus of AI advancements. Civil society and environmental organizations must advocate for ethical AI policies that align with climate goals and social responsibility.

AI has the potential to be a powerful ally in the fight against climate change, but only if it is developed and deployed with sustainability at its core. As we move forward in the digital age, the responsibility to shape AI's trajectory in an environmentally conscious manner falls on all stakeholders. By embedding sustainability into AI development, we can ensure that AI serves as a cornerstone of climate resilience, economic inclusivity, and responsible technological progress.

The transition to a green AI ecosystem represents a blueprint for the future, one in which technology and sustainability coexist in harmony. If approached with careful planning and collaborative efforts, AI can evolve from being a contributor to environmental concerns to becoming a leading force in global climate resilience. The pursuit of Green AI is not just a technological imperative; it is an ethical obligation to future generations. By aligning AI innovation with sustainability principles, we can ensure that AI continues to drive progress while preserving the planet for years to come.

REFERENCES

Abduljabbar, R., Dia, H., Liyanage, S., & Bagloee, S. A. (2019). Applications of Artificial Intelligence in Transport: An Overview. *Sustainability (Basel), 11*(1), 1. Advance online publication. DOI: 10.3390/su11010189

Cao, L. (2023). AI in Finance: Challenges, Techniques, and Opportunities. *ACM Computing Surveys, 55*(3), 1–38. DOI: 10.1145/3502289

Gupta, K., Mane, P., Rajankar, O. S., Bhowmik, M., Jadhav, R., Yadav, S., Rawandale, S., & Chobe, S. V. (2023). Harnessing AI for Strategic Decision-Making and Business Performance Optimization. *International Journal of Intelligent Systems and Applications in Engineering, 11*(10s), Article 10s.

Nishant, R., Kennedy, M., & Corbett, J. (2020). Artificial intelligence for sustainability: Challenges, opportunities, and a research agenda. *International Journal of Information Management, 53*, 102104. DOI: 10.1016/j.ijinfomgt.2020.102104

Olatunde, T. M., Okwandu, A. C., Akande, D. O., & Sikhakhane, Z. Q.Tosin Michael OlatundeAzubuike Chukwudi OkwanduDorcas Oluwajuwonlo AkandeZamathula Queen Sikhakhane. (2024). REVIEWING THE ROLE OF ARTIFICIAL INTELLIGENCE IN ENERGY EFFICIENCY OPTIMIZATION. *Engineering Science & Technology Journal, 5*(4), 4. Advance online publication. DOI: 10.51594/estj.v5i4.1015

Saraswat, D., Bhattacharya, P., Verma, A., Prasad, V. K., Tanwar, S., Sharma, G., Bokoro, P. N., & Sharma, R. (2022). Explainable AI for Healthcare 5.0: Opportunities and Challenges. *IEEE Access, 10*, 84486–84517. IEEE Access. DOI: 10.1109/ACCESS.2022.3197671

Shaheen, M. Y. (2021). Applications of Artificial Intelligence (AI) in healthcare. *RE:view*. Advance online publication. DOI: 10.14293/S2199-1006.1.SOR-.PPVRY8K.v1

Strubell, E., Ganesh, A., & McCallum, A. (2019a). Energy and Policy Considerations for Deep Learning in NLP. In Korhonen, A., Traum, D., & Màrquez, L. (Eds.), *Proceedings of the 57th Annual Meeting of the Association for Computational Linguistics* (pp. 3645–3650). Association for Computational Linguistics. DOI: 10.18653/v1/P19-1355

Strubell, E., Ganesh, A., & McCallum, A. (2019b). *Energy and Policy Considerations for Deep Learning in NLP* (arXiv:1906.02243). arXiv. /arXiv.1906.02243DOI: 10.18653/v1/P19-1355

Chapter 7
Balancing Innovation and Regulation: Ethical Frameworks for AI Policy and Governance

Dinesh Kumar
https://orcid.org/0000-0001-5943-1444
Woxsen University, India

Nidhi Suthar
https://orcid.org/0009-0000-9791-7349
Woxsen University, India

ABSTRACT

This chapter looks into the critical balancing act achieved by promoting innovation and robust regulation of Artificial Intelligence (AI) governance. While rapid evolution in AI technology brings about ethical, legal and social challenges, as they apply to industries and societal processes, the technologies are also evolving rapidly. The principles covered in the chapter relate to ethical AI governance. Additionally, it lays out policy recommendations for dealing with up and coming challenges and inequalities in the AI access. A roadmap for responsible AI development and dynamic governance models are suggested in the chapter. The overarching objective is to ensure that AI technologies support the alignment to the societal values, distribute equitable benefits and minimize the risks inherent in the AI ecosystem to sustainable and inclusive AI ecosystem for the coming generations.

DOI: 10.4018/979-8-3373-1210-1.ch007

INTRODUCTION

All scientific community including scholars such as Boyd and Holton (2018) and Okunlaya, Syed Abdullah, and Alias (2022) are convinced that AI is now a dominating force of this transformative game changing innovation in industry. Most parts of the life have been optimised with the help of AI in healthcare diagnostics, supply chains, autonomous systems management, (Demir & Paksoy, 2020; Madancian et al., 2023; Rong et al., 2020) but it also brings about very serious ethical, social and legal challenges that need strong governance frameworks. The double imperative of innovation and protecting interests of the society, globally, has catalysed the global discourse on AI policy and regulation (Smuha, 2021).

The rapid pace of AI development raises critical questions about its governance. Unregulated deployment of AI risks exacerbation of societal inequities, perpetuations of algorithmic bias and privacy rights violation (Whittaker et al., 2018). On the other end of the spectrum, too strict regulations will kill innovation. Because the benefits of AI are never realized without allowing its potential harms to be mitigated, policymakers seek to maximize the benefits while mitigating the potential harms (Binns, 2018). The challenge of this is with ethical frameworks that govern AI governance without constricting this creative potential.

AI innovation and regulation are particularly important as a global issue. AI technologies development and deployment does not occur at a national border. The challenges of data privacy, cybersecurity, and ethical AI standards (Jobin, Ienca, & Vayena, 2019) are so shared, that they need international cooperation. But differences in technological capacities and governmental priorities complicate the creation of uniformly governed technologies. These challenges suggest that the need for harmonized and flexible policies is to accommodate a regional context and universal ethical principles.

In this chapter we explore the complex relationship between innovation and AI regulation. It examines the ethical dilemmas of AI development and their regulatory strategies. The chapter identifies best practices and proposes a comprehensive ethical framework for AI policy and governance. The chapter has a larger aim of providing actionable insights for stakeholders such as policymakers, technologists and industry leaders to navigate through the thicket of AI governance complexities.

UNDERSTANDING AI INNOVATION

AI innovation is the creation and use of intelligent systems with or approaching human cognitive performance in tasks, such as decision making, pattern recognition and language understanding. However, this innovation is based on advanced algorithms, large data sets and computing power that can either act autonomously or support human decision making (Jarrahi, 2018). Technological progress, economic impasse and pressing social problems are driving the flourish in AI innovation. Rapid AI advancements are led by an environment of rigorous computational capability, ubiquitous big data and advanced algorithmic designs. Businesses increasingly invest in AI to streamline operations, improve decision-making processes and gain competitive advantages (Samara et al., 2024). Simultaneously, societal demands for solutions to critical issues such as climate change, public health crises and resource optimization drive AI research and development. For instance, AI is used to model climate change scenarios, optimize renewable energy systems and support personalized healthcare interventions.

However, due to its potential for transformational change it also maintains serious ethical and social risks. Some of the unintended consequences to the deployment of AI technologies encompasses: algorithmic biases, a lack of transparency, and a threat to privacy (Whittaker et al., 2018). All of these risks need good oversight and governance to prevent an innovation that is not equitable or responsible. In addition, AI's disparities in access to capabilities and benefits compound global inequities, since resource limited regions often cannot harness AI's possible to its fullest capacity. This is yet another reason why democratic policy to foster consistent inclusive policy, including for the distribution of AI benefits in diverse settings, may be necessary to address ethical concerns.

The opportunities and risks of this AI invention are in balancing and are a core aspect of progress today. The importance of the fact that it can improve quality of life, productivity and solving tough global problems. Yet, as with alignment in ethical considerations and equitable access to the benefits of AI innovation are crucial to assure that the benefits of AI innovation are fairly and responsibly spread across societies. The basis of sustainable AI development is to recognize the dual imperative of driving innovation and protecting and the broader societal interests.

THE NEED FOR REGULATION IN AI

The need for regulation in AI arises from its capacity to impact society in profound and often unpredictable ways. While AI offers immense potential for innovation, unregulated deployment can lead to harmful consequences such as bias, discrimination, loss of privacy and threats to safety and security (Habbal, Ali, & Abuzaraida,

2024; Kumar & Suthar, 2024). As AI systems become more integrated into critical societal processes, the urgency to establish robust regulatory frameworks grows.

The mitigation of risks related to algorithmic decision making is one of the main drivers for AI regulation. Unlike humans, AI systems don't have the capability to modify biases introduced into training data, or in their design, unless a human system makes it. They can serve as perpetuators of systemic discrimination in fields ranging from hiring, to lending and law enforcement (Pan & Froese, 2023; Malik et al., 2020). In addition, the opacity of AI operations limits the possibility of accountability after errors or outcomes that are not desirable. Addressing these challenges can be done through regulatory requirements in the form of standards of fairness, transparency and explainability.

That also raises the issue of regulation as a means to address privacy concerns. Because AI systems rely heavily on large datasets that include sensitive personal information, some are concerned that there is no reason for these systems to exist. This data can be misused without safeguards. Facial recognition technologies have been discussed in relation to surveillance and the loss of freedom (Sarabdeen, 2022; Smith & Miller, 2022). These frameworks can help create a clear set of rules for consuming data and a set of boundaries for regulators for AI applications to follow—and to be sure of respecting basic fundamental rights and freedoms when using the data.

However, like any emerging technological area, challenges arise from the pace of AI development for currently existing legal and ethical standards (Kumar & Suthar, 2024; O'Sullivan et al., 2019). However, traditional regulatory mechanisms may not be able to maintain their pace when it comes to the constant evolution of AI technologies. Unfilled gaps in implementation of AI systems increase the chance of uneven adoption of those systems across sectors or regions. These disparities can only be addressed and consistent standards for AI deployment can be promoted through coordinated regulatory efforts.

The other important aspect of AI regulation is how it will help to build public trust. To be accepted in society, AI is perceived as responsible developed and deployed. Transparent and accountable governance can enhance trust in AI (Lahusen, Maggetti, & Slavkovik, 2024).

In the absence of regulation, there is also a risk of exacerbating global inequalities. Advanced AI systems are often concentrated in technologically advanced nations. Regulatory frameworks can help bridge this divide by encouraging technology transfer, capacity-building and equitable access to AI innovations. Additionally, international cooperation on AI governance can address cross-border issues such as cybersecurity, intellectual property and the ethical implications of AI research and deployment.

In general, we need AI to be regulated. While regulation shouldn't kill innovation, it should also have safeguards in place to make sure AI technologies will be used in the best way for the benefit of the public good. Achieving this balances requires that the principles be nuanced to fit with the practical governance strategies.

ETHICAL FRAMEWORKS FOR AI POLICY AND GOVERNANCE

The adoption of AI is widespread and has caused serious ethical and governance concerns that have required strong frameworks for the development and deployment of AI. Structured principles about potential benefits and risks of AI, and how to balance them, exist in the form of ethical frameworks. These frameworks are essential for ensuring that AI technologies operate within the bounds of societal norms, human rights and sustainable development goals. This section delves into the key principles underpinning ethical AI governance, examines existing frameworks and proposes an integrated approach to creating a comprehensive governance model (see Table 1).

Table 1. Comparison of key frameworks for ethical and regulatory governance of AI

Framework	Key Principles	Strengths	Weaknesses
OECD AI Principles	Transparency, Accountability, Fairness, Human-Cantered Design	Provides global consensus on ethical AI; adopted by 42 countries	Non-binding nature limits enforceability; lacks specific implementation guidelines
EU AI Act	Risk-Based Regulation, Transparency, Accountability, Safety	Comprehensive risk-based approach; clear obligations for high-risk systems	Ambiguities in risk categorization; potential for over-regulation in lower-risk applications
UNESCO AI Ethics	Inclusivity, Sustainability, Human Rights, Ethical Impact Assessments	Emphasis on global inclusivity and sustainability; broad ethical focus	Implementation depends on national adoption; limited enforcement mechanisms
Singapore Model AI Framework	Transparency, Human-Centric Design, Governance Structures	Practical tools for businesses (e.g., self-assessment checklists); industry-friendly	Non-binding guidelines may reduce adoption; limited scope beyond business applications
US Approach (Sectoral)	Innovation-Centric, Industry-Specific Regulations	Encourages innovation with flexible, sector-specific guidelines	Lack of overarching federal policy leads to fragmented and inconsistent governance

Source: By authors

Ethical AI governance is central around the principle of transparency. Transparency provides greater assurance in which ways AI systems work can be understood and watched by those who walk through to scrutinize. First, many AI systems are opaque 'black box' systems with internal workings of algorithms that the developers themselves do not understand (Felzmann et al, 2020). Transparency is a transparent system which allows users and regulators to understand how decisions are made, and also how data is collected, processed and stored. For one, organizations using AI should disclose where their training data comes from and document how their models work to reduce risks of use or harm.

The other foundational principle holds that those responsible for developing and deploying AI systems are held accountable for what they do and what they decide (Jedličková, 2024). Accountability implies that when AI systems generate undesirable outcomes, there is a means to determine who is accountable for that, and how to repair the harm they cause. It also means that mechanisms to regulate the use of AI applications — and enforce ethical standards — need to be set in place. In practice, it may entail the creation of oversight bodies, which review high risk AI deployments, or laws which demand organizations take responsibility for the consequences of their AI systems.

The principle of fairness is equally important. It is important for AI systems to avoid reinforcement or magnification of biases — particularly against those which marginalise vulnerable groups (Wachter et al., 2021). To have fairness in AI, making sure the data we use to train our algorithms represents diverse groups of people in the data, and that the models do not produce discriminatory outcomes is necessary. Today, algorithms used in, for instance, hiring or credit scoring have been criticised as biased to some demographic groups, mostly because the underlying training data reflects historically inequitable patterns. In order for ethical frameworks to resiliency these disparities must be addressed by fairness audits and algorithm design and deployment guidelines.

Privacy is another cornerstone of ethical AI governance. AI systems frequently rely on large datasets that include sensitive personal information and raise concerns about how this data is collected, used and protected. Ethical frameworks must prioritize user consent, data minimization and robust security measures to safeguard privacy (Williamson & Prybutok, 2024). The General Data Protection Regulation (GDPR) in Europe is a perfect example of a regulation setting requirements for data protection, and its integration is a model for creating privacy throughout the governance of AI. As with all other uses of AI, privacy considerations apply including that AI applications such as facial recognition and surveillance systems do not infringe or enable mass surveillance.

The principle of safety and security is about preventing the harmful impacts that AI systems could cause to people, to organizations, to and to society. AI Safety means to make sure that AI systems run as they were expected and do not cause harm by error or unexpected consequences (Habbal et al., 2024). Autonomous vehicles, for example, need to be extensively tested to avoid what would otherwise be accidents resulting from software malfunction. While security is about protecting AI systems against external risks, like cyber attacks that could impair their capability or put them into illicit use, security is about making them more vulnerable to attack oneself. It is important for risk assessment, system testing and security protocols of these risks to be developed in an ethical frameworks.

Despite the hands-off behavior, attempts to operationalize these principles using existing ethical frameworks are productive. The OECD AI Principles, which 42 countries have recently adopted, include the principles of inclusivity, transparency, accountability and sustainability (Castonguay et al., 2024). They serve as a basis for governments to design policies that do not differ from the global ethical standards, but at the same time are able to be tailored to the local contexts. Similarly, the European Union's AI Ethics Guidelines outline requirements for trustworthy AI, including human agency, technical robustness and privacy (Nikolinakos, 2023). The significance of alignment between ethical principles and practical implementation means, i.e. the conduct of impact assessments and promotion of stakeholder engagement, is point out.

The Ethics of AI drawn up by the UNESCO Recommendation on the Ethics of AI is a global position aiming to integrate ethical concerns (Morandín-Ahuerma, 2023). It emphasizes the need for AI to promote human well-being, protect fundamental rights and foster sustainable development.

The UNESCO framework aligns with this principle and extends its reach by advocating for the involvement of diverse stakeholder groups in AI governance, including underrepresented groups and developing nations. The importance of such inclusivity to close the global AI access and benefits gap and to reflect in ethics frameworks, cultural and societal values from a greater breadth is fundamental.

Figure 1. Ethical frameworks for AI governance (Authors)

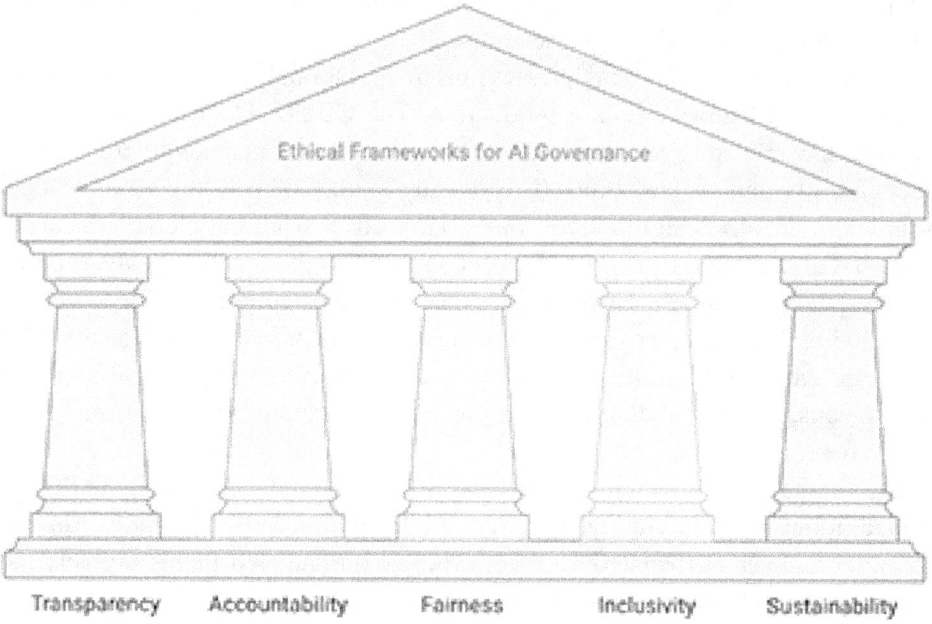

These advancements notwithstanding, existing frameworks struggle with the intricacies of AI governance. The lack of harmonisation across jurisdictions is one big issue. Often other countries and other regions have different ethical standards or different regulatory approaches, so people don't have the same sense of how AI systems should be governed. For example, while the European Union had led with a proposed AI Act, other places have been tardy with taking a comprehensive approach to AI regulation. The diversity of the requirements, however, can result in challenges for multinational organizations undertaking the task of complying with various requirements and also prevent the development of a globally accepted standard.

Thus, we propose the need for a unified ethical framework that spells out the most important principles and reflects its ability to adapt to the nature of AI technologies is evolving. The dynamic features of such a framework should promote flexibility in accommodating updates as ethical challenges and technological advances emerge. Also, it should be flexible enough but enforceable enough so that organizations can innovate while maintaining an ethical guideline. A tiered governance model is another proposed approach: high risk AI applications are subject to more onerous regulatory oversight, while lower risk are governed by industry standards and self-regulation.

It is important that ethical AI frameworks have successful stakeholder engagement. Governance mechanisms have to be developed that are inclusive and representative and policymakers, technologists, civil society organizations and affected individuals must work together to do so. For these reasons, public consultation processes may help to ensure that an ethical framework reflects society's values and includes as many voices as possible in the views on an ethical framework that concern all groups. For instance, AI regulation was taken up through participatory policymaking and citizen panels that inserted public input.

With any luck, ethical impact assessments are integrated into the development and deployment process of ethical AI governance. Such evaluations are analogous to environmental impact assessments in that they can indicate the presence of potential ethical risks and suggested the ways for mitigating these risks before deploying AI systems. An ethical impact assessment can also serve as an implicit basis for continuous monitoring and evaluation and proceed with checking AI systems are aligned with ethical principles during the lifecycle.

And of course, implementation of these frameworks is something that needs education and capacity building. All need to know and skills to understand and apply ethical principles when policymakers, developers and end users work. An example is to include ethics training in the computer science and engineering curricula helping future technologists create AI systems that work for society, first. Like, public awareness campaigns can bring people to informed decisions for AI apps and to ask for ethical governance.

CASE STUDIES IN BALANCING INNOVATION AND REGULATION

AI offers the opportunity to innovate, yet the challenge of the intersection of innovation and regulation creates unique issues with respect to governance that must be addressed to deliver both technological advancement and societal welfare. The case studies of real world examples offer tangible examples of how a balance of these stakeholders can provide insight into how they have navigated such a balance. This addresses successful practices, regulatory gaps and lessons learned, and provides guidance for future policy development (see Table 2).

Table 2. Case studies on the governance and application of AI across different domains

Case Study	Application Area	Governance Approach	Outcomes	Lessons Learned
EU AI Act	Risk-Based AI Regulation	Tiered oversight based on risk categories	Promoted accountability in high-risk applications; supported innovation in low-risk areas	Risk-based frameworks balance innovation and regulation, but require clear risk definitions.
Singapore's Model AI Framework	Business Applications	Non-binding guidelines with self-assessment tools	Encouraged adoption of ethical practices; established trust among businesses	Practical, business-friendly tools foster voluntary compliance without stifling innovation.
Predictive Policing Algorithms	Law Enforcement	Limited oversight; inadequate bias mitigation	Perpetuated biases against minority groups; reduced public trust in AI-driven policing	Lack of transparency and fairness leads to societal harm; audits and fairness checks are critical.
Autonomous Vehicles in the US	Transportation	State-level regulations; no federal framework	Promoted innovation in some states; inconsistencies in safety and liability standards	Uniform, national policies are needed to address safety and ethical concerns comprehensively.
Facial Recognition in San Francisco	Public Security	Municipal ban on government use of facial recognition	Prevented potential misuse of surveillance; sparked global debate on privacy and ethics	Local governance can address immediate concerns but may lead to fragmented regulations.

Source: By authors

One prominent example of balancing innovation and regulation is the European Union's proposed Artificial Intelligence Act (Svantesson, 2022). This framework categorizes AI systems into risk tiers, ranging from minimal to unacceptable with varying levels of regulatory scrutiny. High-risk applications such as those in healthcare or law enforcement are subject to strict requirements, including transparency, accountability and data governance measures. The tiered approach permits low risk applications of AI, which include chatbots or recommendation systems, to run with little or no regulatory overhead. The EU's framework not only shows how regulations can prevent an ethical concern from stifling technological advancement, but also by focusing oversight on levels of risk. Although the framework has been criticized for failing to provide clear definitions of risk categories.

Similar to this is Singapore's Model AI Governance Framework which is a practical guide to developing AI systems. The framework is ethical, human-centric, transparent and provides businesses a clear rulebook on how to ground their AI applications in ethical principles (Goode et al., 2023; Taeihagh 2021). It has tools, such as ethical self-assessment checklists and implementation guides and allows organizations to integrate ethical considerations into processes. Singapore's example shows how regulatory bodies can use flexible, non-mandatory guidelines to encourage responsible innovation. This framework has brought government agencies, industry players and academia together to forge a collaboration on ethical AI governance and cemented Singapore as a platform to pioneer ethical AI governance.

On the other hand, the deployment of predictive policing algorithms in different jurisdictions provide the risks in lack of strict regulation. Historical crime data is used to predict where criminal activity may occur in order to predict potential crime and to optimize law enforcement resources. These systems, if efficient, have come in for criticism for replicating the racial and socioeconomic biases that were encoded in their training data. For example, studies have found that the primary communities of interest for predictive policing algorithms are a minority community (Brantingham et al., 2018). Their opacity and spinelessness further trespass the lack of public trust. The ability to detect faces puts a hefty load on striking the balance between innovation and regulation. Governments and private companies are beginning to apply facial recognition systems to a myriad of purposes intent on security and customer services (Lai & Rau, 2021). However, concerns were rekindled about the ethical dimensions because of the fear that the technologies will infringe upon privacy rights, bolster biases and be abused. As an example, in the United States use of facial recognition by law enforcement has sparked concerns over mass surveillance and wrongful arrests because of inaccuracies identifying members of minority groups. In turn, several cities, such as San Francisco, have banned government use of facial recognition, putting local governance on the front lines of regulatory gaps. In response, several cities, including San Francisco, have banned the use of facial recognition by government agencies and highlights the role of local governance in addressing regulatory gaps. This case highlights the importance of striking a balance between leveraging AI's capabilities and safeguarding fundamental rights, particularly in contexts where public trust is critical.

There is an oppositional view of the deployment of AI in healthcare and a showcase of how innovation and regulation can be made to work together. AI driven diagnostic tools, for example, used to detect diseases as cancer or diabetes, which have shown great promise in improving patient outcomes. Approvals for AI based medical devices have been established by regulatory bodies such as the U.S. Food and Drug Administration (FDA) and are ensured that such medical devices are safe and efficacious prior to their reach to the market (Muralidharan et al., 2024). Collaboration with industry stakeholders through regulator-enabled adoption of innovative artificial intelligence solutions in healthcare has been addressed, while ethical and safety issues have been mitigated. The importance of domain specific regulation that considers the unique risk and benefits of AI applications in this case demonstrates.

AI driven credit scoring systems in the financial area offer us an example of complexity in innovation and regulation. These systems analyse huge amounts of data to determine the creditworthiness of applicants and gives lenders a more efficient and accurate method of evaluating potential applicants. But there's been some calls for algorithmic bias and lack of transparency to come under regulatory oversight. One example would be that of AI models disproportionately denying credit to some of the demographic groups for which fairness and accountability is critical. Proposed regulations, as by the European Commission under the GDPR, are intended to make the AI driven decisions explainable and free of discrimination. The lessons learned are that to allow the benefits of AI to affordably expand financial access without restricting its potential, there must be regulations that are fair and inclusive.

The launch of self-driving vehicles marks the meeting place of innovation and regulation. After all, there are good reasons technologies of driving stand to possibly bring down road traffic accidents, optimize fuel spending, or alter transport systems (Crayton & Meier, 2017; Hosseinian & Mirzahossein, 2024). Perhaps there remain even now moments of doubt regarding this great revolution in technology. If a driverless car causes destruction, who will be responsible? What dilemmas do the algorithms create in making decisions within the context of these dilemmas? The issues concerning various countries' regulations of autonomous vehicles include various forms of governance. For instance, in the US, an approach is almost entirely states-based that allows different states to introduce their own regulations. In Germany there is at least a national framework that tackles some aspects of the ethical dimension. These examples highlight the importance of adaptive and inclusive regulatory processes being available to address emerging challenges to AI innovation.

Across these case studies, several key lessons emerge. First, the importance of stakeholder collaboration is evident in frameworks like Singapore's Model AI Governance Framework and the EU's Artificial Intelligence Act. Engaging diverse stakeholders, including governments, industry, academia and civil society ensures that regulations address the interests and concerns of all affected parties.

The second one is their tiered framework, which besides giving an opportunity to balance innovation and regulation, focuses on overseeing those high-risk applications. Third, is that the push for greater transparency and accountability has pervaded their findings to find expression in theoretical frameworks for a wider focus on the role of public trust. The case studies reveal the gaps and challenges that also need to be addressed.

Although some regional or sector frameworks of AI governance might be unevenly implemented, others would have varying effects on how risk and rewards are shared. Regulators are mostly lagging in taking action toward the rapid developments in AI, retaining them in a reactive context when they should be thinking about proactive governance. Therefore, challenges arise in that the construction of model global harmonized frameworks addressing such issues will still have to consider local contexts in upholding universal ethical principles.

CHALLENGES IN AI REGULATION

Regulation of AI presents a range of challenges due to the complex, dynamic and global nature of this technology. Rapid evolution and diverse applications of AI create significant hurdles for policymakers and stakeholders. These challenges arise from the intrinsic characteristics of AI which creates conflicting interests among stakeholders and the difficulty of aligning regulations across jurisdictions. Addressing these challenges is critical for ensuring that AI technologies are developed and deployed responsibly, equitably and sustainably (See Table 3).

Table 3. Key principles of ethical AI: definitions, applications, and challenges

Principle	Definition	Application Example	Key Challenges
Transparency	Ensuring that AI systems are understandable and their operations are open to scrutiny.	Requiring explainable AI in credit scoring systems.	Overcoming the "black box" nature of complex algorithms and ensuring interpretability for all stakeholders.
Accountability	Holding developers and deployers of AI systems responsible for their outcomes and impacts.	Implementing audits for AI-based hiring tools.	Establishing clear liability frameworks and ensuring compliance with ethical guidelines.
Fairness	Preventing discrimination and ensuring equitable outcomes for all demographic groups.	Auditing AI models for bias in healthcare diagnostics.	Mitigating biases in training data and achieving consensus on definitions of fairness.
Privacy	Protecting individuals' personal data and ensuring informed consent for its use.	Complying with GDPR standards in facial recognition systems.	Balancing data access for innovation with stringent privacy safeguards.
Inclusivity	Ensuring that AI systems benefit diverse groups and do not marginalize any community.	Developing multilingual AI tools for global education.	Addressing disparities in access to AI resources and involving underrepresented communities in governance.
Safety and Security	Ensuring AI systems do not cause harm and are protected from misuse or cyberattacks.	Testing autonomous vehicles under diverse conditions.	Identifying and mitigating risks in high-stakes AI applications and securing AI systems from cyber threats.

Source: By authors

AI technologies are evolving at a pace that is now quicker than the normal speed with which regulatory frameworks are able to keep up (Scherer, 2015). The sheer speed with which AI technologies continue to develop means that there is always a race against time to put in place regulations governing emerging AI technology if any meaningful regulation is to take place. For example, generative AI raises ethical concern related to misinformation, use of intellectual property, and misuse. Keeping a check on the bad practices by regulators proves to be a daunting task. There is space for such an adaptive and flexible regulatory approach that can match well with technological advancements.

The black box nature of AI systems brings unique regulatory challenges. Many AI algorithms, especially deep learning algorithms, work as black boxes in which even their own developers cannot unscramble the decision-making process (Adadi & Berrada, 2018). This opacity makes it difficult to know whether a given decision of an AI system has biases, is mistaken, or constitutes an ethical breach, thus making convicting even developers/heralds difficult. Hence, transparency and explainability are very important elements of AI regulation. Enforcing these principles requires good technical know-how and often cooperative processes on the part of regulators and AI developers.

Conflicting stakeholder interests further complicate AI regulation (Du & Xie, 2021). On one side, developers and businesses prioritize innovation, market competitiveness and efficiency. On the other, policymakers, civil society and end-users demand safeguards to address ethical concerns, privacy and security risks. These conflicting priorities often result in debates over the extent and nature of regulation.Whereas firms may resist stringent requirements that could reduce or stifle innovation, policymakers perceive this as an urgent requirement to protect public interests. Bridging two diverging paradigms requires discourse, collaboration and mechanisms to balance innovation with accountability.

The other crucial obstacles concerning the application of AI possible limits arise from data privacy and security issues (Ali, 2024; Saura et al., 2023; Williamson & Prybutok, 2024). AI systems are dependent on very large amounts of data to do their jobs; it raises questions about how this data is collected, shared, or utilized. Privacy regulations such as the EU's General Data Protection Regulation are intended to address these issues but have problems with enforcement and scaling. Deployments of such emerging technologies, like facial recognition and predictive analytics, heighten such challenges: their implementation involves sensitive personal information. Regulatory design must ensure a balance between compliance and creation toward a free development of AI.

A further critical challenge stems from the global character of AI development and deployment. AI is uniquely positioned as being a technology that operates without the limits of land borders or countries, affecting more than one jurisdiction

(AllahRakha, 2024; Lee, 2022). This sets the stage for questions regarding the development of coherent regulatory standards and, based on those standards, mechanisms of enforcement. An AI system designed in one jurisdiction, for example, might be operating in another jurisdiction with disparate underlying legal and ethical norms. These cross-border dynamics mean that international cooperation is required to frame a consensus response to shared challenges while supporting regional contexts. However, achieving such collaboration is difficult due to geopolitical tensions, economic disparities and differing priorities among nations.

The risk of regulatory overreach or underreach further complicates AI governance. Excessive regulation might impede innovation, drive away investment and slow down technological progress. Whereas a policy environment easily bereft of clarity will give way for unchecked deployment of AI systems posing risks for people and societies alike. Both creating such a helpful environment form a constant round of back-and-forth between two extremes. Risk-based approaches, wherein the regulatory scrutiny applies in proportion to the potential impact brought about by AI applications, is promising but may prove quite challenging in implementation and will have to rely upon continuous assessment.

Therefore, the uneven distribution of the positive and negative repercussions profanes the moral bearings of regulation. If you see, most of the sophisticated AI systems are bound to be used only in technologically advanced areas, leaving of resources constrained areas devoid of these multitudes of buoyant developments. As such, marginalized communities disproportionately face the brunt of biased or injurious AI applications. Some predictive-policing algorithms, for their part, have been said to work unfairly against minorities, thus incurring deep systemic biases in their designs. To rectify the imbalances, regulation ought to think along the lines of inclusivity, fairness and equitable opportunity to AI technologies.

They say these are challenges in respect of enforcement of AI regulation. In providing these statutory tenets, monitoring and complying become ardent and resource-consuming missions with great technical demands. The behavioral changes and/or evolution of AI owing to machine learning contribute yet another layer of difficulty to enforcement. Regulators oftentimes do lack the required expertise, tools or resources to expound on the greater technicalities of AI, forming yet another gap for neglecting enforcement and naturally causing an element through such shortcomings that violate the efficient execution of existent frameworks.

Lastly, ethical dilemmas in AI governance provide a philosophical twist to the concerns of regulatory challenges. The questions about the moral responsibilities of AI systems, the prioritization of competing values-the juxtaposition of privacy over security-and acceptable limits to AI autonomy remain both an insignia of wisdom gone unproven. These unsolved dilemmas continue complicating the establishment of universally applicable ethical standards and still plead with stakeholder groups for continuous discourses aimed at adapting the regulations to an ever-evolving set of social norms and expectations.

TOWARD HARMONIZED GLOBAL AI GOVERNANCE

The global influence of AI demands regulatory approaches which transcend all borders. Although various nations have AI regulations articulated to their peculiar needs, the very nature of AI development, deployment and implications require harmonized frameworks that govern AI at a global scale. These frameworks ought to attend to such shared challenges, to provide for equitable access to the benefits of AI, to mitigate risks, and to accommodate, where necessary, regional or cultural diversity.

The cross-nationality of those developing and deploying AI is a great motivation for harmonized governance (de Almeida et al., 2021; Emery-Xu et al., 2024; Taeihagh, 2021). Oftentimes, the development of AI technologies occurs in one region, while deployment in another region occurs and usage follows in systems that impact individuals worldwide. For example, the use of AI-algorithm-based social media platforms cross the borders that determine, for good or for bad, public discourse, privacy, and security worldwide. Other supply chains, autonomous vehicles, and healthcare solutions are often driven by AI and also involve multinational stakeholders. In this case, inconsistent regulation correlates with fragmented governance, compliance challenges, and ethical differences. Harmonization would converge around common standards allowing innovation and addressing ethical, legal, and societal issues. This relies on international collaboration to address transnational AI issues. The matters of data privacy, cybersecurity, and algorithmic accountability frequently cut across multiple jurisdictions and require a unified response. Thus, in order to safeguard the privacy of the users of AI systems around the world, it has to agree on many standards on digital data sharing, storage, and use (Kseng, 2024; Menzies et al., 2024). The EU's GDPR is one of the leading influences on data privacy regulation in national law around the world and an expression of how regional regulations can drive efforts to put in place norms that balance compelling conflicting regional issues requiring international regulatory regimes. However, achieving true harmonization requires greater collaboration among nations, particularly in addressing disparities between technologically advanced and developing regions.

The role of international institutions in AI governance is critical for fostering cooperation and setting global standards. Organizations such as the United Nations (UN), the Organisation for Economic Co-operation and Development (OECD) and UNESCO have initiated efforts to develop ethical guidelines and policy recommendations for AI. For example, UNESCO's Recommendation on the Ethics of

Artificial Intelligence emphasizes principles such as inclusivity, transparency and sustainability (Menzies et al., 2024; Morandín-Ahuerma, 2023; van Norren, 2023). The OECD's AI Principles, endorsed by numerous countries, outline policies for trustworthy AI and promote human-centric and accountable development (Yeung, 2020). These initiatives highlight the potential of international institutions to align diverse stakeholders and establish common ground.

Despite these efforts, significant challenges to harmonized governance remain. Geopolitical tensions, economic competition and differing cultural values complicate consensus-building. Nations with advanced AI capabilities may prioritize innovation and economic leadership, while others emphasize ethical considerations or equitable access to technology. For example, debates over facial recognition technology reveal varying approaches: some countries prioritize its use for security, while others focus on its potential for mass surveillance and privacy violations. Bridging these differences requires open dialogue, trust-building and mechanisms for resolving disputes.

Practical steps toward harmonized AI governance involve a combination of standardization, capacity-building and collaborative policymaking. Standardization can establish shared technical and ethical benchmarks, such as common definitions for algorithmic fairness, data privacy and accountability. International standards bodies, such as the International Organization for Standardization (ISO), can play a pivotal role in developing these benchmarks (Benraouane, 2024).

Many countries lack the resources, expertise, or infrastructure needed to engage effectively in global AI discussions. International partnerships can address these disparities by providing technical assistance, funding and knowledge-sharing initiatives. For example, initiatives like the Global Partnership on AI (GPAI) bring together governments, industry leaders and academics to foster international collaboration and share best practices.

Collaborative policymaking involves creating platforms for multilateral dialogue and negotiation. Forums such as the World Economic Forum (WEF) and the United Nations High-Level Panel on Digital Cooperation provide spaces for stakeholders to discuss and align on key issues. These platforms can facilitate agreements on critical governance aspects, such as cross-border data flows, ethical AI principles and mechanisms for addressing global challenges like climate change through AI.

Inclusivity and equity must form the foundation of global AI governance efforts. It is significant to ensure representation from less developed regions of the world with equal and active engagement from communities that have been marginalized in the decision-making processes. Such representation is more enabled if deliberate efforts are made to incorporate a diverse range of stakeholders such as governments and private-sector entities to civil societies and to academics. In this context, citizen panels and public consultations are other participatory mechanisms that can help to ground the governance frameworks in the values and priorities of the global populace.

One emerging concept on global AI governance is the establishment of a transnational AI regulatory body modeled upon IAEA for nuclear energy. Such an organization could oversee compliance with international AI standards, facilitate dispute resolution and provide technical expertise to support member states.

In addition to governance mechanisms, ethical guidelines should guide cooperative action. At the very least, human-centered design, fairness, transparency, and sustainability should be the foundation upon which the global AI governance hinges. These principles could be operationalized through ethical impact assessment, monitoring frameworks, and enforcement mechanisms to ensure conformity to common standards. For example, AI systems in health care could undergo international audits for their safety, effectiveness and ethical alignment.

The success of harmonized AI governance ultimately depends on the commitment of stakeholders to prioritize global cooperation over individual interests. Nations, corporations and organizations must recognize the shared risks and opportunities posed by AI and work collaboratively to address them. The potential benefits of harmonized governance include reduced regulatory fragmentation, enhanced public trust and the equitable distribution of AI's benefits across societies.

POLICY RECOMMENDATIONS

Effective policy recommendations are crucial for ensuring that AI contributes to societal progress while minimizing its risks. These policies must balance innovation with ethical governance to provide a foundation for responsible AI development and deployment. The following recommendations focus on fostering transparency, accountability, inclusivity and adaptability in AI governance and ensure that AI technologies align with societal values and address global challenges (See Table 4).

Table 4. Recommendations for ethical AI governance: Objectives, strategies, and expected outcomes

Recommendation	Objective	Implementation Strategy	Expected Outcomes
Adopt Risk-Based Regulation	Align regulatory oversight with the potential risks of AI systems	Implement tiered frameworks where high-risk applications face stringent requirements	Balanced innovation and risk mitigation; enhanced safety and trust in high-risk applications.
Enhance Transparency	Build trust and ensure accountability	Mandate explainable AI, public documentation and independent audits	Improved public understanding of AI systems; greater accountability for stakeholders.
Strengthen Accountability	Ensure responsibility for AI outcomes	Develop clear liability frameworks; establish independent oversight bodies	Increased organizational responsibility; more robust mechanisms to address grievances.
Promote International Collaboration	Harmonize global standards and address cross-border challenges	Foster partnerships through multilateral agreements and global institutions	Consistent governance across jurisdictions; better handling of global AI challenges.
Invest in Capacity-Building	Empower all stakeholders to engage with AI responsibly	Provide funding for education, training and infrastructure development	Reduced global disparities in AI access; informed and capable workforce and policymakers.

Source: By authors

The recommendation is to embrace risk-based regulatory policies whereby the oversight of such systems reflects the impact of AI. Not all annoyingly technical and fancy applications are necessarily equal in risk; the regulations should reflect this variability. High-risk applications should be geared toward areas like healthcare, law enforcement, or financial decision-making, while low-risk applications should impose the least regulation; for instance, customer service chatbots. Consequently, a balanced, tiered approach to regulation could protect societies' needs while developing technological aspects.

Transparency and explainability must be prioritized in AI governance. Policies should require organizations to disclose information about how AI systems function, the data used in their development and the rationale behind their decisions. This transparency is essential for building public trust and enabling independent audits. Explainability ensures that AI systems are interpretable by users and stakeholders, particularly in high-stakes scenarios such as hiring or medical diagnoses. Policymakers can promote transparency through mandatory documentation, algorithmic audits and the establishment of standards for interpretable AI design.

One of the main policy issues in AI regulation is the establishment of accountability mechanisms. Organizations that implement AI systems should be answerable for the consequences that they, particularly when their consequences can affect people or communities. Policymakers should make sure there is a clear accountability framework in place for determining ultimately who is liable for any mistakes, bias, or harm caused by AI systems. These frameworks can and should establish penalties for violations and give incentives for promoting good practices, and include requirements for logging activity to support accountability. Given the rapid pace of change in AI and continuing public concern about its impact, independent oversight authorities may also be developed for monitoring AI deployments.

To protect data governance and privacy, all of these obligatory policies will have to be developed in the AI Age. Policies should have strict regulations concerning data collection, preservation, and use to protect rights and prevent abuse of it. Such policies will need to demand informed express consent for collection purposes, instilling data minimization, and imposing strong, reliable security measures to avoid breaches. Privacy regulations like the European Union's GDPR provide a strong foundation for safeguarding personal information and similar frameworks could be adapted globally. Policymakers must also address challenges associated with cross-border data flows to ensure that data privacy standards are upheld in international contexts.

Creating and implementing inclusive equitable AI is imperative in establishing an equilibrium within an imbalanced society. Policymakers should advocate for diverse perspectives by encouraging the use of diverse and representative datasets to mitigate possible bias in the AI systems. Companies and organizations that significantly impact on an individual or group should be subjected to fairness audits and impact assessments. Furthermore, governments and organizations need to fund initiatives intended to democratize access to the tools under consideration to ensure that unrepresented regions and communities can benefit from the impact of AI. This means financing education and infrastructure development and empowerment-building programs that will enable marginalized people to engage with AI.

There should be a concerted push for international cooperation to address the common nature of the various AI challenges. In promoting dumbed-down common governance, the main focus of policymakers will be to contribute to multilateral agreements and initiatives. Meanwhile, there will be a need for knowledge-sharing and coordinated policy development via the Global Partnership on AI or via the AI ethics initiatives by UNESCO. International cooperation may in turn ensure that such problems as data governance across borders, threats of cyber security, and the ethical implications posed by AI research and deployment are also addressed.

Encouraging stakeholder engagement is another telling recommendation: Policy-makers should consider a diverse range of stakeholder entities such as technologists, civil society organizations, the academic community, and the general public within AI governance processes. Participatory methods, such as public consultation, citizen panels, and multi-stakeholder forums, assure policy consistency with important societal values as well as consideration for all stakeholders' interests. On the other hand, different and contrasting opinions generate public confidence and legitimacy for the AI governance frameworks. Education and capacity building remain paramount in sharpening the aptitude and capability of opinion leaders, developers and end-users for interacting with the special and complex effects of AI machinery. This will need that the policymakers consider supporting initiatives in which the curriculum for technologists incorporates ethical, governing and technical training. Public awareness campaigns can lead to people making informed decisions in their use of AI and convictions for responsible governance. Beyond that, they offered by governments support funding programs to stimulate the advancement of research into ethical AI that is driven by sound evidence and analysis to retain robust decision-making.

Policies can support the development of ethical impact assessments as standard practice in AI governance, in which such evaluations identify potential risks and propose possible mitigations for AI systems even prior to deployment, just as they do for environmental impact assessments. This may call upon organizations to conduct assessments for high-impact AI applications to ensure ethical considerations in their decision-making processes. Such ethical impact assessments also permit for a continuous cycle of monitoring and evaluation to facilitate adaptive governance in response to emerging challenges.

Hence, adaptive governance and flexible governance come into play in any resolution process where it touches on policy action among the diverse actors that develop structural means-through cooperation- to respond to such fast-changing developments in AI technology. Static regulations stand to be rendered ineffective on a momentous occasion or another: either they wear out due to repeated implementations or suppress innovation as a whole. Some frameworks are dynamic and allow once-in-a-while reviews, lightly-produce pilot implementations, and reformist processes that ensure effective governance is involved. For example, regulatory sandboxes—controlled environments to test AI applications under supervision of relevant authorities—are very convenient mechanisms to balance innovation with compliance.

FUTURE DIRECTIONS

The rapid evolution of AI presents both opportunities and challenges that necessitate forward-looking approaches in policy, governance and technological development. Future directions for AI governance must address emerging trends, adapt to technological advancements and ensure that AI benefits are distributed equitably and responsibly. By focusing on innovation, inclusivity and sustainability, stakeholders can create a robust framework for managing AI's transformative potential while mitigating associated risks

One critical area for future exploration is the development of dynamic governance models. AI technologies evolve rapidly, often outpacing the ability of regulatory frameworks to adapt. Static regulations may become obsolete that leads to gaps in oversight or restrictions on innovation. Future governance must embrace flexibility for allowing for continuous updates to policies based on technological advancements and societal needs. Mechanisms such as iterative policymaking, regulatory sandboxes and ongoing impact assessments can provide the adaptability needed to keep pace with AI's development. These approaches ensure that governance remains relevant and effective in addressing both current and emerging challenges.

Another key direction involves advancing AI's role in addressing global challenges. AI has the potential to contribute significantly to sustainable development, healthcare, climate change mitigation and disaster management. For example, AI-powered systems can optimize renewable energy grids, predict disease outbreaks and enhance disaster response efforts. Policymakers and stakeholders must prioritize investments in AI applications that address these critical issues. It is important for them to ensure that their development aligns with ethical principles and sustainability goals.

The future of AI governance calls for a renewed commitment to international cooperation. AI technologies cross national boundaries, and global collaboration must take place in order to address common risks and opportunities. Work to harmonize AI standards and frameworks must continue with an emphasis on developing inclusive and equitable governance structures. Institutions such as the United Nations, UNESCO and the Global Partnership on AI can play a central role in facilitating dialogue to establish benchmarks and ensuring that diverse perspectives are represented. Enhanced collaboration will also help address disparities in AI access and capabilities to promote a more balanced distribution of benefits.

Providing ethical AI research and development becomes an important practice as AI technologies enter into people's daily lives. Common practices among developers and researchers should involve the creation of systems with transparency, fairness, and accountability as critical aspects. The proposed solutions must thus tackle the issues inclusive of algorithmic bias, explainability, and protection of privacy. In the future, it could be attempted that some form of self-regulating AI could be built. Building up AI competences will foster public confidence in AI as well as ensure alignment with societal values.

The incorporation of AI education and literacy into the wider social structures is equally paramount. Since AI systems have already been incorporated into society on a whole other level in terms of capabilities, it is important for humankind to be knowledgeable about and capable of understanding the technologies. Such educational initiatives should target policymakers, developers, and the broader population in training sessions on AI ethics, governance, and technical foundations. Expanding access to AI education in underrepresented regions will help reduce global inequalities and ensure that diverse communities can contribute to and benefit from AI advancements.

Inclusivity in AI governance and development will be critical to ensuring that AI technologies address the needs of all societal groups. It is vital that efforts are made to include in the governance process the underrepresented communities, which may be from developing countries, disempowered sections, or vulnerable groups. This entails integrating their perspectives within the dialogue concerning any policy that provides resources for local innovation and ensures the AI systems are designed to serve diverse populations. Fairness and increased innovation through broadening thoughts and experiences would follow with inclusion.

Another extremely exciting area for future research will be how AI and other technologies might integrate to present new opportunities. Quantum computing, blockchain, and IoT provide opportunities for considerable enhancement to AI and potentially for expanding the domains they apply to. Some examples of such enhancements include advantages like speedy processing of AI algorithms through quantum computing and enhancements in data transparency and security in AI systems through blockchain. Policymakers and researchers will have to explore these synergies, though managing them for mitigating risks while exercising their opportunities for societal advantages.

Regulating autonomous systems will also become increasingly important as AI technologies gain more autonomy in decision-making. Autonomous vehicles, drones and robotic systems are already challenging traditional regulatory frameworks. Future governance must address ethical dilemmas associated with these systems, such as liability in accidents, moral decision-making algorithms and the implications of fully autonomous operations. Developing clear, globally harmonized policies for autonomous systems will be essential to ensuring their safe and ethical deployment.

Finally, the long-term societal impact of AI must be a central focus of future governance. Policymakers, researchers and stakeholders must anticipate how AI will reshape industries, labour markets and social structures. Strategies for managing workforce transitions, such as reskilling programs and social safety nets, will be crucial in mitigating the disruptive effects of AI-driven automation. Additionally, ongoing dialogue about the ethical implications of AI's role in shaping human experiences, values and relationships will help ensure that its development aligns with long-term societal goals.

CONCLUSION

One of the most difficult problems and an opportunity for the current age lies within the governance of AI. With AI improving its competency, there needs to be a balance between its transformative capabilities on the one hand and ethical and societal considerations. This chapter has emphasized the importance of aligning innovation with strong regulation frameworks underpinned with principles such as transparency, accountability, inclusiveness and fairness. The world cases, ethical principles and policy recommendations have shown that only a cooperative, flexible and globally harmonized approach can help manage the complexity of AI.

The future of the governance of AI will involve international cooperation, education, and capacity-building of all actors to include marginalized groups. These strategies will ensure responsible development of AI, realizing equitable benefits with limited risk. Balancing these will be critical for AI to play its positive role in global progress and human well-being.

REFERENCES

Adadi, A., & Berrada, M. (2018). Peeking inside the black-box: A survey on explainable artificial intelligence (XAI). *IEEE Access : Practical Innovations, Open Solutions*, *6*, 52138–52160. DOI: 10.1109/ACCESS.2018.2870052

AllahRakha, N. (2024). Rethinking digital borders to address jurisdiction and governance in the global digital economy. *International Journal of Law and Policy*, *2*(1).

Benraouane, S. A. (2024). *AI Management System Certification According to the ISO/IEC 42001 Standard: How to Audit, Certify, and Build Responsible AI Systems*. CRC Press. DOI: 10.4324/9781003463979

Binns, R. (2018). Algorithmic accountability and public reason. *Philosophy & Technology*, *31*(4), 543–556. DOI: 10.1007/s13347-017-0263-5 PMID: 30873342

Boyd, R., & Holton, R. J. (2018). Technology, innovation, employment and power: Does robotics and artificial intelligence really mean social transformation? *Journal of Sociology (Melbourne, Vic.)*, *54*(3), 331–345. DOI: 10.1177/1440783317726591

Brantingham, P. J., Valasik, M., & Mohler, G. O. (2018). Does predictive policing lead to biased arrests? Results from a randomized controlled trial. *Statistics and Public Policy (Philadelphia, Pa.)*, *5*(1), 1–6. DOI: 10.1080/2330443X.2018.1438940

Castonguay, A., Wagner, G., Motulsky, A., & Paré, G. (2024). AI maturity in health care: An overview of 10 OECD countries. *Health Policy (Amsterdam)*, *140*, 104938. DOI: 10.1016/j.healthpol.2023.104938 PMID: 38157771

Crayton, T. J., & Meier, B. M. (2017). Autonomous vehicles: Developing a public health research agenda to frame the future of transportation policy. *Journal of Transport & Health*, *6*, 245–252. DOI: 10.1016/j.jth.2017.04.004

de Almeida, P. G. R., dos Santos, C. D., & Farias, J. S. (2021). Artificial intelligence regulation: A framework for governance. *Ethics and Information Technology*, *23*(3), 505–525. DOI: 10.1007/s10676-021-09593-z

Demir, S., & Paksoy, T. (2020). Ai, robotics and autonomous systems in scm. *Logistics (Basel)*, *4*, 156.

Du, S., & Xie, C. (2021). Paradoxes of artificial intelligence in consumer markets: Ethical challenges and opportunities. *Journal of Business Research*, *129*, 961–974. DOI: 10.1016/j.jbusres.2020.08.024

Emery-Xu, N., Jordan, R., & Trager, R. (2024). International governance of advancing artificial intelligence. *AI & Society*, •••, 1–26.

Felzmann, H., Fosch-Villaronga, E., Lutz, C., & Tamò-Larrieux, A. (2020). Towards transparency by design for artificial intelligence. *Science and Engineering Ethics*, *26*(6), 3333–3361. DOI: 10.1007/s11948-020-00276-4 PMID: 33196975

Goode, K., Kim, H. M., & Deng, M. (2023). Examining Singapore's AI progress. *Center for Security and Emerging Technology, 19.*

Habbal, A., Ali, M. K., & Abuzaraida, M. A. (2024). Artificial Intelligence Trust, risk and security management (AI trism): Frameworks, applications, challenges and future research directions. *Expert Systems with Applications*, *240*, 122442. DOI: 10.1016/j.eswa.2023.122442

Hosseinian, S. M., & Mirzahossein, H. (2024). Efficiency and safety of traffic networks under the effect of autonomous vehicles. *Civil Engineering (Shiraz)*, *48*(4), 1861–1885. DOI: 10.1007/s40996-023-01291-8

Jarrahi, M. H. (2018). Artificial intelligence and the future of work: Human-AI symbiosis in organizational decision making. *Business Horizons*, *61*(4), 577–586. DOI: 10.1016/j.bushor.2018.03.007

Jedličková, A. (2024). Ethical approaches in designing autonomous and intelligent systems: A comprehensive survey towards responsible development. *AI & Society*, •••, 1–14.

Jobin, A., Ienca, M., & Vayena, E. (2019). The global landscape of AI ethics guidelines. *Nature Machine Intelligence*, *1*(9), 389–399. DOI: 10.1038/s42256-019-0088-2

Kseng, S. (2024). International Collaboration in AI Research and Development. *International IT Journal of Research*, *2*(1), 1–7.

Kumar, D., Dhalwal, R., & Chaudhary, A. (2024). Exploring the Ethical Implications of Generative AI in Healthcare. In *The Ethical Frontier of AI and Data Analysis* (pp. 180–195). IGI Global. DOI: 10.4018/979-8-3693-2964-1.ch011

Kumar, D., Kumar, S., & Joshi, A. (2023). Assessing the viability of blockchain technology for enhancing court operations. *International Journal of Law and Management*, *65*(5), 425–439. DOI: 10.1108/IJLMA-03-2023-0046

Kumar, D., & Suthar, N. (2024). Ethical and legal challenges of AI in marketing: An exploration of solutions. *Journal of Information. Communication and Ethics in Society*, *22*(1), 124–144. DOI: 10.1108/JICES-05-2023-0068

Kumar, D., & Suthar, N. (2025a). AI-Enabled Humanoid Devices Bridging Personalized Learning and Inclusive Education for Cyber Nomads. In *Educational AI Humanoid Computing Devices for Cyber Nomads* (pp. 41–72). IGI Global Scientific Publishing. DOI: 10.4018/979-8-3693-8985-0.ch003

Kumar, D., & Suthar, N. (2025b). Assessing the prospects and constraints of blockchain technology for intellectual property management. *The Journal of World Intellectual Property*, *28*(1), 124–140. DOI: 10.1111/jwip.12324

Lahusen, C., Maggetti, M., & Slavkovik, M. (2024). Trust, trustworthiness and AI governance. *Scientific Reports*, *14*(1), 20752. DOI: 10.1038/s41598-024-71761-0 PMID: 39237635

Lai, X., & Rau, P. L. P. (2021). Has facial recognition technology been misused? A public perception model of facial recognition scenarios. *Computers in Human Behavior*, *124*, 106894. DOI: 10.1016/j.chb.2021.106894

Lee, J. (2022). *Artificial intelligence and international law*. Springer. DOI: 10.1007/978-981-19-1496-6

Madancian, M., Taherdoost, H., Javadi, M., Khan, I. U., Kalantari, A., & Kumar, D. (2023, November). The Impact of Artificial Intelligence on Supply Chain Management in Modern Business. In *The International Conference on Artificial Intelligence and Smart Environment* (pp. 566-573). Cham: Springer Nature Switzerland.

Malik, A., Srikanth, N. R., & Budhwar, P. (2020). Digitisation, artificial intelligence (AI) and HRM. *Human resource management: Strategic and international perspectives, 88*, 103.

Menzies, J., Sabert, B., Hassan, R., & Mensah, P. K. (2024). Artificial intelligence for international business: Its use, challenges, and suggestions for future research and practice. *Thunderbird International Business Review*, *66*(2), 185–200. DOI: 10.1002/tie.22370

Morandín-Ahuerma, F. (2023). Ten UNESCO Recommendations on the Ethics of Artificial Intelligence.

Muralidharan, V., Adewale, B. A., Huang, C. J., Nta, M. T., Ademiju, P. O., Pathmarajah, P., & Olatunji, T. (2024). A scoping review of reporting gaps in FDA-approved AI medical devices. *npj. Digital Medicine*, *7*(1), 273. PMID: 39362934

Nikolinakos, N. T. (2023). The European Parliament's 2020 Resolution: Proposal for a Regulation on Ethical Principles for the Development, Deployment and Use of Artificial Intelligence, Robotics and Related Technologies. In *EU Policy and Legal Framework for Artificial Intelligence, Robotics and Related Technologies-The AI Act* (pp. 281–306). Springer International Publishing. DOI: 10.1007/978-3-031-27953-9_6

O'Sullivan, S., Nevejans, N., Allen, C., Blyth, A., Leonard, S., Pagallo, U., Holzinger, K., Holzinger, A., Sajid, M. I., & Ashrafian, H. (2019). Legal, regulatory, and ethical frameworks for development of standards in artificial intelligence (AI) and autonomous robotic surgery. *International Journal of Medical Robotics and Computer Assisted Surgery*, *15*(1), e1968. DOI: 10.1002/rcs.1968 PMID: 30397993

Okunlaya, R. O., Syed Abdullah, N., & Alias, R. A. (2022). Artificial intelligence (AI) library services innovative conceptual framework for the digital transformation of university education. *Library Hi Tech*, *40*(6), 1869–1892. DOI: 10.1108/LHT-07-2021-0242

Pan, Y., & Froese, F. J. (2023). An interdisciplinary review of AI and HRM: Challenges and future directions. *Human Resource Management Review*, *33*(1), 100924. DOI: 10.1016/j.hrmr.2022.100924

Rong, G., Mendez, A., Assi, E. B., Zhao, B., & Sawan, M. (2020). Artificial intelligence in healthcare: Review and prediction case studies. *Engineering (Beijing)*, *6*(3), 291–301. DOI: 10.1016/j.eng.2019.08.015

Samara, F. Y. A., Taha, A. H. A., Massa, N. M., Jamie, T. N. A., Harara, F. E., Abu-Nasser, B. S., & Abu-Naser, S. S. (2024). The Role of AI in Enhancing Business Decision-Making: Innovations and Implications.

Sarabdeen, J. (2022). Protection of the rights of the individual when using facial recognition technology. *Heliyon*, *8*(3), e09086. DOI: 10.1016/j.heliyon.2022.e09086 PMID: 35309394

Saura, J. R., Ribeiro-Soriano, D., & Palacios-Marqués, D. (2022). Assessing behavioral data science privacy issues in government artificial intelligence deployment. *Government Information Quarterly*, *39*(4), 101679. DOI: 10.1016/j.giq.2022.101679

Scherer, M. U. (2015). Regulating artificial intelligence systems: Risks, challenges, competencies, and strategies. *SSRN*, *29*, 353. DOI: 10.2139/ssrn.2609777

Smith, M., & Miller, S. (2022). The ethical application of biometric facial recognition technology. *AI & Society*, *37*(1), 167–175. DOI: 10.1007/s00146-021-01199-9 PMID: 33867693

Smuha, N. A. (2021). From a ‘race to AI’to a ’race to AI regulation’: Regulatory competition for artificial intelligence. *Law, Innovation and Technology, 13*(1), 57–84. DOI: 10.1080/17579961.2021.1898300

Svantesson, D. (2022). The European Union artificial intelligence act: Potential implications for Australia. *Alternative Law Journal, 47*(1), 4–9. DOI: 10.1177/1037969X211052339

Taeihagh, A. (2021). Governance of artificial intelligence. *Policy and Society, 40*(2), 137–157. DOI: 10.1080/14494035.2021.1928377

Taherdoost, H., Drazenovic, G., Farhaoui, Y., Madanchian, M., Mohamed, N., & Kumar, D. (2025). Navigating the AI Era in Startup Business Development. In *Future Tech Startups and Innovation in the Age of AI* (pp. 191–208). CRC Press.

van Norren, D. E. (2023). The ethics of artificial intelligence, UNESCO and the African Ubuntu perspective. *Journal of Information. Communication and Ethics in Society, 21*(1), 112–128. DOI: 10.1108/JICES-04-2022-0037

Wachter, S., Mittelstadt, B., & Russell, C. (2021). Why fairness cannot be automated: Bridging the gap between EU non-discrimination law and AI. *Computer Law & Security Review, 41*, 105567. DOI: 10.1016/j.clsr.2021.105567

Whittaker, M., Crawford, K., Dobbe, R., Fried, G., Kaziunas, E., Mathur, V., & Schwartz, O. (2018). *AI now report 2018*. AI Now Institute at New York University.

Williamson, S. M., & Prybutok, V. (2024). Balancing privacy and progress: A review of privacy challenges, systemic oversight, and patient perceptions in AI-driven healthcare. *Applied Sciences (Basel, Switzerland), 14*(2), 675. DOI: 10.3390/app14020675

Yeung, K. (2020). Recommendation of the council on artificial intelligence (OECD). *International legal materials, 59*(1), 27-34.

Chapter 8
Navigating AI Governance:
National and International Legal and Regulatory Frameworks

Baidya Nath Mukherjee
https://orcid.org/0000-0002-1165-3432
AURO University, India

ABSTRACT

The rapid growth of Artificial Intelligence (AI) has driven global discussions on regulatory frameworks to ensure ethical and responsible use. Nationally, AI governance varies: the European Union's AI Act prioritizes transparency and accountability, while the United States adopts a sector-specific approach balancing innovation and risk management. Internationally, organizations like the United Nations, OECD, and GPAI aim to harmonize AI governance, addressing risks such as bias, privacy violations, and misuse while fostering global collaboration. This article examines these regulatory strategies, highlighting convergence and divergence across jurisdictions. It underscores the need for a balanced approach that promotes AI innovation while safeguarding ethical standards and public interest. Ultimately, it advocates for a collaborative global effort to develop adaptable regulatory strategies that evolve with AI technologies, ensuring responsible and effective governance.

INTRODUCTION

Since Alan Turing sowed the seed of AI, it has continued to evolve, especially with the advent of Generative AI. AI significantly impacts millions of lives and businesses globally and potentially brings about a paradigm shift and transformation.

DOI: 10.4018/979-8-3373-1210-1.ch008

Due to its rapid pace and transformative potential, AI poses unprecedented challenges to the community. Given the uncertainties and the competitive race among nations to lead in AI development, a flexible and cohesive approach is required to address these challenges. The rapid growth of AI its decision-making capabilities and the significant impact of its outcomes demands regulations grounded in human oversight, understanding, and ethical reasoning. The goal is to build trust and ensure that AI systems align with human values. Its unpredictable and uncontrollable progress and potential risk necessitate a legal framework. Identified risks include AI systems influencing human behaviour, exploiting vulnerabilities, and assessing citizens' trustworthiness. As regulations are crucial to mitigate risk, they should not be aimed at stifling innovation or technological progress. Effective governance should balance promoting development with addressing ethical, societal, and safety concerns. While national and local regulations focus on developing domestic AI industries and addressing localized ethical and societal challenges, they may not adequately handle cross-border issues. Therefore, a global framework is required to address transnational challenges, providing model laws and fostering harmonisation across nations. Despite this clear need, nations often hesitate to commit to universal rules and institutions due to concerns about sovereignty and the prioritization of local interests. However, a harmonized regime built on collaborative international efforts could serve as a vital step toward creating consistent, effective, and fair AI governance worldwide (Sourdin, 2023).

The advancement in AI has prompted significant investments by nations and corporations worldwide. While these investments drive innovation and economic growth, they also highlight a stark disparity between developed nations and developing or least developed countries. The latter may find themselves excluded from the benefits of AI development due to their limited technological capacities and infrastructure, further exacerbating existing inequalities. For nations with robust AI ecosystem, this technology is often perceived as a state-controlled resource critical to national security and economic dominance. Conversely, countries with restrictive AI development capabilities may advocate for a global perspective, proposing that AI be treated as a "common heritage of mankind". This ideological divide underscores the challenges in crafting a unified regulatory framework for AI internationally. The regulatory landscape is further complicated by competing priorities. On one side, nations and entities driven by economic and technological ambitions may resist stringent regulations, arguing that such measures could stifle innovation and competitiveness. On the other side, stakeholders emphasizing ethical considerations, human rights, and equitable development may call for a cautious and principled approach to regulation.

To address these challenges, a coordinated global effort is essential. Establishing an international AI regulatory authority could provide the platform needed to tackle the multifaceted issues emerging in this domain. Such an authority would be tasked with anticipating and responding to the rapidly evolving technological landscape, balancing the interests of diverse stakeholders, and fostering an equitable distribution of AI's benefits.

THE RISE OF AI AND THE IMPERATIVE FOR GOVERNANCE

The rise of Artificial Intelligence heralds a transformative era, akin to the advent of electricity, reshaping industries, economies, and societal landscapes. AI's capabilities promise immense benefits, from enhancing healthcare diagnostics to driving autonomous vehicles. However, its rapid development also raises significant concerns. The extent and severity of these concerns largely depend on the level of AI development and the degree of human oversight in its deployment(Turchin & Denkenberger, 2020). One of the most instant concerns surrounding AI is its potential to disrupt labour markets and contribute to social instability. AI-driven automation threatens job security across multiple industries including healthcare, finance, entertainment, and manufacturing. Widespread job loss may lead to economic disparities, heightened unemployment rates, and an increase in social unrest. Additionally, AI's role in decision-making processes raises concerns regarding fairness, accountability, and transparency. Algorithmic bias embedded in AI systems can lead to discrimination and reinforce existing inequalities(Marr, 2023). AI's increasing application in defense and security sectors raises significant concerns about global stability. Autonomous weapons and AI-powered military systems could be deployed in conflict zones, potentially escalating warfare and reducing human oversight in critical decision-making. Moreover, AI-driven cyber threats pose a risk to national and international security. Governments and organizations face an increasing threat of cyberattacks, ransomware, and biohacking viruses, which could compromise critical infrastructure, including power grids, food supply chains, and transportation networks(Ovink, 2024). AI-powered surveillance technologies present additional risks, as governments may exploit them for mass surveillance, eroding privacy rights and enabling authoritarian control over populations. The possibility of AI being used for state-sponsored cyber warfare or for launching sophisticated cyberattacks on financial institutions, government databases, and public services further highlights the urgency of establishing international safeguards.

Beyond immediate security risks, AI presents deeper existential concerns related to human agency and control over technology. There are fears that unchecked AI development could lead to dangerous scientific advancements, brain modification technologies, and even the emergence of a transnational totalitarian AI system. Moreover, the manipulation of information through AI-generated misinformation and deepfakes threatens democratic processes and societal trust. AI-powered propaganda tools have the potential to influence public opinion, exacerbate political polarization, and undermine the credibility of institutions. Without stringent regulatory measures, the unchecked spread of AI-generated disinformation could destabilize global governance structures.

AI's role in military advancements has intensified geopolitical tensions, with nations engaging in an AI arms race to develop superior autonomous weaponry. The deployment of AI-driven warfare technology raises concerns about unintended conflicts and escalation, as machines take on roles traditionally reserved for human decision-makers. Additionally, the risk of AI-controlled systems being hacked or manipulated by hostile entities could have catastrophic consequences, including large-scale destruction of infrastructure and loss of life(Turchin & Denkenberger, 2020).

Given the profound risks associated with AI, it is imperative to establish comprehensive international regulations that ensure responsible AI development and deployment. A coordinated global response is necessary to mitigate the potential for economic inequality, cyber warfare, ethical violations, and existential threats. Policies must address issues of accountability, fairness, interpretability, security, and compliance while ensuring that AI remains a tool for progress rather than a source of instability and control. As AI continues to evolve, proactive measures must be taken to prevent unintended consequences and to safeguard human rights, democratic values, and global security. By fostering international collaboration and ethical AI governance, the world can harness AI's potential while minimizing the threats it poses to humanity.

Regulating AI requires collaborative efforts involving various stakeholders, including national and international policymakers, legal experts, and academics. Effective AI regulation need to address key legal and ethical concerns such as human rights protection, sovereignty, state responsibility, dispute resolution, and the widening North-South technological divide(Lee, 2022). Provided the global nature of AI development, where computational resources and research networks transcend national borders, international cooperation is not just desirable but essential(Trager et al., 2023). One of the fundamental principles guiding AI regulation is that AI entities must remain under human oversight. However, if AI governance is left solely to national governments and private corporations, there is a risk that economic and political interests will take precedence over broader ethical considerations(Burri, 2017). Additionally, an ad hoc, case-by-case approach to AI-related legal disputes would lead to inconsistency and uncertainty, making it difficult to establish clear precedents.

A major challenge in regulating AI is that domestic laws apply only within national territories, while efforts to extend regulations extraterritorially often face accusations of legal imperialism. Many national legal frameworks struggle to provide a clear, unified definition of AI, fail to address key risks comprehensively, and lack enforceable compliance mechanisms(Ratcliff, 2023). Recognizing these gaps, international organizations and private regulatory bodies have started acknowledging the necessity of transnational AI regulations. However, the limitations of these efforts remain evident, as existing regulatory frameworks often fail to address the unique challenges posed by AI's rapid evolution (Nindler, 2019). As AI continues to evolve, the need for robust, globally coordinated regulations will only intensify. By fostering international collaboration and establishing legally binding standards, policymakers can ensure that AI serves as a force for progress rather than a source of unchecked risks and ethical dilemmas.

NATIONAL LEGAL AND REGULATORY FRAMEWORKS: OVERVIEW OF MOST PERTINENT LEGAL INITIATIVE AND REGULATIONS

United States

The United States has adopted a sector-specific approach to regulating artificial intelligence (AI), focusing on targeted legislative measures and policy initiatives rather than a single, overarching framework. Unlike the European Union, which has moved toward a comprehensive AI regulatory framework, the U.S. approach emphasizes flexibility, encouraging innovation while addressing AI-related risks in specific industries such as finance, healthcare, and national security. This decentralized regulatory model reflects the U.S. government's efforts to maintain a competitive edge in AI development while ensuring ethical considerations, transparency, and accountability (Zaidan & Ibrahim, 2024).

Key Legislative and Policy Measures

a) Algorithmic Accountability Act (Proposed)

The Algorithmic Accountability Act is a proposed legislative measure aimed at improving transparency, fairness, and accountability in AI decision-making processes. If enacted, it would require companies deploying AI-driven systems to conduct bias assessments, ensuring that automated decisions do not lead to discrimination or unintended harmful consequences. The proposed law primarily targets businesses that use AI in critical sectors such as employment, finance, healthcare, and law enforcement, where biased algorithms could negatively impact individuals' rights and economic opportunities.

This proposal comes in response to growing concerns over algorithmic biases in AI applications. Studies and real-world cases have demonstrated how machine learning models, when trained on biased data, can perpetuate or even exacerbate existing societal inequalities. By mandating companies to assess and mitigate biases in AI systems, the Algorithmic Accountability Act seeks to enhance trust and fairness in automated decision-making. (Zaidan & Ibrahim, 2024).

b) National AI Initiative Act (2020)

Enacted in 2020, the National AI Initiative Act established a coordinated federal effort to advance AI research, development, and applications. The legislation led to the creation of the National AI Initiative Office, which serves as the central body overseeing AI-related programs across various government agencies. The act aims to:

- Strengthen AI research and innovation by supporting public-private partnerships in AI development.
- Enhance AI-related education and workforce training to ensure that the U.S. retains its leadership in AI-driven industries.
- Promote ethical AI deployment by ensuring that AI systems align with democratic values, human rights, and national security interests.

By formalizing a national AI strategy, this act underscores the U.S. government's recognition of AI as a strategic asset with broad implications for economic growth, military applications, and technological competitiveness.

Executive Orders on AI

Executive Orders and Federal Directives on AI

The U.S. has also taken a policy-driven approach to AI regulation through a series of executive orders and federal directives issued by different administrations. These executive actions emphasize:

- Federal investment in AI research and development, ensuring that government agencies adopt AI responsibly and effectively.
- Encouraging AI leadership while prioritizing ethics and transparency in AI-driven decision-making.

- Addressing AI-related risks in national security, particularly in the areas of cybersecurity, defense, and misinformation management.

For instance, the White House AI Bill of Rights, introduced as a guiding framework, outlines key principles for responsible AI development. This initiative focuses on protecting individuals from harmful AI applications, emphasizing principles such as:

- Safe and Effective AI Systems – Ensuring AI technologies are rigorously tested before deployment.
- Algorithmic Discrimination Protections – Preventing AI-driven biases that could disproportionately affect marginalized communities.
- Data Privacy – Safeguarding personal information against AI-driven exploitation.

Despite these efforts, the lack of a unified AI regulatory framework remains a significant challenge. The fragmented approach across industries and government agencies has led to inconsistencies in AI governance. Furthermore, concerns over data privacy, cybersecurity, and the role of private corporations in AI decision-making highlight the need for a more cohesive strategy.

Scholars argue that international cooperation is necessary to address cross-border AI risks effectively. As the global AI landscape evolves, the United States may need to engage in transnational AI regulatory efforts, similar to those undertaken by the European Union and the United Nations.

The U.S. approach to AI regulation reflects a deliberate effort to foster innovation while mitigating risks. While sector-specific policies provide flexibility, calls for a comprehensive regulatory framework are increasing, especially as AI technologies become more powerful and pervasive. The success of AI governance in the U.S. will depend on continued collaboration between policymakers, industry leaders, and international organizations to ensure AI serves the public interest while driving technological progress.

European Union

The EU positions itself at the forefront of AI regulation. The European Union (EU) has been at the vanguard of AI regulation, aiming to ensure the responsible development and deployment of artificial intelligence (AI). The EU's comprehensive framework includes the proposed EU AI Act, the General Data Protection Regulation (GDPR), and the Ethics Guidelines for Trustworthy AI.

a) EU AI Act (Proposed)

The EU AI Act represents a landmark effort to categorize AI applications based on their associated risk levels. This regulatory approach is designed to mitigate potential harms while fostering innovation. The AI Act classifies AI systems into four risk categories: unacceptable, high, limited, and minimal.

i. Unacceptable Risk: AI systems that pose a significant threat to safety or fundamental rights are outright banned. Examples include AI technologies used for social scoring by governments, which can lead to discriminatory practices and undermine individual freedoms. The prohibition of such systems reflects the EU's commitment to protecting human dignity and rights.
ii. High Risk: AI systems that operate in critical domains are subject to rigorous regulatory requirements. This category includes AI applications in healthcare, transportation, finance, and critical infrastructure. For instance, AI used in medical diagnostics must comply with stringent standards to ensure accuracy, safety, and reliability. High-risk AI systems must undergo thorough testing, certification, and continuous monitoring to mitigate potential risks.
iii. Limited Risk: AI systems with limited risk are required to adhere to specific transparency and disclosure obligations. These systems are not as heavily regulated as high-risk applications but still require safeguards to prevent misuse. Examples include chatbots and AI-generated content, where users must be informed that they are interacting with an AI system. This transparency helps maintain user trust and prevents deception.
iv. Minimal Risk: AI systems with minimal risk, such as AI-powered video games and spam filters, are largely exempt from regulatory requirements. These applications are considered to pose negligible risks to individuals and society. The minimal regulation of these systems is intended to encourage innovation and the development of non-critical AI technologies.

General Data Protection Regulation (GDPR)

Although not specifically focused on AI, the GDPR has a significant impact on AI through its stringent data protection and privacy requirements. AI systems often rely on large amounts of data, including personal data, to function effectively. The GDPR ensures that individuals have greater control over their personal data and that organizations follow strict guidelines for data collection, processing, and storage.

Key aspects of the GDPR that impact AI include:

i. Data Minimization: Organizations must ensure that they only collect data that is necessary for the specific purpose of the AI system.

ii. Consent and Transparency: Individuals must be informed about how their data will be used, and consent must be obtained.
iii. Right to Access and Erasure: Individuals have the right to access their data and request its deletion.
iv. Data Security: Organizations must implement strong data security measures to protect personal data from breaches.

Ethics Guidelines for Trustworthy AI

The Ethics Guidelines for Trustworthy AI, issued by the High-Level Expert Group on AI, outline fundamental principles to guide the development and deployment of AI systems. These guidelines emphasize the importance of human-centric AI that aligns with ethical values and societal goals.

Key principles of the Ethics Guidelines include:

- **Human Agency and Oversight**: AI systems should enhance human capabilities and respect human autonomy. There should be mechanisms for human oversight to ensure that AI decisions can be reviewed and intervened upon if necessary.
- **Technical Robustness and Safety**: AI systems should be designed to be secure and resilient against adversarial attacks. They must function reliably under normal and unexpected conditions, minimizing risks of harm.
- **Privacy and Data Governance**: AI systems must uphold data protection and privacy. This includes ensuring that data used by AI is handled responsibly and in compliance with regulations like the GDPR.
- **Transparency**: AI systems should be transparent and explainable. This means that users should understand how AI decisions are made, and there should be clear documentation of AI processes.
- **Diversity, Non-Discrimination, and Fairness**: AI systems should be designed to avoid biases and discrimination. This promotes inclusivity and fairness, ensuring that AI benefits all segments of society.
- **Societal and Environmental Well-being**: AI systems should contribute positively to society and consider environmental impacts. This includes promoting sustainable development and ethical use of AI technologies.
- **Accountability**: Organizations and individuals involved in AI development and deployment should be accountable for the outcomes of AI systems. There should be mechanisms to address grievances and rectify any harm caused by AI.

China

China's strategy for artificial intelligence (AI) development is characterized by ambitious goals and stringent regulations, reflecting a unique blend of rapid technological advancement and state oversight(FLIA, 2017). This approach aims to position China as a global leader in AI by 2030 while ensuring that AI technologies align with national interests and social stability(Webster et al., 2017).

New Generation AI Development Plan (2017)

In July 2017, the Chinese State Council issued the New Generation Artificial Intelligence Development Plan, outlining a comprehensive blueprint for AI development up to 2030. The plan sets forth ambitious goals to establish China as a global innovation center in AI, emphasizing the importance of AI in driving economic growth, enhancing national security, and improving social governance.

Key objectives of the plan include:

- **Technological Leadership**: China aims to achieve breakthroughs in core AI technologies, such as deep learning, big data, and quantum computing.
- **Industrial Applications**: The plan encourages the integration of AI into various industries, including manufacturing, healthcare, and transportation, to boost productivity and efficiency.
- **International Collaboration**: China seeks to strengthen international cooperation in AI research and development, fostering partnerships with other countries and organizations.

In March 2022, China introduced the **Regulations on the Administration of Internet Information Service Recommendation Algorithms**, which came into effect on March 1, 2022. These regulations aim to ensure transparency and accountability in the use of recommendation algorithms, addressing concerns about their potential impact on national security and social order.

Regulations on Recommendation Algorithms (2022)

In March 2022, China introduced the **Regulations on the Administration of Internet Information Service Recommendation Algorithms**, which came into effect on March 1, 2022. These regulations aim to ensure transparency and accountability in the use of recommendation algorithms, addressing concerns about their potential impact on national security and social order4.

Key provisions of the regulations include:

- **Transparency**: Algorithmic recommendation service providers must disclose their algorithms' principles, mechanisms, and outcomes to users.
- **Prohibition of Harmful Practices**: The regulations prohibit the use of algorithms to spread false information, incite violence, or engage in illegal activities.
- **Social Responsibility**: Providers are required to promote positive values and prevent the dissemination of harmful content.

Social Credit System

China's **Social Credit System** is a national credit rating and blacklist system that evaluates the trustworthiness of individuals, businesses, and government entities. The system aims to enhance social trust and regulate behavior by rewarding compliance with laws and regulations and penalizing violations6.

Key features of the Social Credit System include:

- **Trustworthiness Assessment**: The system assigns scores based on individuals' and organizations' behavior, including financial transactions, legal compliance, and social interactions.
- **Consequences of Scores**: High scores can result in benefits such as easier access to loans and travel, while low scores can lead to penalties such as restricted access to services and public shaming.
- **National Security and Social Stability**: The system is designed to prevent activities that threaten national security and social order, such as fraud, corruption, and illegal activities

Japan's approach to AI regulation is rooted in the social principles of Human Centric AI, introduced in the year 2019. The principle emphasises three core values, i.e., **Human Dignity**, ensuring AI serves humanity and respects individual rights; **Diversity and Inclusion**, encouraging fairness and non-discrimination; **Sustainability,** aligning AI with environmental and societal goals. These principles align with international frameworks such as the OECD AI Principles and the G20 AI Principles, underscoring Japan's commitment to a balanced approach that integrates AI into society rather than restricting it excessively.

Regulation on AI: A Soft-Law Approach

Unlike the European Union, which has opted for stringent AI regulations (e.g., the EU AI Act), Japan favors a soft-law approach. This includes nonbinding guidelines, industry self-regulation, and transparency requirements rather than rigid legal constraints. The AI Governance in Japan Ver. 1.1 Report by the Ministry of Economy, Trade, and Industry (METI) underscores that legally binding horizontal AI regulations are currently unnecessary due to the dynamic nature of AI innovation. Instead, Japan encourages voluntary compliance and agile governance, which allows for iterative policy updates based on emerging challenges and technological advancements.

Sector-specific regulations exist, such as:

- **Digital Platform Transparency Act** – Ensuring fair competition in online marketplaces.
- **Financial Instruments and Exchange Act** – Mandating risk management for algorithmic trading.
- **Act on the Protection of Personal Information (APPI)** – Regulating data privacy, including provisions for pseudonymized data to facilitate AI research.

Regulation for AI: Enabling Innovation

Japan also actively promotes AI adoption through legal reforms and incentives. Notable legislative initiatives include:

- **Road Traffic Act (2020, 2023)** – Legalizing Level 3 and 4 autonomous vehicles.
- **Installment Sales Act (2020)** – Allowing AI-driven credit risk assessment.
- **Copyright Act (2017, 2019)** – Facilitating AI training on copyrighted data.

Additionally, the **Digital Rincho Commission**, launched in 2021, aims to revise over 5,000 regulations to remove outdated compliance requirements that hinder AI-driven digital transformation.

Japan's AI governance model deliberately balances regulation and innovation. Its risk-based, soft-law approach ensures AI development remains dynamic while addressing societal concerns through ethical guidelines and sector-specific oversight. As AI technology evolves, Japan's leadership in multistakeholder governance, international cooperation, and regulatory adaptability will shape the future of AI regulation on a global scale.

INTERNATIONAL LEGAL AND REGULATORY FRAMEWORKS

United Nations Initiatives

Recognising the transboundary impact of AI technologies and their potential implications on humanity, the United Nations has established a framework for AI governance. In October 2023, the UN formed the High-level Advisory Body on AI to analyze and advance recommendations for the international governance of AI. This multi-stakeholder body was established following the UN Secretary-General's Roadmap for Digital Cooperation and focuses on:

1. Identifying governance gaps
2. Enhancing global cooperation
3. Promoting AI applications aligned with human rights and SDGs

The report highlights three major gaps in global AI governance:

1. Representation Gaps – Many countries, particularly in the Global South, have limited participation in international AI governance discussions.
2. Coordination Gaps – A lack of coherence among AI governance initiatives and institutions, leading to fragmented regulatory frameworks.
3. Implementation Gaps – Challenges in translating AI governance commitments into tangible policies and enforcement mechanisms.

To address these gaps, the UN proposes a globally networked, agile, and flexible governance approach, structured around the following key initiatives:

1. Common Understanding
    a. International Scientific Panel on AI – Modeled after the Intergovernmental Panel on Climate Change (IPCC), this panel will provide impartial scientific knowledge on AI capabilities, risks, and trends.
    b. Policy Dialogue on AI Governance – A twice-yearly forum under the UN's aegis to share best practices, develop regulatory interoperability, and discuss AI-related incidents.
2. Common Ground
    a. AI Standards Exchange – A platform to harmonize AI-related standards and definitions, ensuring interoperability and ethical compliance across global frameworks.

b. Global AI Data Framework – Establishing common principles for AI training data governance, fostering data commons, and promoting fair data stewardship.

3. Common Benefits

   a. AI Capacity Development Network – An UN-affiliated AI training and research center network to enhance AI literacy, governance capacity, and innovation in underrepresented regions.

   b. Global Fund for AI – A funding mechanism to ensure equitable access to AI infrastructure, computational resources, and capacity-building initiatives, particularly for developing nations.

4. Coherent Effort

   a. AI Office within the UN Secretariat – A dedicated UN office tasked with coordinating AI governance initiatives, advising the Secretary-General, and facilitating multi-stakeholder engagement.

The UN's current AI governance framework emphasizes a networked, multi-stakeholder approach. However, as AI technology evolves, the report acknowledges the possibility of establishing a formal International AI Agency with enforcement capabilities. The effectiveness of the proposed initiatives will be continually assessed to determine whether stronger institutional mechanisms are required. The initiatives aim to foster a globally inclusive, accountable, and ethical AI ecosystem. By addressing governance gaps and promoting international cooperation, these efforts seek to maximize AI's benefits while mitigating its risks, ensuring that AI serves humanity equitably and responsibly.

G20 and Other Multilateral Efforts

The G20, as a forum of major economies, has taken a central role in fostering AI governance initiatives. The G20, which includes 19 major economies, the European Union, and the African Union, accounts for a significant portion of global AI research, investment, and regulatory influence.

The G20 has pursued a multipronged approach to AI governance, balancing the need for ethical considerations with the promotion of innovation. Some key initiatives include:

1. G20 AI Principles (2019): The adoption of AI ethics guidelines aligned with OECD principles. These principles focus on transparency, accountability, security, and inclusivity.

2. 2023 G20 New Delhi Leaders' Declaration: This declaration emphasized the responsible development and deployment of AI, particularly in fostering sustainable development and digital economic growth. It reinforced the commitment to global collaboration in AI governance and highlighted AI's role in achieving the Sustainable Development Goals (SDGs).
3. Brazil's 2024 G20 Presidency and AI Focus: Under Brazil's presidency, the G20 has prioritized AI governance with a particular focus on:
   a. AI for Sustainable Development: Encouraging AI solutions to address economic inequality and climate change.
   b. Global South Representation: Ensuring that developing nations play an active role in shaping AI policies.
   c. Public-Private Partnerships: Facilitating cooperation between governments, international organizations, and major AI firms to create fair regulatory frameworks.
4. Coordination with UN and Other Multilateral Bodies: The G20 has supported AI governance discussions at the UN, working alongside UNESCO, OECD, and the Council of Europe to establish ethical and regulatory guidelines.
5. AI Safety and Ethical Use: The G20 has engaged in dialogues on AI safety, recognizing potential risks such as bias, misinformation, and job displacement. Collaborative efforts include:
   a. The promotion of AI safety guidelines inspired by initiatives such as the Bletchley AI Safety Summit.
   b. Developing shared standards for responsible AI practices and security measures.

The G20 has the potential to be a key driver in shaping global AI governance by coordinating efforts among major economies and multilateral institutions. However, achieving a cohesive and equitable AI governance system requires overcoming geopolitical, regulatory, and economic challenges. Moving forward, the G20's leadership in AI governance must emphasize inclusivity, sustainability, and ethical AI development.

Multilateral AI Governance Initiatives

AI governance efforts extend beyond the G20, involving various international institutions and frameworks:

1. OECD AI Principles (2019, updated 2023): The Organization for Economic Cooperation and Development (OECD) established a set of AI principles that serve as a global benchmark for responsible AI. These principles focus on in-

clusivity, accountability, robustness, and transparency in AI development and deployment. The OECD AI Policy Observatory monitors AI policy trends and implementation across member states.

2. UNESCO AI Ethics Recommendation (2021): The United Nations Educational, Scientific and Cultural Organization (UNESCO) introduced a framework to guide AI governance with human rights and ethical considerations. This recommendation outlines principles such as fairness, privacy protection, and non-discrimination while emphasizing AI's potential benefits in education, healthcare, and sustainable development.
3. EU AI Act (2024): The European Union became the first governing body to implement a legally binding AI regulatory framework. The EU AI Act categorizes AI systems based on risk levels, placing strict requirements on high-risk applications, such as those used in law enforcement and healthcare. The act also establishes penalties for non-compliance and encourages transparency in AI algorithms.
4. Council of Europe's Framework Convention on AI (2024): The Council of Europe introduced a binding legal framework addressing AI's impact on human rights, democracy, and the rule of law. The framework aims to ensure AI deployment aligns with fundamental freedoms while preventing the misuse of AI in surveillance, discrimination, and human rights violations.
5. Bletchley AI Safety Summit (2023, 2024): The Bletchley AI Safety Summit, initiated by the United Kingdom, brought together global leaders, AI researchers, and policymakers to discuss AI safety and security concerns. The summit led to international AI safety commitments, emphasizing risk mitigation, accountability, and the establishment of AI governance frameworks for advanced AI systems. The second edition in 2024 further strengthened global cooperation on AI safety regulations.

CHALLENGES IN AI GOVERNANCE GLOBALLY: LAW ADOPTION AND ENFORCEMENT MONITORING

While AI's potential of doing good is virtually limitless, so is the potential of harm intended or otherwise. Given its disruptive power, this technology needs strong, human-driven governance and regulations to ensure it's used responsibly and for the greater good. Despite international efforts to regulate AI, the process of law adoption and enforcement monitoring is inconsistent and fragmented. This section examines the challenges faced in AI governance, focusing on legal adoption and the enforcement mechanisms required to ensure compliance.

Challenges in AI Law Adoption

One of the major challenges in AI law adoption is the absence of a unified global AI framework. Every country has its varied priorities—some focusing on innovation, while others emphasize risk mitigation. The European Union's AI Act (2024) seeks to regulate high-risk AI applications, whereas China has implemented strict algorithmic regulations to control online content. The United States, in contrast, follows a sectoral approach, relying on private-sector initiatives and state-level regulations. This divergence complicates efforts to establish common global standards, leading to regulatory fragmentation and difficulties in cross-border AI governance.

Moreover, Countries prioritize their own economic and security interests when formulating AI laws. Developing nations argue that AI should be a common heritage of humanity, ensuring equitable access and benefits. In contrast, technologically advanced nations seek to maintain control over AI development, considering it a strategic asset for national security and economic growth. This conflicting stance creates barriers to international cooperation, making it difficult to establish a unified AI governance body.

AI technology is evolving at an unprecedented pace, making it difficult for legislators to keep up. By the time regulations are drafted, AI capabilities may have already surpassed the existing legal framework, leading to regulatory gaps. Additionally, AI's complexity, involving machine learning, neural networks, and autonomous decision-making, makes it challenging for regulators to predict potential risks and draft proactive legal safeguards.

Most existing AI regulations are non-binding, relying on ethical guidelines and voluntary compliance. Organizations like the United Nations (UNESCO AI Ethics Framework) and the OECD have proposed AI governance principles, but without legally binding mechanisms, enforcement remains weak. Countries implement AI laws based on their domestic priorities, leading to inconsistencies in AI governance globally.

Challenges in AI enforcement monitoring

The enforcement of AI laws is primarily a national responsibility, with limited international oversight. There is currently no global AI regulatory authority with the mandate to monitor compliance across borders. This results in a fragmented regulatory landscape where AI companies operate in multiple jurisdictions with varying compliance requirements, leading to regulatory loopholes and uneven enforcement.

Even where AI regulations exist, enforcement remains a challenge due to limited resources, political will, and the complexity of AI applications. Regulatory bodies often lack technical expertise and the tools to effectively monitor AI systems. AI-driven surveillance tools, for example, have been criticized for violating privacy rights, but enforcement agencies struggle to ensure compliance. Furthermore, penalties for non-compliance vary significantly, reducing the deterrence effect of AI laws.

AI decision-making processes are often opaque, making it difficult to determine liability in cases of harm or bias. Many AI systems operate as "black boxes," where their decision-making processes are not fully understood even by their developers. This opacity raises concerns about algorithmic accountability, fairness, and ethical AI deployment, necessitating stringent transparency requirements and explainability standards in AI regulations.

Tech companies play a significant role in shaping AI regulations, sometimes to the detriment of public interest. Major AI developers engage in lobbying efforts to influence regulatory frameworks, often leading to weak enforcement measures or self-regulation mechanisms that prioritize corporate interests over ethical concerns. The lack of independent oversight exacerbates this issue, allowing industries to dictate AI governance policies that may not adequately address societal risks.

The need for Global regulatory authority

Given these challenges, there is a strong case for the establishment of a global AI regulatory authority. Such an entity could:

1. Develop and enforce international AI laws based on ethical principles and risk assessments to ensure AI safety and accountability.
2. Facilitate global collaboration among governments, corporations, and civil society to create standardized AI governance frameworks.
3. Monitor AI applications to ensure compliance with human rights standards, prevent potential abuses, and promote fairness and transparency.
4. Standardize AI governance frameworks to prevent regulatory fragmentation and jurisdictional conflicts. This would enable harmonization of AI laws across countries, ensuring consistent enforcement mechanisms.

THE PATH AHEAD

Despite the growing recognition of the need for international legislation to govern artificial intelligence, the field remains in its early stages, raising numerous complex legal questions. These questions extend beyond the mere applicability of existing legal frameworks and include fundamental concerns regarding the responsibilities, roles, and accountability of key stakeholders such as states, civil society organizations, individuals, corporations, and international institutions. A crucial issue pertains to the classification and legal status of AI as a technology. There is an ongoing debate about whether AI should be considered merely a tool under existing legal regimes or whether its increasing autonomy requires the creation of a distinct legal identity. This question is particularly urgent given AI's ability to operate independently, make decisions, and even learn from its experiences, raising concerns about liability, accountability, and personhood in legal discourse. Furthermore, the mechanisms for regulating and controlling AI remain unresolved. Scholars argue that traditional legal instruments may be inadequate, necessitating the adaptation or even a fundamental rethinking of international legal principles. The rapid evolution of AI technologies represents a paradigm shift that challenges the adequacy of current regulatory frameworks, leading to potential gaps in legal scope and rendering specific legal provisions obsolete. Beyond these structural concerns, the regulation of AI is also fraught with both traditional and emerging legal challenges. While some challenges echo those seen in earlier technological advancements—such as data protection, privacy, and liability—others are unique to AI. The prospect of AI acquiring significant autonomy has sparked discussions about whether it should be granted legal personhood or other novel legal statuses that reflect its evolving capabilities.

Another critical challenge lies in the transnational nature of AI deployment. AI systems are not confined within national borders; they operate across jurisdictions, necessitating international consensus on regulatory standards. Effective governance will require states to negotiate and adopt legally binding treaties, agreements, and enforcement mechanisms that establish uniform rules applicable across nations. However, the question of enforcement remains unresolved, as compliance with transnational norms depends on the willingness of states to integrate such obligations into their domestic legal systems.

Finally, an important perspective in this debate suggests that legal regulation alone is inadequate to address the complexities of AI governance. The interaction between technological advancements and social dynamics requires a multidimensional approach that incorporates ethical, technical, and policy-driven considerations. The challenge, therefore, is not merely legal but also one of balancing regulatory oversight with innovation while ensuring AI's safe and ethical integration into society.

In summary, although international law establishes a foundation for AI regulation, it must adapt to meet the complex and evolving challenges presented by this transformative technology. The ongoing discussion highlights the need for innovative legal solutions that strike a balance between flexibility and enforceability, ultimately ensuring that AI benefits humanity while mitigating its associated risks.

CONCLUSION

The governance of Artificial Intelligence (AI) presents one of the most critical challenges of our time, requiring a balance between fostering innovation and protecting fundamental rights and ethical principles. The rapid advancement of AI technologies has the potential to revolutionize industries, boost productivity, and enhance decision-making. However, this progress also introduces risks such as bias, privacy violations, economic inequality, security threats, and ethical dilemmas. As demonstrated in this article, both national and international legal frameworks have attempted to address these challenges, yet significant gaps remain in ensuring comprehensive, enforceable, and globally cohesive AI governance.

At the national level, different jurisdictions have adopted various approaches to AI regulation, reflecting their legal traditions, economic interests, and societal values. The European Union's AI Act serves as a pioneering legislative effort, emphasizing a risk-based framework to regulate AI applications while ensuring transparency and accountability. In contrast, the United States has pursued a sectoral approach, using existing laws to regulate AI across different industries without imposing a unified legislative framework. China has adopted a more centralized and stringent approach, integrating AI regulations into its broader surveillance and national security strategies. Meanwhile, Japan has chosen a soft-law approach, prioritizing ethical AI development through voluntary compliance and industry-driven guidelines.

On the international stage, organizations such as the United Nations, the G20, and the OECD have initiated frameworks to harmonize AI governance, recognizing the need for cross-border collaboration. The United Nations' initiatives, including the High-Level Advisory Body on AI, have emphasized the importance of global cooperation in establishing AI governance mechanisms. The G20's involvement with AI governance, particularly through ethical AI principles and policy coordination, highlights the growing acknowledgment of AI's global implications. The OECD AI Principles, embraced by numerous nations, offer foundational guidelines for responsible AI development and deployment. However, these efforts, while significant, largely remain non-binding and depend on voluntary compliance, raising concerns about their effectiveness in addressing AI's transnational risks.

One of the primary challenges in AI governance is the fragmented and inconsistent application of laws and regulations across different jurisdictions. While national governments prioritize their sovereignty and economic competitiveness, the lack of a unified global AI framework leads to regulatory divergence, making it difficult to enforce common standards. AI systems operate beyond national borders, impacting individuals and businesses worldwide, necessitating international cooperation. A cohesive regulatory approach is essential to prevent regulatory arbitrage, where companies seek jurisdictions with the least stringent AI laws to develop and deploy potentially harmful technologies.

Another critical concern is the ethical dimension of AI, which extends beyond legal compliance to broader societal implications. Issues such as algorithmic bias, discrimination, and the use of AI in surveillance and warfare demand stringent ethical oversight. Without clear ethical standards, the deployment of AI could exacerbate existing social inequalities and undermine democratic principles. Governments and international bodies must prioritize ethical considerations in AI governance, ensuring that AI technologies align with human rights, fairness, and accountability.

Moreover, the enforcement of AI regulations remains a persistent challenge. National regulatory bodies often lack the technical expertise and resources to monitor and assess AI systems effectively. The opacity of AI decision-making processes, commonly referred to as the 'black box' problem, further complicates accountability and liability determinations. Addressing these challenges requires a multi-stakeholder approach involving governments, technology companies, civil society organizations, and academic institutions. Establishing independent AI oversight bodies, equipped with the authority to audit and evaluate AI systems, could enhance compliance and ensure that AI technologies operate within ethical and legal boundaries.

As AI continues to evolve, its governance frameworks must evolve as well. The dynamic nature of AI development requires adaptable regulatory mechanisms that can respond to emerging risks while fostering technological innovation. Regulatory sandboxes, which allow controlled experimentation with AI technologies under regulatory supervision, present a promising approach to balancing innovation and governance. Additionally, ongoing dialogue between policymakers, industry leaders, and researchers is crucial for refining AI regulations and addressing unforeseen challenges.

Looking ahead, the path toward effective AI governance necessitates greater international collaboration. The idea of a global AI regulatory authority has gained traction as a potential solution to harmonize AI governance and ensure the equitable distribution of AI benefits. Such an authority could establish universal standards, facilitate information sharing, and monitor compliance across jurisdictions. While geopolitical and economic interests may hinder the establishment of a binding global AI treaty, incremental steps toward regulatory alignment and cooperation can contribute to a more cohesive governance landscape.

In conclusion, AI governance remains a complex and evolving field that requires a delicate balance between regulation and innovation. Although national and international regulatory efforts are progressing, they still face significant challenges in ensuring the responsible development and deployment of AI. To address these challenges, a collaborative, multi-stakeholder approach is essential, emphasizing ethical considerations, accountability, and transparency. By fostering cooperation among governments, international organizations, industry stakeholders, and civil society, we can navigate the complexities of AI governance and harness AI's transformative potential while mitigating its risks. The future of AI governance depends on our collective ability to craft adaptable, enforceable, and globally coordinated frameworks that safeguard human rights, promote ethical AI practices, and ensure that AI serves the broader public interest.

REFERENCES

Burri, T. (2017). International law and artificial intelligence. *Jahrbuch für Internationales Recht. German Yearbook of International Law*, *60*(1), 91–108. DOI: 10.3790/gyil.60.1.91

FLIA. (2017). *China's New Generation of Artificial Intelligence Development Plan - Foundation for Law and International Affairs*. https://flia.org/notice-state-council-issuing-new-generation-artificial-intelligence-development-plan/

Lee, J. (2022). *Artificial Intelligence and International Law*. Springer. DOI: 10.1007/978-981-19-1496-6

Marr, B. (2023, June 2). The 15 Biggest Risks Of Artificial Intelligence. *Forbes*.

Nindler, R. (2019). The United Nation's Capability to Manage Existential Risks with a Focus on Artificial Intelligence. *International Community Law Review*, *21*(1), 5–34. DOI: 10.1163/18719732-12341388

Ovink, C. (2024). *AI risks for international peace and security*. ORF. https://www.orfonline.org/expert-speak/ai-risks-for-international-peace-and-security

Ratcliff, C. J. (2023, November 8). *Who will write the rules for AI? How nations are racing to regulate artificial intelligence*. The Conversation. https://theconversation.com/who-will-write-the-rules-for-ai-how-nations-are-racing-to-regulate-artificial-intelligence-216900

Sourdin, T. (2023). Cambridge Handbook of Artificial Intelligence: Global Perspectives on Law and Ethics. *Prometheus*, *39*(1), 60–65. DOI: 10.13169/prometheus.39.1.0060

Trager, R., Harack, B., Reuel, A., Carnegie, A., Heim, L., Ho, L., Kreps, S., Lall, R., & Larter, O. Ó hÉigeartaigh, S., Staffell, S., & Villalobos Ruiz, J. J. (2023). International Governance of Civilian AI: A Jurisdictional Certification Approach. SSRN *Electronic Journal*, 1–51. DOI: 10.2139/ssrn.4579899

Turchin, A., & Denkenberger, D. (2020). Classification of global catastrophic risks connected with artificial intelligence. *AI & Society*, *35*(1), 147–163. DOI: 10.1007/s00146-018-0845-5

Webster, G., Creemers, R., Kania, E., & Triolo, P. (2017). *Full Translation: China's 'New Generation Artificial Intelligence Development Plan' (2017)*. DIGICHINA.

Zaidan, E., & Ibrahim, I. A. (2024). AI Governance in a Complex and Rapidly Changing Regulatory Landscape: A Global Perspective. *Humanities & Social Sciences Communications*, *11*(1), 1121. DOI: 10.1057/s41599-024-03560-x

Chapter 9
Global AI Governance and Collaboration: The Role of International Bodies in AI Regulation

Vishambhar Raghuwanshi
https://orcid.org/0009-0009-1365-1850
Manipal University Jaipur, India

Pranjal Khare
https://orcid.org/0000-0002-9937-9588
O.P. Jindal Global University, India

Paridhi Sharma
O.P. Jindal Global University, India

ABSTRACT

Global governance of artificial intelligence (AI) is crucial due to its transformative potential and inherent risks. The rapid advancement of AI necessitates international cooperation to establish unified ethical norms and legal standards, mitigating adverse effects like privacy violations and biased algorithms. Existing national policies are insufficient to address the global nature of AI, leading to fragmented regulations. International organizations like the UN, OECD, and EU play a vital role in developing AI principles and standards, promoting ethical, transparent, and human-centric AI. However, challenges persist, including conflicting national interests, the rapid pace of technological advancement, ethical divergences stemming from varying cultural norms, geopolitical rivalries, economic disparities, and institutional limitations. Overcoming these challenges requires a multifaceted approach that balances innovation with accountability, fosters international collaboration,

DOI: 10.4018/979-8-3373-1210-1.ch009

and addresses the global implications of this transformative technology.

INTRODUCTION

The application of Artificial Intelligence (AI) signals a new era for humanity development, from technological revolution to industrial revolution, and now an intellectual revolution has started to include Artificial Intelligence that is revolutionizing the world's industries, economies, and societies. From changing the approach to diagnosing various diseases and managing supplies flow to creating more accurate climate models, AI took the role of a cornerstone of the modern technological advance. However, as its applications permeate nearly every aspect of daily life, the pressing question arises: how can this powerful technology be governed effectively? The emergent nature of AI is as problematic as it is beneficial, or at the least, questionable, especially conversantly with regulation and governance frameworks that fully capture the ethical, social, and economic implications of AI. It is against this background that more effort needs to be invested in the promotion of good governance structures that are capable of addressing innovation, accountability and inclusion.

Investing in global AI governance is not exclusively an administrative or regulatory affair, but a deeply relevant social necessity. AI is by its very virtue international in form since the systems it incorporates to process and analyze information are international. Mixing this interconnectedness increases the probability of adverse effects of unmoderated AI, including invasions of privacy, high likelihood of prejudicial biases and the proliferation of social imbalances. Furthermore, its application in surveillance systems, cyber warfare, fake news spread, and in many other areas threaten democracy and human rights existence almost to extinction. And it lies precisely here that the nature and function of global governance acquires a reason to be so. Although national policies can offer localized solutions, social applications being a global phenomenon require international cooperation to develop unification of laws and ethical norms. The lack of such global governance may result in fragmented rules and trends within regions that will promote disparate and highly inefficient environments across jurisdictions (Tallberg et al., 2023).

The necessity of international management of AI is due to the continually growing rate of technologies' development, which puts pressure on the ability of current legislation to adapt to the pace of innovations. Legal and policy systems in their conventional sense are not very helpful when it comes to some of the emerging questions that arise while developing and deploying AI, like establishing legal responsibility of self-driving cars, or addressing issues of explainability of machine learning. These challenges are however compounded by the fact that AI technologies are known to be complex 'black boxes', which enables the users to have little to no insight into the outcomes the system delivers. The stated consequence reduces one's level of trust both amongst users and regulators, a fact that inevitably hinders the more extensive implementation of AI in various industries. Hence it becomes incumbent upon international authorities to play an active part in setting and implementing the necessary governance policies for combating these issues and at the same time availing technology to all without making it detrimental to world sustainability (Schmitt, 2022).

Therefore, this chapter positions itself and analyses AI policy, technology, and governance by giving special attention to the international organizations' place in AI regulation. Global grouping like the United Nations, the Organization for Economic Co-operation and Development (OECD) and the World Economic Forum (WEF) have begun the process of developing principles and standards for the use of Al. However, these macro-micro initiatives come with enforcement issues, stakeholder management, and political upheavals. This chapter examines how international collaboration can fill the gaps in the existing governance architecture, how it can provide directions to manage and amplify the opportunities and threats associated with AI. Using case studies and the available literature, this chapter synthesizes and discusses the key findings of the current practices for the cross-cultural transfer of governance models as well as outlining practical suggestions for future work (Zaidan & Ibrahim, 2024).

The study is relevant now as the global society continues to discuss the moral, technological, and global problems of AI regulation. It has become conventional to observe that encouraging innovation is accompanied with challenges in maintaining accountability, which has caused an archaic type of policy fragmentation resulting in different regulatory approaches. For instance, the European Union has recently provided the Artificial Intelligence Act which is now the most complex effort in the regulation of AI technologies within the EU jurisdiction, and it is yet observed that the rest of the world has not come up with any similar attempts. Such a situation causes problems for multinational organizations and developers to deal with a lot of conflicting regulations. Again, the absence of this means global synchronization also poses the risk of regulatory arbitrage where actors take advantage of jurisdictions that have less strict legal measures to saddle AI development and usage with responsibility.

It is for this reason that this chapter postulates that such institutions assist in the development of international solutions with the challenges tackled at international levels to foster harmonization. AI governance has become a critical topic due to the increase in the development of smart technologies, and the development of proper policies (universal principles) of leveraging such technology and their principles like transparency, fairness, and accountability must involve governments, private companies, and other stakeholders. In addition, the fact that truly international actors have the capacity to balance competing interests and priorities makes them valuable players in the governance game. But to harness such potential, it is possible to embrace several challenges such as geopolitical competition, inadequacy of resources, and absence of legal recourse (Samson, 2023).

This chapter builds upon the identified governance frameworks to provide critiques of their adequacy and what can be done to enhance them. The non-technical approach it embraces integrates policy ideas from technology policy, cultural legal analysis, and ethics, making it easier to understand the diverse aspects of global AI governance. It posits that while collaboration is key the system needs to be governed in tandem with the intended technological solutions with special emphasis on flexibility and adaptability for the anticipated changes. Further, the chapter is also about the representation of the global south in the governance processes of non-state actors and marginalized populations.

Consequently, this chapter seeks to add to the contemporary academic discourse on AI governance by presenting a multifaceted analysis of the function of international organizations in the management of AI. It underlines the need for joint international efforts to monitor AI with the potential to provide solutions to the various interconnected problems while protecting the innovation capacity of the new technology. The subsequent subdivisions provide a further analysis of AI opportunities and threats, developmental conceptual paradigms, international organizations' role, and how to make regulation faster and fairer. To this end, this chapter adopts a holistic approach to showcase the confluence of policy, technology, and governance of AI, as well as providing strategies in the process for the academicians, the policymakers, and the practitioners.

OPPORTUNITIES AND CHALLENGES IN THE RISE OF ARTIFICIAL INTELLIGENCE

Technological advancement of Artificial Intelligence (AI) is among the world's rapid transformations, and by far among the most impactful in human history. In this regard, AI technology has become an integrated part of nearly every facet of post-industrial societies with a positive impact on making everyday experiences better and promoting transformations in industries. Now it is considered a valuable instrument, responding to the emerging challenges integrated with problem solving, innovation, and economic development. To its essence AI refers to the ability of a machine to behave in a manner similar to a human being through having the ability to learn, reason as well as correcting itself. Originating as a part of computing science and in close relation with algorithms and data processing, AI quickly went from mere ideas into practices bearing tremendous potential. However, as with any such disruptive technology, AI brings to the table equally massive opportunities as it does difficulties, this is why an acute and multi-faceted approach to the issue of AI's governance is called for (Yang et al., 2024).

AI has numerous potentials, which are vast and closely significant. In healthcare in particular, AI diagnostic equipment is changing the manner in which diseases are diagnosed and treated. It can give doctors an opportunity to detect some diseases in the early stages, for example, cancer or some rare genetic disease which a regular practitioner might miss seeing due to massive amounts of data that learning algorithms can go through. Furthermore, AI-based applications are applicable to the areas of medicine where specific adjustments can be made to the treatment regimen corresponding to a patient's genomic predisposition, habits, and past experiences. Likewise in the agricultural industry, advanced AI is making productivity and efficiency measurable. Applications of AI in smart farming apply advanced technologies in soil analysis, weather, and crop quality to make better use of the resources and improve productivity. Such innovations are important in solving the world's problems such as food scarcity and climate change.

In the corporate and industrial field, the incorporation has brought existing unparallelled productivity by means of automation. Beginning with the supply chain and going as far as the manufacture of the product, AI lowers cost and eliminates potential mistakes. Different industries that implement predictive analytics can forecast the market trends and identify risks that exist so as to develop an edge in their business. Similarly, within the financial sector AI applications are used for areas like fraud detection, credit scoring, algorithmic trading, which helps build a safer financial environment around the world. AI is also making its significant entry into creative fields where AI encompasses art making, music production, and content generation (Csernatoni, 2024). These innovations show that in addition to assisting individuals in improving their activities, AI is also capable of developing new ideas.

They also go beyond the traditional economic and industrial forms in order to tackle global challenges. For instance, application of AI in climate change representation assists climate scientists make meaningful recommendations and predictions towards averted climactic adversities. In disaster response and preparedness, thus, an AI system may be used to offer early warning and response arrangements with regards to earthquake data, weather data and past experiences. In like manner, the AI system in education is helping to erase disparities in accessibility and attainment. In some areas, it gives individualized instruction to learners across the globe; in other areas, translation and voice recognition help make more diverse languages accessible. Such examples illustrate AI's continued positive impact on sustainable development and enhanced quality of human lives across the world (Ajami & Karimi, 2023).

Nevertheless, new opportunities as vast as the AI development itself create problems that should be solved for development of proportional and dispensable artificial intelligence. The first one is the ethical consideration to do with the use of AI applications that are an essential component of the Smart Nation project proposed by Singapore. The case of employing AI in surveillance is questionable in terms of their violation of privacy and peoples' rights. Facial recognition technologies and data analysis are used by governments and various corporations but a lot of the time such entities work in environments that lack regulation and can therefore misuse power. In the same way, the application of AI in police work and criminal justice systems is another potential point of negative emphasis of AI because the algorithms designed for applying justice are programmed with prejudices based on experience and may even increase the existing prejudice. This is why such cases are clear examples of why there is a dire need for well-structured supervision frameworks that will maintain the standard of ethical use of AI systems (Buttazzo, 2023).

The fact that the software that underlies AI is impenetrable only adds to the ethical issue. Another limitation traces its roots from machine learning, or rather, deep learning where most algorithms are opaque in that it is almost impossible to explain how or why a certain decision was made. This lack of transparency weakens the confidence people have in the working of AI brings to the regulators, developers, and the buyers' interface a paradox between AI-performance efficiency and AI-responsibility. There is no simple solution to this problem (Neves & Almeida, 2023). It means that a great deal of effort is needed to construct systems that can help stakeholders to scrutinize those decisions and work with algorithms in a more effective manner.

This chapter also demonstrates that AI presents unique threats to employment and the socio-economic environment. Improvement in the automation of work processes and machines poses the risk of replacing workers in even industries that sell goods and services, transportation, and logistics among others. On the positive side, new jobs and career fields appear with the use of AI, in the meantime, technological progress generates higher demands on skills and frequently this process is faster than it can be met by workers. There are two objectives that the governments and policymakers are to achieve, i.e., encourage innovations and address the negative impacts of automation. The outcomes, especially the impact of AI are that government and corporate strategies in areas like reskilling initiatives, social safety nets, and education reforms are functional mechanisms that guarantee that the advantages of AI are disseminated to all embracing late applications that may not benefit from government overheads.

Furthermore, AI increases global disparities especially between the developed and the developing countries. The countries and regions with widespread technology adoption and high research and development spends are likely to gain from AI while developing countries mostly trail behind. This digital divide poses the danger of aggravating socio-economic inequalities at the center of scrutiny is unfairness and exclusion. A key point of discussion today needs to be that international cooperation and the development of capacity as a global commodity needs to remain open and serve as a tool for growth and not as a distinguisher of human identity.

The impact that AI brings to the world introduces another level of politics: geopolitics. Leading countries' AI competition affects the level of safety and stability in the international system in the future. In today's global geopolitical systems, countries headed towards AI development often tend to protect their employment in the sector and apply competitive strategies rather than cooperation; thus, there can appear inconsistent and even conflicting policies and regulation. The civilian and military duality of most AI technologies add another layer of the problem to the mix. For example, self-directed robotic weapons and cyber weapons have existential implications that need immediate global governance (Padmaja & Sadasivuni, 2024). Hence, the difficulty is to create an international system for governance that works within the confines of national interest while serving the supreme interest of security for all nations across the world.

Misinformation and fake content, made available by the help of AI technologies, are also considered to remain some of the major threats to society. Technology like deepfake, a tool that generates realistic fake audio as well as video can be very dangerous for society as they are likely to cause loss of confidence and manipulation of society. When used by malicious actors, AI is capable of damaging democracy and social cohesiveness: through the promotion of fake news during an election period and by fueling division. To overcome these risks, a complex model should be implemented safeguarding by technology, increasing population's media literacy and developing strong legislation.

Consequently, for these challenges to be dealt with appropriately, AI governance cannot do with a single, narrow approach. It is crucial to encourage coordination between policymakers, technology experts and civil society to create conceptual models regarding the rights approaches of AI. At the national level, governments must implement rules which govern emerging problems like data privacy and algorithmic transparency, as well as employment changes. At the same time, it shall also be the international organizations that should undertake the main responsibilities of the standardization and integration processes. Frameworks like the OECD's AI Principles, the European Union's AI Act present promising beginnings toward the formation of a comprehensive AI governance system but much work still needs to be done (Dwivedi et al., 2023).

Besides accuracy and efficiency of outcome, there is a need to incorporate the public into AI's decision-making process. All the stakeholders have to embrace the responsibility of awareness creation for developing AI technologies and clearing societal concerns. Equal to it, those who design and create AI should adopt values of responsible attitudes to the technology and incorporate ethical strategies into the developing and deploying stages. Moreover, the multidisciplinary cooperation connecting technology, law and ethics is essential for an effective approach at the present to the complex issues connected with AI.

As such the new persistent by way of artificial intelligence can be described as a threatened opportunity in equal measure. AI is innovation that responds effectively across multiple fields, but there are some responsible trends in developing and implementing AI. This chapter raises the apparent dilemma of promoting innovation whilst also encouraging accountability that should shape efforts to address this issue. This way, socio-economic challenges and ethical questions connected with the utilization of AI by humanity will allow humanity to improve the world with the help of AI. In conclusion, it means that further evolution of AI will not only depend on innovations but also on global intent to make the tech future more fair, environmentally friendly, and people-respecting.

CONCEPTUAL FRAMEWORK FOR GLOBAL AI GOVERNANCE

Artificial intelligence has been found to be a greatly disruptive innovation tool as it redefines societies and economies at an unimaginable speed and magnitude. However, the existing global trends regarding the progress of AI develop a need for international AI governance that leans towards the fact that technology has no borders. AI governance on an international level remains a work in progress and an endeavor that requires cooperation, the integration of universal ethical standards and frameworks, and the development of accurate architecture of recommendation and regulation that ensures equity, responsibility and inclusiveness at its core. In this chapter, the author aims at analyzing such aspects as the general principles of governance, the ways for its realization, the participation of various international actors. This is important as AI comes with a bag and baggage of multifaceted issucs that require a systematic and dynamic response.

Some of the basic determinants of the architecture of any global governance structure, is an agreed upon set of norms that capture societal goals and people's values. When it comes to AI, the need to focus on ethical issues is even more relevant because the function of AI is to work in the realms which are the guarantors of people's rights, privacy, and social justice. Pervasive in these principles, is the principle of non-discrimination, which aims at preventing bias amplification by AI systems. Algorithmic fairness will need constant monitoring on which data to use while training a model, how to build and deploy models capable of producing non-discriminatory results. For instance, AI systems used in hiring or credit scoring usually contain biases that perpetuate past unfair discriminations and hence call for intense monitoring with accountability measures being put in place (Budhwar et al., 2022).

Another promising factor to be discussed extensively in the further AI regulation process is the non-operations concept of transparency. Here, deep learning methods, which are popular AI architectures, present practical difficulties for trust and responsibility. The contingent choices in AI systems must be justifiable especially in domains that involve critical decision making like diagnosing diseases, recommending a new legislation or deploying an autonomous weapon. Transparency requires the stewardship of new modular models known as explainable AI to help others understand and evaluate the conclusions reached. Also, it refers to the duties to provide information on data sources, the training process, and aims at applying AI. In turn, such a requirement encourages transparency and responsibility.

Diversity shapes the third leg of international AI regulation. Due to socio-economic, cultural and political differences that exist in the world today, governance frameworks have to understand and tolerate differences. This involves stakeholders from the developed and the developing countries, civil society, universities, businesses and poor strata of society. Diversity also encompasses making the opportunities of AI and related technologies, and their outcomes, accessible to all the four corners of the globe, bridging the digital divide that is even more significant in the developing world. Failing that, there is a very real danger that the technologies are going to end up reinforcing rather than reducing inequalities between nations and people (Wubineh et al., 2024).

It is therefore imperative to have sound mechanisms and institutions to effectively and practically realize global AI governance with the above established principles. One of the important issues facing this process is the problem of the convergence of the regulation standards. This means that while some countries have instituted very high standard rules regarding the conduct of clinical research some are not regulated adequately. It means that while endeavoring to adapt the requirements to the national settings, it is equally important to have common mechanisms to address the threats of regulatory competition. Global organizations including the United Nations, the Organization for Economic Cooperation and Development and others, as well as multilateral regional blocs and the like engage in determining conditions for dialogue or consensus aiming at attaining said goal (Roberts et al., 2024).

The idea of the AI ethical boards and the independent overseeing bodies is part of the governance frameworks. They, as interdisciplinary committees, may afford non-biased assessment of AI systems about their conformity with ethical principles or legal norms. It can also take the role of coordinating a dispute and reaching an agreement regarding the issue specified by them concerning the use of artificial intelligence (Jiang et al., 2021). Also, private public sector collaborations are critical for the generation of innovation with health accreditation.

The study also presented the complexity in the interface between AI and governance due to AI's dynamic and adaptive characteristics. In many cases, the traditional risk-regulating approaches, which are much too rigid and slow in adapting to changes, are completely insufficient to govern the development of AI systems and technologies. As a result, governance frameworks cannot afford to eschew principles of flexibility and incrementalism. For example, regulatory sandboxes enable a range of testing and activities within a safely specified framework so that, after learning from outcomes, relevant policies may be adjusted. Similarly, horizon scanning of the nature of AI applications that are likely to gain prominence in the future enables the formulation of appropriate risks and benefits linked to their application thus enabling proactive rather than reactive measures regarding their governance (Kuleto et al., 2021).

At the international level, the contributions of international organizations in AI regulation are central. Leading members of the international community such as the United Nations in their High-Level Panel on Digital Cooperation have called for a commitment to a multinational approach in solving the challenges advanced by Artificial Intelligence. Perhaps the creation of global compacts or treaties regarding AI ethics and its governance can serve a cohesive catalytic purpose. On the other hand, the recently launched OECD's artificial intelligence principles signed by over 50 countries are a step towards actionable guidelines for good AI. These principles include focus on humans, justice and owing of information, which are important principles of forming and adopting national and international policies (Gill & Germann, 2021).

The European Union has stepped up as one of the leaders of regulatory daring with its proposed Artificial Intelligence Act. Thus, the Act aims at achieving innovation in the field of AI systems while placing the systems under distinct risk categories at the same time. The EU's leadership conveys the message, which reflects the potential of regional actors to shape the international rules at the world level, primarily in cases where their standards are recognized as reference ones by other actors (Rajagopal et al., 2023). In the same way, it is the focus on these regional dimensions that is the key to guaranteeing that the other dimensions of these governance frameworks are inclusive as well.

International actors in the form of corporations, academic institutions and non-governmental organizations also have important roles to play in the direction of governance of artificial intelligence. Technology firms which engage in the development of AI, and which utilize the technology in various projects have essential roles to play when it comes to ethics. Not substituting for regulations, voluntary codes of conduct and industry standards can help the authorities promote accountability and develop new ideas. Scholarly literature enriches the knowledge regarding the nature of AI and its implications; on the other hand, NGOs represent the welfare of marginalized groups and put pressure on companies. The relations between these actors prove that global AI governance is a complex multistakeholder process (Sharma et al., 2020).

Still there are some quite serious gaps and problems in the formation and development of the comprehensive system of governance. The fact that most of these technologies are dual-use systems in nature that are formed essentially for civil use but leveraged under some circumstances for military purposes, presents Volker's challenge of global security. Such as the case with autonomous weapons, one digs into the ethical and legal tolerance of the accountable agent in conflicts. Likewise, either in cyber warfare or surveillance, the application of AI adds tension between nations, imperative regulation to monitor the usage of AI in security areas.

Misinformation and disinformation that have been promoted lately have become another concern that concerns AI technologies. Deepfake and fake news which are generated and promoted through algorithm amplification erode the credibility of information systems and destabilize democratic politics and social cohesion. Solving these problems is possible only with the help of technological protection, media education, and legislative activities (Taeihagh, 2021). People all over the world must unite to fight against cross-border threats and argue that the integrity of information networks is key.

To sum up, global AI governance is needed and possible on the threshold of new breakthroughs in post-industrial technological growth. Therefore, having structured governance frameworks with ethics, transparency, and inclusiveness as their core, the global village can transverse the global AI landscape and gain the full potential of the technology. International organizations, national governments, and non-state actors' actions are expected to be coordinated to set out standardization regimes, flexibility, and stewardship frameworks. Al thus the need for collaborative and future-oriented governance increases as changes in the AI field stay on the rise.

ROLE OF INTERNATIONAL BODIES IN AI REGULATION

As has been pointed out with the development of new technologies like artificial intelligence AI the issue of governance is complex and multi-dimensional and as such requires an international approach. As AI technologies expand beyond territorial borders, they impact international jurisdictions on issues to do with security, human rights and economic justice and ethical issues. Here, decision makers have a critical role in setting up consistent standards as well as in creating an institutional structure on a global level for an adequate utilization that reflects the common requirements and responsibility of the world community about the technical progress in terms of artificial intelligence. It shall analyze the input of international organizations and associations, regional one and multilateral collaborations to AI regulation, its assets, drawbacks and possibility of optimal cooperation.

The UN, OECD, WEF and others, all these global institutions have gone through a lot in terms of developing the basic framework of the future AI regulation. As has been already mentioned before, the United Nations has highlighted multilateralism as the key to addressing the ethical, legal and societal considerations regarding AI. The high-level panel on digital cooperation, set up under the UN Secretary-General, has urged for more open discussions of how governments should regulate AI and acknowledged the signaling need for developing common norms and guidelines. One of the brilliant suggestions it makes is the global digital compact which targets marshal governments, business and civil society to agree on minimal standards of conduct when it comes to AI. This effort demonstrates that the UN can mobilize different actors and coordinate people to agree on certain issues, central to global AI regulation.

The OECD has been most active in the international process of developing the prescriptive norms that regulate the use of AI. On May 22, 2019, the OECD published its Principles on Artificial Intelligence AI, which was embraced by over 50 countries, some of which are not members of the OECD. These principles focus on human-like AI, non-opaque AI, one that is answerable for its actions and atheist AI that will not exclude any aspect or process in its function and can be used as the first principles of ethical artificial intelligence. The achievement of the OECD principles has strongly contributed to the coherency of regulation systems adopted across different legal systems of member states and has acted as a guideline for the formation of regional and international norms (Almeida et al., 2021). However, the methods of putting into practice these principles differ so much from country to country depending on the political, economic and cultural system of the country in which these principles are being implemented.

Sub-national actors, especially the EU, have also gained an important role in regulating the development of artificial intelligence around the world. The EU's proposed Artificial Intelligence Act is a pioneering legislation that proposes the classification of AI systems depending on the risk associated with them and the regulatory framework linked to these categories. New genres of AI applications like biometric identification systems are associated with very high risks and are governed by the law mandating businesses to conduct risk assessments and declare compliance obligations. Thus, the risk-based approach used by the EU aims to achieve innovation with proper protection from the negative consequences. It is for the very reason that the extraterritorial application of the AI Act is so important that the treaty has the potential to set the course globally: companies that want to enter the

EU market must adhere to the provisions of the AI Act. This phenomenon has come to be known as the Brussels Effect; thus, regional regulation can socially influence localization efforts and mold the practices of transnational business organizations as well as influence policies in different jurisdictions (Kashefi et al., 2024).

Much as these efforts continue, there are still major challenges that need to be filled so as to strive to establish a coherent international law of artificial intelligence. One of the main issues on the way to sustainable development remains the conflict of interests and needs of various countries. The countries that are advanced in utilizing AI may adopt the economic objectives of AI as well as support the restricted regulation of AI. Whereas the developing nations may focus on fairness in providing access to such technologies; in addition, addressing the problems that relate to unfavorable effects on susceptible groups. These divergences only offer compelling reasons that the international community should encourage fairness and accountability so that all people who have legitimate grievances with their leaders, especially those in distant corners of the globe, have proper recourse (Erdelyi & Goldsmith, 2022).

International bodies actually do not just create norms targeting the members; they also help them in building their capacity and exchanging information. The United Nations Educational, Scientific, and Cultural Organization (UNESCO) and the International Telecommunication Union (ITU) have recently started campaigns for education and skill building around AI, especially in the developing world. For example, UNESCO's Recommendation on the Ethics of Artificial Intelligence states that raising public awareness of AI, as well as developing organizational capacities that will allow all countries to effectively engage in global AI regulation, should remain a priority. Likewise, the ITU has come up with guidelines on ethics of artificial intelligence in important and sensitive areas like health and emergency and offers technical support to its member states (Cha, 2024). Such actions show the possibility of international organizations to alleviate the problem of digital exclusion and be effective in AI governance.

Some other significance toward the realization of international AI regulation are the multilateral cooperation and affiliation among international and national governments themselves and other entities, as well as international and national organizations and the private sector. While the partnership on AI and the more recent Global Partnership on Artificial Intelligence (GPAI) are notable examples of how stakeholders themselves can collaborate in the development of an adequate set of approaches to tackle emerging challenges together. The GPAI which is backed by countries including but not limited to Canada, France, as well as India emphasizes on the promotion and development of research and innovation in AI that will complement their deployment in compliance with the right and ethical impacts among the society (Walter, 2024). Such relationships promote the sharing of knowledge and assets in efforts to allow countries to harmonize on the right policies and effectively solve mutual problems.

Nevertheless, there is indispensability in the regulation of AI from the international bodies, and this is trapped by structural and operations challenges. This however remains a major challenge due to the absence of compliance enforcement tools since most of the international arrangements and regulations are non-binding and based on consensus. This is because such implementation is often voluntary, and this means that international bodies may not be well placed to effectively tackle instances of non-compliance as we shall see later. Also, the speed of AI advancement is sometimes fast, leaving international institutions unable to catch up with these changes, which explains why there needs to be relevant, innovative, and effective modes of governance.

A third concern is of course the fact that many of these AI applications are dual use in nature meaning they can be applied in a civil as well as in a military context. The threat of autonomous weapons systems and AI-enabled surveillance systems as an increasingly significant potential to provoke political and military crises has obvious ethical questions and security concerns; therefore, they need international regulations. The UN's Group of Governmental Experts on Lethal Autonomous Weapons Systems has been trying to tackle these challenges for some time, but the process of achieving progress has been unreasonably slow thanks to geopolitical conflicts and, of course, the differences in the interests of the participating countries. This can only underline the need for diplomatic work aimed at increasing trust between countries to achieve sustainable agreements on the use of AI in the sphere of security (Pacholska, 2023).

Superimposing these global economic cyclical interactions on artificial intelligence adds another level of difficulty to the regulatory field. AI technologies can be pathological in provoking various forms of inequality both in individual societies and between different countries. The current innovations in AI are mostly controlled by developed high-income nations and multinational corporations resulting in the development of high levels of inequalities in the aggregate benefits of AI. Multilateral organizations have to address such disparities through fair trade, pressure for technology transfer and supporting innovative systems in developing countries. Such measures are needed to prevent AI's effect from being the reinforcement of current global economic imbalances (Emery-Xu et al., 2024).

Therefore, it can be asserted that the international and supranational organizations are an indispensable factor that affects the development of regulation in the sphere of AI. It is crucial that they do this because of the transnationality of AI's issues and the need to make the gains that come with its application to be available to everyone in the world. However, the major barriers to robust international AI management include self-interest, systemic arrangements, and the fact that AI tools are both beneficial and dangerous. As a result, these complexities can be addressed and managed by the international organization that contributes to set up the regulatory foundation for ethical, transparent and human-centric AI. The involvement of international institutions in the AI regulation is not a mere technical or process that has to be followed, but a vision for the desired equitable future AI landscape.

CHALLENGES IN INTERNATIONAL AI GOVERNANCE

Setting out, defining and regulating artificial intelligence (AI) involves enormous global issue-architecting questions that are beyond the reach of national statecraft. Nonetheless, the development of an integrated global governance architecture to governance AI entails formidable challenges. International disagreements on how AI ought to be regulated stem from the proliferations of political systems, economic and cultural perspectives. In addition, the development of AI technologies is extremely fast, and ever-increasing, which overloads policymakers and furthers the challenges faced by unregulated or poorly regulated AI technologies. This section expands on various problems associated with the functioning of the international AI governance and the specific challenges that are the ethical dilemmas, geopolitical vise, economic inequality, technological evolution, and the deficit of institutional capacity.

At the center of the main difficulties encountered by international AI governance lies the absence of any shared and unambiguous ethical postulates and normative orientations. Obviously, the AI systems introduced are designed with the local cultural and societal norms informed by the creators of these significant technological inventions. Therefore, the meaning of ethical AI varies from country to country, including with regard to such specific discursive points as surveillance, privacy, and AI in the military context. For example, while the European Union and its member states formally value privacy and ethical standards that are woven into the country's legal framework and promoted through the GDPR and the proposed AI Act, different parts of the world, for example, China, focus on the critical and economic opportunities of AI and use it for massive surveillance and control over citizens. This divergence poses a problem by limiting the ways in which stakeholders set harmonized ethical standards across the nations because countries may not agree to alternative rules that are antithetical to their strategic plans and cultural norms (Villarino, 2023).

What aggravates the issues of global AI regulation is these are geopolitical rivalries. Today, the AI market looks rather unified, and the number of technologically developed countries using AI as a strategic resource crucial for competition in the world economy, including the United States and China, is constantly growing. This has created an environment of an AI arms race, since every country wants to be ahead in the development of AI. They include disagreements on common standards, objectives, and policies relating to technologies as well as proprietary national interests; as a result, international agreements on regulation are limited by the unwillingness of nations to surrender control of what they consider strategic assets and technology. For example, some members continue to argue over export controls of AI technologies and services in international trade since some nations do not want to relax restrictions to preserve their market leadership. These geopolitical dynamics lay on the fact that it becomes a great challenge for countries to trust each other and work together in the governance of AI (Bastit et al., 2023).

Another challenge facing international AI governance is the uneven economic development of nations particularly the developing countries against the backdrop of the developed ones. The leading implementers and innovators in AI are the developed HICs, owning well-developed technologies, intellectual capital, and financial resources. On the other hand, most developing countries do not have adequate capital or technological knowledge to engage in an active AI global market. This results in a digital divide where the developing nations mostly do not have a say on the governance of AI or are passive holders of AI technologies developed for and owned by other parties. It is a level of concern when AI distributes its goods and services unequally, or it will deepen the inequalities in societies across the globe. These problems must be solved within the framework of international organizations strengthening efforts on capacity building, transfer of technologies, and pro-development decision making that give developing countries a chance to invest in AI development and receive benefits from it.

One such challenge is the dynamic rate of technology in AI, that offers a real threat of obsolescence. Machine learning technologies are still relatively new and are advancing rapidly, as is the case with many other AI applications, faster than the current policymakers are capable of dealing with comprehensively. Technologies like generative AI, deep learning and autonomous systems present ethics, law and more significant social questions which existing laws cannot address well. For instance, deep fakes for manipulative purposes such as fake news and identity theft and the question of robots deciding on the use of force related to AI controlled autonomous weapons systems. The multiple challenges surround the concept of AI and require flexible approaches to governance that will enable an adequate response to novelties and risks at the same time. But still, due to the absence of technical skills among policymakers and time barriers in legislation processes, a number of regulatory voids that weaken the governance efforts remain unfilled (Gu, 2023).

This is even more so since AI technologies are dual-use technologies, making the governance efforts even more challenging. Such applications of Artificial Intelligence can be used in both civilian and military situations and raise a name for more than one ethical and security concern. Systems such as Lethal Autonomous Weapon Systems, have been widely discussed in international organizations: while some argue for the complete prohibition of automation of weapons systems, the others speak about benefits accruing from the efficient use of these systems. Unfortunately, the United Nations' Group of Governmental Experts on Lethal Autonomous Weapons Systems has been rather inconclusive with these issues mostly due to political agendas and the conflicting self-interests of participating nations. In the same way, application of AI in security has raised some questions about the relationship between security and privacy. Some countries have been using AI to monitor their people (Okolo, 2023). Both these examples bear testimony to the dual use nature of AI and make the case for having strong norms in the international domain that can check misuse of AI while facilitating its genuine usage.

Suboptimal governance of International AI is also characterized by lack of enforcement mechanisms as well as institutional limitations. Most conventions and recommendations on AI are soft or recommendatory meaning that states only have made recommendations required of them. Still, such frameworks have their merits, although their results are frequently restrained by the lack of the enactment of specific rules. For example, The Principles on Artificial Intelligence developed by the Organization for Economic Co-operation and Development (OECD) has got many supporters but no enforcement structures to compel organizations which are party to the principles to adhere to them or face repercussions if they infringe on them. Likewise, the United Nations' attempts at gaining broader digital cooperation mean that the big picture principles are widely recognized but not always implemented. The reliance on voluntary measures reflects a broader challenge in international governance: the problem of harmony between sovereignty and cooperation. Having set up normative standards of organizational behavior, effective governance entails the establishment of ways and means of publicizing, enforcing and sanctioning non-compliance (Wagner et al., 2024).

One of the greatest concerns is that some countries and stakeholders are left out of the discussion processes that shape AI governance internationally. Most of the mechanisms of governance are managed by developed countries that put the needs of their own constituents before those of vulnerable peoples. The second reason is exclusion, which skews governance frameworks and deprives them of the support of the large number of people around the globe. Reducing AI bias consequently requires civil society organizations, indigenous communities and other structurally disenfranchised populations to be provided with a greater voice in governance debates. This has not only implications for shifts in governance structures but also for attempts to enhance these actors' ability to effectively participate in highly technical and political policy processes.

Finally, it comes to pragmatic implications and, once again, the variety of problems related to the international governance of AI matches the heterogeneity of the technologies to be governed. Ethical issues, politics, social, technological and institutional factors make it challenging to foster appropriate global governance solutions for the world. Therefore, tackling these challenges entails a systems approach that, among others, entails functioning as a team, being inclusive and recognizing the dynamic nature of the tasks given the evolving characteristics of the AI technologies. As they rightfully pointed out that getting to the right approach to governance is a challenging task, however, this journey is not optional because the stakes are too high. Asian countries' success in AI governance will define not only the future of AI advancement, but also its possible human consequences and effects on international security and equity. The five identified challenges can thus be effectively addressed and this way the international community can promote the idea of the new governance model for maximization of the benefits of AI and minimization of harms.

RECOMMENDATIONS FOR STRENGTHENING AI GOVERNANCE

AI technologies are deepening complexification in global systems thus the need for a strong framework but one that is fair and has visions for the future. The ineffectiveness of existing frameworks, primarily due to their failure to adapt to the scale and speed of developing AI technology, and failure to account for conflicting national interest, was found to this call for fresh ideas for the governance of AI. The following recommendations seek to fill the mentioned gaps in the existing framework and focus on developing a theoretically coherent and practical and multifaceted governance framework that can be integrated into ethical and sustainable global development goals.

The first measure for the enhancement of the Global AI Governance regime is creating an Inter-governmental regulatory body on AI regulation and cooperation. Despite attempts from the UN and OECD to start the regulation of AI, their existing charters and capabilities are not well suited to tackling the challenges that AI presents as a unique technology, effectively calling for a new global institution. It was also suggested that at least a trade-like structure like WTO or IAEA should exist to act as the central decision-making and discussion center of AI Governing policies. Such an entity would also help countries coordinate on how best to implement regulatory frameworks while also making sure that the frameworks are dynamic enough to capture the fast-changing AI market. This body could set international standards and legal requirements to which states can be held accountable and enforce those standards with consequences for the non-compliance, while missing components create enforcement gaps that compromise the existing models of governance.

Equally important is the multi-stakeholder approach as the guiding model for the management of AI. Due to the broad and layered characteristics of AI technologies, its development and management must involve a broad set of stakeholders, such as government institutions, business and industry, civil society organizations and academia, and other vulnerable populations. Since most debates on AI regulation involve governments and corporations, it is crucial to involve marginalized groups because any governance framework that is developed must reflect the circumstances of all consumers and producers. For example, civil society organizations would offer insights on ethical and social ramifications of AI and academia on the other hand would offer supporting research, analysis and advice. Moreover, the shutdown of representative governance deprives marginalized communities, which are on the receiving end of unfair AI discrimination, of any worthwhile say in the continuity of their oppression by AI. This on one hand has necessitated calls for changes in the structures to guarantee such persons a seat at the discussion table but also the implementation of capacity enhancement measures that would prepare such persons for technical and policy debates. It is recommended that a multistakeholder governance model will act as an improvement to the current legitimacy, inclusiveness, and effectiveness of AI governance globally.

Transparency and accountability should also be considered to catalyze trust and engagement in the AI regulation process. One main issue in the nature of AI systems has been the black-box nature especially of systems using machine learning and deep learning. It remains that to avoid these problems, global governance frameworks should require that reliable transparency mechanisms are implemented, including algorithmic auditing, interpretability, and the communicating of data origins and usage. Also, some monitoring and reporting responsibilities need to be created for developers, deployers, and users of AI systems as they are answerable for the results of their technologies. Such structures may be legal responsibilities, professional standards, and a body of ethics or other autonomous authorities. It is evident that transparency and accountability should be applied to Artificial Intelligence regulation as both ethical principles and as rational actions to take into consideration the stakeholders that should trust such systems.

Opponents of a prompt implementation of AI argue that the technology is not yet accessible to a broad scope of populations, and that developing nations are being left behind in terms of technological advancement and infrastructure, which, in turn, results in an AI 'divide'. The high levels of accumulation of artificial intelligence definition and AI assets in the technologically advanced nations increase the inequalities enhancing the impacts of abrupt technological disconnection between AI leaders and emerging nations. To address this problem, international organizations must ensure all projects that contribute to AI development also increase the capability of developing nations to interact with these technologies. This could include grants for research and development, grants for training AI professionals of the future and the incubation of regional AI centers of excellence. More specifically, such persuasions may involve technology transfer agreements to complement current elements of intellectual property rights reforms as a way of enhancing the spread of AI inventions to other areas of the globe that may not have been beneficiaries in the first attempt. These steps would not only allow the developing nations to leverage the opportunities within the AI domain for their country's growth but also come in handy to the benefit of the global knowledge pool and innovation.

Similarly, there is a need to enhance ethical and normative foundations to support the use and application of AI solutions. As informative as existing guidelines may be, including the recent OECD Principles on Artificial Intelligence and the UNESCO Recommendation on the Ethics of Artificial Intelligence, they may lack enforceability and still prove insufficiently comprehensive to cover all the issue areas arising from artificial intelligence. A new international convention, in the same way as the UDHR, could be adopted as a single standard of ethics for using the AI, including the questions of fairness, responsibility for actions, openness and respect for human rights. This should be done alongside developing country specific ethical codes to address differences in regional ethical concerns because of differences in culture and context. In addition, mainstream implementation of ethical knowledge into the courses and training related to Artificial Intelligence would guarantee that developers and policymakers have the necessary competencies required in the sphere of dealing with the ethical non-layman issues of AI solutions.

The fact that AI technologies are used in both military and surveillance settings require the design of strict measures to avoid the exploitation of the capabilities. Issues of efficiency can still be seen in certain fields such as autonomous weapons and AI surveillance systems which elicit major ethical, legal as well as security concerns in relation to their development as well as deployment on the international platforms hence the cooperation agencies need to develop international agreements among themselves. UNCCW could be stepped up with additions regarding AI solutions in the military domain to define concrete prohibitions as for their application. Likewise, the relations between AI and international agreement should cover the question of the utilization of AI to conduct mass surveillance while noting the respective security concerns and protection of individual's rights and freedoms. These safeguards, therefore, should be accompanied by constant monitoring to deal with the violation cases appropriately. Crystal, and in particular, its dual-use technologies are among the most crucial areas of AI governance around the globe as their abuse threatens global security and order.

Lastly, international cooperation and knowledge exchange should be considered a critical measure to address the highly fragmented nature of present-day approaches to AI governance. Creation of new different kinds of artificial intelligence is quite a separate process, and there are few communications and experiences shared between different countries and organizations. To meet this challenge, specific avenues through which stakeholders can deliberate information and coordinate their strategies must be developed on an international level. There are some good starting places, including the GPAI, and the World Economic Forum's AI initiatives but these have to be scaled up. Moreover, increasing collaborations between the public and private sectors and between developed and developing countries would improve the global management of AI due to increased geographical participation of experts and assets.

Consequently, the improvement of AI global governance is a task that needs to be solved with a multifaceted strategy in regard to ethically, technically, and geopolitically of using AI technologies. This widely acknowledged endeavor can only be accomplished if such measures as the creation of a separate international agency, facilitation of global transparency and accountability, improvement of capacity and technology sharing, creation of strict ethical standards, regulation of technologies with dual uses, and international collaboration were developed. With the help of these changes, the international community will establish constructive relationships between AI and the process of human development, ensuring the reduction of risks and making use of the AI benefits for creation of an effective and efficient system of governance for humanity. As AI advances and recalculates the global arena, it becomes more crucial to solve the mentioned governance challenges. Change is now possible only through societal engagement, creativity and collaboration on the vision that AI is to be an agent of positive transformation instead of a driver of more discord.

REFERENCES

Ajami, R. A., & Karimi, H. A. (2023). Artificial Intelligence: Opportunities and Challenges. *Journal of Asia-Pacific Business*, *24*(2), 73–75. DOI: 10.1080/10599231.2023.2210239

Almeida, P., Santos, C. D. S., & Farias, J. S. (2021). *Artificial Intelligence Regulation: a framework for governance*. ResearchGate., DOI: 10.1007/s10676-021-09593-z

Bastit, B., Fernandez, M., Kesh, S., & Tsui, D. (2023). The AI Governance Challenge. *S&P Global*. https://www.spglobal.com/en/research-insights/special-reports/the-ai-governance-challenge

Budhwar, P., Malik, A., De Silva, M. T. T., & Thevisuthan, P. (2022). Artificial intelligence – challenges and opportunities for international HRM: A review and research agenda. *International Journal of Human Resource Management*, *33*(6), 1065–1097. DOI: 10.1080/09585192.2022.2035161

Buttazzo, G. (2023). Rise of artificial general intelligence: risks and opportunities. *Frontiers*. https://www.frontiersin.org/journals/artificial-intelligence/articles/10.3389/frai.2023.1226990/full

Cha, S. (2024). Towards an international regulatory framework for AI safety: Lessons from the IAEA's nuclear safety regulations. *Humanities & Social Sciences Communications*, *11*(1), 506. DOI: 10.1057/s41599-024-03017-1

Csernatoni, R. (2024). The AI Governance Arms Race: From Summit Pageantry to Progress? *Carnegie Endowment.*https://carnegieendowment.org/research/2024/10/the-ai-governance-arms-race-from-summit-pageantry-to-progress?lang=en&center=europe

Dwivedi, Y. K., Sharma, A., Rana, N. P., Giannakis, M., Goel, P., & Dutot, V. (2023). Evolution of artificial intelligence research in Technological Forecasting and Social Change: Research topics, trends, and future directions. *Technological Forecasting and Social Change*, *192*, 122579. DOI: 10.1016/j.techfore.2023.122579

Emery-Xu, N., Jordan, R., & Trager, R. (2025, April). International governance of advancing artificial intelligence. *AI & Society*, *40*(4), 3019–3044. Advance online publication. DOI: 10.1007/s00146-024-02050-7

Erdelyi, O. J., & Goldsmith, J. (2022). Regulating artificial intelligence: Proposal for a global solution. *Government Information Quarterly*, *39*(4), 101748. DOI: 10.1016/j.giq.2022.101748

Gill, A. S., & Germann, S. (2022). Conceptual and normative approaches to AI governance for a global digital ecosystem supportive of the UN Sustainable Development Goals (SDGs). *AI and Ethics, 2*(2), 293–301. DOI: 10.1007/s43681-021-00058-z PMID: 34790947

Gu, P. (2023). Global Artificial Intelligence Governance: Challenges and Complications. *ResearchGate*. https://www.researchgate.net/publication/372083906_Global_Artificial_Intelligence_Governance_Challenges_and_Complications

Jiang, L., Wu, Z., Xu, X., Zhan, Y., Jin, X., Wang, L., & Qiu, Y. (2021). Opportunities and challenges of artificial intelligence in the medical field: Current application, emerging problems, and problem-solving strategies. *The Journal of International Medical Research, 49*(3), 03000605211000157. Advance online publication. DOI: 10.1177/03000605211000157 PMID: 33771068

Kashefi, P., Kashefi, Y., Hossein, A., & Mirsaraei, G. (2024). Shaping the future of AI: Balancing innovation and ethics in global regulation. *Uniform Law Review, 29*(3), 524–548. DOI: 10.1093/ulr/unae040

Kuleto, V., Ilic, M., Dumangiu, M., Rankovic, M., Martins, O. M. D., Paun, D., & Mihoreanu, L. (2021). Exploring Opportunities and Challenges of Artificial Intelligence and Machine Learning in Higher Education Institutions. *Sustainability (Basel), 13*(18), 10424. DOI: 10.3390/su131810424

Neves, M. P., & Almeida, A. B. D. (2023). Before and Beyond Artificial Intelligence: Opportunities and Challenges, *ResearchGate*. https://www.researchgate.net/publication/376852554_Before_and_Beyond_Artificial_Intelligence_Opportunities_and_Challenges

Okolo, C. T. (2023). AI in the Global South: Opportunities and challenges towards more inclusive governance. *Brookings*. https://www.brookings.edu/articles/ai-in-the-global-south-opportunities-and-challenges-towards-more-inclusive-governance/

Pacholska, M. (2023). Many Hands in the Black Box: Artificial Intelligence and the Responsibility of International Organizations. *SSRN*. https://papers.ssrn.com/sol3/papers.cfm?abstract_id=4501072

Padmaja, V. R., & Sadasivuni, L. (2024). The rise of AI: A comprehensive research review. *International Journal of Artificial Intelligence, 13*(2), 2226. DOI: 10.11591/ijai.v13.i2.pp2226-2235

Rajagopal, M., Sivasakthivel, R., Ramar, G., & Karuppasamy, S.K. (2023) A Conceptual Framework for AI Governance in Public Administration – A Smart Governance Perspective. *IEEE Xplore*, 488-495. https://doi.org/DOI: 0.1109/I-SMAC58438.2023.10290366

Roberts, H., Hine, E., Taddeo, M., & Floridi, L. (2024). Global AI governance: Barriers and pathways forward. *International Affairs, 100*(3), 1275–1286. DOI: 10.1093/ia/iiae073

Samson, P. (2023). On Advancing Global AI Governance. *Centre for International Governance Innovation.* https://www.cigionline.org/articles/on-advancing-global-ai-governance/

Schmitt, L. (2022). Mapping global AI governance: A nascent regime in a fragmented landscape. *AI and Ethics*, *2*(2), 303–314. DOI: 10.1007/s43681-021-00083-y

Sharma, G. D., Yadav, A., & Chopra, R. (2023). Artificial intelligence and effective governance: A review, critique and research agenda Author links open overlay panel. *Sustainable Futures : An Applied Journal of Technology, Environment and Society*, *2*, 100004. DOI: 10.1016/j.sftr.2019.100004

Taeihagh, A. (2021). Governance of artificial intelligence. *Policy and Society*, *40*(2), 137–157. DOI: 10.1080/14494035.2021.1928377

Tallberg, J., Erman, E., Furendal, M., Geith, J., Klamberg, M., & Lundgren, M. (2023). The Global Governance of Artificial Intelligence: Next Steps for Empirical and Normative Research. *International Studies Review*, *25*(3), viad040. Advance online publication. DOI: 10.1093/isr/viad040

Villarino, J. M. B. (2023). Global Standard-Setting for Artificial Intelligence: Para-regulating International Law for AI? *Brill.* https://brill.com/view/journals/auso/41/1/article-p157_7.xml?language=en

Wagner, J. K., Doerr, M., & Schmit, C. D. (2024). AI Governance: A Challenge for Public Health. *JMIR Public Health and Surveillance*, *10*, e58358. DOI: 10.2196/58358 PMID: 39347615

Walter, Y. (2024). Managing the race to the moon: Global policy and governance in Artificial Intelligence regulation-A contemporary overview and an analysis of socioeconomic consequences. *Discover Artificial Intelligence*, *4*(1), 14. DOI: 10.1007/s44163-024-00109-4

Wubineh, B. Z., Deriba, F. G., & Woldeyohannis, M. M. (2024). Exploring the opportunities and challenges of implementing artificial intelligence in healthcare: A systematic literature review. *Urologic Oncology*, *42*(3), 48–56. DOI: 10.1016/j.urolonc.2023.11.019 PMID: 38101991

Yang, X., Jia, J., Zhou, X., & Wang, S. (2024). The future of artificial intelligence: Time to embrace more international collaboration. *Innovation (Cambridge (Mass.))*, *5*(6), 100703. DOI: 10.1016/j.xinn.2024.100703 PMID: 39403172

Zaidan, E., & Ibrahim, I. A. (2024). AI Governance in a Complex and Rapidly Changing Regulatory Landscape: A Global Perspective. *Humanities & Social Sciences Communications*, *11*(1), 1121. DOI: 10.1057/s41599-024-03560-x

Chapter 10
Navigating the Intersection of AI Models, State Surveillance, National Security, and AI Regulation in the Indian Technological Landscape

Manu Mariyan Abraham
https://orcid.org/0000-0002-2196-3645
Christ University, Bangalore, India

Shampa Dev
Christ University, Bangalore, India

ABSTRACT

AI models like DeepSeek are revolutionising the industry with their novel development methods and low production and operation costs. Generative AI offers extraordinary capabilities in its application in different sectors. Despite this, the AI models pose serious threats to national security if allowed to operate without any checks. This paper analyses the components of AI, the type of foundational models, and the challenges it poses in regulating AI. The paper also dissects the effect of AI models on national security, surveillance apparatus and law enforcement. The apparent risk of AI models like the 'R1' posing considerable challenges to national security is discussed in the paper, along with the possibility of violating citizens' rights by the AI models implemented by the state in different sectors. The paper also makes an effort to propose the foundation for a feasible framework for AI regulation by

DOI: 10.4018/979-8-3373-1210-1.ch010

analysing the existing framework in other countries.

INTRODUCTION

DeepSeek, a Chinese AI research and development company, released DeepSeek R1, a reasoning model, to compete with ChatGPT and Gemini. DeepSeek immediately became the talk of the town due to the significantly low development and operation costs (Liao, 2025). Further, it stands out from other major Large Language Models (LLM) due to its open-source foundation model. Even though there are other models like Llama and Mistral, DeepSeek's R1 version remarkably outperforms major players like OpenAI's ChatGPT. The company claims to have introduced a novel approach to developing R1, including reinforcement learning and reward engineering. The introduction of the R1 model provides a considerable stimulus for building artificial general intelligence, which can replicate human cognition and decision-making. The imminent and immeasurable success story of DeepSeek has raised some concerns as well. Research labs have made several attempts to test the R1 model against several security metrics. DeepSeek is accused of failing these security tests, questioning its ability to provide safeguards against malicious attacks. There are also privacy concerns with respect to the amount of personal data collected by the AI model and the alleged access provided to the Chinese government (Mercer et al., 2025).

We are witnessing a rapid advancement in technology with the efforts to attain artificial general intelligence capable of emulating human cognition (Raman et al., 2025). This potential growth ushers in tremendous possibilities in applying such technology. The indoctrination of AI models into several industries has already borne fruit in terms of productivity and efficiency (Gao & Feng, 2023). However, it is clamant that the concerns raised with respect to the AI systems be addressed as early as possible.

India has made fewer efforts to develop an AI model that could compete in the global market (Suri, 2025). India recently launched an AI mission to promote the development of indigenous AI stacks and systems to compete globally (Ministry of Electronics & IT, 2025a). It is also imperative that a regulatory framework that stipulates India's AI policy be formulated wherein specific safeguards are ingrained into the law to address privacy and security concerns. Nevertheless, even the much-advanced AI system can only perform specific tasks under certain parameters (Katare et al., 2018). An AI model that can train itself to make decisions in different contexts and parameters without the intervention of humans at any stage is still theoretical. Hence, it can be alluded that AI can only handle tasks that would typically be done by a human being but with better efficacy. This has led to the argument that the current regulatory framework is sufficient for governing AI systems (Liu, 2023). For example, the compliance requirement in the provisions of the Digital Personal Data Protection (DPDP) Act, 2023 would be applicable to an AI model with respect to the collection, processing and storage of data. However, it should be noted that the Indian legislative framework is inadequate in certain scenarios, such as laws governing state surveillance and the misuse of blanket exemptions like national security.

This paper analyses the components of AI, the type of foundational models, and the challenges it poses in regulating AI. The paper also dissects the impact of AI models on national security, surveillance apparatus and law enforcement. The apparent risk of AI models like the 'R1' posing considerable challenges to national security is discussed in the paper, along with the possibility of a potential violation of citizens' rights by the AI models implemented by the state in different sectors. The paper also makes an effort to propose the foundation for a feasible framework for AI regulation by analysing the existing framework in other countries.

AI: HISTORY, SPHERE OF INFLUENCE AND PROSPECTS

Alan Turing was more curious than perplexed when he catechised the question, 'Can machines think?'. He went on to write an entire research paper on it (Turing, 1950). His work 'Computing Machinery and Intelligence' is considered to have established foundations for artificial intelligence and machine learning. The Turing Test, or the Imitation Game, as he would call it, is set out to determine if a machine could fool an uninformed human judge. If it succeeds, then it could be categorised as an artificial intelligence. While listing his findings, Turing believed that machines are dangerously close to passing the test more than seventy percent of the time. We have come a long way since Turing published his findings in 1950. An enormous amount of finance and resources has been injected into the research and development of AI and related areas throughout the backend of the 20th century and the beginning of the 21st (Haenlein & Kaplan, 2019).

The concept of artificial intelligence could be traced back to the idea of automation of functions. Greek philosophers, especially, were intrigued by the possibility of mechanisation of certain functions, a machine that could repeatedly carry out a specific set of instructions. Some of them put their thoughts into action and, over the course of history, provided us with automatons (self-operating machines), from which many complex machines were developed. But artificial intelligence was much more than just mere automation. The proponents of AI required the machine to think on its feet and make complex decisions, much like human intelligence, hence the term 'artificial' intelligence. Demanding a machine or a system to make human cognition its cottage industry is no small feat.

Some would like to think that we have reached the summit of it all. With the introduction of generative AI models like ChatGPT, Gemini, and DeepSeek, AI research and tech could be considered at their peak (Bulowski, 2024). However, it is also exigent to note that AI in its pubescent stage has only been able to be deployed mainly as artificial narrow intelligence, which can be identified in reactive machine AI systems and limited memory AI systems. Reactive systems work on an available data set without the ability to recollect past actions, decisions or outcomes (Bassan et al., 2023)—for example, the chess engines like Deep Blue. Limited memory AI systems can recollect previous decisions and outcomes. However, such memory cannot be stored and be used for long periods. For example, Generative language models like ChatGPT and other chatbots provide specific services. Artificial General Intelligence, wherein the AI is equipped to perform human cognitive functions, and Artificial Super Intelligence, which performs functions better than humans, are still purely academic and theoretical. Hence, it is somewhat indubitable that we have yet to reach the peak with respect to AI research and application.

Any automation is meant to assist humans. It was evident from the outset that any attempt at creating a machine that could operate itself would be meant to make people's lives easier. Therefore, ideally, an attempt at creating any AI system would be to help people, governments, industries and other sectors. This can be discerned from the inculcation of AI in different sectors and industries. AI has been ingrained in manufacturing, R&D, drug design, genetic data analytics, health surveillance and digital health, and various other sectors that are different from the previous one. AI's primary objective or discernible purpose is to circumvent the complexity of the processes involved and save time. This is easily understood from the utilisation of AI in the corporate sector. The operations of a company are huge and expensive. An entire cordon of staff is employed to find penny leaks and unwanted expenditures. The inclusion of AI into this process, which involves performance reports, analysis of investment patterns, operations management and many other activities, helps in quick and accurate data analysis (Zong & Guan, 2024). Subsequently, decision-making becomes more manageable and faster. A much more cynical school of thought looks to find an ulterior motive in the AI models and their applications. The concerns regarding DeepSeek and its considerable inadequacies in security metrics can be read along the same lines (Pearl et al., 2025). State-funded AI models, or the servers of which that can be accessed by the state, pose several security and privacy risks. The efforts of nations to promote data localisation and protect the sensitive personal data of their citizens would be adversely affected as a result. Hence, the underlying concern would be the safety and security of these AI language models and AI systems, which could outweigh their convenience.

AI: COMPONENTS AND FOUNDATIONAL MODELS

The commercial application of Artificial intelligence is rapidly increasing. As mentioned earlier, each industry is utilising AI for various purposes. However, the essential components of AI remain the same. It operates through learning, language processing, and reasoning, leading to decision-making and perception. Learning in AI is comparable to the human acquisition of knowledge. Natural language processing (NLP) is another critical component of AI. It aims at the comprehension of ideas from words and texts. Sentiment analysis is an example of NLP, wherein the AI system analyses whether the underlying sentiment behind the respective text is positive, negative or neutral. AI makes informed decisions based on reasoning. Depending on the problem situation, the best possible route is chosen to achieve the desired result.

The efforts at understanding the capabilities and functionalities of AI also involve identifying the foundational models of each AI system. Each AI system can have either an open-source foundation or a closed model. This particular difference in foundational models doesn't create a clear distinction. Instead, it is believed to have developed a spectrum. To explain it further, the developers of an AI model could make it completely open source by releasing the training data, underlying parameters, and the code running the interface or application (Dahlgren, 2024). For example, TensorFlow and PyTorch are considered open-source models since their underlying parameters and code are available to the public. Another example would be Meta's AI initiative, Llama, which has its components made available to the public. On the contrary, Google DeepMind's Flamingo does not provide any information regarding their components, code or parameters, making them a wholly closed model. Models like GPT-4, primarily closed, release certain data, such as their proprietary application and user interface, placing them closer to the middle of the spectrum rather than at an extreme.

The ongoing debate between the two types of foundational models is imperative in formulating policy and regulatory frameworks. The idea behind open foundational models is one of social benefit. The developers of open-source AI models aim to provide the components of their models to the public so that researchers and developers from diverse backgrounds can suggest and modify the existing system, making it much more efficient. It is argued that open-source models help better understand the model's functionalities and ethical considerations. The proponents of closed AI models suggest that releasing details of their models would lead to the misuse of the code and parameters. It is argued that certain bad actors could utilise the underlying code of the open AI models to manipulate and create other models which provide unrestricted and harmful information to the end user. For example, an AI model created with malicious intention, once prompted, could provide information about biological warfare, equipping chemical weapons, terrorist activities and other harmful elements. This concern is further aggravated by certain AI regulations like California's Safe and Secure Innovation for Frontier Artificial Intelligence Models Act (SB 1047). The Act places the responsibility of malicious AI models on the original developer since a person who has only spent less than 10 million US dollars to produce an AI model based on another larger model is not considered a developer under the Act. In addition, the compliance cost and the fear of bad actors using their models for harmful purposes restrict the developers from releasing the details of their models to the public. It is also argued that a closed model with changes and modifications made exclusively internally helps maintain the superiority of their product in the market, compared to an AI model that is already open source.

Some experts believe the abovementioned concerns are only limited to open-source models. They suggest further research to unravel the effects of novel foundation models to see if the security risks are unique to open-source models since there is nothing to indicate that they are.

AI: DATA PRIVACY, SURVEILLANCE AND NATIONAL SECURITY

The introduction of DeepSeek into the market has opened the Pandora's box. It has an open foundational model with comparatively lower production costs. Despite all this, it is computationally as powerful as ChatGPT. This is supposed to be an excellent piece of news for the developers. DeepSeek has proved that AI models can be developed with low production and operation costs, which are as powerful as their competitors. This provides much encouragement to future programmers. However, it is essential not to overlook the security concerns surrounding DeepSeek. One major concern is the Chinese government's alleged access to DeepSeek servers. It is claimed that sensitive personal data, chat history, user IP address, and keystrokes are directly transferred to the Chinese government. If such an allegation is found to be accurate, the AI model can have enormous implications for privacy and national security. As a precautionary measure, several countries have banned the operation of DeepSeek within their boundaries.

Security of the State and Data Localisation

It is common practice for sovereign nations to address matters of national security with an iron fist. Most forms of aggression with the idea of dismantling the security of the state have been on the cyber front in recent times. To that effect, the ban on suspicious apps and the sale of devices and software have become standard practices. The ban on TikTok in India in 2020 is an example of the scrapping of applications that are prejudicial to the nation's sovereignty. It is alleged and proved to an extent (Ryan et al., 2020) that TikTok and several other apps based in China were funnelling the personal data of its users to the PRC. The same allegation led to a lawsuit against ByteDance, who owns TikTok, in 2019 (*In re TikTok*, 2022).

Along with concerns with respect to consumer privacy, the allegation that the PRC was equipped to conduct surveillance of Indian nationals through the data that was alleged to be transferred out of the country. It is also exigent to note that this was a period in which India did not have privacy legislation requiring a certain amount of compliance from the body corporates that process citizens' data. The Digital Personal Data Protection Act of 2023 allows the government to restrict cross-border data transfer, promoting data localisation. However, the government has not yet mandated such a restriction on data transfer. It is feared that DeepSeek raises similar concerns regarding data privacy and national security. Due to these safety concerns, the Finance Ministry of India has mandated its staff not to utilise the AI model. It is possible that DeepSeek, with the amount of sensitive data that their AI model could access, would transfer such data outside of India. This could open the doors for security issues such as surveillance, profiling, biopolitics, political polarisation of the population and several other activities aimed at thwarting the security of the state.

It is apparent that a limpid stand with respect to data localisation norms could alleviate the concerns regarding the processing of sensitive personal data of Indian citizens to be sent across the border. It is also unclear that such an activity, although highly probable on the face of it, is occurring. Extensive research into the functionalities of such conspicuous applications and AI models would shed some light on the alleged activities.

Prevention of Crime, Investigation and Policing

On the other hand, the Indian government and several state governments have been utilising AI in traffic regulations, investigations, and general policing. Face recognition systems, drone surveillance, Central Monitoring System (CMS) and National Intelligence Grid (NATGRID) allegedly utilise Artificial Intelligence. India was quick to recognise the possibilities of the application of AI in defence and law enforcement. In 2018, an AI task force was constituted by the Ministry of Defence (MoD) to realise AI's capabilities in the defence sector. Likewise, the efforts to ingrain AI into law enforcement have borne fruit recently. Police departments in several states have started utilising locally developed applications that use AI in crime detection, prevention, and policing. The workload of police officials has since been significantly reduced. It can be argued that since none of the existing models are capable of human cognition, AI is not employed to make informed decisions, replacing the need for police personnel. Instead, it assists the officials with data analysis and automation of processes. These are the basic functionalities of policing exercised by police officials and assisted by AI-powered mechanisms. For example, the Karnataka police are utilising AI-powered systems to automate certain tasks like licence plate recognition in case of a traffic rules violation and use facial recognition system coupled with AI to flag down individuals with a criminal history and assist in patrolling a sensitive area by identifying suspicious behaviour. Kerala police use AI to identify vehicles that violate traffic rules and generate challans against their registrations. Last year, Ahmedabad became the first city in India to employ an AI-powered surveillance system. The Maharashtra Research and Vigilance for Enhanced Law Enforcement (MARVEL) has been constituted to utilise AI's capabilities in crime detection and prevention.

The surveillance framework in India is governed by the Telecommunications Act of 2023 (wherein the Telegraph Act of 1885 and subsequent rules were repealed) and the Information Technology Act of 2000. Under Section 17(2), the Digital Personal Data Protection Act 2023 provides exemptions to the state, enabling non-consensual data processing by certain "instrumentalities" of the state. This empowers Investigating agencies to carry on with the surveillance activities under the existing surveillance framework. The long-standing criticism of the existing framework is the lack of judicial oversight and the lack of clear and precise interpretation of terms such as national security, which are the enabling grounds. The authorisation and review of an order for surveillance is presided over by members of the executive (Figure 1). The judiciary is not involved at any stage.

Figure 1. Operation of surveillance mechanism

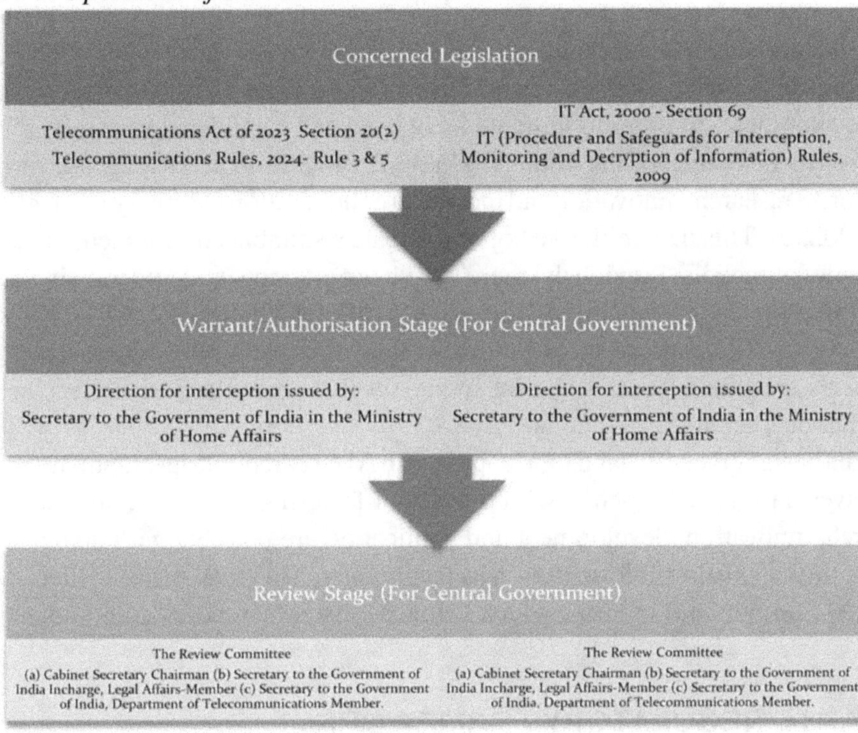

It could be argued that the inoculation of AI in India's surveillance mechanism could exponentially increase the efficiency in investigation, prevention of crime and protecting national security. The Supreme Court opined that employing surveillance mechanisms is common among nations to fight terrorism and crime. The Court also suggested that intelligence agencies can resort to different and novel forms of surveillance in matters involving the security of the state, as long as such activity is legal and authorised (*Manohar Lal Sharma v. Union of India,* 2023). The state agencies must be allowed to utilise novel technologies available to them in the prevention of crime and for investigation. It is equally significant for lawmakers to put in place regulations and safeguards that protect the rights of citizens. Technological advancements such as AI could be utilised maliciously in biopolitics and political polarisation of demography. In the digital age, where data is considered a form of currency, it is compelling that regulations are enacted to protect one's rights.

INDIAN STRIDES

As mentioned earlier, India cannot boast an indigenously developed AI model that can compete globally. The country is at its nascent stage with respect to AI research and development. In order to mitigate its belated entry and lacklustre research, the government has launched the 'IndiaAI Mission', which aims at creating an ecosystem to foster AI research, innovation and industrial collaboration (Ministry of Electronics & IT, 2025b). This new initiative hopes to create a suitable environment to develop foundational models. Previously, there have been attempts at democratising access to AI, like the 2018 National Strategy for Artificial Intelligence by NITI Aayog (NITI Ayog, 2018), aimed at AI innovation and application in various sectors and industries and the proposed Digital India Act that would effectively replace the Information Technology Act, 2000.

India has embraced a 'hands-on' approach to AI research and development. Several initiatives have been launched with the aim of fostering an ecosystem wherein AI research, innovation, development and application are possible with democratised access to the existing information and technology. This was made evident in the 2025 AI Summit held in Paris, which Prime Minister Narendra Modi co-hosted.

A VIABLE REGULATORY FRAMEWORK

Nations are already scrambling to assert themselves in the new era of artificial intelligence and machine learning. There are diminutive efforts to constitute methods of legal scrutiny upon the ever-evolving AI systems. The European Union AI Act (2024), the Executive Order on Safe, Secure, and Trustworthy Development and Use of Artificial Intelligence (2023) (United States' attempt at realising its goals regarding AI), California Senate Bill 1047 are some attempts at actual regulation of AI and its applications. There is a multitude of policies surrounding AI, largely focusing on the promotion of AI research and development, fostering a creative and democratic ecosystem to realise the potential of AI models and to create a notion of participation and collaboration among global peers. However, very few jurisdictions are actually concerned with establishing safeguards and legal oversight. There are several perceivable reasons for this approach. Their relatively recent entry into the AI world has evidently made the nations to be cautious about premature attempts at enacting legislation that would ultimately 'kneecap' the potential applications of AI models. The caution exercised by nations with the thought of keeping the competitive advantage and allowing their developers to fight it out on the global stage in building computationally superior AI models has yielded results. The USA and the UK had refused to concur with their counterparts in responsible AI development aimed at democratising access to tools and innovations (Paris AI Summit, 2025). Both nations are heedful of the fact that such an agreement would hurt their plans to dominate the market economy in the coming decades.

A Theoretical Framework for India

Let us look at the nature of regulations India should potentially bring in the future with comprehensive legislation concerning AI and the respective challenges. Evidently, the chary approach of jurisdictions in regulating AI and its applications comes from the 'hands-off until the trouble' idea. A considerable amount of debate has taken place with respect to the timing, nature of liability, objective and scope of such regulations (Mohanty & Sahu, 2024).

Regarding the 'timing', it has been argued that law has been playing a game of catching up with technology for a long time (Wallach, 2015). In his book, Wallach envisages the moral issues posed by rapid technological growth. The question of accountability and responsibility with respect to such advancements perplexed him. Some have called it the 'pacing problem' (Thierer, 2018), where the law is inept in tackling the convolutions of technology or even giving answers to questions that are not even brought under the purview of law in the first place. Drawing a parallel, we could identify an apparent ambiguity, a grey area, concerning accountability and responsibility once the AI models take a wrong turn. The start of preparations for formulating a regulative framework for technological advancement should be concurrent with its development stage. It is when the vulnerabilities of a system are revealed. Treading on the heels and waiting for a mistake to happen could prove costly as assigning the responsibilities, in case of failure, at a later stage would be much more difficult. Concerning AI models, a diligent and direct approach to regulations is advisable. As the EU AI Act adapted to the requirements of regulating generative AI at a later point in time, it is suggestive that changes can be made to cater to the newer applications and capabilities of AI systems.

Regarding the 'objective and scope' of the potential regulations, along with establishing clear directions on accountability, lawmakers need to establish provisions that regulate the commercial aspects of the application of AI systems to stop monopoly, manipulation, and fair competition by mitigating abuse of market power. It is also important to identify AI models or applications that provide misinformation and outputs that cause harm to the users (for example, creating malicious content using deepfake powered by generative AI). A potential compliance provision in which training data of generative AI models and systems along with traditional AI applications utilised in high-risk ecosystems is subjected to strict scrutiny where the officials could determine that the model is not 'trained' with malicious intent. It is also crucial to note that there is a debate circling the copyright concerns of such training data. It is claimed that most of the training data are publicly available and that no recommunication of the same data is involved. It would be helpful to analyse the training data to determine whether such copyright claims hold water if they are ever interpreted to be violated by developers while training their AI models. Several complexities are involved in constituting such a compliance requirement, as most developers prefer to have a closed-source foundational model for their AI systems. Acquiring training data or any underlying code of a closed AI model would be highly problematic for the government from a legal standpoint. However, without analysing training data or underlying code, the government could not determine whether the particular AI model does not provide outputs or results that would undermine national security (say, provide information on creating chemical weapons) or cause harm to individuals. Mutual trust between the state and developers will be key to the coexistence of regulations and technological innovation. Another area of concern concerning AI models is the 'black box' problem. It is challenging to understand the reasoning behind a decision made by an AI model. Researchers have taken the example of a self-driving car hitting a pedestrian crossing a road instead of braking in time (Blouin, 2023). They argue that even by analysing the training data, it is nearly impossible to provide reasoning for certain decisions taken by AI systems. Since no hypothetical black box is available for the developers to determine the 'thought process' of the AI model, experts suggest that deploying AI models in high-risk, high-stakes ecosystems would project several complexities (Office of General Counsel, 2024). Another point of deliberation would be understanding the subject of the regulations. Patently, the developers and AI models of all kinds would come under the ambit of potential legislation. However, researchers opine that regulating all aspects of an AI model on a shared line is not advisable. Instead, a clear distinction created between the regulation of training data and source code (input), decisions taken by AI models (outputs) and the AI models and applications (processes) would better equip the state to govern the different aspects of AI. In 2024, the Additional Secretary to India's Ministry of Electronics and Information Technology suggested that the government is looking to regulate applications of AI rather than the technology itself, endorsing the approach suggested earlier (Mimansa, 2024).

Regarding 'Liability', accountability is generally assigned to developers and deployers of AI models in various jurisdictions. The California SB 1047 requires the developers to state the security measures employed on their AI models. It also holds the original open-source developer (someone who has spent around 100 million USD) accountable for the outcomes of their models and not the developer who might have deployed the model after making certain modifications that might have violated the regulations. With great difficulty, developers can be classified as 'intermediaries' or 'publishers' under the IT Act and the Information Technology

Intermediary Rules, 2021, respectively. Although it provides a stopgap for the meantime, the definitions would create confusion if it is applied to developers of AI models. Regulations concerning developers and deployers and the preceding definitions could form the basis of accountability and liability concerning AI models.

Suggested Approaches

Any bid to create an AI regulatory framework generally follows a strict or flexible approach. The idea of restraining a prominent technological advancement that would potentially boost the economies and add to the GDP does not appeal to most nations. This cautious approach has culminated in countries identifying three different methods of regulation. Some experts claim that the idea of self-regulation is sufficient to address the existing concerns related to AI for the time being. This would mean that the developers of AI would form an accord to consciously ingrain regulations during their models' development and application stage. The purpose of self-regulation is to allow the experts and creators of such models to regulate themselves since they have the utmost knowledge about the functionalities and implications of their models. This approach would not impede the evolution of AI models in the future. Incentives can be announced to developers who follow self-regulation requirements, similar to the approach adopted by the Indian government in digital advertising. One of the main challenges to this approach is that a level of trust between the developers and the state is contingent. The approach would see certain regulatory concepts inculcated into the design principles of the AI models (Figure 2). For example, privacy concerns are addressed in most nations by requiring developers or body corporates to employ privacy by design, wherein their products comply with privacy mandates during production. Employing regulatory requirements in an AI model by design would cater to the self-regulation argument.

Figure 2. Self-regulation through design principles

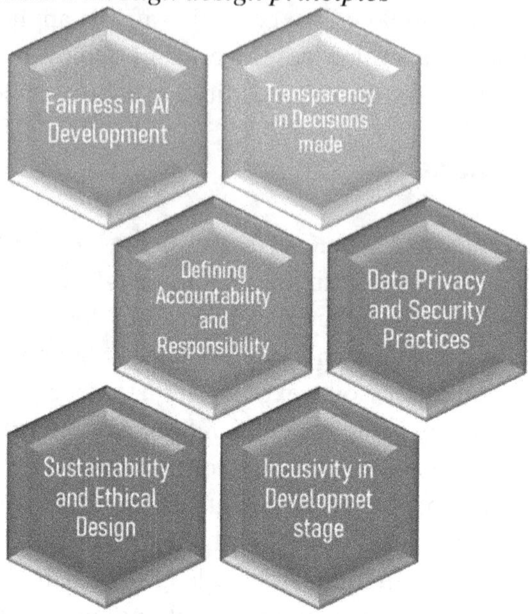

Enacting comprehensive legislation is another approach to regulatory efforts. This would enable the government to mandate that developers follow certain guidelines when developing, deploying, and applying their AI models. The government would also be empowered to restrain the application of an AI model in high-risk environments. In a research paper produced under Carnegie India's Technology and Society Program, the researchers classified AI risks into harmful content, privacy violations, discrimination, national security, and several others (Mohanty & Sahu, 2024). The EU AI Act is an example of this strict and risk-based approach. It classifies critical infrastructures and sectors into high-risk categories where the application of AI is subject to strict scrutiny. The Act classifies the risk categories into unacceptable (application of AI is banned), high risk (application of AI is subjected to specific legal mandates), limited risk (application of AI is subjected to limited obligations), minimal or no risk (application of AI is not subject to regulations). It is argued that a strict approach would hamper the potential of AI systems but give more weight to protecting the rights of individuals.

On the other hand, some experts and nations appreciate a collaborative approach to regulation. This would mean that fully-fledged government legislation would not be put in place; instead, the government and the developers would work together to harmonise advancement and regulation. For example, the UK is aiming to create a flexible regulatory framework that would foster the development of AI and its applications. A Policy paper was released in 2023 titled 'A pro-innovation approach to AI regulation', where a context-specific approach is proposed (Department for Science, Innovation & Technology, 2023). The paper suggests that restricting the deployment of AI in critical infrastructure due to high risk would come at a significant opportunity cost. Instead, the paper proposes a proportional analysis that weighs risks against opportunity costs in high-risk sectors. The proposed legislation would require regulators to display sensitivity to contexts and to exercise a proportional analysis of risks against innovation. The proponents of the flexible approach to regulating AI argue that banning AI applications in a critical industry or sector due to risk classifications would hamper the evolution of such sectors without access to AI.

The existing approaches to a regulatory framework pave the way for various opportunities. The strict approach, which calls for comprehensive legislation, would ensure that citizens' rights are protected by stifling some of the progress that can be made on the development front. On the contrary, the flexible approach can lead to the potential violation of the rights of individuals due to the lack of compliance with self-regulation. It is suggested that there are elements of AI and its application that are already regulated by existing laws, which need not be further brought under a potential regulatory framework. For example, AI utilised to defame a person would be dealt with under Section 356 of Bharatiya Nyaya Sanhita (BNS); impersonation of a person using deepfake technology would be under the ambit of the IT Act and BNS. Similarly, there are laws in India that would deal with certain offences committed using AI, like transmission of obscene content, copyright aspects, and reliability of services. It is also claimed that India would look at a substantial economic boost due to the inculcation of AI in different sectors. Hence, following a strict approach that would hinder such an economic opportunity is not advisable.

Regarding the risk-based approach, it is imperative to conduct an empirical study to assess the impact of the application of AI in high-risk sectors. Such an impact assessment would help to realise the potential opportunity cost that would be incurred for not having AI in a respective sector. The quantitative data would also assist in realising the difference in profit margins and cost of operation after implementing AI in each sector. The study would give valuable insights into the kind of regulatory approach that India should adopt. It would also provide crucial information about the operation of AI in each sector, helping the developers, deployers, and companies that employ the operation of AI to identify issues in its workings.

A Risk-Based Analysis of AI in Law Enforcement and Surveillance

As mentioned earlier, there are several concerns regarding law enforcement agencies' use of AI. This would involve privacy concerns and secretive and enhanced surveillance. AI provides tremendous opportunities in law enforcement, defence and intelligence operations. A risk-based approach is recommended for finding and classifying areas of high, unacceptable and low risks.

For example, AI in state surveillance can be classified as a high-risk ecosystem. Enhancement of surveillance mechanisms with the addition of AI results in significantly higher amounts of data collected within a short span of time. This raises concerns about targeted surveillance and privacy. Nevertheless, state surveillance is imperative to national security. Appropriating a context-based approach similar to the UK would help weigh up the risks involved with the opportunity it provides to prevent credible threats to national security. To explain further, the security risk involved in not utilising AI in assisting the patrolling of a sensitive area during a civil unrest outweighs the risk of violating certain rights of the individuals subject to such surveillance, which would justify the use of AI in that particular case. Likewise, AI can be utilised to counter challenges in DNA analysis to help the investigation of a crime. There would be DNA samples of multiple individuals available from a scene of crime. It is challenging to identify the DNA of the offender through traditional methods. However, recent research shows that AI could help better analyse such samples. Conversely, the use of AI in criminal profiling, categorisation based on profiling, and subsequent surveillance of individuals are questionable use cases. It is argued that the AI models trained with biased data could display biased outputs, resulting in prejudicial profiling and targeting individuals of a specific community (Cekic, 2024).

Another point of discussion should be the requirement of judicial scrutiny over surveillance activity. The existing legal framework on surveillance does not provide for judicial oversight or scrutiny at any stage. With the enhancement of the surveillance mechanism when coupled with AI, it could be argued that there is a potential risk of violating citizens' privacy rights. The involvement of the judiciary either at the warrant/authorisation stage (ex-ante – prior judicial scrutiny by examining the request for surveillance) or during the review stage (ex-post – an involvement of judiciary at the review stage scrutinising the surveillance operation) would succour in implementing the risk-based approach.

CONCLUSION

Foucault's understanding of power changes course in his works. Initially, the idea was that power resided in Institutions rather than men (Foucault, 1977). This 'disindividualised' version of power was explained through the 'panopticon'. Foucault maintained that the institution of the panopticon held power and control over its subjects. Similarly, for him, power resided in institutions like factories, schools, and governments rather than the individuals who constituted such institutions. Likewise, it could be argued that modern governments manifest the 'disinvidualised' versions of power. They exercise their authority over the citizens through surveillance mechanisms. The people under constant fear of surveillance and subsequent punishment are, hence, policed. Thus, a parallel can be drawn to the current forms of surveillance to the panopticon. However, Foucault, in his later writings, realises that power resides in individuals as well, 'even those who are surveilled or punished' (Armstrong, 1992). This could be realised by the rights of the citizens in the present scenario. 'Power' took a new meaning during the Cold War, as there was a race among nations to acquire nuclear power. The global competition for AI dominance is the modern way of attaining power.

There is a race for dominance in Artificial intelligence research, development and applications. Almost all nations are vying to create their own foundational AI models that could help them secure a foothold in this new digital race. It is possible that security concerns can be overlooked when creating such a foothold. The excitement that DeepSeek provided and the consequent findings on its dispiriting performance in security tests and metrics to the aforementioned oversight. There is a threat of secretive surveillance through these generative AI models, which could conflict with national security interests. Also, nations may lose sight of the fundamental idea behind procuring such a technology for themselves, that it is ultimately for the benefit of its citizens. Introducing AI into different sectors and industries would violate citizens' rights without a proper policy framework or regulation. Nevertheless, the law has always been reactive rather than proactive.

Artificial intelligence shows us a new horizon. Through its application, it paves the way for extraordinary innovation and advancement in each sector. The government and its agencies can utilise novel technologies and mechanisms that would further increase efficacy in its functionalities. Introducing DeepSeek and other AI models has alerted India on the necessity of entering the race for AI dominance. At the same time, it has shown the government and the public alike, the security implications of such models, which do not perform well against security tests and parameters. AI offers extraordinary power to individuals and institutions that utilise it. It is evident that without proper mandates and regulations expounding accountability and responsibilities, the risks that AI models pose are exponential.

REFERENCES

Armstrong, W. G. (1992). Punishment, surveillance, and discipline in paradise lost. *Studies in English Literature 1500-1900, 32*(1), 91. https://doi.org/DOI: 10.2307/450942

Ayog, N. I. T. I. (2018). *National strategy for Artificial Intelligence*. National Institution for Transforming India.

Bassan, S., Amir, G., Corsi, D., Refaeli, I., & Katz, G. (2023, October). Formally explaining neural networks within reactive systems. In *2023 Formal Methods in Computer-Aided Design (FMCAD)* (pp. 1-13). IEEE.

Blouin, L. (2023, March 6). AI's mysterious 'black box' problem, explained. *University of Michigan- Dearborn News*. https://umdearborn.edu/news/ais-mysterious-black-box-problem-explained

Bulowski, P. (2024, December 23). *The AI Data Crunch: Are We Reaching "Peak Data?"*. Medium. https://medium.com/@meshuggah22/the-ai-data-crunch-are-we-reaching-peak-data-4a801df2cd91

Cekic, E. (2024). The impact of artificial intelligence tools on criminal psychological profiling. *International Journal of Academic Research in Psychology, 110*(1), 01–13.

Dahlgren, M. (2024). Defense priorities in the open-source ai debate: a preliminary assessment. *arXiv preprint arXiv:2408.10026.*

Department for Science. Innovation & Technology. (2023). *A pro-innovation approach to AI regulation* [White Paper]. Crown. https://www.gov.uk/government/publications/ai-regulation-a-pro-innovation-approach/white-paper

Foucault, M. (1977). *Discipline and punish: the birth of the prison* (1st American ed.). Pantheon Books.

Gao, X., & Feng, H. (2023). AI-Driven Productivity Gains: Artificial Intelligence and Firm Productivity. *Sustainability (Basel), 15*(11), 8934. DOI: 10.3390/su15118934

Haenlein, M., & Kaplan, A. (2019). A brief history of artificial intelligence: On the past, present, and future of artificial intelligence. *California Management Review, 61*(4), 5–14. DOI: 10.1177/0008125619864925

In re TikTok, Inc. 565 F. Supp. 3d 1076

Katare, G., Padihar, G., & Qureshi, Z. (2018). Challenges in the integration of artificial intelligence and internet of things. *International Journal of System and Software Engineering*, *6*(2), 10–15.

Liao, H. (2025). DeepSeek large-scale model: Technical analysis and development prospect. *Journal of Computer Science and Electrical Engineering*, *7*(1), 33–37.

Liu, S. (2023). India's AI regulation dilemma. *The Diplomat*. Retrieved March 20, 2025, from https://thediplomat.com/2023/10/indias-ai-regulation-dilemma/

Manohar Lal Sharma v. Union of India (2023) 11 SCC 401

Mercer, S., Spillard, S., & Martin, D. P. (2025). Brief analysis of DeepSeek R1 and its implications for Generative AI. *SuperIntelligence - Robotics - Safety & Alignment*, *2*(1). https://doi.org/DOI: 10.70777/si.v2i1.11097

Mimansa. (2024, September 11). Govt is looking to regulate AI applications, not AI technology: Additional Secretary to IT Ministry. MediaNama. https://www.medianama.com/2024/09/223-government-regulating-ai-application-not-ai-technology-meity-additional-secretary/

Ministry of Electronics & IT (India). (2025a, March 19). *Government of India Expands AI-Driven Skilling* [Press release]. https://pib.gov.in/PressReleasePage.aspx?PRID=2113095

Ministry of Electronics & IT (India). (2025b, March 6). *India's AI Revolution* [Press release]. https://pib.gov.in/PressReleasePage.aspx?PRID=2108810

Mohanty, A., & Sahu, S. (2024). *India's advance on AI regulation*. Carnegie India. https://carnegieendowment.org/research/2024/11/indias-advance-onai-regulation?lang=en&center=india

Office of General Counsel. (2024). *AI best practices guidelines*. MacEwan University. https://www.macewan.ca/c/documents/ai-best-practices-guidelines.pdf

Pearl, M., Brock, J., & Kumar, A. (2025). *Delving into the dangers of DeepSeek*. Center for Strategic and International Studies (CSIS). https://www.csis.org/analysis/delving-dangers-deepseek

Raman, R., Kowalski, R., Achuthan, K., Iyer, A., & Nedungadi, P. (2025). Navigating artificial general intelligence development: Societal, technological, ethical, and brain-inspired pathways. *Scientific Reports*, *15*(1), 1–22. DOI: 10.1038/s41598-025-92190-7 PMID: 40069265

Ryan, F., Fritz, A., & Impiombato, D. (2020). TikTok privacy concerns and data collection. In *TikTok and WeChat: Curating and controlling global information flows* (pp. 36–42). Australian Strategic Policy Institute.

Suri, A. (2025). *The missing pieces in India's ai puzzle: Talent, data, and R&D.* Carnegie India. https://carnegieendowment.org/research/2025/02/the-missing-pieces-in-indias-ai-puzzle-talent-data-and-randd?lang=en

Thierer, A. (2018). The pacing problem and the future of technology regulation. *Mercatus Center: The Bridge*. https://www.mercatus.org/bridge/commentary/pacing-problem-and-future-technology-regulation

Turing, A. M. (1950). I.—Computing machinery and intelligence. *Mind*, *LIX*(236), 433–460. DOI: 10.1093/mind/LIX.236.433

Wallach, W. (2015). *A Dangerous Master: How to Keep Technology from Slipping Beyond Our Control*. Basic Books.

Zong, Z., & Guan, Y. (2024). AI-driven intelligent data analytics and predictive analysis in industry 4.0: Transforming knowledge, innovation, and efficiency. *Journal of the Knowledge Economy*, *16*(1), 1–40. DOI: 10.1007/s13132-024-02001-z

Compilation of References

Aaronson, S. (2013). *Quantum Computing Since Democritus*. Cambridge University Press. DOI: 10.1017/CBO9780511979309

Abbasi, M., Bernardo, M. V., Váz, P., Silva, J., & Martins, P. (2024). Adaptive and Scalable Database Management with Machine Learning Integration: A PostgreSQL Case Study. *Information (Basel)*, *15*(9), 574.

Abduljabbar, R., Dia, H., Liyanage, S., & Bagloee, S. A. (2019). Applications of Artificial Intelligence in Transport: An Overview. *Sustainability (Basel)*, *11*(1), 1. Advance online publication. DOI: 10.3390/su11010189

Adadi, A., & Berrada, M. (2018). Peeking inside the black-box: A survey on explainable artificial intelligence (XAI). *IEEE Access : Practical Innovations, Open Solutions*, *6*, 52138–52160. DOI: 10.1109/ACCESS.2018.2870052

Ajami, R. A., & Karimi, H. A. (2023). Artificial Intelligence: Opportunities and Challenges. *Journal of Asia-Pacific Business*, *24*(2), 73–75. DOI: 10.1080/10599231.2023.2210239

Alexander Sukharevsky. (2025). *The state of AI: How organizations are rewiring to capture value.*

Aliferis, P., & Preskill, J. (2008). Fault-Tolerant Quantum Computation Against Biased Noise. *Physical Review A*, *78*(5), 052331. DOI: 10.1103/PhysRevA.78.052331

Al-Khassawneh, Y. A. (2023). A review of artificial intelligence in security and privacy: Research advances, applications, opportunities, and challenges. *Indonesian Journal of Science and Technology*, *8*(1), 79–96. DOI: 10.17509/ijost.v8i1.52709

AllahRakha, N. (2024). Rethinking digital borders to address jurisdiction and governance in the global digital economy. *International Journal of Law and Policy*, *2*(1).

Al-Rasheed, A., Ksibi, A., Ayadi, M., Alzahrani, A. I. A., Zakariah, M., & Ali Hakami, N. (2022). An Ensemble of Transfer Learning Models for the Prediction of Skin Cancers with Conditional Generative Adversarial Networks. *Diagnostics (Basel), 12*(12), 3145. Advance online publication. DOI: 10.3390/diagnostics12123145 PMID: 36553152

Alumni, A. (2022). *PathAI – Can we create a better, more robust pathologist.*

Anderson, C. L., Biscaye, P. E., & Reynolds, T. W. (2017). National ID programs: A multi-country review and analysis of policy and practical challenges. In Data for Policy 2017 Conference: Government by Algorithm.

Andrea Renda, N. B. (2023). *AI Risk & Accountability*. https://oecd.ai/en/site/risk-accountability

Anna Tong. (2023). *OpenAI's Sam Altman launches Worldcoin crypto project.*

Armstrong, W. G. (1992). Punishment, surveillance, and discipline in paradise lost. *Studies in English Literature 1500-1900, 32*(1), 91. https://doi.org/DOI: 10.2307/450942

Artificial Intelligence Index Report 2023 Introduction to the AI Index Report 2023. (n.d.).

Arute, F., Arya, K., Babbush, R., Bacon, D., Bardin, J. C., Barends, R., Biswas, R., Boixo, S., Brandao, F. G. S. L., Buell, D. A., Burkett, B., Chen, Y., Chen, Z., Chiaro, B., Collins, R., Courtney, W., Dunsworth, A., Farhi, E., Foxen, B., & Martinis, J. M. (2019). Quantum supremacy using a programmable superconducting processor. *Nature, 574*(7779), 505–510. DOI: 10.1038/s41586-019-1666-5 PMID: 31645734

Aspuru-Guzik, A., Dutoi, A. D., Love, P. J., & Head-Gordon, M. (2005). Simulated quantum computation of molecular energies. *Science, 309*(5741), 1704–1707. DOI: 10.1126/science.1113479 PMID: 16151006

Atzori, L., Iera, A., & Morabito, G. (2010). The Internet of Things: A survey. *Computer Networks, 54*(15), 2787–2805. DOI: 10.1016/j.comnet.2010.05.010

Ayog, N. I. T. I. (2018). *National strategy for Artificial Intelligence*. National Institution for Transforming India.

Babbush, R.. (2021). Quantum Algorithms for Scientific Applications. *Science Advances, 7*(25), eabg5656.

Bai, D. (2023, December). Design of Artificial Intelligence Information System Using NoSQL Database and Ajax Technology. In *2023 International Conference on Applied Physics and Computing (ICAPC)* (pp. 678-683). IEEE.

Barenco, A., Bennett, C. H., Cleve, R., DiVincenzo, D. P., Margolus, N., Shor, P., Sleator, T., Smolin, J. A., & Weinfurter, H. (1995). Elementary gates for quantum computation. *Physical Review A, 52*(5), 3457–3467. DOI: 10.1103/PhysRevA.52.3457 PMID: 9912645

Basak, S., Kar, S., Saha, S., Khaidem, L., & Dey, S. R. (2019). Predicting the direction of stock market prices using tree-based classifiers. *The North American Journal of Economics and Finance, 47*, 552–567. DOI: 10.1016/j.najef.2018.06.013

Bassan, S., Amir, G., Corsi, D., Refaeli, I., & Katz, G. (2023, October). Formally explaining neural networks within reactive systems. In *2023 Formal Methods in Computer-Aided Design (FMCAD)* (pp. 1-13). IEEE.

Bastit, B., Fernandez, M., Kesh, S., & Tsui, D. (2023). The AI Governance Challenge. *S&P Global*. https://www.spglobal.com/en/research-insights/special-reports/the-ai-governance-challenge

Bates, T., Cobo, C., Mariño, O., & Wheeler, S. (2020). Can artificial intelligence transform higher education? *International Journal of Educational Technology in Higher Education, 17*(1), 1–12. DOI: 10.1186/s41239-020-00218-x

Batty, M., Axhausen, K. W., Giannotti, F., Pozdnoukhov, A., Bazzani, A., Wachowicz, M., Ouzounis, G., & Portugali, Y. (2012). Smart cities of the future. *The European Physical Journal. Special Topics, 214*(1), 481–518. DOI: 10.1140/epjst/e2012-01703-3

Bauer, B., Wecker, D., Hastings, M. B., & Troyer, M. (2016). Hybrid Quantum-Classical Approach to Quantum Dynamics. *Physical Review X, 6*(3), 031015. DOI: 10.1103/PhysRevX.6.031045

Baur, C., Albarqouni, S., & Navab, N. (2018). *MelanoGANs: High Resolution Skin Lesion Synthesis with GANs*. http://arxiv.org/abs/1804.04338

BBC Verify: Viral Donald Trump Jr audio highly likely AI fake. (2025).

BBC. (2016). *Google's DeepMind to peek at NHS eye scans for disease analysis*.

Begüm Yavuzdoğan Okumuş, Y. U. T. S. T. (2024). *Türkiye'de Yapay Zekanın Düzenlenmesine İlişkin Gelişmeler*.

Bennett, C. H., & Brassard, G. "Quantum Cryptography: Public Key Distribution and Coin Tossing." *Proceedings of IEEE International Conference on Computers, Systems and Signal Processing*, Bangalore, India, 1984, pp. 175–179.

Benraouane, S. A. (2024). *AI Management System Certification According to the ISO/IEC 42001 Standard: How to Audit, Certify, and Build Responsible AI Systems*. CRC Press. DOI: 10.4324/9781003463979

Bharti, K., Cervera-Lierta, A., Kyaw, T., Haug, T., Alperin-Lea, S., Anand, A., Degroote, M., Heimonen, H., Kottmann, J. S., Menke, T., Mok, W.-K., Sim, S., Kwek, L.-C., & Aspuru-Guzik, A. (2022). Noisy Intermediate-Scale Quantum Algorithms. *Reviews of Modern Physics*, *94*(1), 015004. DOI: 10.1103/RevModPhys.94.015004

Biamonte, J., Wittek, P., Pancotti, N., Rebentrost, P., Wiebe, N., & Lloyd, S. (2017). Quantum Machine Learning. *Nature*, *549*(7671), 195–202. DOI: 10.1038/nature23474 PMID: 28905917

Binns, R. (2018). Algorithmic accountability and public reason. *Philosophy & Technology*, *31*(4), 543–556. DOI: 10.1007/s13347-017-0263-5 PMID: 30873342

Blais, A., Grimsmo, A. L., Girvin, S. M., & Wallraff, A. (2021). Circuit quantum electrodynamics. *Reviews of Modern Physics*, *93*(2), 025005. DOI: 10.1103/RevModPhys.93.025005

Blouin, L. (2023, March 6). AI's mysterious 'black box' problem, explained. *University of Michigan- Dearborn News*. https://umdearborn.edu/news/ais-mysterious-black-box-problem-explained

Bombin, H., & Martin-Delgado, M. A. (2006). Topological Quantum Distillation. *Physical Review Letters*, *97*(18), 180501. DOI: 10.1103/PhysRevLett.97.180501 PMID: 17155532

Boniface, M., Carmichael, L., Hall, W., Pickering, B., Stalla-Bourdillon, S., & Taylor, S. (2022). The Social Data Foundation model: Facilitating health and social care transformation through *datatrust services.Data & Policy*, *4*, e6. DOI: 10.1017/dap.2022.1

Boscardin, C. K., Gin, B., Golde, P. B., & Hauer, K. E. (2024). ChatGPT and Generative Artificial Intelligence for Medical Education: Potential Impact and Opportunity. *Academic Medicine*, *99*(1), 22–27. DOI: 10.1097/ACM.0000000000005439 PMID: 37651677

Bouwmeester, D., Pan, J.-W., Mattle, K., Eibl, M., Weinfurter, H., & Zeilinger, A. (1997). Experimental Quantum Teleportation. *Nature*, *390*(6660), 575–579. DOI: 10.1038/37539

Boyd, R., & Holton, R. J. (2018). Technology, innovation, employment and power: Does robotics and artificial intelligence really mean social transformation? *Journal of Sociology (Melbourne, Vic.)*, *54*(3), 331–345. DOI: 10.1177/1440783317726591

Brantingham, P. J., Valasik, M., & Mohler, G. O. (2018). Does predictive policing lead to biased arrests? Results from a randomized controlled trial. *Statistics and Public Policy (Philadelphia, Pa.)*, *5*(1), 1–6. DOI: 10.1080/2330443X.2018.1438940

Breque, M., De Nul, L., & Petridis, A. (2021). Industry 5.0: Towards a sustainable, human-centric, and resilient European industry. European Commission Report.

Briegel, H. J., Dür, W., Cirac, J. I., & Zoller, P. (1998). Quantum Repeaters: The Role of Imperfect Local Operations in Quantum Communication. *Physical Review Letters*, *81*(26), 5932–5935. DOI: 10.1103/PhysRevLett.81.5932

Broussard, M. (2019). *Artificial unintelligence : how computers misunderstand the world*. The MIT Press.

Brown, B. J.. (2019). Fault-Tolerant Handling of Qubit Loss in Surface Codes. *Physical Review X*, *9*(3), 031041.

Brown, T. B., Mann, B., Ryder, N., Subbiah, M., Kaplan, J., Dhariwal, P., Neelakantan, A., Shyam, P., Sastry, G., Askell, A., Agarwal, S., Herbert-Voss, A., Krueger, G., Henighan, T., Child, R., Ramesh, A., Ziegler, D. M., Wu, J., Winter, C., & Amodei, D. (2020). *Language Models are Few-Shot Learners*. http://arxiv.org/abs/2005.14165

Budhwar, P., Malik, A., De Silva, M. T. T., & Thevisuthan, P. (2022). Artificial intelligence – challenges and opportunities for international HRM: A review and research agenda. *International Journal of Human Resource Management*, *33*(6), 1065–1097. DOI: 10.1080/09585192.2022.2035161

Bulowski, P. (2024, December 23). *The AI Data Crunch: Are We Reaching "Peak Data?"*. Medium. https://medium.com/@meshuggah22/the-ai-data-crunch-are-we-reaching-peak-data-4a801df2cd91

Burri, T. (2017). International law and artificial intelligence. *Jahrbuch für Internationales Recht. German Yearbook of International Law*, *60*(1), 91–108. DOI: 10.3790/gyil.60.1.91

Buttazzo, G. (2023). Rise of artificial general intelligence: risks and opportunities. *Frontiers*. https://www.frontiersin.org/journals/artificial-intelligence/articles/10.3389/frai.2023.1226990/full

Cao, X., Ge, B., Li, M., Wang, H., & Ren, J. (2022, November). Database Protection Techniques for Electromagnetic Radiation Based on Machine Learning. In 2022 IEEE 10th Asia-Pacific Conference on Antennas and Propagation (APCAP) (pp. 1-2). IEEE.

Cao, H., Tan, C., Gao, Z., Xu, Y., Chen, G., Heng, P.-A., & Li, S. Z. (2022). *A Survey on Generative Diffusion Model*. http://arxiv.org/abs/2209.02646

Cao, L. (2023). AI in Finance: Challenges, Techniques, and Opportunities. *ACM Computing Surveys*, *55*(3), 1–38. DOI: 10.1145/3502289

Casino, F., Dasaklis, T. K., & Patsakis, C. (2019). A systematic literature review of blockchain-based applications: Current status, classification, and open issues. *Telematics and Informatics*, *36*, 55–81. DOI: 10.1016/j.tele.2018.11.006

Castonguay, A., Wagner, G., Motulsky, A., & Paré, G. (2024). AI maturity in health care: An overview of 10 OECD countries. *Health Policy (Amsterdam)*, *140*, 104938. DOI: 10.1016/j.healthpol.2023.104938 PMID: 38157771

Cebi, C. B., Bulut, F. S., Firat, H., Sahingoz, O. K., & Karatas, G. (2020). Deep learning based security management of information systems: A comparative study. *Journal of Advances in Information Technology*, *11*, 3. DOI: 10.12720/jait.11.3.135-142

Cekic, E. (2024). The impact of artificial intelligence tools on criminal psychological profiling. *International Journal of Academic Research in Psychology*, *110*(1), 01–13.

Charles Owen-Jackson. (2024). *Open source, open risks: The growing dangers of unregulated generative AI*. IBM.

Cha, S. (2024). Towards an international regulatory framework for AI safety: Lessons from the IAEA's nuclear safety regulations. *Humanities & Social Sciences Communications*, *11*(1), 506. DOI: 10.1057/s41599-024-03017-1

ChatGPT on Palestine and Israel - What do you make of this? (2023).

Chaudhary, M., & Bhotta, D. (2023). Online student engagement and innovative teaching strategies post COVID-19. *International Journal of Innovation in Education*, *8*(2-4), 96–111. DOI: 10.1504/IJIIE.2023.136160

Chaudhuri, S. (1998). Data mining and database systems: Where is the intersection? *IEEE Data Eng. Bull.*, *21*(1), 4–8.

Chen, Y.. (2020). Variational quantum simulation of the Heisenberg model on a superconducting quantum processor. *Physical Review. A*, *101*(3), 032329.

Childs, A. M.. (2002). Quantum algorithms for algebraic problems. *Quantum Information & Computation*, *2*(3), 181–191. DOI: 10.26421/QIC2.3-1

Choi, T. M., Wallace, S. W., & Wang, Y. (2018). Big data analytics in operations management. *Production and Operations Management*, *27*(10), 1868–1881. DOI: 10.1111/poms.12838

Christidis, K., & Devetsikiotis, M. (2016). Blockchains and smart contracts for the Internet of Things. *IEEE Access : Practical Innovations, Open Solutions*, *4*, 2292–2303. DOI: 10.1109/ACCESS.2016.2566339

Chuma, E. L., & De Oliveira, G. G. (2023). Generative AI for Business Decision-Making: A Case of ChatGPT. *Management Science and Business Decisions*, *3*(1), 5–11. DOI: 10.52812/msbd.63

Cooper, I., & Yon, J. (2019). Ethical Issues in Biometrics. *Science Insights*, *30*(2), 63–69. DOI: 10.15354/si.19.re095

Crayton, T. J., & Meier, B. M. (2017). Autonomous vehicles: Developing a public health research agenda to frame the future of transportation policy. *Journal of Transport & Health*, *6*, 245–252. DOI: 10.1016/j.jth.2017.04.004

Crompton, H., & Burke, D. (2023). Artificial intelligence in higher education: The state of the field. *International Journal of Educational Technology in Higher Education*, *20*(1), 22. DOI: 10.1186/s41239-023-00392-8

Csernatoni, R. (2024). The AI Governance Arms Race: From Summit Pageantry to Progress? *Carnegie Endowment.*https://carnegieendowment.org/research/2024/10/the-ai-governance-arms-race-from-summit-pageantry-to-progress?lang=en&center=europe

Dahlgren, M. (2024). Defense priorities in the open-source ai debate: a preliminary assessment. *arXiv preprint arXiv:2408.10026.*

Dan Jurafsky and James H. Martin. (2025). *Speech and Language Processing: An Introduction to Natural Language Processing*. Computational Linguistics, and Speech Recognition with Language Models.

de Almeida, P. G. R., dos Santos, C. D., & Farias, J. S. (2021). Artificial intelligence regulation: A framework for governance. *Ethics and Information Technology*, *23*(3), 505–525. DOI: 10.1007/s10676-021-09593-z

Deepfake footage purports to show Ukrainian president capitulating. (2022).

Deepfakes Are Coming for the Financial Sector. (2024).

DeepMinde. (2019). *AlphaStar: Mastering the real-time strategy game StarCraft II.* .

Demir, S., & Paksoy, T. (2020). Ai, robotics and autonomous systems in scm. *Logistics (Basel)*, *4*, 156.

Dennis, E., Kitaev, A., Landahl, A., & Preskill, J. (2002). Topological Quantum Memory. *Journal of Mathematical Physics*, *43*(9), 4452–4505. DOI: 10.1063/1.1499754

Department for Science. Innovation & Technology. (2023). *A pro-innovation approach to AI regulation* [White Paper]. Crown. https://www.gov.uk/government/publications/ai-regulation-a-pro-innovation-approach/white-paper

Deutsch, D. (1985). Quantum theory, the Church–Turing principle and the universal quantum computer. Proceedings of the Royal Society of London. A. Mathematical and Physical Sciences, 400(1818), 97-117.

Development Co-operation Report 2021. (2021). OECD. DOI: 10.1787/ce08832f-en

Ding, B., Das, S., Marcus, R., Wu, W., Chaudhuri, S., & Narasayya, V. R. (2019, June). Ai meets ai: Leveraging query executions to improve index recommendations. In *Proceedings of the 2019 International Conference on Management of Data* (pp. 1241-1258).

DiVincenzo, D. P. (2000). The physical implementation of quantum computation. *Fortschritte der Physik*, *48*(9-11), 771–783. DOI: 10.1002/1521-3978(200009)48:9/11<771::AID-PROP771>3.0.CO;2-E

Du, S., & Xie, C. (2021). Paradoxes of artificial intelligence in consumer markets: Ethical challenges and opportunities. *Journal of Business Research*, *129*, 961–974. DOI: 10.1016/j.jbusres.2020.08.024

Dwivedi, Y. K., Sharma, A., Rana, N. P., Giannakis, M., Goel, P., & Dutot, V. (2023). Evolution of artificial intelligence research in Technological Forecasting and Social Change: Research topics, trends, and future directions. *Technological Forecasting and Social Change*, *192*, 122579. DOI: 10.1016/j.techfore.2023.122579

EEA. (2022). *Ethical guidelines on the use of artificial intelligence and data in teaching and learning for educators.*

Einstein, A., Podolsky, B., & Rosen, N. (1935). Can Quantum-Mechanical Description of Physical Reality Be Considered Complete? *Physical Review*, *47*(10), 777–780. DOI: 10.1103/PhysRev.47.777

Eman A. Alasadi and Carlos R. Baiz*. (2023). *Generative AI in Education and Research: Opportunities, Concerns, and Solutions.*

Emery-Xu, N., Jordan, R., & Trager, R. (2024). International governance of advancing artificial intelligence. *AI & Society*, •••, 1–26.

Erdelyi, O. J., & Goldsmith, J. (2022). Regulating artificial intelligence: Proposal for a global solution. *Government Information Quarterly*, *39*(4), 101748. DOI: 10.1016/j.giq.2022.101748

Eric David. (2017). *Google DeepMind announces new research partnership to fight breast cancer with AI.*

Europa, E. C. (n.d.). *AI Act A risk-based approach The AI Act defines 4 levels of risk for AI systems.* https://ec.europa.eu/commission/presscorner/detail/en/ip_24_383

European Commission. (2021). *Proposal for a Regulation Laying Down Harmonized Rules on Artificial Intelligence.* EUR-Lex.

Farhi, E., Goldstone, J., & Gutmann, S. (2014). A quantum approximate optimization algorithm. arXiv preprint arXiv:1411.4028.

Farrelly, T., & Baker, N. (2023). Generative Artificial Intelligence: Implications and Considerations for Higher Education Practice. *Education Sciences, 13*(11), 1109. DOI: 10.3390/educsci13111109

Felzmann, H., Fosch-Villaronga, E., Lutz, C., & Tamò-Larrieux, A. (2020). Towards transparency by design for artificial intelligence. *Science and Engineering Ethics, 26*(6), 3333–3361. DOI: 10.1007/s11948-020-00276-4 PMID: 33196975

Feynman, R. P. (1986). Quantum mechanical computers. *Foundations of Physics, 16*(6), 507–531. DOI: 10.1007/BF01886518

FLIA. (2017). *China's New Generation of Artificial Intelligence Development Plan - Foundation for Law and International Affairs.* https://flia.org/notice-state-council-issuing-new-generation-artificial-intelligence-development-plan/

Floridi, L., Cowls, J., Beltrametti, M., Chatila, R., Chazerand, P., Dignum, V., Luetge, C., Madelin, R., Pagallo, U., Rossi, F., Schafer, B., Valcke, P., & Vayena, E. (2018). AI4People—An ethical framework for a good AI society: Opportunities, risks, principles, and recommendations. *Minds and Machines, 28*(4), 689–707. DOI: 10.1007/s11023-018-9482-5 PMID: 30930541

Foucault, M. (1977). *Discipline and punish: the birth of the prison* (1st American ed.). Pantheon Books.

Fu, Z., Teng, Q., Wang, X., & Wu, X. (2021). Analysis for the Robotic process automation firm's future development based on the business model. *BCP Business & Management, 14*, 208–215. DOI: 10.54691/bcpbm.v14i.146

G R Mukesh. (2024). *Are We Ready For This? Dutch Journalist Demonstrates "Real-Time AI Facial Recognition."*

Gadde, H. (2024). AI-Augmented Database Management Systems for Real-Time Data Analytics. *Revista de Inteligencia Artificial en Medicina, 15*(1), 616–649.

Gambetta, J. M., Chow, J. M., & Steffen, M. (2017). Building logical qubits in a superconducting quantum computing system. npj quantum information, 3(1), 2.

Gao, X., & Feng, H. (2023). AI-Driven Productivity Gains: Artificial Intelligence and Firm Productivity. *Sustainability (Basel), 15*(11), 8934. DOI: 10.3390/su15118934

Georgescu, I. M., Ashhab, S., & Nori, F. (2014). Quantum Simulation. *Reviews of Modern Physics, 86*(1), 153–185. DOI: 10.1103/RevModPhys.86.153

Getlago. (2025). *Why DeepSeek had to be open-source (and why it won't defeat OpenAI).*

Ghouse, S. M., & Chaudhary, M. (2024). Artificial Intelligence (AI) for Tourism Start-Ups. In *Innovative Technologies for Increasing Service Productivity* (pp. 161-178). IGI Global.

Gill, A. S., & Germann, S. (2022). Conceptual and normative approaches to AI governance for a global digital ecosystem supportive of the UN Sustainable Development Goals (SDGs). *AI and Ethics, 2*(2), 293–301. DOI: 10.1007/s43681-021-00058-z PMID: 34790947

Goode, K., Kim, H. M., & Deng, M. (2023). Examining Singapore's AI progress. *Center for Security and Emerging Technology, 19.*

Goodfellow, I. Bengio, Yoshua., & Courville, Aaron. (2017). *Deep learning*. The MIT Press.

Goodfellow, I. J., Pouget-Abadie, J., Mirza, M., Xu, B., Warde-Farley, D., Ozair, S., Courville, A., & Bengio, Y. (2014a). Generative adversarial nets. *Advances in Neural Information Processing Systems, 3*(January), 73–76. Advance online publication. DOI: 10.1007/978-3-658-40442-0_9

Goodfellow, I. J., Pouget-Abadie, J., Mirza, M., Xu, B., Warde-Farley, D., Ozair, S., Courville, A., & Bengio, Y. (2014b). *Generative Adversarial Networks*. http://arxiv.org/abs/1406.2661

Gottesman, D. (1996). Class of Quantum Error-Correcting Codes Saturating the Quantum Hamming Bound. *Physical Review A, 54*(3), 1862–1868. DOI: 10.1103/PhysRevA.54.1862 PMID: 9913672

Grover, L. K. (1996, July). A fast quantum mechanical algorithm for database search. In *Proceedings of the twenty-eighth annual ACM symposium on Theory of computing* (pp. 212-219).

Gu, P. (2023). Global Artificial Intelligence Governance: Challenges and Complications. *ResearchGate*. https://www.researchgate.net/publication/372083906_Global_Artificial_Intelligence_Governance_Challenges_and_Complications

Guan, C., Mou, J., & Jiang, Z. (2020). Artificial intelligence innovation in education: A twenty-year data-driven historical analysis. *International Journal of Innovation Studies, 4*(4), 134–147. DOI: 10.1016/j.ijis.2020.09.001

Gubbi, J., Buyya, R., Marusic, S., & Palaniswami, M. (2013). Internet of Things (IoT): A vision, architectural elements, and future directions. *Future Generation Computer Systems, 29*(7), 1645–1660. DOI: 10.1016/j.future.2013.01.010

Gunning, D., & Aha, D. W. (2019). DARPA's explainable artificial intelligence (XAI) program. *AI Magazine, 40*(2), 44–58. DOI: 10.1609/aimag.v40i2.2850

Gupta, K., Mane, P., Rajankar, O. S., Bhowmik, M., Jadhav, R., Yadav, S., Rawandale, S., & Chobe, S. V. (2023). Harnessing AI for Strategic Decision-Making and Business Performance Optimization. *International Journal of Intelligent Systems and Applications in Engineering, 11*(10s), Article 10s.

Habbal, A., Ali, M. K., & Abuzaraida, M. A. (2024). Artificial Intelligence Trust, risk and security management (AI trism): Frameworks, applications, challenges and future research directions. *Expert Systems with Applications, 240*, 122442. DOI: 10.1016/j.eswa.2023.122442

Haenlein, M., & Kaplan, A. (2019). A brief history of artificial intelligence: On the past, present, and future of artificial intelligence. *California Management Review, 61*(4), 5–14. DOI: 10.1177/0008125619864925

Hao, H. (2021, October). Database Mining Information System Based on Artificial Intelligence Algorithm. In *2021 IEEE International Conference on Data Science and Computer Application (ICDSCA)* (pp. 181-185). IEEE.

Hare, R., & Tang, Y. (2023). Player Modeling and Adaptation Methods Within Adaptive Serious Games. *IEEE Transactions on Computational Social Systems, 10*(4), 1939–1950. DOI: 10.1109/TCSS.2022.3203926

Harrow, A. W., Hassidim, A., & Lloyd, S. (2009). Quantum algorithm for linear systems of equations. *Physical Review Letters, 103*(15), 150502. DOI: 10.1103/PhysRevLett.103.150502 PMID: 19905613

Harvard Business Review, M. E. P. T. H. D. P. D. H. J. W. (2019). *HBR's 10 Must Reads on AI, Analytics, and the New Machine Age.*

Hashim, S., Omar, M. K., Ab Jalil, H., & Sharef, N. M. (2022). Trends on technologies and artificial intelligence in education for personalized learning: Systematic literature. *Journal of Academic Research in Progressive Education and Development, 12*(1), 884–903. DOI: 10.6007/IJARPED/v11-i1/12230

Heather Chen and Kathleen Magramo. (2024). *Finance worker pays out $25 million after video call with deepfake 'chief financial officer*. CNN.

Helen Briggs. (2020). *One of biology's biggest mysteries "largely solved" by AI.*

Henman, P. (n.d.). *The computer says "DEBT": Towards a critical sociology of algorithms and algorithmic governance*. DOI: 10.5281/ZENODO.884117

Ho, J., Jain, A., & Abbeel, P. (2020). Denoising Diffusion Probabilistic Models. *Advances in Neural Information Processing Systems, 33*, 6840–6851. https://proceedings.neurips.cc/paper/2020/hash/4c5bcfec8584af0d967f1ab10179ca4b-Abstract.html

Holmes, W. (2016). *Intelligence Unleashed: An argument for AI in Education.* https://www.researchgate.net/publication/299561597

Hosseinian, S. M., & Mirzahossein, H. (2024). Efficiency and safety of traffic networks under the effect of autonomous vehicles. *Civil Engineering (Shiraz), 48*(4), 1861–1885. DOI: 10.1007/s40996-023-01291-8

Huang, J., Saleh, S., & Liu, Y. (2021). A review on artificial intelligence in education. *Academic Journal of Interdisciplinary Studies, 10*(3).

Huang, X., Gao, X., & Chen, G. (2024, January). Ditune: A reinforcement learning based framework for automated database index selection. In 2024 18th International Conference on Ubiquitous Information Management and Communication (IMCOM) (pp. 1-8). IEEE.

ian bremme. (2023, October 16). *Asking chatgpt about justice for israel/palestine generates vastly different responses.* Https://Twitter.Com/Ianbremmer/Status/1713985163191837045

IBM. (2023). *The CEO's Guide to Generative AI.*

IBM. (2024). How to establish. *AI and Ethics.*

IBM. (n.d.). *CEO decision-making in the age of AI.*

IEEE Standards Association. (2021). *Advancing interoperability in AI systems.* IEEE Reports.

Igbokwe, I. C. (2023). Application of artificial intelligence (AI) in educational management. *International Journal of Scientific and Research Publications*, *13*(3), 300–307. DOI: 10.29322/IJSRP.13.03.2023.p13536

In re TikTok, Inc. 565 F. Supp. 3d 1076

International journal of arts, humanities & social science. (2020).

International Science Council. (2023). *A framework for evaluating rapidly developing digital and related technologies: AI, Large Language Models and beyond.*

International Science Council. (2025). *Preparing National Research Ecosystems for AI.*

Ivanov, D., & Dolgui, A. (2020). Viability of intertwined supply networks: Extending the supply chain resilience angles towards survivability. A position paper motivated by COVID-19 outbreak. *International Journal of Production Research*, *58*(10), 2904–2915. DOI: 10.1080/00207543.2020.1750727

Ivanov, S. (2023). The dark side of artificial intelligence in higher education. *Service Industries Journal*, *43*(15-16), 1055–1082. DOI: 10.1080/02642069.2023.2258799

Jain, P. K., Pamula, R., & Srivastava, G. (2021). A systematic literature review on machine learning applications for consumer sentiment analysis using online reviews. *Computer Science Review*, *41*, 100413. DOI: 10.1016/j.cosrev.2021.100413

Jain, S. K., Goel, P., & Jain, S. (2024). Understanding Consumer Sentiments Towards Marketing: An Investigation in Indian Context. *Vision (Basel)*, *28*(2), 210–224. DOI: 10.1177/09722629211027327

Jarrahi, M. H. (2018). Artificial intelligence and the future of work: Human-AI symbiosis in organizational decision making. *Business Horizons*, *61*(4), 577–586. DOI: 10.1016/j.bushor.2018.03.007

Jedličková, A. (2024). Ethical approaches in designing autonomous and intelligent systems: A comprehensive survey towards responsible development. *AI & Society*, •••, 1–14.

Jiang, L., Wu, Z., Xu, X., Zhan, Y., Jin, X., Wang, L., & Qiu, Y. (2021). Opportunities and challenges of artificial intelligence in the medical field: Current application, emerging problems, and problem-solving strategies. *The Journal of International Medical Research*, *49*(3), 03000605211000157. Advance online publication. DOI: 10.1177/03000605211000157 PMID: 33771068

Jobin, A., Ienca, M., & Vayena, E. (2019). The global landscape of AI ethics guidelines. *Nature Machine Intelligence*, *1*(9), 389–399. DOI: 10.1038/s42256-019-0088-2

John Gapper. (2018). *Cambridge Analytica exploited Facebook data with style.*

Kadowaki, T., & Nishimori, H. (1998). Quantum Annealing in the Transverse Ising Model. *Physical Review E: Statistical Physics, Plasmas, Fluids, and Related Interdisciplinary Topics*, *58*(5), 5355–5363. DOI: 10.1103/PhysRevE.58.5355

Kandala, A., Mezzacapo, A., Temme, K., Takita, M., Brink, M., Chow, J. M., & Gambetta, J. M. (2017). Hardware-efficient variational quantum eigensolver for small molecules and quantum magnets. *Nature*, *549*(7671), 242–246. DOI: 10.1038/nature23879 PMID: 28905916

Kandolo, W. (2024). Ensuring ai data access control in rdbms: A comprehensive review. In *Proceedings of the IEEE/CVF Conference on Computer Vision and Pattern Recognition* (pp. 8400-8407).

Kaplan, J., McCandlish, S., Henighan, T., Brown, T. B., Chess, B., Child, R., Gray, S., Radford, A., Wu, J., & Amodei, D. (2020). *Scaling Laws for Neural Language Models.* http://arxiv.org/abs/2001.08361

Karan, B., & Angadi, G. R. (2023). Potential Risks of Artificial Intelligence Integration into School Education: A Systematic Review. *Bulletin of Science, Technology & Society*, *43*(3-4), 67–85. DOI: 10.1177/02704676231224705

Kashefi, P., Kashefi, Y., Hossein, A., & Mirsaraei, G. (2024). Shaping the future of AI: Balancing innovation and ethics in global regulation. *Uniform Law Review*, *29*(3), 524–548. DOI: 10.1093/ulr/unae040

Katare, G., Padihar, G., & Qureshi, Z. (2018). Challenges in the integration of artificial intelligence and internet of things. *International Journal of System and Software Engineering*, *6*(2), 10–15.

Kellstedt, P. M., Linn, S., & Hannah, A. L. (2015). The usefulness of consumer sentiment: Assessing construct and measurement. *Public Opinion Quarterly*, *79*(1), 181–203. DOI: 10.1093/poq/nfu056

Kılınç, H. K., & Keçecioğlu, Ö. F. (2024). Generative Artificial Intelligence: A Historical and Future Perspective. *Academic Platform Journal of Engineering and Smart Systems*, *12*(2), 47–58. DOI: 10.21541/apjess.1398155

Kitaev, A. Y. (2003). Fault-Tolerant Quantum Computation by Anyons. *Annals of Physics*, *303*(1), 2–30. DOI: 10.1016/S0003-4916(02)00018-0

Kjaergaard, M., Schwartz, M. E., Braumüller, J., Krantz, P., Wang, J. I., Gustavsson, S., & Oliver, W. D. (2020). Superconducting Qubits: Current State of Play. *Annual Review of Condensed Matter Physics, 11*(1), 369–395. DOI: 10.1146/annurev-conmatphys-031119-050605

Knill, E.. (1996). Resilient Quantum Computation: Error Correction or Purification? *Physical Review Letters, 77*(13), 2575–2578.

Krantz, P., Kjaergaard, M., Yan, F., Orlando, T. P., Gustavsson, S., & Oliver, W. D. (2019). A quantum engineer's guide to superconducting qubits. *Applied Physics Reviews, 6*(2), 021318. DOI: 10.1063/1.5089550

Kryshtafovych, A., Schwede, T., Topf, M., Fidelis, K., & Moult, J. (2019). Critical assessment of methods of protein structure prediction (CASP)—Round XIII. *Proteins, 87*(12), 1011–1020. DOI: 10.1002/prot.25823 PMID: 31589781

Kseng, S. (2024). International Collaboration in AI Research and Development. *International IT Journal of Research, 2*(1), 1–7.

Kuleto, V., Ilic, M., Dumangiu, M., Rankovic, M., Martins, O. M. D., Paun, D., & Mihoreanu, L. (2021). Exploring Opportunities and Challenges of Artificial Intelligence and Machine Learning in Higher Education Institutions. *Sustainability (Basel), 13*(18), 10424. DOI: 10.3390/su131810424

Kumar, A., Boehm, M., & Yang, J. (2017, May). Data management in machine learning: Challenges, techniques, and systems. In *Proceedings of the 2017 ACM International Conference on Management of Data* (pp. 1717-1722).

Kumar, D., Dhalwal, R., & Chaudhary, A. (2024). Exploring the Ethical Implications of Generative AI in Healthcare. In *The Ethical Frontier of AI and Data Analysis* (pp. 180–195). IGI Global. DOI: 10.4018/979-8-3693-2964-1.ch011

Kumar, D., Kumar, S., & Joshi, A. (2023). Assessing the viability of blockchain technology for enhancing court operations. *International Journal of Law and Management, 65*(5), 425–439. DOI: 10.1108/IJLMA-03-2023-0046

Kumar, D., & Suthar, N. (2024). Ethical and legal challenges of AI in marketing: An exploration of solutions. *Journal of Information. Communication and Ethics in Society, 22*(1), 124–144. DOI: 10.1108/JICES-05-2023-0068

Kumar, D., & Suthar, N. (2025a). AI-Enabled Humanoid Devices Bridging Personalized Learning and Inclusive Education for Cyber Nomads. In *Educational AI Humanoid Computing Devices for Cyber Nomads* (pp. 41–72). IGI Global Scientific Publishing. DOI: 10.4018/979-8-3693-8985-0.ch003

Kumar, D., & Suthar, N. (2025b). Assessing the prospects and constraints of blockchain technology for intellectual property management. *The Journal of World Intellectual Property*, *28*(1), 124–140. DOI: 10.1111/jwip.12324

Lahusen, C., Maggetti, M., & Slavkovik, M. (2024). Trust, trustworthiness and AI governance. *Scientific Reports*, *14*(1), 20752. DOI: 10.1038/s41598-024-71761-0 PMID: 39237635

Lai, X., & Rau, P. L. P. (2021). Has facial recognition technology been misused? A public perception model of facial recognition scenarios. *Computers in Human Behavior*, *124*, 106894. DOI: 10.1016/j.chb.2021.106894

Lee, J. (2022). *Artificial intelligence and international law*. Springer. DOI: 10.1007/978-981-19-1496-6

Lee, J., Bagheri, B., & Kao, H. A. (2019). A cyber-physical systems architecture for Industry 4.0-based manufacturing systems. *Manufacturing Letters*, *3*(1), 18–23.

Liao, H. (2025). DeepSeek large-scale model: Technical analysis and development prospect. *Journal of Computer Science and Electrical Engineering*, *7*(1), 33–37.

Liapis, A., Yannakakis, G. N., Nelson, M. J., Preuss, M., & Bidarra, R. (2019). Orchestrating game generation. *IEEE Transactions on Games*, *11*(1), 48–68. DOI: 10.1109/TG.2018.2870876

Li, G., Zhou, X., & Cao, L. (2021, October). Machine learning for databases. In *Proceedings of the First International Conference on AI-ML Systems* (pp. 1-2).

Li, J., Miao, B., Wang, S., Dong, W., Xu, H., & Si, C.Hiplot Consortium. (2022). Hiplot: A comprehensive and easy-to-use web service for boosting publication-ready biomedical data visualization. *Briefings in Bioinformatics*, *23*(4), bbac261.

Li, S., Da Xu, L., & Zhao, S. (2018). The Internet of Things: A survey. *Information Systems Frontiers*, *17*(2), 243–259. DOI: 10.1007/s10796-014-9492-7

Li, T., Sahu, A. K., Talwalkar, A., & Smith, V. (2020). Federated learning: Challenges, methods, and future directions. *IEEE Signal Processing Magazine*, *37*(3), 50–60. DOI: 10.1109/MSP.2020.2975749

Liu, S. (2023). India's AI regulation dilemma. *The Diplomat*. Retrieved March 20, 2025, from https://thediplomat.com/2023/10/indias-ai-regulation-dilemma/

Lloyd, S. (1996). Universal Quantum Simulators. *Science*, *273*(5278), 1073–1078. DOI: 10.1126/science.273.5278.1073 PMID: 8688088

Madancian, M., Taherdoost, H., Javadi, M., Khan, I. U., Kalantari, A., & Kumar, D. (2023, November). The Impact of Artificial Intelligence on Supply Chain Management in Modern Business. In *The International Conference on Artificial Intelligence and Smart Environment* (pp. 566-573). Cham: Springer Nature Switzerland.

Mahsun, M., Ali, M., Ekaningrum, I. R., & Ibda, H. (2024). Trend of Using ChatGPT in Learning Process and Character Education: A Systematic Literature Review. *International Journal of Learning. Teaching and Educational Research, 23*(5), 387–402. DOI: 10.26803/ijlter.23.5.20

Ma, J. (2022, July). Research on Intelligent Management System of Practical Courses Based on Artificial Intelligence Technology. In *2022 International Conference on Artificial Intelligence and Autonomous Robot Systems (AIARS)* (pp. 315-318). IEEE.

Ma, L., & Sun, B. (2020). Machine learning and AI in marketing–Connecting computing power to human insights. *International Journal of Research in Marketing, 37*(3), 481–504. DOI: 10.1016/j.ijresmar.2020.04.005

Malik, A., Srikanth, N. R., & Budhwar, P. (2020). Digitisation, artificial intelligence (AI) and HRM. *Human resource management: Strategic and international perspectives, 88*, 103.

Manohar Lal Sharma v. Union of India (2023) 11 SCC 401

Marr, B. (2023, June 2). The 15 Biggest Risks Of Artificial Intelligence. *Forbes.*

Mazen Baroudi, S. C. F. A. W. (2023). *What happened to "All human beings are born free"? Reflections on a ChatGPT "experiment."*

McArdle, S.. (2020). Quantum Chemistry on Quantum Computers. *Reviews of Modern Physics, 92*(1), 015003. DOI: 10.1103/RevModPhys.92.015003

McEwen, M.. (2019). Gate performance characterization of the Hadamard operation on superconducting qubits. *Physical Review Applied, 12*(2), 024043.

Mehrabi, N., Morstatter, F., Saxena, N., Lerman, K., & Galstyan, A. (2021). A survey on bias and fairness in machine learning. *ACM Computing Surveys, 54*(6), 1–35. DOI: 10.1145/3457607

Menzies, J., Sabert, B., Hassan, R., & Mensah, P. K. (2024). Artificial intelligence for international business: Its use, challenges, and suggestions for future research and practice. *Thunderbird International Business Review, 66*(2), 185–200. DOI: 10.1002/tie.22370

Mercer, S., Spillard, S., & Martin, D. P. (2025). Brief analysis of DeepSeek R1 and its implications for Generative AI. *SuperIntelligence - Robotics - Safety & Alignment, 2*(1). https://doi.org/DOI: 10.70777/si.v2i1.11097

Mermin, N. (2007). *David. Quantum Computer Science: An Introduction*. Cambridge University Press. DOI: 10.1017/CBO9780511813870

Miao, H., Li, A., Davis, L. S., & Deshpande, A. (2017, April). Towards unified data and lifecycle management for deep learning. In 2017 IEEE 33rd International Conference on Data Engineering (ICDE) (pp. 571-582). IEEE.

Mimansa. (2024, September 11). Govt is looking to regulate AI applications, not AI technology: Additional Secretary to IT Ministry. MediaNama. https://www.medianama.com/2024/09/223-government-regulating-ai-application-not-ai-technology-meity-additional-secretary/

Ministry of Electronics & IT (India). (2025a, March 19). *Government of India Expands AI-Driven Skilling* [Press release]. https://pib.gov.in/PressReleasePage.aspx?PRID=2113095

Ministry of Electronics & IT (India). (2025b, March 6). *India's AI Revolution* [Press release]. https://pib.gov.in/PressReleasePage.aspx?PRID=2108810

Mohanty, A., & Sahu, S. (2024). *India's advance on AI regulation*. Carnegie India. https://carnegieendowment.org/research/2024/11/indias-advance-onai-regulation?lang=en&center=india

Mona Chalabi. (2023, October 16). *Asking ChatGPT about israel/Palastine*.

Montanaro, A. (2016). Quantum algorithms: an overview. npj Quantum Information, 2(1), 1-8.

Morandín-Ahuerma, F. (2023). Ten UNESCO Recommendations on the Ethics of Artificial Intelligence.

Moult, J., Pedersen, J. T., Judson, R., & Fidelis, K. (1995). A large-scale experiment to assess protein structure prediction methods. *Proteins, 23*(3). Advance online publication. DOI: 10.1002/prot.340230303 PMID: 8710822

Muhammad Zulhusni. (2025). *Sam Altman's World Network introduces messaging feature with identity verification*.

Multinational loses HK$200 million to deepfake video conference scam, Hong Kong police say. (2024).

Munappy, A., Bosch, J., Olsson, H. H., Arpteg, A., & Brinne, B. (2019, August). Data management challenges for deep learning. In 2019 45th Euromicro conference on software engineering and advanced applications (SEAA) (pp. 140-147). IEEE.

Muralidharan, V., Adewale, B. A., Huang, C. J., Nta, M. T., Ademiju, P. O., Pathmarajah, P., & Olatunji, T. (2024). A scoping review of reporting gaps in FDA-approved AI medical devices. *npj. Digital Medicine*, *7*(1), 273. PMID: 39362934

Muvija M. (2025). *Google develops AI co-scientist to aid researchers.*

Nain, H., & Chaudhary, M. (2022). Internet Usage by Young Kids in India. *Fwu Journal of Social Sciences, 16*(3).

Nakamoto, S. (2008). Bitcoin: A Peer-to-Peer Electronic Cash System. *Bitcoin.org*.

Nanda, A., Bajaj, S. B., & Gupta, S. (2020, June). A Comprehensive Survey of Machine Learning in Scheduling of Transactions. In 2020 4th International Conference on Trends in Electronics and Informatics (ICOEI)(48184) (pp. 740-745). IEEE.

Neves, M. P., & Almeida, A. B. D. (2023). Before and Beyond Artificial Intelligence: Opportunities and Challenges, *ResearchGate*. https://www.researchgate.net/publication/376852554_Before_and_Beyond_Artificial_Intelligence_Opportunities_and_Challenges

Nguyen, Q. K.. (2020). A survey on blockchain applications in IoT. *IEEE Access : Practical Innovations, Open Solutions*, *7*, 164–173.

Nielsen, M. A., & Chuang, I. L. (2010). *Quantum Computation and Quantum Information*. Cambridge University Press.

Niemi, H. (2021). AI in learning: Preparing grounds for future learning. *Journal of Pacific Rim Psychology*, *15*, 18344909211038105. DOI: 10.1177/18344909211038105

Nihalani, N., Silakari, S., & Motwani, M. (2009, July). Integration of artificial intelligence and database management system: an inventive approach for intelligent databases. In *2009 First International Conference on Computational Intelligence, Communication Systems and Networks* (pp. 35-40). IEEE.

Nikolinakos, N. T. (2023). The European Parliament's 2020 Resolution: Proposal for a Regulation on Ethical Principles for the Development, Deployment and Use of Artificial Intelligence, Robotics and Related Technologies. In *EU Policy and Legal Framework for Artificial Intelligence, Robotics and Related Technologies-The AI Act* (pp. 281–306). Springer International Publishing. DOI: 10.1007/978-3-031-27953-9_6

Nindler, R. (2019). The United Nation's Capability to Manage Existential Risks with a Focus on Artificial Intelligence. *International Community Law Review, 21*(1), 5–34. DOI: 10.1163/18719732-12341388

Nishant, R., Kennedy, M., & Corbett, J. (2020). Artificial intelligence for sustainability: Challenges, opportunities, and a research agenda. *International Journal of Information Management, 53*, 102104. DOI: 10.1016/j.ijinfomgt.2020.102104

Nookala, G. (2021). Automated Data Warehouse Optimization Using Machine Learning Algorithms. *Journal of Computational Innovation, 1*, 1.

NVDIA. (2024). *NVIDIA Studio | Built for Creators.*

O'Sullivan, S., Nevejans, N., Allen, C., Blyth, A., Leonard, S., Pagallo, U., Holzinger, K., Holzinger, A., Sajid, M. I., & Ashrafian, H. (2019). Legal, regulatory, and ethical frameworks for development of standards in artificial intelligence (AI) and autonomous robotic surgery. *International Journal of Medical Robotics and Computer Assisted Surgery, 15*(1), e1968. DOI: 10.1002/rcs.1968 PMID: 30397993

OECD. (2019). *OECD AI Principles overview.* https://oecd.ai/en/ai-principles

Office of General Counsel. (2024). *AI best practices guidelines.* MacEwan University. https://www.macewan.ca/c/documents/ai-best-practices-guidelines.pdf

Okolo, C. T. (2023). AI in the Global South: Opportunities and challenges towards more inclusive governance. *Brookings.* https://www.brookings.edu/articles/ai-in-the-global-south-opportunities-and-challenges-towards-more-inclusive-governance/

Okunlaya, R. O., Syed Abdullah, N., & Alias, R. A. (2022). Artificial intelligence (AI) library services innovative conceptual framework for the digital transformation of university education. *Library Hi Tech, 40*(6), 1869–1892. DOI: 10.1108/LHT-07-2021-0242

Olatunde, T. M., Okwandu, A. C., Akande, D. O., & Sikhakhane, Z. Q.Tosin Michael OlatundeAzubuike Chukwudi OkwanduDorcas Oluwajuwonlo AkandeZamathula Queen Sikhakhane. (2024). REVIEWING THE ROLE OF ARTIFICIAL INTELLIGENCE IN ENERGY EFFICIENCY OPTIMIZATION. *Engineering Science & Technology Journal, 5*(4), 4. Advance online publication. DOI: 10.51594/estj.v5i4.1015

Openko, P. V., Hohoniants, S. Y., Starkova, O. V., Herasymenko, K. V., Yastrebov, M. I., & Prudchenko, A. O. (2019, December). Problem of choosing a dbms in modern information system. In *2019 IEEE International Conference on Advanced Trends in Information Theory (ATIT)* (pp. 171-174). IEEE.

Orús, R.. (2020). Quantum Computing for Finance: Overview and Prospects. *Reviews in Physics*, *5*, 100–115.

Ovink, C. (2024). *AI risks for international peace and security*. ORF. https://www.orfonline.org/expert-speak/ai-risks-for-international-peace-and-security

Pacholska, M. (2023). Many Hands in the Black Box: Artificial Intelligence and the Responsibility of International Organizations. *SSRN*. https://papers.ssrn.com/sol3/papers.cfm?abstract_id=4501072

Padmaja, V. R., & Sadasivuni, L. (2024). The rise of AI: A comprehensive research review. *International Journal of Artificial Intelligence*, *13*(2), 2226. DOI: 10.11591/ijai.v13.i2.pp2226-2235

Paganelli, M., Sottovia, P., Park, K., Interlandi, M., & Guerra, F. (2023). Pushing ML Predictions Into DBMSs. *IEEE Transactions on Knowledge and Data Engineering*, *35*(10), 10295–10308. DOI: 10.1109/TKDE.2023.3269592 PMID: 37954972

Pan, J.-W.. (2010). Experimental Free-Space Quantum Teleportation. *Nature Photonics*, *4*(6), 376–381. DOI: 10.1038/nphoton.2010.87

Pan, Y., & Froese, F. J. (2023). An interdisciplinary review of AI and HRM: Challenges and future directions. *Human Resource Management Review*, *33*(1), 100924. DOI: 10.1016/j.hrmr.2022.100924

Pearl, M., Brock, J., & Kumar, A. (2025). *Delving into the dangers of DeepSeek*. Center for Strategic and International Studies (CSIS). https://www.csis.org/analysis/delving-dangers-deepseek

Pirandola, S., Andersen, U. L., Banchi, L., Berta, M., Bunandar, D., Colbeck, R., Englund, D., Gehring, T., Lupo, C., Ottaviani, C., Pereira, J. L., Razavi, M., Shamsul Shaari, J., Tomamichel, M., Usenko, V. C., Vallone, G., Villoresi, P., & Wallden, P. (2020). Advances in Quantum Cryptography. *Advances in Optics and Photonics*, *12*(4), 1012–1236. DOI: 10.1364/AOP.361502

Preskill, J. (1998). *Fault-tolerant quantum computation*. Introduction to Quantum Computation and Information. DOI: 10.1142/9789812385253_0008

Pulivarthy, P. (2024). Gen AI Impact on the Database Industry Innovations. *International Journal of Advances in Engineering Research*, *28*(3), 1–10.

QuantumFind. (2024). *NVIDIA Canvas: Astonishing Digital Art with AI in 2024*. https://quantumfind.ai/nvidia-canvas/

Rajagopal, M., Sivasakthivel, R., Ramar, G., & Karuppasamy, S.K. (2023) A Conceptual Framework for AI Governance in Public Administration – A Smart Governance Perspective. *IEEE Xplore*, 488-495. https://doi.org/DOI: 0.1109/I-SMAC58438.2023.10290366

Ramakrishnan, R., & Gehrke, J. (2002). *Database management systems*. McGraw-Hill, Inc.

Raman, R., Kowalski, R., Achuthan, K., Iyer, A., & Nedungadi, P. (2025). Navigating artificial general intelligence development: Societal, technological, ethical, and brain-inspired pathways. *Scientific Reports*, *15*(1), 1–22. DOI: 10.1038/s41598-025-92190-7 PMID: 40069265

Ramesh, A., Dhariwal, P., Nichol, A., Chu, C., & Chen, M. (2022). *Hierarchical Text-Conditional Image Generation with CLIP Latents*. http://arxiv.org/abs/2204.06125

Ramesh, A., Kambhampati, C., Monson, J. R. T., & Drew, P. J. (2020). Artificial intelligence in medicine. *Annals of the Royal College of Surgeons of England*, *86*(5), 334–338. DOI: 10.1308/147870804290 PMID: 15333167

Ratcliff, C. J. (2023, November 8). *Who will write the rules for AI? How nations are racing to regulate artificial intelligence*. The Conversation. https://theconversation.com/who-will-write-the-rules-for-ai-how-nations-are-racing-to-regulate-artificial-intelligence-216900

Rathore, B. (2020). Personalization and Profits: The Impact of AI on Targeted Digital Marketing. *International Journal of Transcontinental Discoveries*, *7*(1), 1–14.

Ren, J.-G., Xu, P., Yong, H.-L., Zhang, L., Liao, S.-K., Yin, J., Liu, W.-Y., Cai, W.-Q., Yang, M., Li, L., Yang, K.-X., Han, X., Yao, Y.-Q., Li, J., Wu, H.-Y., Wan, S., Liu, L., Liu, D.-Q., Kuang, Y.-W., & Pan, J.-W. (2017). Ground-to-Satellite Quantum Teleportation. *Nature*, *549*(7670), 70–73. DOI: 10.1038/nature23675 PMID: 28825708

REPUBLIC OF TÜRKİYE COUNCIL OF HIGHER EDUCATION. (n.d.). *ETHICS GUIDE OF GENERATIVE ARTIFICIAL INTELLIGENCE USE IN THE SCIENTIFIC RESEARCH AND PUBLICATION PROCESS OF HIGHER EDUCATION INSTITUTIONS*. Retrieved April 3, 2025, from https://www.yok.gov.tr/en/Documents/2024/ethics-guide-of-generative-ai-use-in-the-scientific-research-and-publication-process.pdf

Retro. (2025). *We're Adding 10 Years to Healthy Human Lifespan*.

reuters. (2025). Bogus video of Trump and Musk briefly appears on screens at US government office. *Reuters*.

Reyna, A., Martín, C., Chen, J., Soler, E., & Díaz, M. (2018). On blockchain and its integration with IoT. Challenges and opportunities. *Future Generation Computer Systems*, *88*, 173–190. DOI: 10.1016/j.future.2018.05.046

Roberts, H., Hine, E., Taddeo, M., & Floridi, L. (2024). Global AI governance: Barriers and pathways forward. *International Affairs*, *100*(3), 1275–1286. DOI: 10.1093/ia/iiae073

Roman, R.. (2018). Privacy and security in the Internet of Things: A review. *Future Generation Computer Systems*, *78*, 826–837.

Rong, G., Mendez, A., Assi, E. B., Zhao, B., & Sawan, M. (2020). Artificial intelligence in healthcare: Review and prediction case studies. *Engineering (Beijing)*, *6*(3), 291–301. DOI: 10.1016/j.eng.2019.08.015

Rosa, C.. (2024). Integrating Novel Machine Learning for Big Data Analytics and IoT Technology in Intelligent Database Management Systems. *Journal of Internet Services and Information Security*, *14*(1), 206–218. DOI: 10.58346/JISIS.2024.I1.014

Russell, S., & Norvig, P. (2020). *Artificial Intelligence: A Modern Approach* (4th ed.). Pearson.

Ryan, F., Fritz, A., & Impiombato, D. (2020). TikTok privacy concerns and data collection. In *TikTok and WeChat: Curating and controlling global information flows* (pp. 36–42). Australian Strategic Policy Institute.

Saharia, C., Chan, W., Saxena, S., Li, L., Whang, J., Denton, E., Ghasemipour, S. K. S., Ayan, B. K., Mahdavi, S. S., Lopes, R. G., Salimans, T., Ho, J., Fleet, D. J., & Norouzi, M. (2022). *Photorealistic Text-to-Image Diffusion Models with Deep Language Understanding*. http://arxiv.org/abs/2205.11487

Samara, F. Y. A., Taha, A. H. A., Massa, N. M., Jamie, T. N. A., Harara, F. E., Abu-Nasser, B. S., & Abu-Naser, S. S. (2024). The Role of AI in Enhancing Business Decision-Making: Innovations and Implications.

Samson, P. (2023). On Advancing Global AI Governance. *Centre for International Governance Innovation*. https://www.cigionline.org/articles/on-advancing-global-ai-governance/

Sanca, V., & Ailamaki, A. (2024). Efficient Model-Relational Data Management: Challenges and Opportunities. *IEEE Transactions on Knowledge and Data Engineering*, *36*(12), 7399–7409. DOI: 10.1109/TKDE.2024.3384276

Saputra, Y. M., Ali, E. Y., & Fadhli, R. (2023). Implementation of Artificial Intelligence (AI) Technology in Students' Academic and Non-Academic Activities in Higher Education: A Wright Map Analysis. *Journal for ReAttach Therapy and Developmental Diversities*, *6*(10s), 1183–1193.

Sarabdeen, J. (2022). Protection of the rights of the individual when using facial recognition technology. *Heliyon*, *8*(3), e09086. DOI: 10.1016/j.heliyon.2022.e09086 PMID: 35309394

Saraswat, D., Bhattacharya, P., Verma, A., Prasad, V. K., Tanwar, S., Sharma, G., Bokoro, P. N., & Sharma, R. (2022). Explainable AI for Healthcare 5.0: Opportunities and Challenges. *IEEE Access, 10*, 84486–84517. IEEE Access. DOI: 10.1109/ACCESS.2022.3197671

Sarkar, M., Ayon, E. H., Mia, M. T., Ray, R. K., Chowdhury, M. S., Ghosh, B. P., & Puja, A. R. (2023). Optimizing E-Commerce Profits: A Comprehensive Machine Learning Framework for Dynamic Pricing and Predicting Online Purchases. *Journal of Computer Science and Technology Studies*, *5*(4), 186–193. DOI: 10.32996/jcsts.2023.5.4.19

Saura, J. R., Ribeiro-Soriano, D., & Palacios-Marqués, D. (2022). Assessing behavioral data science privacy issues in government artificial intelligence deployment. *Government Information Quarterly*, *39*(4), 101679. DOI: 10.1016/j.giq.2022.101679

Scarani, V., Bechmann-Pasquinucci, H., Cerf, N. J., Dušek, M., Lütkenhaus, N., & Peev, M. (2009). The Security of Practical Quantum Key Distribution. *Reviews of Modern Physics*, *81*(3), 1301–1350. DOI: 10.1103/RevModPhys.81.1301

Scherer, M. U. (2015). Regulating artificial intelligence systems: Risks, challenges, competencies, and strategies. *SSRN*, *29*, 353. DOI: 10.2139/ssrn.2609777

Schmitt, L. (2022). Mapping global AI governance: A nascent regime in a fragmented landscape. *AI and Ethics*, *2*(2), 303–314. DOI: 10.1007/s43681-021-00083-y

Schuhmann, C., Beaumont, R., Vencu, R., Gordon, C., Wightman, R., Cherti, M., Coombes, T., Katta, A., Mullis, C., Wortsman, M., Schramowski, P., Kundurthy, S., Crowson, K., Schmidt, L., Kaczmarczyk, R., & Jitsev, J. (2022). *LAION-5B: An open large-scale dataset for training next generation image-text models*. http://arxiv.org/abs/2210.08402

Schuld, M., & Petruccione, F. (2018). *Supervised Learning with Quantum Computers*. Springer. DOI: 10.1007/978-3-319-96424-9

Schwabe, M., Pastori, L., de Vega, I., Gentine, P., Iapichino, L., Lahtinen, V., . . . Eyring, V. (2025). Opportunities and challenges of quantum computing for climate modelling. arXiv preprint arXiv:2502.10488.

Shaheen, M. Y. (2021). Applications of Artificial Intelligence (AI) in healthcare. *RE:view*. Advance online publication. DOI: 10.14293/S2199-1006.1.SOR-.PPVRY8K.v1

Sharma, G. D., Yadav, A., & Chopra, R. (2023). Artificial intelligence and effective governance: A review, critique and research agenda Author links open overlay panel. *Sustainable Futures : An Applied Journal of Technology, Environment and Society*, *2*, 100004. DOI: 10.1016/j.sftr.2019.100004

Shen, H., Li, Y., Tian, X., Chen, X., Li, C., Bian, Q., Wang, Z., & Wang, W. (2022). Mass data processing and multidimensional database management based on deep learning. *Open Computer Science*, *12*(1), 300–313. DOI: 10.1515/comp-2022-0251

Shi, W., Cao, J., Zhang, Q., Li, Y., & Xu, L. (2016). Edge computing: Vision and challenges. *IEEE Internet of Things Journal*, *3*(5), 637–646. DOI: 10.1109/JIOT.2016.2579198

Shor, P. W. (1994, November). Algorithms for quantum computation: discrete logarithms and factoring. In *Proceedings 35th annual symposium on foundations of computer science* (pp. 124-134). Ieee.

Shor, P. W. (1996, October). Fault-tolerant quantum computation. In *Proceedings of 37th conference on foundations of computer science* (pp. 56-65). IEEE.

Shor, P. W. (1997). Polynomial-time algorithms for prime factorization and discrete logarithms on a quantum computer. *SIAM Journal on Computing*, *26*(5), 1484–1509. DOI: 10.1137/S0097539795293172

Simonofski, A., Tombal, T., De Terwangne, C., Willem, P., Frenay, B., & Janssen, M. (2022). Balancing fraud analytics with legal requirements: Governance practices and trade-offs in public administrations. *Data & Policy*, *4*, e14. DOI: 10.1017/dap.2022.6

Singh, U., Saraswat, A., Azad, H. K., Abhishek, K., & Shitharth, S. (2022). Towards improving e-commerce customer review analysis for sentiment detection. *Scientific Reports*, *12*(1), 21983. DOI: 10.1038/s41598-022-26432-3 PMID: 36539524

Skandarani, Y., Jodoin, P.-M., & Lalande, A. (2023). GANs for Medical Image Synthesis: An Empirical Study. *Journal of Imaging*, *9*(3), 69. DOI: 10.3390/jimaging9030069 PMID: 36976120

Slattery, P. (2025). *What are the risks from Artificial Intelligence*. https://airisk.mit.edu

Smith, A., & Hutson, J. (2024). From concept to creation: The role of generative artificial intelligence in the new age of digital marketing. *Design, 1*(1), 4776. DOI: 10.36922/dp.4776

Smith, M., & Miller, S. (2022). The ethical application of biometric facial recognition technology. *AI & Society, 37*(1), 167–175. DOI: 10.1007/s00146-021-01199-9 PMID: 33867693

Smuha, N. A. (2021). From a 'race to AI'to a 'race to AI regulation': Regulatory competition for artificial intelligence. *Law, Innovation and Technology, 13*(1), 57–84. DOI: 10.1080/17579961.2021.1898300

Sourdin, T. (2023). Cambridge Handbook of Artificial Intelligence: Global Perspectives on Law and Ethics. *Prometheus, 39*(1), 60–65. DOI: 10.13169/prometheus.39.1.0060

Spiegelhalter, D. (2020). Should We Trust Algorithms? *Harvard Data Science Review*. Advance online publication. DOI: 10.1162/99608f92.cb91a35a

Steane, A. (1996). Error Correcting Codes in Quantum Theory. *Physical Review Letters, 77*(5), 793–797. DOI: 10.1103/PhysRevLett.77.793 PMID: 10062908

Steven Lee Myers. (2025). *DeepSeek's Answers Include Chinese Propaganda, Researchers Say*. https://www.nytimes.com/2025/01/31/technology/deepseek-chinese-propaganda.html

Stitch Fix. (2023). *How We're Revolutionizing Personal Styling with Generative AI.*

Strubell, E., Ganesh, A., & McCallum, A. (2019a). Energy and Policy Considerations for Deep Learning in NLP. In Korhonen, A., Traum, D., & Màrquez, L. (Eds.), *Proceedings of the 57th Annual Meeting of the Association for Computational Linguistics* (pp. 3645–3650). Association for Computational Linguistics. DOI: 10.18653/v1/P19-1355

Stuart Russell and Peter Norvig. (2011). *Artificial Intelligence A Modern Approach* (3rd ed.).

Surden, H. (2019). *Artificial Intelligence and Law: An Overview, 35 GA*. https://scholar.law.colorado.edu/faculty-articles

Suri, A. (2025). *The missing pieces in India's ai puzzle: Talent, data, and R&D.* Carnegie India. https://carnegieendowment.org/research/2025/02/the-missing-pieces-in-indias-ai-puzzle-talent-data-and-randd?lang=en

Svantesson, D. (2022). The European Union artificial intelligence act: Potential implications for Australia. *Alternative Law Journal*, *47*(1), 4–9. DOI: 10.1177/1037969X211052339

Ta, R., & West, D. M. (2023). Should schools ban or integrate generative AI in the classroom?.

Taeihagh, A. (2021). Governance of artificial intelligence. *Policy and Society*, *40*(2), 137–157. DOI: 10.1080/14494035.2021.1928377

Taherdoost, H., Drazenovic, G., Farhaoui, Y., Madanchian, M., Mohamed, N., & Kumar, D. (2025). Navigating the AI Era in Startup Business Development. In *Future Tech Startups and Innovation in the Age of AI* (pp. 191–208). CRC Press.

Tallberg, J., Erman, E., Furendal, M., Geith, J., Klamberg, M., & Lundgren, M. (2023). The Global Governance of Artificial Intelligence: Next Steps for Empirical and Normative Research. *International Studies Review*, *25*(3), viad040. Advance online publication. DOI: 10.1093/isr/viad040

Tennie, F., & Palmer, T. N. (2023). Quantum Computers for Weather and Climate Prediction: The Good, the Bad, and the Noisy. *Bulletin of the American Meteorological Society*, *104*(2), E488–E500. DOI: 10.1175/BAMS-D-22-0031.1

Terhal, B. M. (2015). Quantum Error Correction for Quantum Memories. *Reviews of Modern Physics*, *87*(2), 307–346. DOI: 10.1103/RevModPhys.87.307

The AlphaFold team. (2020). *AlphaFold: a solution to a 50-year-old grand challenge in biology.*

The Risk of Automation for Jobs in OECD Countries (OECD Social, Employment and Migration Working Papers, Vol. 189). (2016). DOI: 10.1787/1815199X

Thierer, A. (2018). The pacing problem and the future of technology regulation. *Mercatus Center: The Bridge*. https://www.mercatus.org/bridge/commentary/pacing-problem-and-future-technology-regulation

Tiwari, S., Bharadwaj, S., & Joshi, S. (2021). A study of impact of cloud computing and artificial intelligence on banking services, profitability and operational benefits. [TURCOMAT]. *Turkish Journal of Computer and Mathematics Education*, *12*(6), 1617–1627.

Topol, E. J. (2019). *Deep Medicine: How Artificial Intelligence Can Make Healthcare Human Again.*

Trager, R., Harack, B., Reuel, A., Carnegie, A., Heim, L., Ho, L., Kreps, S., Lall, R., & Larter, O. Ó hÉigeartaigh, S., Staffell, S., & Villalobos Ruiz, J. J. (2023). International Governance of Civilian AI: A Jurisdictional Certification Approach. SSRN *Electronic Journal*, 1–51. DOI: 10.2139/ssrn.4579899

Trunk, A., Birkel, H., & Hartmann, E. (2020). On the current state of combining human and artificial intelligence for strategic organizational decision making. *Business Research*, *13*(3), 875–919. DOI: 10.1007/s40685-020-00133-x

Tsesmelis, D., & Simitsis, A. (2022, May). Database optimizers in the era of learning. In 2022 IEEE 38th International Conference on Data Engineering (ICDE) (pp. 3213-3216). IEEE.

Turchin, A., & Denkenberger, D. (2020). Classification of global catastrophic risks connected with artificial intelligence. *AI & Society*, *35*(1), 147–163. DOI: 10.1007/s00146-018-0845-5

Turing, A. M. (1950). I.—Computing machinery and intelligence. *Mind*, *LIX*(236), 433–460. DOI: 10.1093/mind/LIX.236.433

TVs at US government building show AI video of Trump kissing Musk's feet. (2025).

Unuriode, A., Durojaiye, O., Yusuf, B., & Okunade, L. (2023). The Integration of Artificial I Intelligence Into D Database Systems (Ai-Db Integration Review). Available at *SSRN* 4744549.

Unusual CEO Fraud via Deepfake Audio Steals US$243,000 From UK Company. (2019).

Upwork. (2024). *Using the Upwork chatbot.*

Van Aken, D., Pavlo, A., Gordon, G. J., & Zhang, B. (2017, May). Automatic database management system tuning through large-scale machine learning. In *Proceedings of the 2017 ACM international conference on management of data* (pp. 1009-1024).

van Norren, D. E. (2023). The ethics of artificial intelligence, UNESCO and the African Ubuntu perspective. *Journal of Information. Communication and Ethics in Society*, *21*(1), 112–128. DOI: 10.1108/JICES-04-2022-0037

Varian, H. (2018). Artificial Intelligence, Economics, and Industrial Organization. *NBER Chapters*, 399–419. https://ideas.repec.org/h/nbr/nberch/14017.html

Villarino, J. M. B. (2023). Global Standard-Setting for Artificial Intelligence: Para-regulating International Law for AI? *Brill*. https://brill.com/view/journals/auso/41/1/article-p157_7.xml?language=en

Vincent, J. (2017). *DeepMind's Go-playing AI doesn't need human help to beat us anymore.*

Wachter, S., Mittelstadt, B., & Russell, C. (2021). Why fairness cannot be automated: Bridging the gap between EU non-discrimination law and AI. *Computer Law & Security Review, 41*, 105567. DOI: 10.1016/j.clsr.2021.105567

Wagner, J. K., Doerr, M., & Schmit, C. D. (2024). AI Governance: A Challenge for Public Health. *JMIR Public Health and Surveillance, 10*, e58358. DOI: 10.2196/58358 PMID: 39347615

Wallach, W. (2015). *A Dangerous Master: How to Keep Technology from Slipping Beyond Our Control.* Basic Books.

Walter, Y. (2024). Managing the race to the moon: Global policy and governance in Artificial Intelligence regulation-A contemporary overview and an analysis of socioeconomic consequences. *Discover Artificial Intelligence, 4*(1), 14. DOI: 10.1007/s44163-024-00109-4

Wang, W., Zhang, M., Chen, G., Jagadish, H. V., Ooi, B. C., & Tan, K.-L. (2016). Database meets deep learning: Challenges and opportunities. *SIGMOD Record, 45*(2), 17–22. DOI: 10.1145/3003665.3003669

Wang, Y.. (2020). High-Fidelity Phase Gates for Superconducting Qubits. *Physical Review Applied, 12*(3), 034034.

Wang, Y., Bourhis, P., Rouvoy, R., & Royer, P. (2024, October). Challenges & Opportunities in Automating DBMS: A Qualitative Study. In *Proceedings of the 39th IEEE/ACM International Conference on Automated Software Engineering* (pp. 2013-2023).

Wannalai, N., & Mekruksavanich, S. (2019, January). The application of intelligent database for modern information management. In 2019 Joint International Conference on Digital Arts, Media and Technology with ECTI Northern Section Conference on Electrical, Electronics, Computer and Telecommunications Engineering (ECTI DAMT-NCON) (pp. 105-108). IEEE.

Watrous, J. (2018). *The Theory of Quantum Information.* Cambridge University Press. DOI: 10.1017/9781316848142

Webster, G., Creemers, R., Kania, E., & Triolo, P. (2017). *Full Translation: China's 'New Generation Artificial Intelligence Development Plan' (2017).* DIGICHINA.

Wenhua, Z., Qamar, F., Abdali, T. A. N., Hassan, R., Jafri, S. T. A., & Nguyen, Q. N. (2023). Blockchain Technology: Security Issues, Healthcare Applications, Challenges and Future Trends. In *Electronics (Switzerland)* (Vol. 12, Issue 3). MDPI. DOI: 10.3390/electronics12030546

Whittaker, M., Crawford, K., Dobbe, R., Fried, G., Kaziunas, E., Mathur, V., & Schwartz, O. (2018). *AI now report 2018*. AI Now Institute at New York University.

Williamson, S. M., & Prybutok, V. (2024). Balancing privacy and progress: A review of privacy challenges, systemic oversight, and patient perceptions in AI-driven healthcare. *Applied Sciences (Basel, Switzerland)*, *14*(2), 675. DOI: 10.3390/app14020675

World Economic Forum. (2020). The Global Technology Governance Report 2020. World Economic Forum.

World Economic Forum-The Global Risks Report 2024. (2024). www.weforum.org

World Team. (2024). *World ID is a privacy-preserving proof of human for age of AI.*

Wubineh, B. Z., Deriba, F. G., & Woldeyohannis, M. M. (2024). Exploring the opportunities and challenges of implementing artificial intelligence in healthcare: A systematic literature review. *Urologic Oncology*, *42*(3), 48–56. DOI: 10.1016/j.urolonc.2023.11.019 PMID: 38101991

Yang, X., Jia, J., Zhou, X., & Wang, S. (2024). The future of artificial intelligence: Time to embrace more international collaboration. *Innovation (Cambridge (Mass.))*, *5*(6), 100703. DOI: 10.1016/j.xinn.2024.100703 PMID: 39403172

Yeung, K. (2020). Recommendation of the council on artificial intelligence (OECD). *International legal materials, 59*(1), 27-34.

Yilmaz, R., & Yilmaz, F. G. K. (2023). The effect of generative artificial intelligence (AI)-based tool use on students' computational thinking skills, programming self-efficacy and motivation. *Computers and Education: Artificial Intelligence*, *4*, 100147. DOI: 10.1016/j.caeai.2023.100147

Yuan, X., Lu, Y., & Wang, X. (2020). Quantum-enhanced Blockchain and its applications. *Quantum Engineering*, *2*(1), e49.

Zaidan, E., & Ibrahim, I. A. (2024). AI Governance in a Complex and Rapidly Changing Regulatory Landscape: A Global Perspective. *Humanities & Social Sciences Communications*, *11*(1), 1121. DOI: 10.1057/s41599-024-03560-x

Zeilinger, A.. (2007). Quantum Entanglement and Teleportation. *Reviews of Modern Physics*, *79*(3), 777–787.

Zhang, J.. (2020). Experimental quantum simulation of fermion-antifermion scattering via boson exchange in a superconducting quantum circuit. *Nature Communications*, *11*(1), 1–8. PMID: 31911652

Zhang, P., White, J., Schmidt, D. C., Lenz, G., & Rosenbloom, S. T. (2021). FHIR-Chain: Applying Blockchain to securely and scalably share clinical data. *Computers in Biology and Medicine*, *104*, 132–141.

Zhang, Y., Zhang, S., & Wang, X. (2021). Quantum Optimization for Complex Systems. *Journal of Quantum Information*, *7*(2), 45–67.

Zhou, N., Zhang, C.-T., Lv, H.-Y., Hao, C.-X., Li, T.-J., Zhu, J.-J., Zhu, H., Jiang, M., Liu, K.-W., Hou, H.-L., Liu, D., Li, A.-Q., Zhang, G.-Q., Tian, Z.-B., & Zhang, X.-C. (2019). Concordance Study Between IBM Watson for Oncology and Clinical Practice for Patients with Cancer in China. *The Oncologist*, *24*(6), 812–819. DOI: 10.1634/theoncologist.2018-0255 PMID: 30181315

Zhou, X., Chai, C., Li, G., & Sun, J. (2020). Database meets artificial intelligence: A survey. *IEEE Transactions on Knowledge and Data Engineering*, *34*(3), 1096–1116. DOI: 10.1109/TKDE.2020.2994641

Zohuri, B. (2023). Charting the Future The Synergy of Generative AI, Quantum Computing, and the Transformative Impact on Economy, Society, Jobs Market, and the Emergence of Artificial Super Intelligence. [CTES]. *Current Trends in Engineering Science*, *3*(7), 1–4. DOI: 10.54026/CTES/1050

Zong, Z., & Guan, Y. (2024). AI-driven intelligent data analytics and predictive analysis in industry 4.0: Transforming knowledge, innovation, and efficiency. *Journal of the Knowledge Economy*, *16*(1), 1–40. DOI: 10.1007/s13132-024-02001-z

Zurek, W. H. (2003). Decoherence, einselection, and the quantum origins of the classical. *Reviews of Modern Physics*, *75*(3), 715–775. DOI: 10.1103/RevModPhys.75.715

About the Contributors

Ayse Arslan is a researcher and a policy analyst in Silicon Valley. She currently serves at the Berkeley AI Initiative. Previously, she gained extensive experience in Silicon Valley tech companies such as Google and Apple as both a researcher and an individual contributor. She participated in various projects in partnership with international organizations such as UN, NATO and the EU. She got a Masters and a Phd-level research degree from the Oxford University (UK) and a Masters from the Cambridge University (UK).

***

Manu Abraham is a Research Scholar from School of Law, CHRIST (Deemed to be University), Bangalore, India. The author graduated from Karnataka State Law University in BALLB. He completed his master's degree in law from CHRIST (Deemed to be University), Bangalore, India. Author's research focuses on laws governing the surveillance framework in India and the implications on right to privacy.

Asral Bin Bahari is an Associate Professor at the Faculty of Electronic Engineering Technology, Universiti Malaysia Perlis (UniMAP), Malaysia. He also serves as the Head of the Centre of Excellence for Micro System Technology (MiCTEC) at UniMAP. With over 20 years of experience in both industry and academia, Dr. Jambek specializes in the design of very large-scale integration (VLSI) circuits and systems. His research interests encompass integrated circuits and systems, sensor node design for the Internet of Things (IoT), artificial intelligence (AI), system-on-chip (SoC) development, image and video processing algorithms and architectures, data compression algorithms and architectures, and low-energy circuits and systems. He is an active member of the IEEE Circuit and System Society (CAS), serving as the Chair of the Malaysia Chapter. Dr. Jambek has made significant contributions to the field of electronic engineering through his research, publications, and mentorship of postgraduate students. His work focuses on developing low-energy algorithms and architectures for ultra-portable devices, including circuits and systems for IoT devices, AI, SoC, and signal/image/video processing. He has supervised numerous postgraduate students, guiding them in various research projects related to microelectronic engineering. Dr. Jambek's contributions have been recognized within the academic community, and he continues to play a pivotal role in advancing research and development in electronic engineering technology.

Monica Chaudhary is the Deputy Head and an Associate Professor at School of Business, Melbourne Institute of Technology, Sydney, Australia. She is a postgraduate in economics, MBA and PhD in Marketing with more than 17 years' experience in academics, research, consulting and industry. In the past, she had worked with MNCs in the area of data analytics and business intelligence. She is an active researcher and has authored several refereed research papers in reputed research.

Shampa Dev is a Professor of Law at the School of Law, CHRIST University. She completed her graduation from Nagpur University in 1995. Following graduation, she joined the offices of Justice Sirpurkar, where she engaged primarily in writ petitions, civil suits, and family law matters; and studied for a Master of Law at the Post Graduate Teaching Department, Nagpur University. Having topped in master's, she received an invitation to teach at the same department, which launched her into a career of teaching, learning, and research. Professor Dev regularly teaches, Legal Research Methodology and Jurisprudence, and has taught courses on Constitutional Law, Election Laws, Family Law, Human Rights, Interpretation of Statutes, and the Right to Information. Her scholarship focuses on exploring rights jurisprudence in the domains of privacy, human rights, gender justice, environmental rights, and disability rights. Her significant contributions are in initiating quality improvement measures at the law school as head of the Internal Quality Assurance Cell, Holistic Education Cell, Teaching Learning Enhancement Cell, and Curriculum Development Cell.

Ökkeş Fatih Keçecioğlu is a faculty member at Kahramanmaraş Sütçü İmam University, Department of Electrical and Electronics Engineering. He received his BSc, MSc, and PhD degrees in Electrical and Electronics Engineering from the same institution. His research interests include power quality, harmonic compensation, reactive power control, fuzzy logic systems, and renewable energy systems. He has contributed to various national and international research projects and has published numerous articles in SCI/SCI-Expanded indexed journals. He is a member of

IEEE and the Chamber of Electrical Engineers (EMO) and has received several awards, including the TÜBİTAK Publication Incentive Award and KSÜ Academic Productivity Award.

Pranjal Khare is a distinguished corporate lawyer and is currently working as a law faculty at O.P. Jindal Global University, India. He specializes in Property Law, Corporate laws, Intellectual Property Rights, and International law. Mr. Pranjal is a highly regarded scholar and has published on numerous issues related to international affairs, economy, politics, data & privacy, artificial intelligence and IP disputes. He is also a frequent speaker at legal conferences and has served as a consultant to numerous law firms and corporations.

Bahauddin Atiq Khatib is a entrepreneur running a manufacturing unit Modustone. He received a bachelor's degree in economics from S P Jain school of global management in Sydney, Australia. His current field placement is with Next level working as a assistance consultant.

Hatice Kübra Kılınç is a PhD student in Electrical and Electronics Engineering at Kahramanmaraş Sütçü İmam University. She holds a master's degree in Electronics and Computer Engineering from Hasan Kalyoncu University and a bachelor's degree in Computer Engineering. Her current research focuses on generative AI, specifically GANs and diffusion models. She received certified training from NVIDIA and published a review article on generative AI. She previously worked on fake news detection using deep learning and machine learning techniques. She also volunteers in AI education projects and outreach through organizations such as Young Academia.

Dinesh Kumar is an accomplished professional with extensive expertise in the military, academia, business, and charity sectors. He holds a PhD from the esteemed Indian Institute of Technology (IIT) Roorkee and has received admission offers for the Fellow Program in Management from the Indian Institute of Management (IIM) Ranchi that made him the first Indian soldier to secure doctoral admission offers from both IIT and IIM. He is the founder of Pomento and Mission Dost-E-Jahan. He is the propounder of 'Lifestyle Social Work.' Currently, he is a business analytics faculty member at the School of Business, Woxsen University, India.

Baidya Nath Mukherjee, PhD, LLM, is an academic, solicitor, practitioner, and researcher specializing in Constitutional Law, Criminal Law, and Police Studies, with over seven years of educational experience. He has made significant contributions to discussions on police accountability, judicial interventions in policing, and wrongful convictions. Beyond academia, he actively collaborates with law enforcement agencies, having trained Sub-Inspectors and Investigating Police Officers in India. His expertise also includes organizing legal seminars, conferences, and publishing books. Committed to police reforms and the administration of justice, he examines frameworks that balance law enforcement efficiency with human rights protection while advocating for independent oversight, enhanced training, and legislative reforms. His interdisciplinary approach combines legal analysis, criminology, and public policy to shape effective and accountable policing models.

Akshaya Siripuram is a 2nd year student in CSE Department, B V Raju Institute of Technology, Narsapur. She is currently working in Quantum cost optimization architectures.

Nidhi Suthar holds a PhD from MPUAT, Rajasthan, India. She has worked for more than a decade in academia and industry. She is a management faculty member in the School of Business, Woxsen University, India.

Srivardhan Vadla is a 2nd year student in CSE Department, B V Raju Institute of Technology, Narsapur. He is currently working in Quantum cost optimization architectures.

Ziyi Wang is an Economics PhD and JD researcher at Cornell University. She holds a Bachelor of Science in Foreign Service from Georgetown University's School of Foreign Service in Washington, D.C. Her research interests include Economic Development, Industrial Organization, Innovation, Platform Economics, and Empirical Legal Studies. She is a Research Associate at the UN75 Global Governance Forum.

Index

A

B

C

D

E

F

G

H

I

M

N

P

Q

R

S

T

www.ingramcontent.com/pod-product-compliance
Lightning Source LLC
LaVergne TN
LVHW061543290926
849162LV00004B/889